THE
EASTERN
EUROPE
COLLECTION

SLAVONIC EUROPE

R. Nisbet Bain

ARNO PRESS & THE NEW YORK TIMES
New York - 1971

Reprint Edition 1971 by Arno Press Inc.

Reprinted from a copy in
The Harvard University Library

LC# 76-135790

ISBN 0-405-02732-X

The Eastern Europe Collection

ISBN for complete set: 0-405-02730-3

Manufactured in the United States of America

Cambridge Historical Series.

EDITED BY G. W. PROTHERO, Litt.D.

HONORARY FELLOW OF KING'S COLLEGE, CAMBRIDGE.

SLAVONIC EUROPE

CAMBRIDGE UNIVERSITY PRESS WAREHOUSE,
C. F. CLAY, Manager.
London: FETTER LANE, E.C.
Glasgow: 50, WELLINGTON STREET.

Leipzig: F. A. BROCKHAUS.
New York: G. P. PUTNAM'S SONS.
Bombay and Calcutta: MACMILLAN AND CO., Ltd.

SLAVONIC EUROPE

A POLITICAL HISTORY OF POLAND AND RUSSIA FROM 1447 to 1796

BY

R. NISBET BAIN,

Assistant Librarian, British Museum,
Author of *Scandinavia*, *The First Romanovs*, *Gustavus III
and his contemporaries*, etc., etc.

CAMBRIDGE :
at the University Press
1908

GENERAL PREFACE.

The aim of this series is to sketch the history of Modern Europe, with that of its chief colonies and conquests, from about the end of the fifteenth century down to the present time. In one or two cases the story commences at an earlier date: in the case of the colonies it generally begins later. The histories of the different countries are described, as a rule, separately; for it is believed that, except in epochs like that of the French Revolution and Napoleon I, the connection of events will thus be better understood and the continuity of historical development more clearly displayed.

The series is intended for the use of all persons anxious to understand the nature of existing political conditions. " The roots of the present lie deep in the past" ; and the real significance of contemporary events cannot be grasped unless the historical causes which have led to them are known. The plan adopted makes it possible to treat the history of the last four centuries in considerable detail, and to embody the most important results of modern research. It is hoped therefore that the series will be useful not only to beginners but to students who have already acquired some general knowledge of European History. For those who wish to carry their studies further, the bibliography appended to each volume will act as a guide to original sources of information and works more detailed and authoritative.

Considerable attention is paid to political geography, and each volume is furnished with such maps and plans as may be requisite for the illustration of the text.

G. W. PROTHERO.

PREFACE.

THIS book is, I believe, the only existing compendium, in English, of the political history of Poland and Russia, from the middle of the fifteenth to the end of the eighteenth century, when the Polish Republic disappeared from the map of Europe and the Russian Empire took its place as the head and right arm of the Slavonic world. The unfamiliarity of our scholars with the two leading Slavonic languages is, no doubt, the primary cause of this long neglect of the history of eastern Europe, some acquaintance with which is, nevertheless, absolutely indispensable to a right knowledge of the lands which lie nearer home.

It has been no easy matter to compress so vast and complicated a subject within the narrow limits of nineteen, necessarily brief, chapters, each one of which might very well be expanded into one or more volumes. The utmost that could be done was to present a clear and connected outline of the whole panorama of events, omitting nothing essential, giving due prominence to the human element which, after all, must ever be the determining factor of history, and throwing into clear relief, by the light of the most recent criticism, many murky and nebulous districts of this immense and hitherto but partially explored region.

R. NISBET BAIN.

November, 1907.

CONTENTS.

Contents

MAPS.

CHAPTER I.

INTRODUCTORY.

FROM the vague indications of the ancient *lyetopisi*, or Slavonic chronicles, it would seem that, about the middle of the ninth century, what is now, roughly speaking, Russia, was then divided between two races, a north-western race paying a tribute of pelts to the Varangians or Northmen, and a south-eastern race paying a similar tribute to the Kozars or Chazars, a mixed race, living in tent-waggons, on the confines of Europe and Asia, principally along the Volga, whose Kagan or King was a Jew. Somewhat later, the northern tribes, Finns and Slavonians alike, invited the Varangian chieftain, Ruric, to come and rule over their hopelessly distracted tribal communities; and with the coming of Ruric (*circa* 862) Russian history may be said to begin. Ruric endeavoured to curb and concentrate the tribes by building fortress towns; and his successor, Oleg (*circa* 872), extended the new dominion southwards, the tribes who there had hitherto borne the heavy yoke of the Chazars, willingly exchanging it for Oleg's comparatively light one. Oleg made Kiev his capital. Here was the best soil and the most equable climate. Its situation also tempted him. Kiev commanded the Dnieper, the easiest route to the Euxine. It also abutted immediately upon the vast south-eastern steppe. Thus it was an ideal starting-point, and resting-place, for predatory barbarians with a taste for adventure. Thence, by water, Askold and Dir (*circa* 866) led the first raid of the Northmen against Constantinople. The raid failed. But in 907 Oleg himself united all the tribes in a military expedition against the imperial city, and exacted a heavy tribute[1]. The subsequent expeditions of Igor (912–945), Oleg's successor, were less fortunate; and in 945 he made a perpetual peace with the Greeks.

It is in Igor's reign that we hear, for the first time, of "the land of Rus," a sign that the country was growing in political cohesion. Christianity was also beginning to permeate among the Slavs. Thus the Greek historians now begin to differentiate the christian from the heathen Rus, and we hear of the Church of St Elias at Kiev. "The wise Olga," who ruled the Rus during the minority of her son Svyatoslav (945–957), was actually baptised at Constantinople by the Patriarch Polyeuktes, in the presence of the Emperor Constantine Porphyrogenitus, who has left us an account of the ceremony; but it was not till the eighth year of the reign of her grandson, Vladimir (980-1015), that the Rus were formally received into the Orthodox Eastern Church. Vladimir, after a singularly irregular and turbulent youth, seems to have deliberately chosen Christianity for his religion in preference to both Judaism and Mohammedanism, with both of which he had become acquainted during his numerous wars with the barbarians of the eastern steppe. Judaism repelled him as being the religion of a people without a country and therefore, obviously, under the wrath of God. Mohammedanism was objectionable because it proscribed fermented liquors. Christianity, already recommendable as the faith of his grandmother Olga, "the wisest of us all," impressed him by the majesty of its ritual. It also promised obvious political advantages. It was as the ally of the Greek Emperor, whose daughter Anne he wedded at the same time, that Vladimir

---

[1] From the form of the names of Oleg's fifteen ambassadors it is plain that the Viking element still predominated in the Russian army.

was baptised at Korsun in the Crimea (988).   Two years
later, the Kievlians were immersed in the waters of the Dnieper
by Greek missionary priests.   Thus the narrow strip of territory
from Kiev to Novgorod became the nucleus of a new Christian
State, environed and hard pressed by savage pagans, the most
formidable of whom were the Pechenegs, a Mongolian race,
who, some fifty years before, had annihilated and supplanted
the Chazars.   They are described by the German missionary,
Bruno, who lived among them (*circa* 1007), as the cruellest
of the heathen, and were very evil neighbours to Russia for
generations to come.   Meanwhile, another enemy had arisen
in the West behind the Bug, now the boundary of the two
States, in the shape of the young kingdom of Poland.

We possess no certain historical data relating to Poland
till the end of the tenth century.   It would seem that the
progenitors of the Poles, originally established on the Danube,
were driven thence to the still wilder wildernesses of central
Europe, settling finally among the forests and morasses of
the basin of the upper Oder and Vistula, where they dwelt,
in loosely-connected communities, as hunters, herdsmen, and
tillers of the soil, till the pressure of rapacious neighbours
compelled them to combine for mutual defence, and form
the semi-mythical kingdom of the Piasts, from Piast its
supposed founder.   The Piasts wrested Chrobacya, a province
extending from the Carpathians to the Bug, from the shadowy
Moravian Empire, which subsequently collapsed before the
intrusion of the Magyars, itself a capital fact in European
history resulting in the permanent separation of the south-
eastern from the north-western Slavs.   Under Mieszko I
(962–992), Poland nominally accepted Christianity from the
Eastern Church, but was re-converted by the Roman Church
at the instigation of Boleslaus I (992–1025) in order that he
might obtain the protection of the Holy See against the persistent pressure of the Germans from the West.   It was
Boleslaus who founded the primatial see of Gnesen with

jurisdiction over the bishoprics of Cracow, Breslau and Kolberg, all three of which were in territory conquered by Boleslaus; for, hitherto, Cracow and Breslau had been Bohemian cities, while Kolberg was founded to curb the lately subjugated Pomeranians. Boleslaus was also the first Polish Prince to bear the royal title (*circa* 1000); and he founded an empire which extended from the Baltic to the Carpathians, and from the Elbe to the Bug, an empire which twenty years after his death collapsed before a combined attack of all Poland's enemies. Simultaneously a terrible pagan reaction swept away the poor remnants of christianity and civilisation. Under Boleslaus II (1058–1079) and Boleslaus III (1102–1138) some of the lost provinces, notably Silesia and Pomerania, were temporarily recovered, and Poland was at least able to maintain her independence against the ever-hostile Germans; but, on the death of Boleslaus III, whose last act was to divide his territories among his numerous sons, a period of disintegration ("the partitional period" of Polish historians) began, lasting from 1138 to 1305, during which the land was divided into a dozen independent principalities, and lost all political significance.

Russia and Poland first came into serious collision on the death of Vladimir the Great (1015), when Boleslaus intervened energetically to place Vladimir's eldest son, Svyatopulk, on the throne of Kiev. But, according to the *lyetopisi*, both *Rusya*[1] and *Slavonya*[2] were on the side of Yaroslav, a younger son of Vladimir, who may consequently be regarded as the national candidate. In a great battle fought on the Alta, Yaroslav defeated and slew Svyatopulk and became sole ruler (1019–1054). His long and glorious reign was very beneficial to Russia. He extended his sway to Lake Peipus, building the town of Yur'ev[3], later Dorpat, to secure his conquests (1030);

[1] The inhabitants of South Russia.
[2] The inhabitants of Novgorod and the North.
[3] *i.e.*, "George's City." He was christened "George."

incorporated part of Finland; subdued the Pechenegs; and
established an ecclesiastical hierarchy at Kiev, independent
of the Constantinopolitan Patriarch.   We hear great things of
his stately capital enriched by the Greek trade; of his famous
druzhina (bodyguard) and his brilliant court; of his love of
scholars who resorted to the learned Prince laden with MSS,
which he helped them to translate into Slavonic; of the
marriages of three of his daughters to the Kings of France,
Hungary, and Norway respectively.   From his reign too dates
the first Russian civil law, the so-called *Ruskaya Pravda.*

Yaroslav divided his dominions among his five sons, exhorting them, on his deathbed, to look up to and love their
elder brother, Izyaslav, whom he placed on the throne of Kiev.
This was the beginning of that singular family system which
differentiated the Russian Government from all the Governments of the West, and was the principal obstacle to the
establishment of feudalism in the east Slavonic lands.   According to this system, all the Russian lands, taken together,
belonged theoretically to the members of the whole princely
family.   The senior Prince, subsequently called the *Veliki
Knyaz,* or *Dux principalis,* reigned in the metropolitan city
of Kiev; and his "younger brothers," in other words all the
junior members of the family, deferred to him, not as
the common sovereign, for each was autonomous in his own
principality, but as the common father.   Each member of
the princely line might become senior in turn and therefore
be entitled to sit on the primatial throne of Kiev.   But no
Prince could become the eldest of the line if his father before
him had never attained to the seniority, that is to say if he,
the father, had died while *his* eldest brother was still *Veliki
Knyaz.*   In such cases the seniority passed to the next eldest
brother of the last Grand Duke.   Such excluded Princes were
called *izgovuie,* or "the expelled"; and, as time went on, a
second class of *izgovuie* arose, consisting of Princes who had
been deprived of their right of seniority, often arbitrarily

enough, for other reasons. On the death of the senior Prince
a general exchange of thrones immediately ensued. The next
senior Prince was duly installed, or, most often, installed
himself, at Kiev, with his *druzhina*; and the other principalities
were redistributed according to the dignity or power of their
respective holders. Originally, for the whole subject is very
obscure, there seem to have been six principalities, Kiev,
Polock, Chernigov, Pereyaslavl, Smolensk, and Vladimir
Voluinsk. Great Novgorod, at first dependent on Kiev,
presently set up a Republic of her own. As the *izgovuie*
carved out separate dominions, other principalities arose, such
as Ryazan, Vladimir on the Klyazma, Rostov, Suzdal, and
Halich, so that, towards the end of this period (*circa* 1240),
the Russian lands extended, roughly speaking, from the
Gulf of Finland to the Dnieperian steppes, and from the
Carpathians to the Upper Volga. Such a system made
for anarchy; and, indeed, the history of this *dyelnoe* or
"divisional period," as Russian historians call it (1014–1240),
is one interminable record of internecine wars. Now and
again the bright and gracious figure of some valiant champion,
or saintly ruler, crosses the darkling scene. Such an one was
the great national hero, Vladimir Monomakh (1107–1125),
whose great victory at Salnitsa (1109) beyond the Don,
temporarily freed Russia from the yoke of the Polovtsui,
the supplanters of the Pechenegs, who tormented the Russian
lands till they themselves were supplanted by the Tatars.
Kiev preserved its ascendency till 1170, when it was taken
and burnt by Andrew Bogolyubski, Prince of Suzdal, who
thereupon established himself at Vladimir. From this event
is to be dated the decline of the family system and the enmity
between the *Russkie Dyetskie* (Russian children), as the
chronicle now calls the southern Princes, and their northern
rivals. Autocracy was first definitely established in the north
by Vsevolod III (1176–1212), who also subdued most of the
south, and enforced allegiance not only to himself but *to*

his children, a significant innovation. Meanwhile the extreme south-western principalities, Halich and Volhynia, had gone their own way, and, despite the constant interference of Hungary and Poland, seemed about to establish new centres of Russian influence and civilisation at Lemberg and Vladimir Voluinsk. Daniel Romanovich, Prince of Halich (1247–1261), is especially memorable for his prowess and enterprise.

The terrible Tatar invasions (1224–1242) profoundly influenced the fate of the Slavonic lands. Its immediate effect upon Poland was to introduce a middle-class element there for the first time. The only way of filling up the gaps in the population, due to the ravages of Batu, was to invite foreign immigrants of a superior sort, chapmen and handicraftsmen capable of building strong cities and defending them afterwards. Such immigrants, naturally, could only be obtained from the civilised West on their own terms. Immediately dependent upon the Prince from whom they obtained their privileges, these traders soon became an important factor in the State, balancing, to some extent, the influence of the gentry and enriching the land by developing its resources. But these were not the only Germans with whom the young Polish State had now to deal. In the first year of the thirteenth century, the Knights of the Sword had been founded in Livonia to convert the pagan Letts; and in 1208 the still more powerful Teutonic Order was invited by Prince Conrad of Masovia to settle in the district of Culm (roughly corresponding to the modern West Prussia) to protect his territories from the incursions of the barbarian Prussians. The Teutonic Order, which had just been expelled from Hungary by Andrew II, joyfully accepted this new domicile; and its position in the North was definitely established by the compact of Kruszewicz (1230). A second Tatar invasion, in 1239, still further depressed Poland; and, simultaneously, another enemy appeared on her north-eastern border—the Lithuanians. This interesting people originally dwelt among the impenetrable forests and marshes of the Upper Niemen, where they were able to preserve their original savagery longer than any of their neighbours, and foster a tenacious and enterprising valour which made them very formidable to all the surrounding States. They first emerge into the light of history at the time of the settlement of the Teutonic Order in the North. Rumours of the war of extermination, waged by the Knights against their near kinsfolk the wild Prussians, first awoke the Lithuanians to a sense of their own danger. They immediately abandoned their loose communal system for a monarchical form of government, and under a series of exceptionally capable Princes, notably Mendovg (1240–1263) and Gedymin (1315–1341), began an astonishing career of conquest, mainly at the expense of Russia, so that at the death of Gedymin the Grand Duchy of Lithuania, as it was now called, extended from Courland to the Carpathians and from the Bug to the Desna, including the old Russian principalities of Polock, Kiev and Chernigov. Indeed, at one time, it seemed as if this new, non-Slavonic, State was about to eclipse and absorb all the Slavonic States to the east and west of her. Poland just then seemed to be dropping to pieces. Even the urgent and reiterated exhortations of the Popes failed to make her score of Princes unite for mutual defence; and, towards the end of the fourteenth century, it seemed highly probable that she would become either a dependency of the new Bohemian Empire of Waclaw II, or the prey of the Teutonic Knights. From both dangers she was saved by the valour and genius of Wladislaus I, *Lokietek*, "Span-long," so called from his diminutive stature (1309–1339), who re-united Great and Little Poland, revived the royal dignity (1320), and taught the Poles, on the bloody field of Plowce, (1332) that the Knights were not invincible. The fruits of his labours were richly reaped by his son Casimir III (1333–1370), Poland's first great statesman, who, by a most skilful system of matrimonial alliances, re-introduced his long isolated country into the European family and gave it a beneficial rest of

37 years. A born ruler, he introduced a whole series of administrative and economical reforms, protected the townsmen (whom he admitted to the franchise) against the tyranny of the nobles, and added the greater part of Galicia to the Polish dominions.

Very different was the fate of Russia. The Tatar invasions so weakened her southern principalities that, one by one, they submitted to the yoke of Lithuania. The current of the national life was now forced to flow north-eastwards instead of following its natural south-western course as heretofore. It was in the rude climate and amidst the vast virgin forests of the plain of the Upper Volga that the Russian Princes, entirely cut off from western civilisation, began with characteristic doggedness, painfully and laboriously, to build up again the Russian State. At first their position was desperate. For some time to come they were the tributaries of the Grand-Khan who ruled the Golden Horde at Sarai on the Volga (founded 1242); Tatar *Bashkaks* made regular censuses of the taxable population ; and the pretenders to the various Russian thrones went personally to the Horde to receive their *yarluiki*, or articles of investiture. Even the greatest of these early northern Princes, Alexander Nevsky, who defeated a league of the German Knights, Swedes and Lithuanians at the famous " Ice-Battle " on Lake Peipus (1242), and first established the sway of Russia over the Baltic Provinces, even Alexander Nevsky accepted his crown from the Grand-Khan Sartak. The most grinding period of the Tatar rule was between 1235 and 1260. Subsequently the grip of the Horde gradually relaxed, especially after the victories of the Lithuanian Princes, who pursued them into the very heart of the steppe. They now became as much the confederates as the tyrants of the constantly contending Russian Princes, as the Pechenegs and the Polovtsui had been before them. It was now (*circa* 1270) that the dominant Russian Dukes began to assume the title of Grand Dukes, and to aggrandise themselves at the expense of the weaker principalities. Vladimir, Tver, and Moscow were, successively, or alternately, the seats of these new Grand Dukes; while Novgorod, whose territories and colonies then extended from Lake Ilmen and the Gulf of Finland to the Arctic Ocean and the northern Urals, set up a quasi-independent Republic of its own, more or less dependent upon the Lithuanian Grand Dukes whom they, not unskilfully, played off against the Russian Princes. The ascendency of Moscow dates from Ivan I *Kalita*[1] (1330–1339), in whose reign the Russian Metropolitan transferred his See from Vladimir to Moscow[2] to the great advantage of the latter city and its rulers, who freely employed his ecclesiastical authority to promote their not very scrupulous political ambition. Kalita's son Simeon *Gordy*[3] (1340–1353) still further improved the position of Moscow, and was even admitted into Great Novgorod as the protector of that city.

The further progress of Moscow was, for some time, seriously impeded by the warlike Princes of Lithuania, who, by now, had extended their dominions to the shores of the Black Sea. One of them, Olgierd, twice besieged Moscow (1363 and 1370) though unsuccessfully. On the other hand, the Golden Horde (*circa* 1360) split up into three contending sections, which encouraged the Grand Duke Demetrius of Moscow (1362–1389) to lead a combination of all the northern Russian Princes into the steppe to fight the Tatars. He vanquished them at Kulikovo on Don (Sept. 30, 1380), but paid very dearly for his victory the following year, when the Khan Toktamuish led a punitive expedition against Moscow, which he took and burned. Tver and Vladimir shared the same fate. But in 1395 Tamerlane treated the Tatars as the Tatars had treated the Russians; and during

[1] Money-Bag.
[2] In 1229 the Metropolitan had moved from Kiev to Vladimir.
[3] The Proud.

the next twelve years the Horde was too feeble to extort the usual tribute. But now Witowt, Grand Duke of Lithuania, seized upon Smolensk and other Russian territory; and the Grand Duke Vasily I of Moscow (1389–1425) was glad to make an ally of his rival by marrying his daughter Sophia. Vasily I's son and successor, Vasily II *Temny*[1] (1425–1462), suffered greatly at the hands of the Tatars, who worried him perpetually and burnt and blackmailed Moscow in 1444. But he suffered still more from his rebellious magnates, who blinded and deposed him (1446). The same year he was restored to his throne by the clergy and people, and devoted the remainder of his long reign to gathering together under one sceptre all the northern and central Russian lands, a process which began with the incorporation of Mozhaisk in 1454 and ended with the incorporation of Vyatka in 1459. Thus, by the middle of the fifteenth century, the political life of north-eastern Russia had concentrated in and around Moscow, which was to give its name to the new State till Peter the Great converted Moscovy into Russia. South-western Russia meanwhile had been merged in another great Slavonic State, whose existence also dates from the fifteenth century—the century which saw the collapse of mediævalism and the beginning of the nationalities of modern Europe.

For nearly twenty years after the death of Casimir the Great (1370–1386) Poland was, technically, part of the vast Hungarian Empire of the Angevins, but, in 1383, Jadwiga, the youthful granddaughter of Wladislaus Lokietek, and the niece of Casimir the Great, was elected Queen by the Poles. In 1386 she was married to Jagiello, Grand Duke of Lithuania, who, three days previously, had been baptised and crowned King of Poland at Cracow, under the title of Wladislaus II. The union of Poland and Lithuania, as two independent States under a common King, had been brought about by their common fear of the Teutonic Order. But the trans-

[1] The Blind.

formation of the pagan Lithuanian chieftain into a Catholic King was a serious blow to the Knights also. The inevitable and immediate consequence of this great event was the formal reception of the Lithuanian nation into the fold of the Church. What the Knights had vainly endeavoured to bring about by fire and sword during two centuries, was, nominally and peaceably, brought about by Jagiello in the course of a single generation. The conversion of Lithuania menaced the very existence of the Knights. Originally planted on the Baltic shore for the express purpose of christianising their savage neighbours, these crusading monks had freely exploited the wealth and the valour of the West, originally in the cause of religion, but latterly for the purpose of founding a dominion of their own. This dominion was now little more than a German military outpost, extending from Pomerania to the Niemen, excluding the Slavs from the sea and thriving at their expense. But, if the Order had now become an anachronism, it was still the strongest military organisation in Europe. The pick of the feudal chivalry composed its ranks; with all Christendom to draw upon, its resources seemed inexhaustible; and centuries of political experience had made it as formidable in diplomacy as in warfare.

In the circumstances, war between Poland and the Knights was inevitable. It began in 1391 and was waged with varying success till 1410, when Wladislaus and his cousin Witowt (to whom, by the compact of Wilna, 1401, he had surrendered the Grand Duchy of Lithuania on the understanding that the two States were to have a common policy and jointly elected Sovereigns) inflicted a crushing defeat upon the Knights at Grünewald or Tannenburg (July 15), which brought about the surrender of the towns of Thorn, Elbing, Brunsberg, and Dantzig to the Polish King. But the excessive caution of Jagiello after the victory, the withdrawal of Witowt to oppose a Tatar invasion in the East, and the unruliness of the Polish levies, gave the Knights time to recover somewhat from the blow. At the first Peace of Thorn (Feb. 11, 1411) they only ceded Samogitia and Dobrzyn and paid a war indemnity of 100,000 marks. One important result of this war was the Union of Horodlo (Oct. 2, 1413) for the purpose of binding Poland and Lithuania still more closely together. It enacted that henceforth there should be an absolute parity of the institutions, the official hierarchy, and the nobility of the two States. The Lithuanian Grand Duke was declared to be the equal in all respects of the Polish King and only eligible by the Senates of Poland and Lithuania conjointly, just as the King of Poland could only be elected by the Senates of Lithuania and Poland. The privileges of the newly-created Lithuanian nobility were, however, to be conditional upon their profession of Catholicism, experience having demonstrated that difference of religion in Lithuania meant difference of politics, the majority of the Lithuanian Boyars inhabiting the old Russian lands being of the Greek Orthodox confession, with a consequent tendency towards Moscow.

During the remainder of the reign of Wladislaus II, the repeated attempts of the Teutonic Order to evade the obligations of the Treaty of Thorn gave Poland much trouble. The long contest, mainly fought with diplomatic weapons at Rome and elsewhere, was still undecided at the death of Wladislaus in 1434. During his long reign of 49 years, Poland had gradually risen to the rank of a great power—a result due in no small measure to the sagacity, tact and patience of the first of the Jagiellos. Wladislaus had sacrificed every other consideration to the vital necessity of welding the central Slavs into a compact and homogeneous State; and his success had been commensurate with his efforts. The next ten years tested severely the stability of his great work. But neither a turbulent minority, nor the neglect of an absentee King, nor the revival of separatist tendencies in Lithuania, nor the outbreak of aristocratic lawlessness in Poland, could do more than shake slightly the superstructure of the imposing edifice. Fortunately too, after the death at Varna, in 1444, of Jagiello's eldest son and immediate successor, Wladislaus III (whose history belongs rather to Hungary than to Poland), another great statesman, in no wise inferior to Wladislaus II, was at hand at a critical juncture, to complete and consolidate his father's work. This was Wladislaus' second son, Casimir IV, with whom the modern history of Poland properly begins.

CHAPTER II.

CASIMIR IV, 1447–1492.

THE sudden death of Wladislaus III on the field of Varna (Nov. 1444) had, at first, a paralysing effect on the more northerly of his two kingdoms. The last letter which the Polish Senate despatched to the heroic young King (he was but twenty when he fell), and which never reached him, was full of warnings, entreaties and even threats. If, it declared, he did not return instantly, to repair the dilapidation of the realm, his Polish subjects would feel justified in renouncing their allegiance. The ensuing three years' interregnum did not improve matters. The most convenient candidate for the vacant throne was Wladislaus' younger brother Casimir, since 1440 Grand Duke of Lithuania, a precociously sagacious youth of seventeen, who was by no means disposed to exchange an absolute sway in his beloved Grand Duchy, for a relatively limited authority in a kingdom which he had never visited. Only after exasperating negotiations, only after the Poles had threatened him with a rival in Boleslaus, Prince of Masovia, would Casimir give way. Then he stipulated that the disputed border provinces of Volhynia and Podolia should previously be adjudged to Lithuania (Treaty of Brezsc Litewsk, March 23, 1446), and even after his coronation at Cracow (June 1447) he continued to spend the greater part of his time in Lithuania. For the next seven years he quietly but steadfastly resisted all the petitions of the Polish nobles for a confirmation of their ancient privileges, till they threatened to form a confederation against him. Then he yielded his consent (Diet of Piotrkow, 1453)[1], but in such general terms as to make it of little or no value. Casimir's firmness had important political consequences. The *Szlachta*[2] were impressed by his resolution, but they mistrusted him ever afterwards as a pro-Lithuanian, and henceforth made it a point of honour to give him nothing gratis.

A natural partiality for the land of his birth was, no doubt, partly responsible for Casimir's original reserve towards Poland; but behind this partiality lay the unshakable conviction that the fate both of the dynasty and the dual state depended on the maintenance of the union. He rightly held that to this fundamental principle everything else must be subordinated. Casimir humoured Lithuania because, at this time, Lithuania was the more restive and uncertain of the two political yoke-fellows. Wild and wayward as Poland might be, she was, nevertheless composed and tranquil as compared with Lithuania. Her population was of one race and religion. Her provincial *Sejmiki*, or Dietines, exercised some control over her turbulent gentry. She had reached a higher degree of civilisation, such as it was, than the Grand Duchy. In Lithuania, on the other hand, there were different nationalities and more than one religion. Samogitia was still semi-pagan; Lithuania Proper, thanks to the propaganda from Wilna, was semi-Catholic; but the remainder of the land[3], five-sixths of the whole, consisting of subjugated Old-Russian territory, was mostly orthodox. Superadded to these religious and ethnological difficulties were strong national rivalries. Lithuania was too ignorant rightly to appreciate the advantages of a union with Poland, and much too sensitive of her past military glories to tolerate any interference

---

[1] On this occasion Podolia was provisionally awarded to Poland and Volhynia to Lithuania.

[2] The generic name of the whole Polish nobility, akin to *Geschlecht*.

[3] *See* map I.

from the Crown[1] in her affairs. From the first, strong separatist tendencies asserted themselves. The immense preponderance of her orthodox population drew her rather to the East than to the West, while her geographical position directly exposed her not only to the ravages but to the intrigues of the Moscovite. To keep the two States at one was the problem of the whole Jagiellonic period; and it is the especial glory of the Jagiellos that they did at last succeed in welding them inseparably together. But it was an ungrateful, troublesome task, requiring constant watchfulness and consummate tact. Fortunately Casimir IV possessed both these qualities in an eminent degree.

In February, 1454, Casimir wedded the Archduchess Elizabeth of Austria, in order to perpetuate the dynasty of which he was now the last surviving member. The Princess bore him six sons, four of whom became Kings, and seven daughters, thus earning the title of "The Mother of the Jagiellos." Highly gifted, both in heart and mind, she was ever an excellent counsellor as well as a devoted wife and mother. She also warmly identified herself with all the aspirations of her adopted country, for which she was rewarded by an extraordinary popularity.

Casimir shewed as much sobriety and discretion in foreign as in domestic affairs. A prince of a more martial temperament might have endeavoured to profit by the political complications in Bohemia and Hungary during the years 1447–1458. But Casimir, who well understood where the proper interests of Poland lay, remained neutral. On the other hand, when, at the instigation of the Grand Duke Vasily of Moscow, the Tatars fell upon Bransk and Wiezma, Casimir retaliated by devastating Mozhaisk and blackmailing Tver. In 1450 he placed his tributary, Alexander, on the Moldavian throne, and in 1457 he acquired, by purchase, the Silesian Duchies of Zator and Oswiecim.

[1] The general term for Poland during the Union.

B.

2

But it was towards the Teutonic Order that his attention was chiefly directed.

The rout of Grünewald had severely shaken the internal organisation of the Teutonic Order. Everywhere else in Europe, except Byzantium and Moscovy, the nobility, clergy and townsmen possessed some share in the government of the country which they defended, educated, and enriched; but in the dominions of the Knights these three classes remained without the slightest political influence. So long as the Order was rich and powerful enough to defend its subjects and spare their pockets, the gentry and the towns acquiesced in their political effacement. But, when the burden of taxation began to increase, unaccompanied by any additional benefit, the gentry and citizens began to look with other eyes upon the Swabians, Franconians and Saxons who came from the distant West, in monkish habits, to exploit and dominate them. The discontent was most violent in the province of Kulm, or Chelm, that is, the district lying between the rivers Vistula, Drewenca and Ossa, where the Polish element largely predominated. In 1397 the malcontents formed a league called the *Jaszczurczycy* or Lizardites, from their adopted emblem, the *Jaszczurka*, or Lizard. At the battle of Grünewald the defection of the Lizards, at the crisis of the struggle, contributed as much as the fury of Witowt and his Lithuanians to the overthrow of the Knights. After the Peace of Thorn the Order recognised the necessity of some concessions to its subjects; and, in 1414, a consultative *Rada Krajowa*, or Landtag, was formed, which gave them a limited veto they were not slow to exercise. In 1440 this Landtag, more and more dissatisfied with the rule of the Knights, formed the Prussian League, consisting of the *Szlachta* and all the towns of the Prussian Provinces; but the Grand Master, Ludwig von Erlichshausen, procured a papal bull threatening the League with excommunication if it did not disperse. In its extremity the League appealed to the Emperor; but, when the Emperor also pronounced against

it, there was nothing for it but to claim the protection
of its nearest powerful neighbour, the King of Poland.
Hitherto, Casimir had remained strictly neutral, though
private negotiations had been proceeding for some time between the Polish Senate and the Prussian League.   But when,
in the beginning of February, 1454, the League publicly renounced its allegiance to the Grand Master and seized fifty-four
towns and strongholds, including Thorn, the King hesitated no
longer.

On February 18, 1454, during the celebration of the nuptials
of Casimir and Elizabeth of Hapsburg, Jan Bazynski, at the
head of an embassy from the Prussian League, appeared at
Cracow and formally offered to surrender the Prussian lands to
the Polish Crown.   He concluded his lengthy oration with
these words : " Your Majesty will not be taking alien possessions.   You will but be recovering what the Crusaders, either
by force of arms or by treaty, in times passed, took away from
Poland."   On March 6 Casimir issued a manifesto incorporating all the Prussian provinces with Poland, confirming
the privileges of the Prussian Estates, exempting them from all
tolls and taxes, granting them local autonomy, and promising
them the same trade privileges already enjoyed by the Polish
cities.   The deputies, on their part, placed in the hand of
the Polish Primate a sealed oath of allegiance to the Polish
King; whereupon Casimir divided the Prussian lands into four
wojwodschafts, or palatinates—Chelm, Pomeria, Elbing, and
Königsberg—and appointed Bazynski Governor General.   All
this was the work of a fortnight; and Casimir IV now prepared,
with a light heart, to enter into possession of his new provinces.
It did not seem an insuperably difficult task.   The Knights
were known to be in sore need of money and allies.   The
majority of the Prussian population was in Casimir's favour.
Then, too, the subjugation of the Knights was vital to the very
existence of Poland.   It meant the excision of a mischievous,
alien element.   It meant the recovery, at little cost, of the

control of the principal rivers of Poland, the Vistula and the Niemen. It meant the obtaining of a sea-board with the corollaries of sea-power and world-wide commerce. Casimir IV was justified in counting upon the ardent support of the whole Polish nation in such a patriotic enterprise. But all his calculations foundered upon the narrow provincialism of the Poles which hampered him at every step, and retarded the incorporation of the Prussian lands for thirteen years. To understand how this came about, we must first glance back, nearly two hundred years, to the origin of the Polish political system.

The origin of the Polish constitution is to be sought in the *wiece*, or council, of the Polish Princes during the partitional period. The privileges conferred upon the magnates, of whom these councils were composed, revolted the less favoured *Szlachta*, or gentry, who, towards the end of the fourteenth century, combined in defence of their rights, in their *Sejmiki*, or local diets, of which, originally, there were five, three in Great Poland, one in Little Poland, and one in Posen-Kalisch, the other Provinces obtaining their Sejmiki somewhat later. Thus, at the period we have reached, Poland was a confederacy of half a dozen semi-independent States, with different and even conflicting interests. Little Poland had for some time enjoyed a sort of primacy in this confederation, due partly to the superior wealth and importance of her capital, Cracow, which was both the coronation city and the seat of the Senate, or central executive government, and partly to the fact that her oligarchs had brought in the reigning dynasty and ruled in its name. The pre-eminence of Little Poland excited the jealousy of the other members of the confederacy; but, besides that, no one province was bound by the decision of any other province. All such essential matters as taxation, military service, and so on, were settled by each province in its own *Sejmik*; the convocation of a *Walny Sejm*, or general Diet, to represent the whole nation, being a very unpopular[1] and therefore a very unusual expedient.

---

[1] Because most of the deputies found the journey too costly.

Casimir IV was now to experience all the inconveniences of this primitive and yet complicated state of things. It had been arranged that the King, after receiving the homage of the Prussian Estates at Thorn and Elbing, should proceed to reduce the cities and fortresses still held by the Knights, beginning with Marienberg and Chojnice. For this purpose the *pospolite ruszenie*, or militia, was summoned to render its one obligation of military service, and take the field. Difficulties at once began. The only province which willingly responded to the summons was Great Poland, which bordered upon the Prussian lands and hoped to profit largely by the war. But even the *Szlachta* of Great Poland would not stir a step till the King had first subscribed 35 articles in their camp at Cerekwica, near Thorn (Sept. 15, 1454), confirming and enlarging their privileges. Three days later they were shamefully routed beneath the walls of Chojnice, so that the King got decidedly the worst of the hard bargain. The process was repeated with the militia of Little Poland. Their assistance was purchased by the articles of Nieszawa (Nov. 1454) whereby the King conferred on the Little Poles privileges similar to those conferred on the Great Poles three months previously. The general effect of all these privileges was to make the local Diets the arbiters of peace and war in future, thus weakening, still further, the executive government which Casimir the Great, alarmed at the centripetal tendency of the *Szlachta*, had originally set up at Cracow with the Senate as its mouthpiece and the King as its right arm. Immediately afterwards (Jan. 1455) Casimir IV again crossed the Vistula at the head of the militia of Little Poland to besiege the fortress of Laszyna, and again he was compelled to retreat with dishonour, the *Szlachta*, so strenuous in the extortion of privileges, demonstrating its incompetence to win battles or take strongholds. The natural consequence of this abortive campaign was that many of the Prussian towns returned to their former allegiance, and the King had to look about him for professional soldiers.

The best mercenaries of those days were the Czechs. The genius of Jan Žižka in the Hussite wars had caused a revolution in military tactics. He had demonstrated that dense masses of light-armed, well trained, mobile infantry were more than a match for all the valour of the clumsy, undisciplined feudal chivalry. The Hussite soldiery soon became indispensable in the northern wars. Žižka's ablest pupils, men like Iskra of Brandeis, for instance, carved out principalities for themselves and won European reputations. Hussites had fought on both sides at Grünewald, and now both Casimir IV and the Knights eagerly competed for their assistance. But, like all mercenaries, the Czechs could be very troublesome to unpunctual paymasters; and the Knights, whose treasury was well-nigh depleted, were the first to experience this disagreeable tendency. On August 15, 1456, the Czech captain, Ulryk Czerwonka, unable to obtain his arrears from the Order, offered to surrender to Casimir the 21 towns and fortresses in his hands, including Marienberg, the capital of the Knights, for 436,000 gulden, payable in three instalments. Casimir, who had already expended 1,200,000 ducats on the war out of his private income, was almost as poor as the Knights, and therefore appealed to the generosity of the nation. What next ensued is not very creditable to the Polish Estates. The *Szlachta* first attempted to lay the whole burden on the shoulders of the clergy, who vigorously protested. Finally, after weeks of wrangling, a *Sejm*, or Diet, assembled at Piotrkow in September, 1416, proposed a two per cent. property tax, the details of which were left to the decision of the local *Sejmiki*, to which the King had also to apply in person. The *Sejmiki* were, as usual, mutinous and obstructive. Only after the King, driven to desperation, had threatened to quit Poland altogether and bury himself in the forests of Lithuania, did they relent. Even when, at last, the subsidy had been grudgingly granted, on condition that it should be placed in the hands of commissioners, it proved so inadequate that

Casimir was forced to supplement it by loans from the Cathedral Chapter of Cracow and other private sources. By these means the first instalment was finally paid by the Polish commissioners to Czerwonka; and on the Saturday before Palm Sunday, 1457, a Polish garrison was admitted into the citadel of Marienberg. But Casimir's humiliations were not yet over. Only a few days after his own triumphal entry, on Wednesday in Holy Week, the burgomaster of Marienberg readmitted the Knights; and the King had again to go, hat in hand, to the *Sejmiki* for money to recover it. Great Poland was complacent enough, but Little Poland, which was well able to put 60,000 men in the field, refused even to pay the wages of the little band of Czech mercenaries encamped around Cracow till they arose and pillaged the city. At a subsequent *Sejm*, assembled at Cracow in September, 1459, Jan Rytwianski, Starosta of Sandomir, took it upon himself to lecture the King severely for his carelessness, incompetence, and undue partiality for Lithuania. He concluded by exhorting his Sovereign to play the man, and wage the war more successfully. To this blustering philippic, whose naïveté was equal to its impertinence, the King drily replied that no war could be waged without money, and money must be found now if the war was to go on at all. The necessary subsidies were then granted without further demur.

Marienberg was ultimately recovered, whereupon the war became a *guerilla* of raids, petty skirmishes and tedious sieges, which did infinitely more damage to the land than half a dozen regular campaigns. By this time the military incompetence of the *Szlachta* had become so manifest, that they themselves willingly voted a five per cent. land tax in commutation of military service, which enabled Casimir to enlist 2000 extra mercenaries for the relief of Danzig, then hardly pressed. The turning point of the war was marked by the battle of Puck (Sept. 17, 1462), when the Czechs severely defeated the Knights, whose resistance, henceforth, visibly slackened. On September 26, 1466, the oft-besieged fortress of Chojnice fell, at last, into the hands of the Polish King. The superior diplomacy of Casimir also contributed materially to the termination of the struggle. The Curia had hitherto been on the side of the Knights. But, now (despite a serious quarrel between the King and the Pope as to the filling up of the See of Cracow, 1461–1463, when Casimir roundly declared that he would rather lose Poland altogether than submit to papal dictation), the Holy Father, from political motives, was inclined to look benevolently upon so considerable a Prince as Casimir was, evidently, becoming. The Order also sought an agreement with its adversary through the mediation of the Hanseatic League; and a peace Congress was accordingly opened at Thorn in 1463. The Knights were now willing to surrender the provinces of Chelm, Thorn and Michailowò, and render tribute and military service for the rest. The King, however, claimed the whole territory as old Polish land, and offered to settle the Knights in Podolia, where, he added, with a touch of irony, they would still be able to perform their original mission of defending Christendom against the Tatars[1]. But the Knights, by no means relishing this proposal to exchange their comfortable quarters for the naked steppes, broke off the negotiations and the war was resumed for three years, when the Order, utterly exhausted, again sued for peace.

A second Congress, under the mediation of a papal nuncio, thereupon met at Thorn on September 23, 1466; and on October 14 the second Peace of Thorn was signed. By this treaty the provinces of Pomerelia, Michailowo, Warmia, Elbing and Marienberg passed to Poland. The remainder of the Knights' territory, roughly corresponding to the modern East Prussia, with its capital at Königsberg, was to be an inseparable but autonomous portion of the Polish realm, united thereto in

---

[1] He had previously suggested to the Pope, much to their alarm, that they should, for the same reason, be transferred to Tenedos or to the neighbourhood of Constantinople.

much the same way as was Lithuania, with this difference : that,
whereas the Grand Duke of Lithuania was the equal, the Grand
Master was to be the subject, of the Polish King, holding his
lands by military tenure and bound, six months after his election, to render homage to his suzerain. In all other respects
he was to be a quasi-independent Prince. He was to occupy
the first place in the Royal Council after the King. No war
was to be declared or peace signed without his consent. His
territories were to be exclusively under his jurisdiction.
The amount of his military service was left, practically, to his
own discretion.

It was a proud moment for Casimir IV when, amidst the
peals of the church bells and salvoes of artillery, and surrounded by the dignitaries of Poland and Lithuania in full
panoply, he received in the market-place of Thorn the homage
of the Grand Master of the Teutonic Order kneeling before the
throne. In the hour of his triumph Casimir treated the vanquished with princely generosity. To the Grand Master he
gave a largess of 15,000 ducats, from his privy purse, to pay
his starving mercenaries ; and, in view of the general misery of
Prussia, he exempted the Order from the obligation of military
service for 20 years. The condition of the land was, indeed,
pitiable. It is estimated that, during the course of the war,
1000 monasteries and churches were ruined, 18,000 out of
21,000 villages were reduced to ashes, and 270,000 of the
inhabitants, not including 170,000 mercenaries, perished
miserably.

It was no fault of Casimir IV's that his victory after all was
but a half-victory. It had been his intention to incorporate all
the Prussian lands with the Polish State, but the stress of circumstances had compelled him to acquiesce in an unnatural and
purely mechanical union with the secular enemies of the Polish
nation. There could be no lasting fellowship, no community
of political interests, between the two peoples ; and presently
religious differences were superadded, and the chasm between

them became unbridgeable. Nevertheless, one half of the Prussian lands had been incorporated; and the economical advantages derived therefrom by Poland were not inconsiderable. She had now, moreover, a sea-board which placed her once more, after an interval of 300 years, in direct commercial communication with the West. She might reasonably hope to secure, in time, her proper share of the lucrative Baltic trade and lay the foundations of a Sea Power.

The Peace of Thorn had scarce been concluded when Pope Paul II offered Casimir the throne of Bohemia on condition that he drove out the reigning heretic King, George Podiebrad. But Casimir, well disposed to George as being a faithful ally, unable to pay the *Szlachta* the covenanted five marks per lance for foreign expeditions, and unwilling to be the tool of the Curia, remained immovable. "I cannot understand," he said to the importunate papal legates, "how a crowned and anointed King can be deposed after this sort." The ambitious young King of Hungary, Matthias Hunyadi, though bound to Podiebrad by ties of kinship and gratitude, was less particular. On May 3, 1469, after winning Moravia by the Battle of Trebicza, he was proclaimed King of Bohemia in the castle of Olmütz; whereupon Podiebrad offered the Bohemian crown to Wladislaus, the eldest son of Casimir IV, on condition that he wedded his daughter Ludomilla and reconciled the Utraquists with the Pope. At the same time, the Emperor Frederick IV's dread and jealousy of Matthias induced him to form an anti-Hungarian League with Casimir (Congress of Willach, 1470). On March 22, 1471, George Podiebrad died, and all eyes were instantly fixed upon the vacant throne of Bohemia. On May 27, 1471, the Utraquist majority of the Bohemian Diet, assembled at Kuttenberg, elected Wladislaus King; and he was crowned at the Cathedral of St Vitus, at Prague, on August 22. But Matthias, who had already been anointed King of Bohemia at Erlau, in Hungary, by the papal legate, Roverella, and now held Silesia (then generally regarded as a part of the Bohemian

Empire) as well as Moravia, refused to withdraw his claims. A league was immediately formed against him, consisting of Casimir IV, the Emperor, the Bohemian Utraquists and the Hungarian malcontents ; and it seemed, at first, as if he must inevitably, be crushed beneath the sheer weight of it. But the subtle genius of Matthias, ever inexhaustible in resources, extricated him out of all his difficulties. It is true that he did not succeed in ousting Wladislaus from Bohemia proper, but he compensated himself by seizing all the hereditary States of the Emperor. His chief weapon against Casimir was the Teutonic Order, which he took under his protection, and twice incited to rebel against its suzerain. He also stirred up the Moscovite and the Tatar against Lithuania. Wherever Casimir had an enemy, Matthias was sure to be behind him. Finally, after a desultory, intermittent war, lasting eight years, in the course of which Casimir tried to place his second son, John Albert, on the Hungarian throne, all the parties to it grew weary of the struggle; and peace, as far as Poland was concerned, was concluded at the Congress of Olmütz, July, 1479, on a *uti possidetis* basis.

There can be little doubt that Casimir's Bohemian-Hungarian adventure was a mistake. For once he seems to have been guided by dynastic rather than by patriotic considerations. Hungary and Bohemia, even under a Jagiellonic sceptre, could not benefit Poland, as subsequent events were to demonstrate. Yet this eccentric excursion did not divert Casimir's attention from pressing matters nearer home. In particular the separatist tendencies of Lithuania were a constant source of uneasiness. For instance, so irritated were the Lithuanians at the provisional annexation of Podolia to Poland that, for a time, they meditated superseding Casimir by Simon, Prince of Kiev, a feudatory of the Grand Duchy. After Simon's death, in 1471, Casimir prevented any such contingency in the future by converting the principality of Kiev into an ordinary *woiwodschaft*, or palatinate. But the chief danger to Lithuania, though still but a remote one, lay in the proximity of Moscovy; and Casimir did his utmost to counteract it by promoting the Catholic propaganda in the Grand Duchy. From a purely political point of view this was wise and just, for the complete union of Lithuania with Poland could only be brought about by gradually permeating the Grand Duchy with the superior civilisation of the West. Such a policy logically excluded the counter-influence of the Greek Church, and was therefore likely to be very unpopular in Lithuania. But here Casimir, naturally tolerant and inclined to indulge the prejudices of the Lithuanian boyars, proceeded very warily. He would not hear of the persecution of the Orthodox. But he favoured the Uniate Churches, established in Lithuania since 1443, by placing them on a footing of perfect equality with the Catholics, a position unattainable by the Orthodox. The same care for centralisation and unity is the explanation of Casimir's constant refusal to appoint a viceroy over Lithuania. He always kept the government of the Grand Duchy in his own hands. Even in his old age he would not suffer his sons to represent him there.

With Moscovy Casimir's relations were friendly enough during the latter years of the Grand Duke Vasily, who, on his deathbed in 1462, confided the care of his children to the Lithuanian Prince. This fatherly solicitude was quite superfluous, as the new Grand Duke of Moscovy, Ivan III, was eminently capable of taking care of himself, and proved to be a troublesome neighbour[1]. Casimir is sometimes accused of regarding the growth of Moscovy with indifference because he did not seriously dispute with her the possession of Great Novgorod. But the distant north did not really fall within Casimir's proper sphere of influence. Besides, what reason had he for apprehending the serious rivalry of an infant State which actually paid tribute to the very Tatar Khans, whom he,

[1] *See* next chapter.

himself, from time to time, set upon their unstable thrones in the Crimea?

Casimir IV was frequently exhorted by the Popes to form or join a general league against the Turks, with whom Poland had not yet come into direct collision[1]. It was not, however, till the latter years of his reign that Casimir was able to turn his attention to the south, and when he did so it was more from political than from religious motives. Moldavia was the object which attracted him thither. The relations of this principality with Poland were peculiar. Poland had established a sort of suzerainty over Moldavia as early as the end of the fourteenth century, but, at best, it was a loose and vague overlordship which the Hospodars repudiated whenever they were strong enough to do so. The Turks were too much occupied elsewhere to pay much attention to the Danubian Principalities till the middle of the fifteenth century. Mohammed II had indeed attempted their subjection, with indifferent success, in 1478, but it was not till 1484 that the Ottomans became inconvenient neighbours to Poland. In that year a Turkish fleet captured the strongholds of Kilia and Akkerman, commanding respectively the mouths of the Danube and Dniester. This aggression seriously threatened the trade of Poland, and induced Casimir IV to accede to a general league then in process of formation against the Porte. In 1485, after driving the Turks out of Moldavia, the Polish king, at the head of 20,000 men, proceeded to Kolomya, on the Pruth; but Bajazid III, embarrassed by the Egyptian War, offered peace. As, however, no agreement as to the captured fortresses could be arrived at, the Turks would only consent to a two years' truce. Meanwhile, the projected anti-Turkish league was frustrated by the intrigues of Matthias of Hungary, who himself had designs upon Moldavia. It is generally supposed that it was at his

[1] Only a small Polish contingent was with Wladislaus II at Varna. It was as King, not of Poland but of Hungary, that Wladislaus undertook the expedition.

instigation that a motley host of Wallachians, Cossacks, Tatars and Magyars now fell suddenly upon Polish Russia[1]; but they were encountered and utterly overthrown by the Polish chivalry under the *Krolewicz*, or Crown Prince, John Albert, at Koposztyna (Sept. 8, 1487). In 1490 the Tatars a second time ravaged Russia, apparently impelled thereto by Matthias, so that the tidings of his sudden death on April 6, the same year, were hailed with relief at the Court of Cracow.

It was during the reign of Casimir IV that the *Szlachta*, or gentry, began to dominate the *Sejmiki*, or local Diets, and impose their will on the country at large. As already indicated, they had added to their original privilege of freedom from every obligation except that of military service, the right of deciding all questions of peace or war and controlling the military levies. As, moreover, they held the power of the purse, they could hamper the executive at every step. Their distrust of the King was fully equalled by their jealousy of the towns. At this time the municipalities of Poland still played a not unimportant part in her history. These cities, notably Cracow, had obtained from the Crown their privileges (such as self-government and freedom from tolls) in return for loans to impecunious Kings, or important public services, such as warding off Tatar raids. The cities of German origin were also protected by the Magdeburg Law. Furthermore, Louis the Great (1370–1382) had placed the burgesses of Cracow on a level with the gentry by granting to the town council jurisdiction over all the serfs in the extra-mural estates of the citizens. Henceforth, deputies from all the chief cities were usually summoned to the *Sejmiki* on all important occasions, *e.g.* the ratification of treaties—a right formally conceded to them by the Sejmik of Radom in 1384. But, as the *Szlachta* grew in power and pride, they chafed against their political partnership

---

[1] The term *Russia* at this period means, generally speaking, the Polish Province of Red Russia, extending from the Upper Bug and its confluents to the Dniester.

with the wealthy plebeian burgesses, though ready enough to claim their assistance in case of need, as when the *Szlachta* of Red Russia combined with the burgesses of Lemberg, in 1464, against the tyrannical Starosta-General, Piotr Odrowanz. Such combinations were, however, very exceptional. Generally speaking, the *Szlachta* was more disposed to injure the towns than to co-operate with them. A memorable instance of patrician arrogance and vindictiveness occurred in 1461.

Andrzy Tenczynski, brother of the Castellan of Cracow, one of the highest dignitaries in the realm, on the eve of his departure for the Prussian War, quarrelled with Klemens, a smith of the city, about the price of repairs to a suit of armour. Tenczynski sent the smith 18 groats. Klemens demanded two gulden, or four times as much. Then Tenczynski first gave Klemens a sound drubbing and afterwards complained of his insolence to the town council. The town council promised to make amends; but, in the meantime, Tenczynski, with a numerous armed retinue, encountered the injured smith in the street. High words ensued on both sides. Finally, Tenczynski's retainers drew their swords upon Klemens, and so wounded him that he was carried home half-dead. The tidings of this outrage quickly spread through the city; and the same day Tenczynski was murdered in the church of the Franciscans, where he had taken refuge, by an infuriated mob of artisans and citizens. All this took place on July 16, when the militia of Little Poland were encamped round Cracow. The nobility at once clamoured for redress; but Casimir prudently postponed the consideration of the matter to the end of the year, when he should have returned from the Prussian campaign. The case was accordingly brought before the Sejmik of Kosczyn on December 6. The town council, through their advocate, questioned the competency of the tribunal, and claimed the privileges of the Magdeburg Law, conferred upon the city by Casimir the Great in 1318 Tenczynski's friends appealed to the recently enacted articles

of Nieszawa, which enjoined that a plebeian assaulting a
gentleman should answer for his offence before the local Diet,
in other words before a tribunal of gentlemen.   The King, who
was absolutely dependent on the *Szlachta* for the subsidies
necessary to continue the war, decided in their favour; the
local Diet tried the case in its own way; and, on January 4,
1462, seven of the town councillors of Cracow were publicly
executed for refusing to hand over the prisoner, who, apparently,
had made his escape in the meantime.   When, however, the
Tenczynskis, not content with this summary art of vengeance,
demanded the imposition of the enormous fine of 80,000 marks
upon the town council, Casimir intervened and reduced the
amount to 2000.

Yet, like all the Jagiellos, Casimir IV, as a rule, both respected and defended the privileges of the towns.   The
following case may be taken as typical.

A *szlachcic*[1], Piotr Bostowski, had attacked the house of
Adam Solcz, a citizen of Cracow, broken open the doors, killed
two of Solcz's servants and done other mischief.   The city
consuls thereupon arrested and brought the culprit before
the town council.   He was duly tried, according to the
Magdeburg Law, condemned to death and publicly executed,
confessing the justice of his sentence.   Immediately afterwards
the Bostowskis summoned the consuls and town council before
the local Diet for the slaying of their kinsman.   The town
council refused to admit the jurisdiction of the provincial court
and appealed to the King for protection.   Casimir summoned
the parties before him at the castle of Cracow, and, after a
careful consideration of the case, decided that the consuls had
acted in strict conformity with the privileges of the city, as
guaranteed by the Magdeburg Law, and were worthy rather
of praise than of blame.

Casimir IV died at Troki, in Lithuania (June 7, 1492), while
on his way from Wilna to Cracow, in his 65th year.   A Prince

[1] *i.e.* a member of the *Szlachta*.

of little learning, simple tastes (he always drank water, and his one recreation was the chase) and pacific temperament, he was not, perhaps, the man to inspire the enthusiasm of an essentially martial people.   Yet no other Polish King ever did so much for Poland.   It was his wisdom, judgment, moral courage, infinite patience, and inexhaustible tenacity which raised Poland to the rank of a great Power.   His task was a difficult one; and he pursued it, from first to last, with a rare devotion and conscientiousness which deserved to the full the respect and gratitude freely rendered to his memory after his death by a nation which was unable to appreciate him during his life-time.

CHAPTER III.

IVAN III AND THE SONS OF CASIMIR, 1462–1506.

IT was as the fortunate inheritor of the fruits of the labours of generations of careful ancestors that Ivan III ascended the grand ducal throne of Moscovy in 1462, in his 23rd year. Roughly speaking, the Grand Duchy proper then embraced the very centre of modern European Russia, with off-shoots extending northwards as far as Lake Byelo and Ustyug on the Sukhona. Round the Grand Duchy were grouped the still nominally independent principalities of Rostov, Tver, and Ryazan, while the semi-dependent Republic of Great Novgorod, with her *zavoloche*, or colonies, extended from Ladoga and the Gulf of Finland to the northern Dwina and the White Sea. Beyond Novgorod, the sturdy rival Republic of Pskov dominated Lake Peipus and district. In the West, Moscovy was hemmed in by Lithuania, whose territory, far exceeding that of Moscovy, reached almost up to Kaluga. Eastward and southwards stretched the interminable steppes of the Volga and the Don, still in the possession of the Tatar Hordes.

Ivan was to be a greater "land-gatherer"[1] than any of his predecessors, but his task was infinitely easier than theirs had been. Circumstances were entirely in his favour. The minor principalities were ripe for dropping into the lap of Moscovy at

---

[1] "Sobiratel"—the highest encomium the *lyetopis* can pay a Prince in those days of anarchy and dispersion.

the least touch.   The Tatar yoke hung very loosely on the shoulders of the Russian Princes ; a single shake might dislodge it.   The whole population looked instinctively to Moscow alone for advancement and protection.   The Polish Kings, engrossed by the Lithuanian problem, or involved in Bohemo-Hungarian complications, were his only rivals, and they had neither the money nor the time to oppose him seriously.   Ivan himself possessed all the acquisitive instincts of his ancestors.   Neither morally nor physically can he be called attractive.   A tall, lean, furtive man, who stooped so much that he seemed to be hump-backed[1], his crooked body was the envelope of a crooked soul. Yet this cunning, stealthy Prince, who carried caution beyond the verge of cowardice, had inherited an inexhaustible fund of patience and tenacity ; and, if he never took any risks, he never made any mistakes.   Nor, to do him justice, was he particularly cruel.

The first to feel the hesitating but retentive grip of Ivan Crookback was the Republic of Great Novgorod.

Great Novgorod held a unique position among the old Russian lands.   Belonging at first to Kiev, from whom she originally received her *Posadniki*, or Presidents, she established her independence about 1135, from which time her Presidents were elected, generally for life, by the *Vyeche*, or General Assembly of the people, over which they presided.   The *Vyeche* was summoned by the ringing of the great bell of the Cathedral of St Sophia, and sat either in the ancient Palace of Yaroslav or in the great square of St Sophia. For a time Novgorod was the most powerful and progressive State in Russia, owing to her favourable position for foreign trade.   She rapidly extended her empire to the White Sea at the expense of the Esths, Finns and Swedes ; successfully resisted more than one hostile league of the Russian Princes, all of whom coveted her wealth ; and, in later times, adroitly played off the North against the South.   She also made a

---

[1] Hence his nickname, *Gorbaty*.

bold stand against the Teutonic Knights. At the beginning of the fourteenth century Great Novgorod was at her prime, but her influence declined as the influence of the autocratic northern Grand Dukes increased. They claimed the right of nominating the *Vladika*, or Archbishop, and often treated the Republic as if she were a subject State; but the subsequent rise of the Lithuanian Grand Duchy once more enabled Novgorod to hold her own by adroitly oscillating between the various Grand Duchies as it suited her convenience. The custom was for the *Vyeche* to summon any Prince who took the popular fancy to settle in the city and protect it with his *druzhina*, or body-guard. But all such Princes held their precarious sway on good behaviour, and were superseded at the discretion of the Republic. They could, moreover, do nothing of consequence without the consent of their co-assessor and coadjutor, the *Posadnik*, who represented popular control in its most stringent form. The Republic also had the absolute control of its foreign policy. All treaties were subscribed on its behalf by the *Posadnik* and the *Vladika*, who also declared war and concluded peace on behalf of the *Vyeche*. From 1393 onwards, the land-gathering policy of Moscovy led to frequent collisions with the Republic, which successfully defended both her colonies and her privileges till 1456, when, by the Peace of Yazhelits, she was obliged to relinquish her great seal, to engage, henceforth, not to harbour the enemies of the Grand Duke, and to pay tribute. In all these contests Novgorod was greatly straitened by the active hostility of the Republic of Pskov, originally a dependency, but now the jealous rival of the older Republic.

The humiliation of Yazhelits rankled in the minds of "the big people" of Novgorod, who could generally command the votes of "the little people" in the *Vyeche*. They realised, too, the danger of the Republic now that all the lesser Grand Duchies, so many possible confederates, had been suppressed, and she stood face to face with Moscovy alone. The turn of

Novgorod was bound to come next, sooner or later, unless she strengthened herself with fresh alliances in the meantime. In this crisis Novgorod naturally looked to Casimir IV for protection. As the son of an orthodox mother, and the ruler over millions of orthodox subjects obedient to the ancient metropolitan See of Kiev, he might fairly be considered as much a Russian Prince as Ivan III, and his clemency and liberality were notorious. A formal alliance was concluded, at the beginning of 1470, between Lithuania and "the free men of Novgorod," Casimir undertaking to hasten to their assistance whenever they might be attacked by Moscovy. Natural caution and complications with the Tatars kept Ivan III away from the west during the first eight years of his reign, though he had frequently to complain of the disrespectful tone of Novgorod and the insults inflicted upon his representatives in the city. He knew, however, that he had a powerful ally in the ignorant and violent orthodoxy of "the little people" of the *Vyeche*, so he awaited his opportunity while the materials for a conflagration were slowly accumulating. The spark of ignition was the insolent behaviour of an embassy from Pskov to Moscovy, which, on its way through Novgorod, offered to mediate between the Grand Duke of Moscovy and "ye, his patrimony," as they phrased it. At this the pride of the Republic of Novgorod was aroused. The great bell summoned the *Vyeche* to the square of St Sophia. "We are free men! we are not the patrimony of the Grand Duke of Moscow" was the prevailing cry. Then there were loud shouts for King Casimir; and the partisans of Moscovy were stoned and driven out of the Assembly. A last effort at mediation, on the part of the metropolitan of Moscow, having been rejected with scorn, Ivan III (May, 1471) sent a formal declaration of war to Novgorod.

By June the first of his huge armies, which included innumerable Tatars and the auxiliaries of Pskov and Tver, fell ravaging into the territory of the Republic. It is clear, from the contemporary *lyetopisi,* that public opinion in Russia generally was on the side of the aggressor. The Novgorodians were regarded not merely as the enemies of the Grand Duke, but as renegades from the Lord God. "After being Christians for so many years, they are now going over to the Latins," naively remarks our chronicler. The Grand Duke, according to this hypothesis, was warring not against fellow-Christians but against heretics and heathens, to whom no sort of mercy could be shewn. He certainly shewed none. The Moscovite hordes burnt and wasted in every direction and haled thousands away into captivity. Casimir, far away on the Bohemian border watching the movements of Matthias Corvinus, and the Livonian Order, appealed to at the eleventh hour, could send no timely help. Nevertheless, Novgorod, left entirely to its own resources, did not submit without a struggle. Despite serious defeats at Korostuina, on Lake Ilman (June 23), and on the Shelona, when 40,000 of them were defeated by 4000 Russians, with the loss of 12,000 men (a defeat due largely to the inveterate insubordination of the Novgorod levies, who would only fight when and how they chose), the men of Novgorod destroyed their suburbs in November and prepared to sustain a long siege. But the supply of corn ran short; the Moscovite faction raised its head again; the authorities lost heart, and finally purchased the mediation of Ivan's Boyars. Peace was concluded at the end of the year on the following terms. Novgorod engaged (1) never to admit a Lithuanian Prince; (2) to remain in perpetual alliance with Moscow; and (3) to pay an indemnity of 15,000 rubles. In the circumstances these terms do not appear to be excessive, especially as Novgorod retained her ancient liberties and nearly all her possessions. But the first article, which isolated her politically, sealed her future fate.

During the next seven years the net cast around Novgorod was gradually drawn in. In 1475 Ivan visited the city "peaceably," on the plea of adjusting differences and extruding pro-Lithuanians, who were sent in chains to Moscow.

On this occasion Ivan scrupulously observed all the ancient laws and customs, did nothing without the co-operation of the *Posadnik*, whom he "advised" to renew the expiring commercial treaty with Sweden, and returned to Moscow laden with gifts. Evidently he went to spy out the nakedness of the land, for, shortly afterwards, he sent to enquire what master the Archbishop and all Great Novgorod would be under, and whether they would now accept the Grand Duke's *tyunui*, or governors, in all their quarters. The reply was open defiance. The *Vyeche* was "rung in"; the Boyars of the Moscovite faction were executed as traitors; and the Republic prepared for war. So strongly did the *Posadnik* fortify the city that, when Ivan's armies environed it, in the course of 1476, it was found to be impregnable by assault. Long, spun-out negotiations ensued; but the best terms the Novgorodians could obtain, in return for absolute submission, were the retention of their local tribunals and immunity from confiscation. The formal oath of allegiance was taken on January 13, 1478. When, on February 17, Ivan quitted his camp and returned to Moscow, he took with him many hostages, all the treaties made between Lithuania and Novgorod, and the famous *vyechevy Kolokol*, or Assembly-Bell, which was hung up in one of the squares of the Kremlin, among larger and louder bells. But Novgorod could not at once forget her ancient glory. In 1477, 1484, 1487 and 1488 she again asserted herself only to be easily and sternly repressed. In 1487 it was considered necessary to remove 50 of her noblest and wealthiest families to Moscovite territory. In 1488, 7000 more of her Boyars and merchants were transplanted to "the lower towns[1]," which had to fill up the gaps out of their own population. After this, Great Novgorod gave no more trouble to Ivan III. Pskov and Ryazan, as a reward for their obsequiousness to the Grand Duke, were permitted to enjoy their ancient liberties a little longer. Tver, on the other hand, was seized

---

[1] *i.e.* Vladimir on the Klyazma, Murom, Nizhny Novgorod.

and incorporated in 1486 for negotiating directly with
Casimir IV.

Eastwards, the progress of Ivan III was halting and variable.
It was easy enough to deal with the savage Permians and the
Voguls in the Upper Kama district. Both these Finnish tribes
were subdued by the end of the fifteenth century; and thus the
limits of the Moscovite Empire were extended to the Urals.
The independent Khanates of Kazan and Astrakhan also
acknowledged the sovereignty of Ivan III for a time,
though they broke away from him towards the end of his
reign. The much reduced Golden Horde still persisted in the
Lower Volgan Steppes. In 1480 the Grand Khan, Achmet,
egged on by Lithuania, advanced against Moscow with his
whole host. Ivan abandoned his army on the Oka and fled
abjectly to the outskirts of Moscow. But for the indignant
remonstrances of Vassion, the high-spirited metropolitan of
Rostov, he would have fled still further, or purchased peace
on almost any terms. An unusually severe winter finally compelled Achmet to retire into the Steppe, and, while encamping
on the Donets, he was surprised and slain in a night attack
(January 6, 1481) by the hostile Khan of the Shaban and
Nogai Tatars. This was virtually the end of the Golden
Horde. Its place was taken by the Crimean Horde, which,
under the Khans of the Girej family, played an important part
in Russian history for the next three centuries. Common
interests drew Moscovy and the Crimean Khan together. The
importance of this alliance to Moscovy may be gauged by the
obsequiousness of Ivan III to Khan Mengli Girei, whom he
generally addresses as his superior, to whom honour and
tribute are due. From 1474, when these friendly relations
first began, Ivan thought it necessary to maintain a resident
ambassador at the Crimea with what we should now call a
secret service fund, consisting, for the most part, of sables and
other precious pelts.

It was through the Khan of the Crimea that Moscovy came

into contact with the Ottoman Empire. In 1475 the Turks conquered the Crimea and made the Khans subject Princes. Their seat of government was the great slave-exporting port of Kaffa ; and the injury the Pachas inflicted on the lucrative Eastern trade of Moscovy induced Ivan, in 1492, to send a letter of remonstrance to Bajazet II through the hands of Mengli. A special Russian envoy, Mikhail Pleshcheev, sent direct to Stambul on the same errand, in 1497, was dismissed as an ignoramus because, in strict obedience to his instructions, he refused to deliver his credentials to any one but the Sultan personally. This *faux-pas* put an end to the diplomatic intercourse between Turkey and Moscovy for some time to come.

Meanwhile, in Poland, a sober statesman had been succeeded by an impetuous warrior. This was John Albert, the third son[1] of Casimir IV, who (August 27, 1492) was elected King of Poland by the Bishops, Palatines and Castellans, and the representatives of the cities of Cracow, Thorn, Lemberg, Dantzic and Posen. The Lithuanians, in direct violation of the Union of Horodlo, had, a month earlier, elected John Albert's younger brother, Alexander, their Grand Duke.

The new King, an energetic, enterprising man in the prime of life, rather resembled his heroic uncle Wladislaus, of Varna, than his prudent father. His ambition was military glory and, as the victor of Koposztyna (1487), he already enjoyed a high military reputation. Unfortunately for his far-reaching plans he was chronically impecunious. His father left him nothing but a heavy load of debt; he could draw no revenue from Lithuania; only a month after his coronation he had to pawn one of his villages to the town council of Kazimierz to furnish his table. The poverty of the King had far-reaching political consequences. Dependent on the *Szlachta* for subsidies, but anxious to get those subsidies without the intolerable necessity of applying in turn to half-a-dozen provincial assemblies, John Albert

[1] The eldest son, Wladislaus, was already King of Bohemia and Hungary. The second son, Casimir, predeceased his father.

conceived the bold idea of superseding the *Sejmiki*, or local Diets, by reviving the *Sejm*, or National Assembly. The obvious advantages of such a reform were the much needed centralisation of the Polish Government and the relegation of the local assemblies to purely local affairs. The first General Diet met at Piotrków on January 18, 1493. As usual, the *Szlachta* insisted on the confirmation of their privileges before considering financial questions. The King signed a new Constitution in 24 articles, but the subsidies he secured in return were so paltry that at the ensuing Diet, which met in 1496, he was as poor as ever. Encouraged by their success three years before, the *Szlachta* had, meanwhile, formulated a whole series of fresh demands (most of them at the expense of the other classes of the community) which became statutes before the Assembly arose. One of these statutes exempted the exports and imports of the *Szlachta* from the payment of all tolls and other impositions; a second deprived burgesses of the right of holding extra-mural estates, and those who already possessed the right were to surrender it within a given time under penalty of heavy fines; a third enacted that, henceforth, prelatures and canonries should be held solely by the descendants on both sides of noble families, except three canonries specially reserved for doctors of theology, canon-law and medicine of plebeian origin. Other statutes restricted the ancient right of the agricultural labourer to migrate to better wage markets, especially at harvest time, and introduced modifications of land-tenure which just stopped short of the socage system[1]. Thus the Diet of 1496 introduced that abnormal condition of things which was, ultimately, one of the chief causes of the collapse of Poland. It elevated the *Szlachta* into a favoured caste apart. The burgesses, forbidden henceforth to hold landed estates, were thereby excluded from all participation in military service with its numerous attendant advantages. In a word, they were excluded as much as

[1] In one province socage had been already introduced. (Sejmik of Krasnymstano, September, 1477.)

possible from the public service, and thus tended to become·
indifferent to the welfare of their country. Nay, more, their
commercial prosperity was seriously imperilled by the fiscal
exemptions now granted to their competitors, the great land-
owners. The yeomanry of Poland, too, were being degraded
into mere serfs and lost much of their ancient spirit. But it
was the State which suffered most. The natural equilibrium
between the various grades of society was disturbed by these
radical changes, and the sources of the national wealth were at
the same time diminished.

In abandoning the lower estates to the *Szlachta*, John Albert
had calculated upon the generosity of the latter to relieve him
from his financial embarrassments. But here he was disappointed.
As a matter of fact, the Diet granted him nothing but an excise
duty, which fell entirely upon the burgesses, and a subsidy of
four groats per hide of land, which was paid by the peasants.
Nevertheless, the King affected to be satisfied, and diverted his
attention to foreign affairs. He seems to have determined first
to win popularity by means of military glory and then to use the
popularity so acquired for the benefit of the Crown. Circumstances at this time seemed especially favourable for a Crusade
against the Turks. Under Bajazet II (1481–1512), a weak Prince,
whose enemies were those of his own household, the strong tide
of Turkish conquest had ceased to flow ; and the Holy See once
more summoned Christendom to arms against the arch enemy
of the faith. At a Congress, held at Leutschau, in Hungary,
attended by the Kings of Poland, Bohemia and Hungary, the
Królewicz Sigismund, Frederick of Brandenburg and some
lesser potentates, a plan of campaign was actually arranged, in
accordance with which John Albert was to march through
Moldavia, retake Kilia and Akkerman, and thus bar the
advance of the Ottomans into Poland. Military preparations
went on unceasingly during 1495 and 1496, the King travelling
from province to province to stimulate the zeal and the liberality
of the *Szlachta*. His energy was rewarded by the marshalling

of the largest army which Poland had ever put into the field. It was at the head of 80,000 militia that John Albert marched to the border. Meanwhile, rumours that the King of Poland was bent upon conquering Moldavia drove the Hospodar Stephen, already flurried by Hungarian intrigues, into the arms of the Turks, whereupon John Albert turned his arms against the Hospodar. From September 25 to October 16 he besieged the fortress of Suceva in vain; and the subsequent retreat of the Poles through the forests of the Bukowina to Sniatyn, harassed at every step by the enemy, completed the ruin of his army. The same year the Tatar bands ravaged Red Russia. In 1498 the Poles, depressed by these reverses, concluded peace with Stephen and recognised his independence. In June, 1500, a fresh anti-Turkish league was formed at Buda between Venice, Poland, Hungary-Bohemia and France; but it came to nothing, owing to the opposition of the Czech and Magyar magnates and the untimely death of the Polish King.

Oddly enough, the collapse of John Albert's military adventure coincided with the sudden increase of his power and popularity. Particulars are wanting, but there can be little doubt, from what followed, that treachery or cowardice on the part of the Polish chivalry must have been one of the main causes of the failure of the campaign of Suceva. Anyhow, immediately after his return, the King proceeded to confiscate the estates of hundreds of the nobility, evidently with the approval of the nation. No protest seems to have been made; the subsequent Diets of 1498 and 1499 were unusually open-handed; while the Diet of 1501, so mischievous in other respects, placed the control of the militia entirely in the King's hands, in order to enable the executive to deal with the chronic danger of Tatar invasions more expeditiously in future. Towards the end of John Albert's reign the ever-mutinous Teutonic Knights grew acutely troublesome. In 1497 Albert of Saxony was elected Grand Master. He was persuaded by the Emperor to refuse to take the oath of allegiance to Poland on the pretext that, as a Prince of the Empire, he was not subject to the obligations of the Peace of Thorn. The difficulties of John Albert prevented him for four years from enforcing his rights as over-lord; but in 1501, accompanied by the national militia, he proceeded to Thorn and categorically summoned his vassal to appear before him. The Grand Master begged for some modification of the terms of the Peace of Thorn; but the King was inexorable. The Grand Master still hesitating, heavy artillery was brought up to the Polish camp and then Albert gave way. On June 11, 1501, he did homage for Prussia. A week later the King died suddenly from a stroke of apoplexy.

We do not possess sufficient materials for judging the character of John Albert. The whole history of his reign is mysterious and obscure. Even the principal events in it are so imperfectly recorded that we have no clue to the unravelling of their meaning. Only one thing is obvious—the growing confidence of the nation in the King in spite of repeated disasters This seems to prove that the disasters were no fault of his. We feel that we are in the presence of a great man whose opportunity has not yet come, but is coming rapidly. Then death intervenes, and Poland is plunged once more into anarchy and confusion.

Meanwhile, Lithuania had been learning from bitter experience that she was no longer able to stand alone. It is remarkable that during the life-time of Casimir IV, Ivan III abstained from regular warfare against the Grand Duchy. The two Princes contented themselves with ravaging each other's border provinces by Tatar mercenaries. But, in the second year of Alexander (1493), Ivan compelled Lithuania to cede altogether to the Moscovite portions of the Chernigov territory which, hitherto, they had divided between them. During the negotiations, and on the signature of the peace, Ivan, instead of using the time-honoured title "Grand Duke of Vladimir and Moscow," suddenly styled himself: "Ivan, by the grace of God, Gosudar[1] of all Russia, etc." This portentous innovation was never recognised by Alexander, even after he had, in accordance with the conditions of the Peace, married the Grand Duke's daughter Elena (1495). Ivan's sensitiveness on this head, even more than the incessant border *guerillas* and the attempts of the Lithuanian Court to convert Elena to the Roman Faith, was the cause of a second war between Lithuania and Moscovy, which began in 1499. The Lithuanians, completely taken by surprise, were routed on the plain of Mitkowa and at Mstislavl, in 1500, and lost a considerable number of towns and districts, including Bryansk, Serpeisk, Mosalsk, Dorogobuzh and Toropets. The war was concluded by a six years' truce, on a *uti possidetis* basis (March 25, 1503); but Alexander, now King of Poland as well as Grand Duke of Lithuania (the two countries had, in 1499, renewed the compact of Horodlo for mutual protection), rejected Ivan's usurped title of "Gosudar of all Russia," as altogether unwarrantable and absurd in the circumstances, which it certainly was[2].

But Ivan III was now sailing, with a prosperous wind, on the full tide of sovereignty. He was not only victorious abroad, but omnipotent at home. If there was one privilege of the Russian Boyars which might be regarded as inalienable, it was the privilege of transmigration from one Prince to another. So long as there were three or four independent and fairly equal Russian Principalities in existence, it occurred to no one to dispute this privilege. It was always assumed, as a matter of course, in all the treaties made between the various Grand Dukes, who divided the north Russian lands between

---

[1] Sovereign.

[2] When, in 1494, Ivan's ambassadors asked him how they were to justify the assumption of a title never borne before by a Russian Grand Duke, they were told to say: " My master so commands. Whoever wants to know more about it had better come to Moscow and there he will be told." An answer which shows equal brutality and embarrassment.

them.   When, however, all the other principalities had bowed
down before Moscovy, it is obvious that none of them would
care to run the risk of offending the Grand Duke of Moscow
by harbouring his fugitive Boyars.   Still, the right of transmigration on the part of the Boyars themselves had never been
called in question; and it therefore came as a shock to Russian
conservatism when Ivan III deliberately violated this ancient
custom by seizing Prince Ivan Obolensky, who had taken refuge
in the territory of the Grand Duke's own brother, Prince Boris
of Volok.   Boris at once invited his three younger brothers to
protest against this act of tyranny; and the protest took the
form of an open rebellion in 1480.   A reconciliation was
patched up by the old Dowager Grand Duchess; and ultimately, in 1486, a new division of property was made between
the Grand Duke and his kinsmen, when, it is needless to say,
the younger brethren got by far the worst of the bargain.
Perhaps it was from resentment at this chicanery that another
brother, Prince Andrew of Uglich, refused, in May, 1491, to
render due service to Ivan against the Tatars.   Anyhow, in
September, the same year, while on a friendly visit to the
Grand Duke at Moscow, he was seized along with his brothers
and nephews, and they were all sent in chains to remote strongholds.   Ivan then seized their lands, excusing his conduct to
the Metropolitan as a prudential measure, designed to prevent
Moscovy from again becoming the slave of the Tatars.

No doubt his behaviour was largely determined by his
ambitious second consort, Sophia Paleologa (daughter of
Thomas, Despot of the Morea, and niece of Constantine, the
last Greek Emperor), whom he espoused in 1472.   This union
was first proposed by Pope Paul II, through Cardinal Bessarion,
as a means of establishing papal influence in Moscovy.   It
assumed that a Princess who had been educated at Rome could
have no insuperable aversion from the Catholic Church, and,
properly manipulated, might even lead her husband into the
right way.   The Princess was accompanied to Russia by

Cardinal Antonio, who gave great offence to the orthodox by avoiding the ikons and blessing the people with his gloves on. He was not permitted to enter Moscow till his processional crucifix had been hidden in his sledge; and when, the day after the wedding (November 12, 1472), he began to speak of the union of the churches, he was hustled out of the country. But the marriage itself was an event of the highest political importance, It gave to the aspiring young autocracy, just emerging from the restraints of ancient custom, an imperial sanction, inasmuch as the rulers of Moscovy henceforth regarded themselves as the political and religious inheritors of the imperial traditions of New Rome, which Sophia Paleologa brought with her to her adopted country. Ivan's contemporaries noticed an ominous change in him after his marriage with the descendant of the Byzantine Emperors. According to them, Ivan, hitherto, had been one of the patriarchal Princes of the olden times, who loved his people, respected the aged, and took frequent and familiar council with his servants. But after the event he suddenly grew into a *grozny gosudar*[1], "an austere sovereign," who held aloof from his subjects, or addressed them (if he addressed them at all) from heights of inaccessible grandeur. Before him the great Boyars, the descendants of Rurik and Gedymin, were expected to do obeisance as reverentially as the meanest *muzhik*. This unwelcome metamorphosis was generally attributed to Sophia; and there can be no doubt that the attribution was just. Sophia was certainly superior, both in craft and courage, to any of her contemporaries, and she seems to have made up her mind, from the first, to have her own way. Yet her influence was good on the whole. But for her, Ivan would never have attempted to shake off the shameful Tatar yoke. On the other hand, she acclimatised the palace intrigue, hitherto peculiar to Byzantium, in

---

[1] Ivan was the first Russian Sovereign to whom the epithet *grozny* was applied. In his case it meant " austere," in the case of his grandson, Ivan IV, it took the darker significance of "terrible."

Moscow, and induced her husband to alter the old order of succession.

By his first wife, Maria of Tver, who died in 1467, Ivan III had one son, Ivan, who was crowned Grand Duke but predeceased his father. He also left one son, Demetrius. By this time, Sophia also had borne her husband an heir, who was christened Vasily Gabriel. The question now arose whether the grandson, or the son by the second marriage, should succeed to the throne. Ivan at first favoured the claims of his grandson, who also had the better right by custom, inasmuch as his father had worn the Grand-Ducal crown. On the other hand, Sophia's son was the inheritor of the imperial escutcheon of New Rome and all that it implied. The Boyars were on the side of Demetrius and his mother, Elena of Moldavia, but the lesser nobility and the clerks of the Council took the part of Sophia and Vasily. In 1497 a conspiracy to remove Demetrius was discovered. Sophia was thereupon charged with witchcraft; her partisans were put to death; and on February 4, 1498, Demetrius was solemnly crowned Autocrat and Gosudar of all Russia at the Uspensky Cathedral, in the presence of the Court. The Boyars of the old school had triumphed, but their triumph was not for long. In January, 1499, the great Boyar families, the Patrikyeevs and the Ryapolovskies, who had been dominant in Moscovy for half a century and represented its most conservative traditions, were arrested, tortured and executed. The discreet contemporary *lyetopisi* do not venture to furnish particulars of this sudden catastrophe; but it is significant that from henceforth Demetrius takes the second place. Finally, on April 11, 1502, he was disinherited; and, three days later, Sophia's son, Vasily, was crowned Gosudar and Grand Duke. The crafty Greek lady had come off victorious in this silent subterranean struggle for pre-eminency.

It is in the reign of Ivan III that Moscovy first comes into contact with the West. Russia was discovered, much about the same time as America, by a German traveller, Ritter Niklas von Poppel, who, in 1486, brought to Vienna the strange tidings that north-eastern Russia was not, as generally supposed, a part of Poland, but a vast independent State far larger than Poland. In 1489 he was accredited to Ivan III, to whom he was to propose a matrimonial alliance, and he brought back with him, as Ivan's ambassador, the Greek, George Trachionotes. There were further attempts, in 1491 and 1504, on the part of the Emperor, to attract this mysterious, potential ally within his political orbit, but Ivan III was far too haughty and suspicious to commit himself to anything definite. Presently Europe had tidings of Moscovy of a more disturbing sort. In 1503 the Grand Master of the Livonian Order Walther von Plettenburg, who, as the ally of Lithuania, had been waging war with Ivan III since 1501, informed the Pope that Moscovy would soon either conquer Livonia or, if the fortresses prevented that, would, at least, reduce it to a wilderness, unless His Holiness proclaimed · a crusade against these merciless barbarians. Sweden had had a still earlier experience of the savagery of a foe who had studied strategy in the school of the Tatars. In 1466 the Moscovites, for reasons unknown, had invaded Finland and fruitlessly besieged Viborg. In 1467 they ravaged Finland up to Tavastahus, and destroyed an army of 7000 men ; whereupon the Swedes retaliated by capturing Ivangorod, a fortress which Ivan had erected on the Narova, when hostilities seem to have been suspended.

Ivan III died on October 27, 1505, in the 67th year of his age and the 44th of his reign, having survived his second consort two years. By his will he divided his territories among his five sons, Vasily, George, Demetrius, Simeon and Andrew, but the younger brothers were enjoined to look up to Vasily as their father and obey him in all things. They had small temptation to do otherwise, as their petty appanages made them utterly impotent.

Ten months after the death of Ivan III, his rival, Alexander of Poland and Lithuania, followed him into the grave (August 19, 1506). Alexander's short reign of five years was a succession of blunders, disasters and humiliations. He was a man of good intentions but feeble character, in whom the family virtues of caution and generosity became slothfulness and prodigality. His election as King of Poland (October 4, 1501) at least put an end to Lithuanian separation, for it was preceded and conditioned by a compact between the Poles and the Lithuanians to the effect that, henceforth, the King of Poland should always be Grand Duke of Lithuania. This, however, was the solitary advantage (though, no doubt, a considerable one) which Poland derived from Alexander, an advantage more than counterbalanced by his incapacity for ruling. During his reign the Senate and the Sejm governed, while the Monarch looked on. The *Pacta conventa* presented to him at Mielnica for signature, before his coronation, and generally known as the Articles of Mielnica, curtailed the prerogative as regards the distribution of offices, deprived the Crown of the control of the Mint and the regalia, and exempted all the members of the Senate from prosecution by the royal courts. The constitution of 1504 enacted that, henceforth, the royal estates should not be mortgaged without the unanimous consent of the Senate, given during Diet; that the King should be constantly attended by a permanent council of 24 Senators, relieving each other in rotas of six every six months; and that the Grand Chancellor and the Vice-Chancellor should only be appointed with the concurrence of the Senate and during the session of the Sejm. These enactments were reinforced in 1505, at the Diet of Radom, by the edict *Nihil Novi*, whereby the King bound himself and his successors never to alter the constitution, or enact any new statute, to the prejudice or injury of the Republic or any member of it, without the previous consent of the Senate and Sejm. The very subsidies granted to the Crown by this Diet had to pass through the hands of Commissioners, who were to examine all receipts paid into the Treasury by the King.

The Senate was justified in protecting the State against the

wastefulness of a helplessly good-natured Prince who never
had the courage to say "no!" Unfortunately, these self-
appointed guardians of the public weal were wrangling
mediocrities, unaccustomed to the exercise of sovereignty.
The consequence was that, by the end of the reign, domestic
affairs, especially financial matters, were in a deplorable condition, while abroad Poland was regarded as politically bankrupt.
So low, indeed, did she fall that minor States, like Moldavia
and Prussia, which had lately been, or still were, her vassals,
became her rivals and despoilers.   Stephen of Moldavia, encouraged by the ever anti-Jagiellonic Hungarian magnates,
occupied the *Woiwodschaft* of Pokucie (the portion of Red
Russia lying between the Carpathians and the Dniester) in 1502.
Only after years of negotiation was the province recovered
from Stephen's son and successor, Bogdan (Treaty of Lublin,
February 16, 1506).   Still more offensive were the pretensions
of the Grand Master of the Teutonic Order, who aimed not
merely at renouncing the homage due to the Polish Crown,
but also at recovering West Prussia.   The whole dispute was
referred to the arbitration of the Holy See, and was still pending
when Alexander died.

The last moments of the unfortunate Polish King were
cheered by at least one gleam of good fortune.   The Peace
with Moscovy had been concluded, and no further trouble
from that quarter was anticipated, when the Crimean Khan,
Mengli, suddenly burst upon defenceless Lithuania with a
countless horde.   The King already lay on his death-bed;
the border palatines were taken completely by surprise; no
resistance seemed possible.   But, at the eleventh hour, 10,000
men were got together for the defence of Wilna; and, on
August 5, 1506, the Tatar host was annihilated at Kleck by
Stanislaus Kiszka and Michael Glinski.   Alexander was already
speechless when the glad tidings were brought to him, but he
expressed his joy by raising grateful hands to heaven.   The
same evening he expired, in his 45th year.

CHAPTER IV.

THE REHABILITATION OF POLAND UNDER SIGISMUND I, 1506–1548.

By his last will, King Alexander had bequeathed his patrimony to his younger brother Sigismund, who put himself in possession thereof without a moment's delay. Ten days after the obsequies of Alexander, Sigismund, who on receiving tidings of his brother's dangerous illness had posted from Glogau to Wilna, was unanimously elected Grand Duke of Lithuania. In the beginning of 1506 a Polish deputation offered him the Kingdom also; and on January 24, 1507, he was crowned at Cracow.

The new Monarch was in his 40th year, and his herculean figure and majestic bearing profoundly impressed all who approached him. He came to Poland with an excellent reputation. While only Duke of Glogau, he had been entrusted by his brother Wladislaus, King of Bohemia and Hungary, with the government of Silesia, which for centuries had been the battle-field of the ceaseless antagonisms of the Slav and the German. His just but iron rule had quickly converted a political Alsatia into a model State, and not only did he clear it of *Raubritter*, but he also made it pay, for the first time, its proper quota into the Bohemian treasury. Sigismund was, indeed, above all things a provident and economical statesman; and one of his first acts after his accession, was to attempt to restore the credit of Poland, which had been all but ruined by the recklessness of John Albert and the prodigality of Alexander. His chosen colleagues in this great work were a few honest and capable citizens of Cracow, merchants and bankers, most of them of German origin, and exiles for conscience sake, men like Kasper Beer, Justus Decyusz, who became his secretary and chronicler, Johann Thurzo, Johann Boner and the Bettmans. They began with the reform of the currency[1]. Under their skilful management, the mint, which hitherto had been more costly than profitable, rendered to the King an annual net income of 210,000 gulden, which enabled Sigismund to pay his predecessor's debts, redeem the royal plate, recover some of the alienated crown lands, and even hire mercenaries to serve as the nucleus of a standing army.

If ever a Prince had constant need of a well-filled treasury and powerful armaments it was Sigismund I during the whole of his long and troubled reign of forty-two years. At the very outset he was confronted by a conspiracy which struck at the very foundation of Poland's political existence, a conspiracy the more dangerous as it was inspired and directed by one whose genius and resolution were scarce inferior to Sigismund's own. The chief personage in Lithuania, at this time, was Prince Michael Glinsky, the Court Marshal and prime favourite of the late King Alexander. The Glinscy came of a Tatar stock which had migrated to the Grand Duchy in the reign of Witowt, and risen rapidly to eminence. Michael, the most illustrious of his family, had travelled and studied in Italy and Spain, spent some time at the court of Maximilian who prized him highly, and returned home learned in all the arts of peace and war. No wonder then, if he easily outshone the simple Lithuanian lords, and so fascinated the impressionable Alexander that, contrary to his coronation oath, he confiscated the estates of Glinsky's rivals in order to enrich him and his brothers, one of whom, Prince Ivan, was made Palatine of Kiev. On the

[1] Polish coins were now dated, for the first time.

death of Alexander, Glinsky possessed one half of Lithuania and was generally suspected of the design of erecting Red Russia into an independent principality for himself. It must be admitted, however, that Glinsky had been consistently loyal to Alexander, to whom he rendered considerable services. There is also no reason to suppose that he had, at first, any evil designs against Sigismund. But, in the circumstances, he was too powerful a vassal to be tolerated by any self-respecting King; and Sigismund had evidently determined to get rid of him on the first opportunity. He began by depriving Ivan Glinsky of the *Woiwodschaft* of Kiev, affected to listen to the insinuations of Michael Glinsky's numerous enemies, refused him redress when he claimed it, and thus drove the angry and humiliated magnate, who disdained to hold the second place in Lithuania after having so long held the first, into the arms of Tsar Vasily III of Moscovy, with whom he proposed to conquer and divide western Russia.

For the next ten years, Glinsky was the ubiquitous, irreconcilable enemy of Sigismund. It was through fear of his influence spreading throughout the Grand Duchy that the Polish King, after a two years' war, came to terms with Vasily by ceding to him, in perpetuity, all the conquests his father Ivan III had made from Alexander. But this peace availed Poland little, for Glinsky, now firmly established at Moscow as the chief Councillor of Vasily III, who had married his niece Helena in 1526, moved heaven and earth to rekindle the war, kept a watchful eye upon all Sigismund's movements, and took advantage of his ever increasing embarrassments to raise up enemies against him in every quarter[1]. Moreover, Glinsky's agents traversed Germany, Bohemia and Silesia to collect mercenaries and modern artillery, which were conveyed to Moscovy by way of Livonia. Towards the end of 1511, Sigismund's difficulties with the Teutonic

---

[1] Hans of Denmark in 1509; Maximilian in 1510; the Prussian Order in 1511.

Order induced Vasily to renew hostilities; and, on December 19, he set forth to besiege the fortress of Smolensk, the key of the Dnieperian district. Notwithstanding his 140 big guns, Vasily had, however, to abandon the siege with the loss of 11,000 men. In 1513, stimulated by Glinsky, Vasily again attacked the fortress and was again repulsed. In 1514 he appeared before Smolensk for the third time. This time his pertinacity was rewarded, chiefly owing to the ability of the master-gunner Stephen; and the place surrendered on June 31. Vasily had promised Smolensk to Glinsky if Glinsky's gunners could take it. Yet, when the place fell, it was at once occupied by a Russian garrison. From Vasily's point of view this seemed, no doubt, a necessary act of precaution ; but it was also a flagrant breach of honour and gratitude which the disillusioned Glinsky was quick to resent. He communicated with Sigismund, offering to transfer his services ; but the correspondence was discovered before Glinsky could undo his own work, and he was sent in chains to Moscow where, however, his eclipse was but transient. Two months later the Poles, under Prince Constantine Ostrogsky, routed the Moscovites at Orsza (Sept. 8, 1514), slaying 30,000 of them and capturing four generals, 27 foreign colonels and 1500 boyars. This victory came too late to save Smolensk, but it damped the martial ardour of the Moscovite generals, who, henceforth, avoided pitched battles, and induced the Moscovite government to open negotiations with the Poles under the mediation of the imperial ambassador, Sigismund Herbertstein, who arrived at Moscow in April 1517. The negotiations began on November 1. The Russian plenipotentiaries demanded Kiev, Polock, Witebsk and, generally speaking, all the other towns and territories constituting the original patrimony of the old Russian Grand Dukes who claimed descent from St Vladimir.

This claim was, henceforth, advanced by Moscovy in all similar negotiations with Lithuania and is of great historical interest. It reveals the true character of the struggle between the two Slavonic sovereigns, one calling himself Grand Duke of Lithuania and Russia, while the other claimed the title of Grand Duke of all Russia. Hopeless, fantastic even, as Moscovy's claim to all the old Russian lands must have seemed in the sixteenth century, it was never omitted from the preliminary conferences lest silence should be construed to mean renunciation. Herbertstein's mission was a failure; and his successors, Francesco da Kollo and Antonio de Conti, were equally unsuccessful. The negotiations were broken off, and Vasily tried to obtain assistance from the Grand Master of the Teutonic Order, to whom (Sept. 1519) he sent sufficient money to equip 10,000 mercenaries. But the Teutonic Order proved but a broken reed to lean upon; and, after a fresh series of savage raids and futile sieges, both parties wearied of the interminable struggle and terminated it (1522) by a five years' truce, renewed repeatedly but never converted into a permanent peace, because Sigismund refused to cede and Vasily to part with Smolensk, which remained provisionally in the hands of the Russians.

Sigismund I may, perhaps, have underestimated the significance of the war of Smolensk, but, after all, the whole Moscovite question was still of secondary importance to Poland. The really vital question of the day, upon which everything then depended, was how to deal with the troublesome and rebellious Teutonic Order.

This Teutonic question, besides weakening Poland internally, seriously hampered her foreign policy. In the first two decades of the sixteenth century the Popes were intent on combining Christendom in a crusade against the Turks; and Hungary and Poland, as being the nearest neighbours of the common foe, were expected to take leading parts in the great enterprise. But Sigismund could not expose his country, during his absence, to the rapacity of his impatient vassal, the Grand Master of Prussia, who was bent upon throwing off the Polish yoke altogether with the support of Poland's enemies.

Chief among these was the Emperor Maximilian, who, at the Peace Congress of Posen (1510), warmly supported the claims of the Knights to absolute independence. A second Congress, held at Thorn (Jan. 1511), proved equally abortive; and the matter was then transferred to the Lateran Council, at which the cause of Poland was eloquently pleaded by her greatest diplomatist, the Primate, Jan Laski, who would have prevailed but for the determined opposition of the imperial ambassadors.

Four years later the subject was reopened at the Congress of Pressburg (1515), which was attended by the Emperor, Sigismund, and Wladislaus of Bohemia and Hungary. By this time Sigismund had recognised the necessity of coming to an understanding with Maximilian. The chief cause of the Emperor's persistent hostility at this time was his fear lest Sigismund might traverse his plans in Hungary. In February 1512, Sigismund yielding to the earnest representations of the Senate that it was his first duty to perpetuate the dynasty, now again in danger of extinction, had married Barbara, daughter of Stephen Zapolya, the most powerful of the Hungarian magnates, compared with whom the reigning King Wladislaus was a mere cipher. Maximilian, who had already conceived the design of acquiring Hungary, *more austriaco*, by a family alliance with the Hungarian Jagiellos, at once took alarm; but Sigismund, at Pressburg, smoothed over the difficulty by consenting to a double marriage between Maximilian and Anne, Wladislaus' daughter and Sigismund's niece, on the one hand[1], and between the Crown Prince Louis of Hungary, then a lad of nine, and the Archduchess Mary, Maximilian's granddaughter, on the other. This arrangement was subsequently confirmed by the compact of Vienna (July, same year). In return for Sigismund's complacency, Maximilian now absolved the Knights from all their obligations to the Empire and left them to get the best terms they could from the Polish King.

---

[1] By a subsequent modification of the original compact, Anne married Maximilian's son Ferdinand I to whom she bore 15 children.

On the death of Maximilian (Jan. 12, 1519), however, the new Emperor, Charles V, seemed inclined to protect the Order; which inclination encouraged the Grand Master, Albert of Brandenburg, to renew all his old pretensions. Sigismund thereupon summoned him to Thorn to render due homage. Albert's reply was a declaration of war, at the beginning of which he captured Braunsburg and other fortresses (1520). But the Polish Diet on this occasion liberally supported the King with men and money; and Sigismund and his generals, after some hard fighting, drove the Grand Master across the Vistula and pressed him so hardly that he sued for peace. For the moment it seemed as if the sway of the Knights had at last come to an end. Unfortunately, at this critical moment, complications with the Porte compelled Sigismund to conclude a four years' truce with the Grand Master (March 22, 1521), who, in the following year, was won over to Protestantism by Osiander at Nürnberg. Acting on the advice of his new friends, Albert now resolved to convert the territories of the Order into a secular hereditary principality vested in his own family. Sigismund, weary of the interminable struggle, made no objection to the secularisation, offensive as it was to the Catholic Powers; and on April 8, 1525, he solemnly received the homage of Albert in the market-place of Cracow. Thus it was that the last Grand Master of the Teutonic Order became the first Duke of Prussia[1].

The pressure of the Teuton had forced Sigismund I to relinquish Smolensk to the despised Moscovite; the pressure of the Turk had forced him to grant the vanquished Teutons terms usually accorded to victors. But, at any rate, both the Moscovite and the Teutonic questions had been settled somehow; and Sigismund was able to turn his attention to the South,

---

[1] Albert bound himself on this occasion to render military service to Poland (100 Knights per annum). In case of the extinction of the four branches of the new ducal family, Prussia was to revert to the Polish Crown.

where portentous events were exciting the apprehension of Europe.

On August 29, 1526, Sigismund's nephew, Louis II of Hungary, perished on the field of Mohács with his whole army. The importance of the actual battle has been exaggerated. It was a far less serious disaster than the capture of Belgrade, six years previously; and the monarchy survived it for fourteen years. But the attending circumstances demonstrated, what very few[1] had hitherto suspected, viz. that feudal Hungary in the sixteenth century was in such a rotten, crazy condition as to be fit for nothing but to be cast into the oven of political dissolution.

Two candidates at once presented themselves for the vacant throne—John Zapolya, Voivode of Transylvania, at the head of an army twice as large as that which had perished at Mohács; and Ferdinand of Austria, grandson of the Emperor Maximilian. Both candidates were crowned by their respective partisans, John in 1526, Ferdinand in 1527; and the country was instantly flooded by German, Italian, Polish and Turkish mercenaries, who reduced half of it to a desert, till the Peace of Grosswardein (1538) established John on the Hungarian throne which, after his death, was to revert to Ferdinand. The whole question profoundly interested but deeply divided Polish politicians. The unusually well-informed King favoured the Austrian candidate, in the belief, amply justified by later events, that Hungary could only remain a permanent barrier against the Turks if closely united with the House of Hapsburg. But a large and powerful party in Poland, headed by the Primate, Jan Laski, and his three nephews, Hieronymus, Jan and Stanislaus, all of them men of extraordinary but somewhat erratic genius, warmly supported Zapolya, principally because he hated the Germans

---

[1] Except the Nuncios and Venetian Ambassadors at Buda. One of the former, ten years earlier, wrote, with perfect truth, that even if the Kingdom could be saved for a few crowns, not one of the wealthy oligarchs would make the sacrifice.

as much as they did. Hieronymus Laski not only supplied Zapolya with army after army, but went the round of all the European Courts on his behalf, finally undertaking the famous embassy to Stambul which resulted in the alliance between Zapolya and the Sultan, against which Ferdinand proved powerless. At the instigation of the Emperor Charles V, Pope Clement VII thereupon excommunicated Zapolya, and addressed such a severe *monitorium* to the Polish Primate that the old man, already depressed by the heterodoxy of his eldest nephew Jan and the disgrace of Hieronymus, whose gratuitous and compromising policy had been severely punished by Sigismund, died, it is said, of a broken heart (May 19, 1531). The alliance between the Jagiellos and the Hapsburgs had already been strengthened by Sigismund's marriage with Bona Sforza[1] (April 1518), who brought with her a *dot* of 200,000 ducats, and the prospect of an inheritance of another half million after the death of her mother Isabella of Aragon. Sigismund's Austrian policy never varied. Even on the death of John Zapolya (1540), when the Queen-Mother, Isabella, Sigismund's own daughter, attempted to secure the Magyar throne for her infant son John Sigismund, her father dissuaded her from so grossly violating the Peace of Grosswardein, and made her hand over the Hungarian regalia to Ferdinand. Finally, in 1543, the Austrian alliance was still further cemented by the marriage of Sigismund's only son, Sigismund Augustus, with the Austrian Archduchess Elizabeth.

With the Porte, Sigismund carefully avoided a collision. It is a common error to suppose that Poland was the buckler of Christendom against Islam. That glorious distinction belonged from the end of the fourteenth to the end of the fifteenth century to Hungary, and to Hungary alone. Till the middle of the sixteenth century Poland had but little to do with Turkey. The *alföld*, or great Hungarian plain, lay between the two States; and Moldavia, beneath the sceptre of Stephen the

[1] Queen Barbara died on October 1, 1515, leaving two daughters.

Great (1458–1504), served as an additional barrier. Just before and during the reign of Sigismund I, however, this geographical remoteness was brought to an end by two events. In 1475 the Turks subjugated the Crimean Tatars; in 1513 the Moldavian Princes submitted to the suzerainty of the Sultan. Henceforth the south-eastern frontier of Poland was conterminous with Turkish territory; and the whole situation became permanently insecure.

As regards Moldavia, Sigismund avoided complications, so far as possible, by scrupulously respecting the Sultan's claims. He gave the most memorable instance of his forbearance in 1530 when the Moldavian Hospodar, Petrylo, seized Pokucie. Sigismund sent against him the Grand Hetman[1] of the Crown, Stanislaus Tarnowski, the first of Poland's great captains, who defeated and slew the Hospodar after a fierce two days' battle at Obertyn (Aug. 21, 22), for which he was awarded a triumph and one-sixth of the year's subsidies. So signal was this victory that all Moldavia lay at the feet of the Grand Hetman. Nevertheless, Sigismund strictly forbade Tarnowski to cross the Moldavian frontier, and even sent a letter of explanation to the Sultan.

With the Tatars it was much more difficult to cope. Since the collapse of the Golden Horde they had become mere free-booters, ravaging indiscriminately Moscovy and Lithuania, in spite of the tribute regularly paid to them by way of insurance money. The Sultan let them loose the more readily upon any State whose hostility he might suspect, because, as the nominal subjects of the Crimean Khan, they could always be officially repudiated at Stambul; and Poland suffered terribly from their endless depredations. The whole of her vast, ill-protected, south-eastern frontier, extending from Kiev to the Dnieper[2], and known as the *dzikie poli*, or "wilderness," lay wide open to their sudden and incalculable attacks; and, generally, they

---

[1] *i.e.* Captain-General. Similarly, the Lithuanian Captain-General was called "the Grand Hetman of Lithuania." [2] See map I.

had disappeared like a whirlwind in the trackless steppe before the border castellans could marshal their widely-scattered levies. In 1510 Prince Constantine Ostrogski defeated them in a great battle fought at Wisniowiec, on St Vitalis' Day, April 28, which was kept as a national festival in Lithuania for generations afterwards. Yet only six years later (1516), another great Tatar raid ravaged the *Woiwodschafts* of Russia, Belsk, and Ljubelsk, carrying off no fewer than 50,000 captives to be sold as slaves at Kertch. In 1519 the Tatars wiped out a whole Polish army-corps 5000 strong. In 1527 they penetrated almost to the walls of Cracow, but this time were overtaken and routed at Kaniow, when 80,000 captives were recovered. As Poland became a great power, the humiliation of these raids was felt even more than their mischief; but it was not till 1533 that the valiant and experienced Lord Marcher, Ostafi Daszkiewicz, was consulted by the Diet as to the best way of securing the Ukrain[1] against these savage attacks. Daszkiewicz advised that the Ukrain should be gradually colonised, and that, in the meantime, the pick of the semi-nomadic orthodox population of the Steppe, the so-called Cossacks[2], consisting mostly of runaway serfs, or poor vagabond gentlemen in search of plunder and adventure, should be enrolled in companies and established permanently on the islands of the Lower Dnieper, which could easily be made impregnable *points d'appui*. This excellent plan, which met all the difficulties of the situation, received no support from the Polish Diet. It was simply shelved. Yet Queen Bona, who, with all her faults, was a model administrator, had already demonstrated the practicability and immense advantage, even on a small scale, of such a plan as Daszkiewicz's. To secure her estates in the Ukrain, she built the little castle of Bar, the defence of which she entrusted to her Silesian steward Bernard Pretficz. Seventy times did he

---

[1] A Ruthenian word meaning, like its Russian equivalent, Okrain, a border or frontier.

[2] From Kazaki, a Tatar word meaning a freebooter.

repulse the Tatar roaming bands, so that, to cite a contemporary chronicler, "in the days of Pan Pretficz the Hagarenes fell back from the frontier." The natural result was that thousands of colonists flocked to the Starosty of Bar, where land reclamation was conducted on a gigantic scale, Bona assisting the good work by making roads, draining marshes, and building bridges. By these means the value of her Ukrainian estates rose a hundredfold in a very short time. But the country benefited also, for Bar became the bastion of Podolia, and the centre of a wealthy agricultural district. The contemporary fortress of Krzemieniec owed its origin to similar causes.

Had the Polish Diet done, from motives of duty and patriotism, what Queen Bona did by way of private investment, the Tatar difficulty would never have swollen into a peril. Unfortunately, the *Szlachta*, which now began to dominate the Diet, was so blinded by considerations of caste and privilege as to be almost incapable of thinking imperially. Throughout the reign of Sigismund I, the Polish State suffered grievously from the pretensions, the jealousies, and above all, from the fatal parsimony of the Sejm. In 1510 the Primate Laski proposed that all the great dignitaries of State, in view of the King's necessities (it was the interval between the first and second Moscovite war), should contribute half of their annual income at once, and one-twentieth part thereof every subsequent year, and that, in future, all legal fines and charges should be paid into the royal treasury. The project was indignantly rejected by the Diet which would only grant subsidies for two years, amounting, nominally, to 40,000 but which diminished during collection to 7000 gulden. At the Diet of 1512 the King proposed to commute military service into a fixed charge of six gulden per head, payable by every nobleman at the beginning of a campaign, the money to be employed in hiring mercenaries. This plan was also rejected. Then the King proposed that the whole kingdom should be divided into five military circles, bound to defend the realm alternately from

Easter to St Martin's Day.   This proposal was so far approved
of by the local diets of Little and Great Poland that St Michael's
Day in each year was fixed upon for the registration and
assessment of the gentry of each province.   Every *armiger*
was free to commute his service at a fixed quota; but his
property was to be liable to confiscation if he had failed to
pay his quota within a given time.   At the eleventh hour, the
whole project foundered on the incurable jealousies of the
Senate and the *Szlachta*, neither being willing to trust the other
with the custody of the registers, whereupon the Diet of 1515
rejected the reform altogether, and the King had to make the
best of the old subsidies, voted for three years.   In 1518–1519
the Poles granted Sigismund only 39,000 gulden, whereas the
Lithuanians gave him 134,000, the superior liberality of the
latter being due to the fact that they were more directly
threatened by the Moscovites and Tatars.   The Poles, moreover, had an irritating habit of accompanying the slightest
pecuniary concession with demands for fresh privileges, mainly
at the expense of the rich burgesses of Cracow and of the
lower classes generally.   In 1513 the local diet of Korczyn went
so far as to extrude from its session the burgomaster and
consuls of Cracow.   But Sigismund promptly reinstated them
and publicly confirmed their privilege of representing the city
in the local diets.

In 1533, and again in 1537, fresh efforts were made
in vain by the *Szlachta* to exclude the deputies of Cracow
from the Diets, and, finally, the King was obliged (1539)
to issue an edict threatening to prosecute for *lèse-majesté*
any gentleman who attempted in future to infringe the rights
of the citizens.   Both this *Sejmik* and the *Sejmik* of Bromberg
in 1520 were also very severe upon the peasantry who were now
compelled to work one day a week gratis on their master's land.
Hitherto, this had been a matter of private arrangement; now
it was made a statutory and universal obligation.   The Diets
of 1522 and 1523 would grant the King nothing for the national

defence ; and he was compelled, with the consent of the Senate, to levy taxes by royal edict. This unpatriotic parsimony was largely due to the *Szlachta's* suspicion of the magnates and senators who surrounded the King and monopolized all the chief offices in the State. The oligarchs, on the other hand, as being experienced and practical statesmen, took a juster view of things ; and one of them, the Primate Andrzej Krzycki (1483–1537), summed up the situation, pretty accurately, in a letter to Sigismund. "All of us know right well," he said, " the great danger that threatens us, so that if your Majesty did not rule this body-politic, like as the soul of a man ruleth his members, we should all fall to pieces."

In 1526 the ranks of the *Szlachta* were reinforced by hundreds of Masovian squires, the Duchy of Masovia, on the extinction of the male ducal line (August 26, 1526), being incorporated with the kingdom. This event was not without considerable political influence. The poor[1], ignorant, but fiery Masovian squires, whose rough grey coats and ragged accoutrements excited the ridicule of contemporary satirists, introduced a strong democratic element into the Polish Diet, which helped to stiffen the opposition. The King, too, was now growing weary of strife. He had out-lived most of his friends and counsellors, and repeated disappointments had saddened and disillusioned him. His chief care now was to pass the Crown on to, and make the future easy for, his beloved and only son Sigismund Augustus. He could still, as we shall see, be very firm in religious matters ; but, politically, his powers of resistance were weakening. In the last years of his reign the *Szlachta* (now nominated to the *Sejm,* or great Diet, by their own local diets, instead of, as heretofore, by the officers of the Crown at the royal courts) became the leading power in the

---

[1] The whole income of the duchy only amounted to 14,000 gulden per annum. It consisted mainly of sand and fir trees, but was densely populated by small landowners. From henceforth its capital Warsaw. thanks to its central position, begins to rise in importance.

State; and the King acquiesced in the transfer of authority from the magnates to the gentry, especially as he himself largely profited thereby. In the districts where the magnates owned all the land, the *Szlachta*, naturally, had no direct influence; but they were gradually becoming the masters of the Diet, and there they circumscribed the authority of the Executive, as represented by the Senate, in every direction. Thus, statutes were passed forbidding the Grand Hetman, or Captain-General, of the Kingdom, to levy troops, the Lord Treasurer to collect taxes, the Grand Chancellor to direct the tribunals; the King and Diet together were hencoforth to attend to all such matters. Military service, moreover, was now declared a universal obligation. In this respect, the mightiest *Pan*, or Lord, was placed on the same level, according to his means, as the poorest grey-coat (1527). This beneficial reform resulted in a large increase of all the local militias. Thus in 1529 Podolia alone raised 3200 horse and 300 foot, the control of which was placed in the hands of the King.

In the remote and still semi-barbarous Lithuania, on the other hand, the Senate was everything, the gentry nothing. Even so late as 1569 the only persons who attended at the Lithuanian *Sejms* were the *Voivode*, or Governor, the *Starosta*, or Judiciary, and the *Chorazy*, or Standard-bearer, with their officials. These dignitaries would then proceed to pass whatever statutes they pleased, commit them to writing, and circulate them among the provincial nobility, who were compelled to sign them under the threat of a flogging. The great obstacle to the spread of civilisation in the Grand Duchy was the war of the two hostile confessions, the Roman Catholic and the Greek Orthodox. From the beginning of the Union, conversion to Catholicism in Lithuania had been rewarded by donations of vast domains and seats in the Senate. The sons of these renegade fathers jealously guarded their predominance, and unmercifully oppressed their despised orthodox brethren, who represented four-fifths of the entire population. When the Lithuanian Chancellor, Gasztold, could describe the illustrious and enlightened Prince Constantine Ostrogski as "a new man of low condition whose ancestors stood at the footstool of my ancestors," we may form some idea of how ordinary orthodox gentlemen were treated in Lithuania. At the beginning of the century things were, naturally, very much worse. In the eyes of the ruling oligarchs, everyone who won promotion by personal services, or royal favour, was an impertinent intruder. Thus, when Sigismund rewarded Ostrogski for his great victory at Orsza, by conferring on him the *Voivody* of Troki, such a storm arose at the subsequent Diet of 1522, that the King had to give a written undertaking that, henceforth, none but a Catholic should have a seat in the Lithuanian Senate. Nevertheless, Sigismund was ever the consistent upholder of tolerance and equity. Devout Catholic though he was, he sternly repressed every attempt at religious persecution on the part of the dominant Catholic minority. The chartered rights of the orthodox population were rigorously maintained, and every injury inflicted on them was promptly punished. In all confessional conflicts, the Orthodox were treated as the equals of the Catholics before the Law. Hence the universal popularity enjoyed by Sigismund in his Grand Duchy, which was very useful to him politically. He was able, with little difficulty, to procure the election of his infant son as Grand Duke (1522); to codify the unwritten and chaotic laws of Lithuania, which code, in the Ruthenian language, was promulgated by the Diet of Wilna in 1529; to abolish socage in Samogitia; and to introduce many far-reaching economic reforms.

The last years of Sigismund I were years of resigned despondency. Externally, thanks to his splendid physique and majestic presence, the old King seemed as hale and vigorous as ever. In reality, he was a weary and broken man. New and disquieting problems came crowding upon him towards the end of his reign, and he knew that his failing powers were unequal to their solution. The most pressing of these problems was

how to prevent the spread of the new religious ideas, which
were beginning to exercise such a peculiar influence upon
Polish politics.

Despite her fidelity to the Holy See, Poland, so early as
1326, had required the assistance of an Inquisitor to protect
her orthodoxy against the onslaughts of the Hussites. Yet she
gave but little trouble to the Curia till the age of Luther ; and,
but for the pretensions and the exactions of her own clergy, it
is very doubtful whether Lutheranism would have gained any
sure footing in the kingdom at all. As a German product,
Lutheranism was naturally distasteful to the Poles ; and the
repressive measures adopted against the new heresy by
Sigismund I were approved by the nation at large, mainly
from political reasons. The first outbreaks of militant Protestantism occurred at Dantzic in 1518 and 1520. Still more
alarming was the rebellion of 1525, when the innovators
purged the town council of Catholics, closed the monasteries,
appropriated the churches, abolished nearly all the taxes, and
introduced free-trade. At Cracow, these disturbances were
at first attributed to the machinations of the ever restive
Teutonic Order. Sigismund lost no time in bringing the
rebels to reason. He came in person to Dantzic at the head
of a large body of troops, hung fifteen of the ring-leaders,
including the aldermen, re-established Catholicism, expelled
the perverts, forbade the dissemination of Lutheran literature
and, contrary to his usual practice, released the gentry from all
civic jurisdiction, not only in Dantzic, but throughout the
Prussian provinces. In Poland proper, anti-Lutheran edicts
were also issued. In 1520 the Edict of Thorn forbade the impor-
tation of German books. The Edict of Grodno confirmed
and extended that of Thorn. The Edict of Cracow (1523)
condemned to confiscation and the stake anyone preaching
Lutheranism. But these edicts, for the most part, remained
inoperative, partly because heretics were few on Polish soil,
but, principally, because the Bishops became more and more

afraid of exercising their coercive functions in view of the increasing hostility of the *Szlachta* freely expressed in the Sejms. Religion had but little to do with the anti-ecclesiastical sentiments of the Polish gentry. No doubt, the very unapostolic lives of the Polish Bishops of the period armed the *Szlachta* with the best of all weapons against their spiritual fathers. But it was the pretensions and the privileges, not the opinions of the Prelates, which gave the most offence. In brief, the spiritual peers had now to submit to the same levelling process as the temporal peers had already undergone; and, as the clergy had always claimed more, they necessarily suffered more than the privileged laity. It was now that the gentry began to refuse to pay tithes, to question the jurisdiction of the spiritual courts, to object to the payment of *Annates* and other papal charges, and, generally, to exalt liberty, as they understood it, above everything else. But, so long as Sigismund I reigned, the Church, supported by the whole weight of the Crown, had little to fear. The *Szlachta* might storm and rage and even threaten Sigismund to his face with rebellion; but the old King remained imperturbable and indifferent, and their threats invariably came to nothing.

It was in the reign of Sigismund that the influence of the Italian Renaissance extended to Poland. Sigismund, always a lover of music and interested in architecture, his one expensive luxury[1], was naturally attracted by the artistic side of the Renaissance; and under the direction of his accomplished second consort, Bona of Ferrara, the Court of Cracow became the focus of Italian culture. There Bona reigned resplendent, winning every heart by her grace and beauty, and every head by her brilliant wit and perfect command of Latin. The satirist Krzycki indited to her his choicest epigrams; the chancellor Tomicki humoured her lightest caprice; the future

---

[1] The stately castle of Cracow was built for him by the best Italian masters.

fathers of the Polish church assiduously sought her patronage. But, beyond the narrow limits of art and literature, Bona's extraordinary ascendency[1] was everywhere mischievous. The Polish nation rightly detested a Princess who did nothing but enrich herself at its expense, and was as much a foreigner when she decamped with her accumulated millions as when she first entered the land as a bride, thirty-seven years before. Her greed of gold was only equalled by her greed of power. She hated her only son as a political rival, and contributed, by her inhuman treatment, to the death of his first consort, the amiable Archduchess Elizabeth of Austria (1543). Bona's political intrigues frequently embarrassed Sigismund in his later years ; but her sway over him prevailed to the end, and when he expired, on April 1, 1548, in his 81st year, it was she who closed his eyes.

[1] Even Krzycki complains that she played the part of Juno to Sigismund's too-complaisant Jove.

CHAPTER V.

THE LAST OF THE JAGIELLOS, 1548—1572.

On April 17, 1548, the magnates and prelates of Lithuania assembled at the castle of Wilna to kiss the hand of their new Grand Duke, Sigismund Augustus, on the eve of his departure to Cracow, to bury his father and receive his father's Crown from the hands of the Polish *Pans*[1] who had elected him King eighteen years previously. At the first hour after noon, Sigismund entered the crowded hall, mounted the throne, and, after greeting the assembled dignitaries, thus addressed them : " Many reasons, meet and right and even weighty, have constrained me, hitherto, to conceal that which I will this day reveal to you all. Barbara Radziwillowna, Wojewodzina of Troki, is my wife, given to me in holy, Christian, wedlock in the presence of her kinsfolk. Know ye therefore that nought on the earth can sever such a tie lawfully contracted among Christians." After this prelude, the King ordered the doors of the hall to be opened, and introduced Barbara, surrounded by a numerous retinue of Lithuanian Senators. The assembly was thunderstruck by this sudden and emphatic announcement of Sigismund's marriage with a lady who was doubly offensive to the oligarchs as being the daughter of Prince Nicholas Radziwill, commonly called " Black Radziwill," the leader of the Calvinists, and herself an ardent Calvinist. But in Lithu-

---

[1] Great Lords.

ania the authority of the semi-absolute Grand Duke prevailed, and no protest was made. Far different was the reception of the tidings in Poland, where Queen Bona, jealous of the beauty and influence of the young bride, used every effort to annul a union "so unequal as to tarnish the King's majesty." As a Lithuanian, Barbara was distasteful to the Poles generally; as a heretic she was especially offensive to the clergy. Not a voice was raised in her defence; and when, on October 31, 1548, the *Sejm* assembled at Piotrków, the only Senator who stood by the King was the Grand Hetman of the Crown, Jan Tarnowski. During the first debate in the Senate, the Grand Marshal, Kmita, moved that the King should not disgrace his order. Two days later a deputation from the *Izba*, or lower House, petitioned Sigismund to "withdraw from his intentions and not call that a marriage which was no marriage." "Every man," replied Sigismund calmly, "has the right to choose his own wife; why cannot the King do the same? Or does the Christian religion allow me to put away her whom I have wedded? It is for you of the clergy, who know better about such things, to convince your brethren on this head. But I will not desert my wife, though she were stripped of everything but her shift." This simple and manly declaration evoked such a storm of abuse that the King was obliged to enjoin silence. The Primate, Dzierzgowski, a creature of Bona's, then fiercely denounced the marriage; and other bishops and senators followed his example. Kmita's language was so venomous that the King bade him hold his tongue. The whole Chamber revolted at such an unusual rebuke from the throne, but Sigismund was not to be frightened. "What hath been done cannot be undone," he said. "I have sworn never to forsake my wife and, so help me God! I mean to keep my oath." Shortly afterwards, Sigismund dissolved the Diet and issued a *Universal*, or manifesto, in which he appealed to the sense of justice of the nation against the violence and tyranny of the Legislature. He knew that he had won a moral victory, and he proceeded, skilfully enough, to make the most of it. Not till May 4, 1550, was a second Diet summoned. By this time public opinion had so completely veered round that not a word was uttered about the royal marriage. Nay, when the Posen deputy, Nicholas Sienicki, accused the King of despotic designs, the Grand Marshal, Kmita, rebuked him roundly for attempting to circumscribe the royal prerogative.

This episode is worth dwelling upon, illustrating as it does both the character of the new King and the peculiar difficulty of the task before him.

Sigismund II, when he ascended the throne, was in his 28th year. Brought up by and among women, in the exotic luxury of an italianate Court which had absorbed everything, good or bad, which the Renaissance could offer, his frail and elegant figure seemed puny and effeminate to the sturdy, homespun gentry who, for nearly fifty years, had followed, often reluctantly enough, in the footsteps of his burly and downright father. Yet Sigismund II was a true Jagiello. He possessed, in an eminent degree, the patience and tenacity which were the characteristic virtues of his family, and he combined with these useful qualities a perspicacity, an intellectual suppleness, and a diplomatic *finesse* (doubtless inherited from his mother) which carried him triumphantly over the worst obstacles of the most difficult situations. "The King," wrote the Austrian Envoy, towards the end of the reign, "most easily turns this most indocile of nations whithersoever he will. Things here ever befall according to his wishes." The Papal nuncio Paggieri renders similar testimony.

The Barbara incident enables us, moreover, to gauge, pretty accurately, the force and direction of the quasi-democratic movement whose beginnings we have already noted in the reign of Sigismund I, and whose representatives claimed the right to interfere in everything. This movement was, originally, of a social-political character. It was a revolt of the *Szlachta*, or gentry, against the usurpations of the *Pans*. Its fundamental object was the so-called *egsekucya praw*, or enforcement of all the statutes which had been passed, from time to time, to arrest the aggrandisement of the magnates, or compel them to fulfil their obligations to the.State.

But now this movement assumed a religious character owing to the *Szlachta's* jealousy of the privileged position of the clergy, accentuated by a strong feeling of personal independence which resented the liability of being haled before the ecclesiastical Courts for inquisitorial purposes. In these circumstances, any opponent of the Established Church was the natural ally of the *Szlachta*. But, although the pride and jealousy of the gentry were the principal, they were by no means the only causes of the early successes of the Reformation in Poland. The scandalous condition of the Polish Church at this time seemed to excuse, and even justify, the far-reaching apostacy which was now to shake her to her very foundations. The bishops, who had grown up beneath the demoralising influence of Queen Bona—elegant triflers, for the most part, as pliant as reeds, with no fixed principles and saturated with a false humanism—were indifferent in matters of faith, and regarded the new doctrines with philosophical toleration. Some of them were notorious ill-livers. " Pint-pot " Latalski, Bishop of Posen, had purchased his office from Bona for 12,000 ducats ; while another of her creatures, Peter, popularly known as "the wencher," was appointed Bishop of Przemysl, and promised the reversion of the wealthy see of Cracow. Moreover, despite her immense wealth (in the Province of Little Poland alone, she owned at this time 26 towns, 83 landed estates and 722 villages), the Church claimed exemption from all public burdens, from all political responsibilities, although her prelates, sitting as they did in the Senate, and holding many of the offices of the State, continued to exercise an altogether disproportionate political influence. Education was shamefully neglected, the masses being left in almost heathen ignorance ; and this, too, at a time when the middle classes were greedily appropriating the ripe fruits of the Renaissance, and when, to use the words of a contemporary, there were "more Latinists in Poland than ever there were in Latium." The Academia Jagiellonika, or University of Cracow, the sole source of knowledge and enlightenment in the vast Polish realm, still moved in the vicious circle of scholastic formularies. The principal schools, dependent upon so decrepit an *alma mater*, were, for the most part, suffered to decay. The sons of the gentry, denied proper instruction at home, betook themselves to the nearest High Schools across the border, to Goldberg in Silesia, to Wittenburg, to Leipzig. Here they fell in with the adherents of the new faith, grave, God-fearing men, who professed to reform the abuses which had grown up in the Church in the course of ages; and they endeavoured, on their return, to propagate these wholesome doctrines, and clamour for the reformation of their own degenerate prelates. Finally, the poorer clergy, cut off from all hope of preferment, and utterly neglected by their own bishops, were also inspired by the spirit of revolt, and eagerly devoured and imparted to their flocks, in their own language, the contents of the religious tracts and treatises which reached them by devious ways, from Goldberg and Königsberg. Nothing indeed did so much to popularise the new doctrines in Poland as this beneficial revival of the long-neglected vernacular by the Reformers.

Such was the situation when Sigismund II began his reign. The King, too good a Catholic and too wise a statesman to weaken the conservative elements of the State in a period of acute crisis, adopted from the first, with consummate skill, the office of mediator between the contending confessions. On December 12, 1550, five days after the coronation of Barbara as Queen of Poland[1] by the Primate Dzierzgowski, he issued the celebrated edict whereby he pledged his royal word to preserve intact the unity of the Church and the privileges of the clergy,

---

[1] She survived the ceremony less than six months, dying of cancer on May 8, 1551, to the inconsolable grief of her broken-hearted consort.

and to enforce the law of the land against heresy. Encouraged by this pleasing symptom of orthodoxy, the bishops, with singular imprudence, instead of first attempting to put their own dilapidated house in order, at once proceeded to summon before their Courts all persons suspected of heresy. The *Szlachta* instantly took the alarm ; and at the stormy Diet of Piotrków, which met in January 1552, even devout Catholics, like Jan Tarnowski, inveighed bitterly against the bishops and questioned their right to summon the gentry before their tribunals. On this head the whole estate of nobles, Catholic and Protestant alike, was unanimously agreed. The bishops, timid and vacillating, bent beneath the storm ; and, when the King proposed, by way of compromise, that the jurisdiction of the Church Courts should be suspended for twelve months, on condition that the gentry continued to pay tithes, the prelates readily sacrificed their convictions to save their revenues.

Henceforth the Reformers began to propagate their opinions openly, and even molested the Catholics. Those of the Protestant gentry who had the right of presentation to benefices began bestowing them upon chaplains and ministers of their own persuasion, in many cases driving out the orthodox incumbents and substituting Protestant for Catholic services. Presently Reformers of every shade of opinion, even those who were tolerated nowhere else, poured into Poland, which speedily became the battle-ground of all the sects of Europe. Most of them now became numerous enough to form ecclesiastical districts of their own. In the *Sejm* itself the Protestants were absolutely supreme ; and they invariably elected a Calvinist, or even a Socinian, to be their marshal or president. At the Diet of 1555 they boldly demanded a national Synod for the cleansing and reforming of the Church, and presented nine points for the consideration of the King and Senate, amounting to a demand for absolute toleration. The bishops naturally refused to entertain this revolutionary programme ; and, the King again intervening as mediator, the existing *interim* was, by mutual consent, indefinitely prolonged. The violent and unscrupulous proceedings of the bigoted Roman Nuncio, Ludovico Lippomano, on this occasion, still further damaged the Catholic cause by provoking universal indignation, even the bishops refusing to obey him.   At the subsequent Diet of Warsaw (1556), the whole of the *Izba*, or Lower Chamber, clamoured furiously against "the Egyptian bondage of the Prelacy," and demanded absolute freedom of discussion in all religious questions.   Again, however, the King adopted a middle course; and, by the Edict of Warsaw (Jan. 1557), it was decreed that things should remain as they were till the following Diet.   At that Diet, which assembled at Piotrków on November 20, 1558, the onslaught of the *Szlachta* on the clergy was fiercer than ever; and a determined attempt was even made to exclude the bishops from the Senate on the principle that no man could serve two masters.   True loyalty and patriotism, it was urged, could not be expected from prelates who were the sworn servants of a foreign potentate—the Pope.   But the King and the Senate, perceiving a danger to the Constitution in the violence of the *Szlachta*, not only took the part of the bishops but quashed a subsequent, reiterated demand for a national Synod.   On February 8, 1559, the Diet dissolved without coming to any resolution.   The King, in his valedictory address, justly threw all the blame for the abortiveness of the session upon the interference and injustice of the *Szlachta*.

The *Sejm* of 1558–1559 indicates the high-water mark of Polish Protestantism.   From henceforth, it began, very gradually, but unmistakably, to subside.   The chief cause of this subsidence was the division among the Reformers themselves.   The almost absolute religious liberty which they enjoyed in Poland proved, in the long run, far more injurious to them than to the Church which they professed to reform.   From the chaos of creeds resulted a chaos of ideas on all imaginable moral and social subjects, which culminated in a violent clashing of the various sects, each one of which naturally strove for the mastery.   An auxiliary cause of the decline of Protestantism in Poland was the beginning of a Catholic reaction there.   Not only the far-seeing, statesmanlike, monarch himself but his chief counsellors also could no longer resist the conviction that the project of a National Church was a mere Utopia.   The bulk of the population still held languidly yet persistently to the faith of its fathers; and the Holy See, awakening at last to the gravity of the situation, gave to the slowly reviving zeal of both clergy and laity the very necessary stimulus from without.   There can be no doubt that, in the first instance, it was the papal Nuncios who re-organised the scattered and faint-hearted battalions of the church militant in Poland and led them back to victory.   The most notable of these re-constructing Nuncios was Berard, Bishop of Camerino, who arrived in 1560 and persuaded the King to send delegates to the council of Trent.   He was less successful at the Diet of 1562.   On this occasion Sigismund completely won the susceptible hearts of the *Szlachta*, by appearing in the grey coat of a Masovian squire.   Needing the subsidies of the Deputies— for the incorporation by Poland of most of the territories of the defunct Order of the Sword had excited the jealousy of Moscovy and the Scandinavian Powers—Sigismund was prepared, as the lesser of two evils, to sacrifice the clergy; and, with his consent, the jurisdiction of the ecclesiastical Courts was practically abolished, it being declared that henceforth no confiscations consequent upon condemnations for heresy could be executed except by the secular Courts as administered by the Starostas or Lord Justices, many of whom were Protestants.   The bishops protested, but the King was inexorable.   "You must," he said, "take the plunge."

Berard was thereupon superseded by Giovanni Francisco Commendone, one of the most experienced and devoted of the Roman diplomatists.   His earlier despatches to Rome (1563–1564) are gloomy enough.   He reported that the higher

Catholic clergy were disunited and disaffected; that the Protestants were guilty, almost daily, of outrages against Catholic ceremonies; and that the childless King seemed intent on a divorce from his third wife (his first wife's sister) the Archduchess Catharine of Austria, whom he had married, for purely political reasons, in 1553, and who was now living apart from him at Radom, an incurable invalid. Nevertheless, the tact and energy of the capable and courageous Nuncio soon worked wonders. The King, despite the strong influence of the Calvinistic Radziwills, and the alluring precedent of Henry VIII, did not press to an issue the much dreaded question of the divorce. In 1564 Commendone persuaded him to accept and promulgate the Tridentine Decrees and issue an edict banishing all foreign heretics from the land. At the Diet of 1565 the Protestants presented a petition for a national pacificatory Synod; but the King rejected it as unnecessary, inasmuch as the Council of Trent had already settled all religious questions. He declared, at the same time, that he was resolved to live and die a Catholic. But the most re-assuring feature of this Diet, from a churchman's point of view, was the presence in the *izba* of a zealous Catholic minority which, while willing enough to keep the clergy within bounds, energetically protested against any attack upon the Church's ceremonies or dogmas. It was quite a new thing to see the Polish gentry marshalled round a papal Nuncio and drawing their sabres, in full session, against the gainsayers of Catholic truth. At the same Diet, Sigismund consented to the introduction into Poland of the most formidable adversaries of the Reformation, the Jesuits. Noskowski, Bishop of Plock, had already installed them at Pultusk; and, after the Diet had separated, the Society was permitted to found establishments in the dioceses of Posen, Ermeland, and Wilna, which henceforth became centres of a vigorous and victorious propaganda.

Unfortunately, this very Diet, in many respects so salutary, marks the mischievous victory of the *Szlachta* over their old

enemies the burgesses.   A death-blow was struck at the prosperity of the towns by the statute which made export trade,
henceforth, the exclusive privilege of the *Szlachta*, and at their
liberty by the statute which placed them under the jurisdiction
of the provincial Starostas.   Henceforth, the Polish towns count
for nothing in Polish politics.

The Catholic revival gained in strength every year, although
the King continued, judiciously, to hold the balance between
the opposing parties and preserved order by occasionally
nominating Protestants to the highest offices of the State, and
always preventing persecution.   Moreover, a new order of
bishops, men of apostolic faith and fervour, were gradually
superseding the indolent and corrupt old prelates of Bona's
creation.   Many of the magnates, too, were, about this time,
re-converted to the Catholic religion, notably Adalbert Laski,
and Jan Sierakowski whom the Protestants could ill afford to
lose.   In the *Sejm* itself, the attacks of the Protestants upon
the Catholics grew feebler every year, ceasing at last altogether.
Nay, at the Diet of 1569, the Protestants actually made
overtures for a union with the Catholics, which the latter
postponed till the reformed sects should have become " quite
agreed among themselves as to what they really believed."   At
the Diet of 1570 Sigismund, strong in the support of a small
but zealous Catholic majority, rejected a petition of the
Protestants that their confession should be placed on a
statutory equality with Catholicism.   Henceforth, all the
efforts of the Protestants were directed towards holding the
ground they had actually won.

By his wisdom and equity, Sigismund II had saved Poland
from the horrors of a religious war in the very age of the Wars
of Religion.   At the same time, his statesmanship, always
circumspect yet profiting by every favourable contingency, was
increasing the prestige of Poland abroad, and enlarging her
boundaries, just where territorial accretions promised to be
most useful to her.

B.

6

Generally speaking, Sigismund was true to the traditional political watchword of the Jagiellos: friendship with the Empire and peace with the Porte. Sigismund was, indeed, well aware of the acquisitive tendencies of the House of Hapsburg. "They mean us no good," he used frequently to say to his diplomatic agents, who were always busy counter-acting real or imaginary intrigues at Rome and elsewhere. But, on the other hand, he regarded Austria as the natural counterpoise to a still more formidable potentate, the Turkish Padishah, with whom he was especially anxious to avoid a collision. Sigismund could always frighten the Court of Vienna into subservience by pretending to espouse the cause of his own nephew, John Sigismund, Prince of Transylvania, a claimant of the Magyar throne, and the semi-feudatory of the Ottoman Empire. The relations between Sigismund and the Emperor Maximilian were, therefore, generally civil though never very cordial; and the unfortunate marriage between Sigismund and the Archduchess Catharine in 1553 was meant to be an additional confirmation of a political alliance which was, at the same time, a guarantee against any league between Austria and the Moscovite.

It was not so easy for Poland to preserve friendly relations with the Porte. Moldavia and Wallachia were the points of contact and peril. Nominally subject to the Turk, the Hospodars of these States were little better than freebooters on a grand scale; and their violations of Polish territory constantly called for reprisals. The Jagiellonic Kings were, however, very careful to stop short at repressing these desperadoes. So late as 1552, when Sigismund found it necessary to depose Stephen VIII of Wallachia and enthrone Peter Lepusnano in his stead, the Vice-Hetman entrusted with this police duty was strictly charged to evacuate the principality immediately afterwards. The King could control the Hetmans, but he was powerless to check the frequent raids into Moldavia and Wallachia of the *Pans* or great lords. From time immemorial the Wallachs had

sought a refuge in Poland from the tyranny of their Hospodars ;
there was a large Wallach population in the south-eastern
Polish provinces ; and the trade between the two countries was
lively and lucrative.   From about the middle of the sixteenth
century onwards, the Lord Marchers of Poland took it upon
themselves to interfere freely in Wallachian and Moldavian
affairs without even consulting the Polish Government.   In
1558 Adalbert Laski assisted the fantastic polyglot adventurer
calling himself " Heraclides, Prince of Samos," to drive Peter
Lepusnano from Moldavia and establish himself there.   Heraclides, however, was speedily expelled by the Turks ; and there
matters would have rested had it not occurred to another Polish
Pan, Prince Demetrius Wisniowiecki, to reinstate Heraclides
by force of arms.   The adventure ended most disastrously.
Heraclides was defeated and tortured to death by the rival candidate ; Wisniowiecki perished miserably at Stambul ; and those
of the Polish captives who were not massacred on the spot, were
sent home minus their ears and noses.   Fortunately for Sigismund, the contemporary disasters of the Turks in Hungary,
which led to the truce of Erlau (1562), disinclined the Sublime
Porte to embark in a war with Poland on this occasion.

These so-called *Kozakowania*[1], always inconvenient and
disquieting, were doubly so at this period, when Sigismund II
was about to embark upon an enterprise which must infallibly
lead to a fresh war with the Moscovite.

At the beginning of the sixteenth century, the dominion of
the ancient Knights of the Sword, which extended, roughly
speaking, from the Gulf of Finland to a little beyond the
Northern Dwina, and from Lake Peipus to the Baltic, was
about to fall to pieces from sheer caducity.   Inflanty, or
Livonia, as it was generally called, had long been one of the
principal markets of Europe, where English, Dutch, and
Scandinavian merchants jostled each other in search of corn,
timber, hides and the other raw products of Lithuania and

[1] *i.e.* embarking in adventures after the manner of Cossacks.

Moscovy. Originally a compact, self-sufficient, unconquerable military colony in the midst of savage and jarring barbarians, the Order had, in the course of ages, sunk into a condition of confusion and decrepitude that tempted the greed of the three great monarchies—Sweden, Moscovy and Poland—which had, in the meantime, grown up around and now pressed hard upon it. The Gulf of Finland still separated the Livonian lands from Sweden, but the Moscovite had only to cross the Narowa, the Polack, the Dwina, to strike at the very heart of the crumbling realm. Livonia was to be an apple of discord between the three northern Powers for generations to come. Each of the three aimed at the domination of the Baltic, and the first step towards the domination of the Baltic was the possession of Livonia.

Poland was the first to intervene. In June, 1556, Wilhelm of Brandenburg, Archbishop of Riga, appealed to Sigismund for help against the Grand Master, Wilhelm von Fürstenberg. Sigismund sent his ambassadors to mediate between the rivals; but, in the meantime, Fürstenberg had besieged and captured the Archbishop in Kokenhausen; and Lancki, one of the Polish envoys, was murdered by the Grand Master's son. This outrage gave Sigismund an excellent excuse for intervening directly. He invaded south Livonia with an overwhelming force of 80,000 men, forcibly reconciled the Archbishop and the Grand Master in his camp at Pozwole (Sept. 1557), and compelled the Order to contract an offensive and defensive alliance with Poland directed against Moscovy. In 1558, when Ivan IV invaded Livonia[1], Fürstenberg fled to Poland, leaving Gotthard von Kettler Grand Master in his stead. In June, 1559, the Estates of Livonia, in terror of the Moscovite, formally placed themselves beneath the protection of the Polish Crown, to which they at the same time ceded their southernmost provinces, Courland and Semigallia (Treaties of Wilna, August 31 and Sept. 15). It is worthy of note

[1] *See* Chapter VII.

that Sigismund concluded these important treaties not as King of Poland but as Grand Duke of Lithuania, the Polish *Sejm* refusing all cooperation and responsibility for an affair which, they said, concerned Lithuania alone. The almost simultaneous occupation of Oesel by the Danes and of Esthonia by the Swedes[1], and the horrible devastation of central Livonia by Ivan IV, accelerated the incorporation of Livonia with Lithuania. In 1561 the Lithuanian Hetman, Prince Nicholas Radziwill, received the submission of the Grand Master and the Archbishop in his camp before Riga. In September of the same year a great Livonian deputation proceeded to Wilna to render homage to Sigismund, and, on November 28, the incorporation of Livonia was accomplished; though the compact of subjection was not signed till February, 1562. Sigismund swore to confirm all the privileges of the Livonian nobility, to relieve them from all military burdens, to recognise the Augsburg Confession in his new domains. Kettler thereupon exchanged Catholicism for Lutheranism, and became a feudatory of Poland under the title of Duke of Courland, which dignity was to be hereditary in his heirs male. Simultaneously, Sweden was disarmed by a compact made with Duke John of Finland who, on October 4, 1562, arrived at Wilna, and was there married to Sigismund's third sister Catharine. Thus the tact and tenacity of Sigismund II had succeeded in excluding Moscovy from the sea. For the first time in her history, Poland had the opportunity of establishing herself as a naval Power. The ablest of Sigismund's counsellors fully understood the importance of the newly acquired provinces. "Methinks," observed the Polish Vice-Chancellor Myszkowski, "that Polish fleets will soon be sailing on the sea, and that the King of Denmark will be more straitened thereon than heretofore."

The last and greatest service which Sigismund II rendered to his country was the amalgamation of Poland and Lithuania.

[1] *See* my *Scandinavia*, in the same series.

All the Princes of the House of Jagiello had aimed at this ; and Sigismund II, taught by their and his own experience, recognised the necessity of such an amalgamation more clearly than any of them. The present loose, weak confederacy included within it all the elements of disruption. The Polish State could never subsist as a great power so long as it was divided into two semi-independent principalities with strong centrifugal tendencies. In Poland itself men were of one mind as to the desirability of a complete and absolute union ; but the Lithuanian magnates, who still exercised absolute authority over the gentry, obstinately opposed a union the first effect of which would be to swamp their comparatively insignificant numbers amidst the countless masses of the Polish gentry. Only the fear of the Moscovite, with whom they were always, more or less, at war, induced the Lithuanians to entertain the proposal at all. The project of a closer union was first debated at the Diet of Warsaw (Nov. 1563—June 1564) to which the Lithuanians sent delegates. The discussion was warm on both sides and ultimately came to nothing ; but the King judiciously prepared the way for future negotiations by voluntarily relinquishing his hereditary title to the throne of Lithuania, so as to place the contending nationalities more on a level to start with. In 1565 died Black Radziwill, the principal opponent of the Union in Lithuania; and the negotiations were reopened, under far more favourable conditions, at the Diet which met at Lublin on January 10, 1569. Nevertheless, in a memorial presented by their Vice-Treasurer, Naruszewicz, the Lithuanians refused to go beyond a personal union, and, on the rejection of their memorial, withdrew from the Diet, leaving two of their dignitaries to watch the proceedings on their behalf. Then the King took a decisive step, and, of his own authority, as ruler of Lithuania, incorporated the border provinces of Volhynia, Podlasia and the Ukraine with the Crown[1], whereupon the Podlasian deputies

[1] The official designation of Poland.

swore the oath of allegiance to him as King of Poland, and took their seats alongside their Polish colleagues. Their example was quickly followed by the Volhynians. Perceiving that further resistance would be useless, the Lithuanian delegates returned to the Diet and accepted the Union as proposed by the King. On July 1 the Act of Union was solemnly sworn to in the church of the Franciscans, whereupon Sigismund, followed by the Senate, proceeded in the pouring rain to the church of the Dominicans and kneeling on the steps of the Altar intoned a " Te Deum." Henceforth, in the words of the statute confirming this great act, " the Crown of Poland and the Grand Duchy of Lithuania is a composite and indivisible body and also one composite and common republic, or the incorporation and welding together of two States into one Nation." They were to have one *Pan*, or Sovereign Lord, elected jointly, one *Sejm*, one and the same currency. Every restriction upon the settlement of Poles in Lithuania or of Lithuanians in Poland was abolished. The Prussian and Livonian provinces were to belong to Poland and Lithuania in common. One relic of her former independence still remained to Lithuania. She retained her own separate dignitaries. Thus, to the very end, the Grand Hetman and the Vice-Hetman, the Grand Chancellor and the Vice-Chancellor of Lithuania, etc., continued to officiate side by side with their colleagues of the Crown.

The last years of Sigismund II were comparatively tranquil. The intermittent, indecisive, Moscovite War dragged on for a time[1], despite the Polish victories at Ula (1564) and Czasniki (1567); but in 1571 it was suspended by the usual truce. With all other Powers Sigismund remained friendly. Yet one poignant grief haunted him perpetually: he had no heir to whom to leave the Kingdom he had so ably guarded and consolidated. None of his three wives and neither of his two mistresses, Barbara Gizanka and Anna

[1] For details *see* Chapter VII.

Zajanczkowska, with whom he successively cohabited in the hope of offspring (which the Diet solemnly engaged to legitimate beforehand), had borne him children. The death of his sickly third wife Catharine (Feb. 28, 1572) released him at last from the bonds of wedlock ; and he thereupon declared his intention of wedding Gizanka, but it was too late. At 8 o'clock on the morning of July 9, Sigismund II expired at his favourite *château* at Knyszyn, in his 52nd year. In his last will and testament he solemnly exhorted the two nations, "whom God hath exalted above all other nations," to live together in peace and harmony and invoked the curse of Heaven on whomsoever should sow discord between them.

. . . .

The Jagiellonic period of Polish history (1386–1572), which terminates with the death of Sigismund II, is the history of the fusion into one political whole of numerous national elements, more or less akin ethnologically, but differing widely in language, religion, and, above all, in degrees of civilisation. Out of the ancient Piast Kingdom, mutilated by the loss of Silesia and the Baltic shore, arose a confederacy consisting, at first, of various loosely-connected entities, naturally centrifugal, but temporarily forced together by the urgent need of combination against a superior foe who threatened them, separately, with extinction. Beneath the guidance of a dynasty of Princes which, curiously enough, was supplied by the least civilised portion of this congeries of nationalities, the nascent confederacy gradually grew into a Power which subjugated its former oppressors and, viewed externally, seemed to bear upon it the promise of Empire. In politics it is always dangerous to prophecy, but all the facts and circumstances before us point irresistibly to the conclusion that had the Jagiellonic Dynasty but endured, this promise of Empire might well have been realised. The extraordinary thing about the Jagiellos was the equable persistency of their genius. Not only were five of the seven statesmen, but they

were statesmen of the same stamp.   We are disturbed by no
such sharp contrasts as are to be found among the Vasas and
the Bourbons.   The Jagiellos were all of the same mould and
pattern, but the mould was a strong one and the pattern
was good.   Their predominant and constant characteristics
were a sober sagacity and a calm tenaciousness.   The
Jagiellos were rarely brilliant, but they were always perspica-
cious; and they alone seem to have had the gift of guiding
successfully along the path of prosperity the most flighty and
self-willed of nations.

CHAPTER VI.

THE FIRST ELECTIVE KINGS, 1572–1588.

THE death of Sigismund II, though long foreseen, came upon Poland unexpectedly, and at an inconvenient and even dangerous moment. Of foreign complications there was happily no fear. The Grand Turk had not yet recovered from the shock of Lepanto (Oct. 7, 1571); and Ivan IV, with a view to obtaining the Polish Crown cheaply, by fair means, had, but recently, concluded a truce with the Polish Government. The Austrian and Swedish Courts had no motive for offending the Poles on the eve of an election in which they were both equally interested. Externally, then, the political horizon was absolutely cloudless. All the more disquieting was the internal situation. The Union of Lublin, barely three years old, was still extremely unpopular in Lithuania. In Poland proper, the *Szlachta* was fiercely opposed to the magnates; and the Protestants seemed bent upon still further castigating the Catholic clergy. At the first moment of surprise and dismay, nobody seemed to know exactly what to do. Even the dead body of the last Jagiello was shamefully neglected. Gizanka, Sigismund's much-beloved mistress, pillaged the royal treasury so effectually that there was not enough left wherewith to clothe the corpse becomingly, as it lay in state; and Fogelweder, Sigismund's German physician, for the sake of decency, took the gold chain off his own neck and placed it round the King's. Yet the Papal

Nuncio, shortly before, had estimated the value of the royal treasures at 10,000,000 ducats, and declared that the jewels of Rome and Venice were as nothing in comparison with those of Cracow.

Worst of all, there existed no recognised authority in the land to curb and control its jarring, centrifugal, political elements. Nothing had been fixed as to the succession; it was nearly 200 years since Poland had last been saddled with an interregnum; and the precedents of 1382 were obsolete. The Primate Uchanski, on hearing of the demise of the Crown, at once invited all the Senators of Great Poland to a conference at Lowicz, but passed over the *Szlachta* altogether. In an instant, the whole Republic was seething like a cauldron. Jan Firlej, the Grand Marshal of the Crown, and the head of the Protestant party, instantly summoned to Cracow an independent confederation of the gentry, which received the support of the Senators of Little Poland who resented the exclusiveness of the Primate's assembly. Fortunately, civil war was averted at the last moment; and a *Konwokacya*, or National Assembly, composed of Senators and deputies from all parts of the Kingdom, assembled at Warsaw in April 1573, for the purpose of electing a new King.

Meanwhile five candidates for the throne were already in the field. Lithuania was in favour of her near neighbour Tsar Ivan IV, whose election would have guaranteed her territories against Moscovite invasion. In Poland, the bishops and most of the Catholic magnates were in favour of an Austrian Archduke. But the House of Hapsburg was so obnoxious to the nation at large, that the *Szlachta* was disposed to accept almost any other candidate except a Moscovite. It was therefore no very difficult task for the adroit and energetic French ambassador, Montluc—who had been sent to Poland (Oct. 1572) by Catherine dei Medici to promote the candidature of her favourite son Henry, Duke of Anjou—to win over the majority of the *Szlachta*, especially as it was notorious that the

Ottoman Porte, while inclined to tolerate a French Prince on the Polish throne, would regard the election of an Austrian Archduke as a *casus belli*. Montluc, well provided with funds, purchased many of the magnates, but he placed his chief reliance in the ignorant and credulous masses of the *Szlachta* in whose hands the issues of the election really lay. He therefore devoted his energies to captivating all the lesser gentry, irrespective of religion. Montluc's popularity reached its height when he strenuously advocated the revival of the semi-barbarous *powszechne prawo glosowania*, or open, popular, mode of election by the gentry *en masse*, as opposed to the usual and more orderly "secret election" by a congress of senators and deputies sitting with closed doors. It was due to his efforts, seconded by the eloquence of the young Jan Zamoyski, now on the threshold of his brilliant career, that the *Sejm* decided in favour of the more popular method. The religious difficulty, meanwhile, had been satisfactorily adjusted by the Compact of Warsaw (Jan. 28, 1573), which granted absolute religious liberty to all non-Catholic denominations ("Dissidentes de Religione" as they now began to be called) without exception, thus exhibiting a far more liberal intention than the Germans had manifested in the religious Peace of Augsburg, eighteen years before. Nevertheless, the Warsaw Compact was eventually vitiated by the clauses which reserved to every master, spiritual or temporal, the right "to punish, according to his judgment," every rebellious servant, even if his rebellion were entirely due to his religious convictions. This unlimited power of arbitrary correction speedily resulted in the absolute serfdom of the rural population; and eventually, when the Protestant proprietors were won back to the church by the Jesuits, their dependents were of course forced to follow their example.

Early in April 1573, the Election Diet began to assemble at Warsaw; and across the newly-built bridge, the first that ever united the banks of the Vistula, flowed a stream of 40,000 electors, hastening to pitch their tents on the plain of Kamicnie, near Warsaw, where the fate of the Kingdom was to be decided. The next fortnight was passed in fierce debates, and in listening to the orations of the various foreign ambassadors on behalf of their respective candidates. The orators of Austria and Sweden were received but coldly because, though they had a great deal to say, they had very little to offer. Montluc, on the other hand, entranced the electors with a speech " worthy of eternal remembrance," which he took care to reinforce by private golden arguments. After this there could be no doubt of the success of the French candidate; and on May 11, 1573, Henry of Valois was elected King of Poland.

Nevertheless, as the prospects of the Duke of Anjou had approached certainty, the more cool-headed of the electors had begun to feel some natural anxiety as to how far this foreign Prince, the offspring of a despotic House, would be likely to respect the liberties of the Republic. They had therefore, by way of precaution, drawn up the so-called "Henrician Articles" which deprived the future King of the privilege of electing his successor, forbade his marrying without the previous consent of the Senate, required him to protect all the religious sects equally, considerably restricted his authority as commander-in-chief, and bound him to accept a permanent council of 14 Senators, elected every two years by the Diet, four of whom, in rotation, were to be in constant attendance upon him. The articles were supplemented, a few days later, by *pacta conventa*, corresponding to our coronation oath, which Montluc signed on behalf of Henry. The new King bound himself thereby to maintain a fleet in the Baltic at his own expense, place 450,000 ducats at the disposal of the Republic, educate 100 young Polish nobles abroad, espouse the late King's sister, the Korolewna Anna, eighteen years his senior[1], and confirm the Compact of Warsaw. Henry was persuaded to accept the *Pacta* at Notre Dame on September 10, 1573;

---

[1] This article Henry refused to confirm.

and on February 21, 1574 he was solemnly crowned King
at the Cathedral of Cracow. His reign, dating from his
arrival in Poland, lasted exactly four months. To a man of
his tastes and inclinations, his new position was intolerable;
and, when the death of his brother Charles IX left him the heir
to the French throne, he resolved to escape from his troublesome and terrifying Polish subjects forthwith. On June 19,
1574, half-an-hour after midnight, he fled from the Castle of
Cracow accompanied by a few French lords. A week later he
was dancing at a ball at Chambéry, to which place he was
pursued by a company of Polish cavaliers who besought him
to return. This he absolutely refused to do; and he was
formally deposed by the Diet which met at Stenczyc in May
1575. When, however, the question arose how to fill the
vacancy, the assembly split up into half a dozen fiercely
antagonistic sections. Anything like agreement was hopeless.
Finally, it was resolved that the whole question should be
referred to another Diet which the Primate, acting as *Interrex*,
summoned to meet at Warsaw on November 7.

A few weeks later, the Poles were taught the evils of anarchy
by a terrible lesson. In the beginning of October the eastern
provinces were ravaged by a Tatar horde, 120,000 strong. The
gentry shut themselves up in their castles; the common people
fled to the nearest stronghold, while "the scourge of God"
swept over the rich plains of the Ukraine, leaving a smoking
wilderness behind them and vanishing into their native steppes
with 55,000 captives, 150,000 horses and countless herds of
cattle. This lesson was not thrown away. At the Diet of
Warsaw a King was really elected—though not the King that
all the world had been led to expect.

Anxious to avoid violence and disorder, the Senate had
issued a proclamation restricting the retinue of each magnate
to 50 persons, and forbidding the *Szlachta* to carry any other
arms than the usual sword and halbert. This proclamation
was absolutely disregarded. Every one of the magnates who

attended the Diet was surrounded by a body-guard of at least 1000 horsemen. The gentry also came armed *cap-à-pied*. The prohibited arquebuses and spiked battle-axes were in everybody's possession, and there were whole forests of lances. All the materials for a bloody civil war were present on the field of election.

From November 13 to 18 audience was given to the orators of the various competitors, who included the Emperor Maximilian, the Archdukes Ernest and Ferdinand of Austria, John III of Sweden, the Duke of Ferrara, and Stephen Báthory, Prince of Transylvania. From November 18 to 25 the whole matter was debated in the Senate, which, profoundly influenced by the papal legate Vincenzo Laureo (who has left us a vivid account of the proceedings), declared in favour of the Emperor Maximilian by a large majority. But the *Izba*, or Lower House, where the debates lasted from November 22 to November 30, would not have a German at any price. This turbulent assembly was dominated by Jan Zamoyski, the most determined foe of the Hapsburgs, who fulminated so eloquently against "the craft and cruelty of the House of Austria" that the *Szlachta* determined, on November 30, by an enormous majority, to elect a *Piast*, or native Pole. As, however, both the noblemen nominated by the *Szlachta* at once declined the dangerous honour, the Senate, on December 10, proclaimed Maximilian King

At sunrise, next morning, 7000 Polish noblemen assembled outside the city to protest, sword in hand, against the election of the Emperor. Yet the embarrassment of the assembly was at least equal to its indignation. The question was, whom were they to elect, for no native candidate dared to come forward against the Hapsburgs. At last, when the confusion was worse confounded, the Palatine of Cracow suddenly arose and proposed Stephen Báthory, Prince of Transylvania. In an instant the name of Báthory was on every lip ; and, on December 14, he was unanimously elected King of Poland and

Grand Duke of Lithuania, on condition that he signed the usual *pacta conventa* and espoused the Princess Anna.   Thus Poland had now two Kings elect, one supported by the Senate, the other by the Diet.

A race for the Crown immediately ensued.   The last act of the Diet was to send a deputation to Transylvania to congratulate Báthory on his election and invite him to come instantly to Poland.   Meanwhile his partisans had not been idle.   Another Diet, summoned by the advice of Zamoyski, assembled at Jendrzejow (Jan. 18, 1576), confirmed the election of Stephen, sent an embassy to Vienna forbidding the Emperor to enter Poland, and then, marching to Cracow, put to flight all the Emperor's partisans.

But a splendid embassy had already been sent by the Senate to Vienna to announce to the Emperor Maximilian his election.   On March 23 Maximilian accepted the Polish Crown ; but, on the following day, deputies from the Diet of Jendrzejow arrived at Vienna to inform the Emperor, officially, that Stephen Báthory was now the lawful King of Poland.   They were speedily followed by a *chiaus* from the Sultan, who declared that any attempt on the part of Maximilian to disturb either the Polish or the Transylvanian possessions of the new Prince would be regarded at Stambul as a *casus belli*.   But the sudden death of Maximilian at the very moment when, in league with the Moscovite, he was about to invade Poland, completely changed the face of things.

King Stephen was now firmly established on his throne.   On Easter Monday (March 23, 1576) he made his state entry into Cracow with great magnificence.   On May 1 he and his wife-elect the Princess Anna were solemnly crowned King and Queen of Poland.   The coronation was followed by the nuptials of the Sovereigns, banquets and tourneys, the distribution of offices and dignities (Zamoyski's appointment to the Vice-Chancellorship was one of the first) and the issue of *universals* summoning a general Diet to Warsaw in the beginning of June.   All who failed to appear there at the appointed time were to be regarded as traitors and rebels. Then Báthory, who was determined, he said, to shew that he was " neither a painted nor a ballad King," set off for Warsaw to meet the Diet.

The leading events of Stephen's glorious reign can here only be very briefly indicated. All armed opposition to him collapsed with the surrender of the great city of Dantzic, since 1454 a self-centred, autonomous, free State. The "Pearl of Poland," encouraged by her immense wealth and almost impregnable fortifications, as well as by the secret support of Denmark and the Emperor, had shut her gates against the new monarch, and was only reduced, December 16, 1577, after a six months' siege, beginning with a pitched battle beneath her walls, in which she lost 5000 of her mercenaries, and the famous banner with the inscription " Aurea Libertas." Dantzic was compelled to pay a fine of 200,000 gulden into the royal treasury, but her civil and religious liberties were wisely confirmed. Stephen was now able to devote himself exclusively to foreign affairs, which demanded equally decided and delicate handling. The difficulties with the Sultan were temporarily adjusted by a truce signed November 5, 1577; and the Diet was at length persuaded, though not without the utmost difficulty, to grant Stephen subsidies for the inevitable war with Moscovy— subsidies which, as usual, proved totally inadequate.

Two campaigns of wearing marches, and still more exhausting sieges, ensued, in which Báthory, although repeatedly hampered by the parsimony of the short-sighted *Szlachta*, which could not be made to see that the whole future fate of Poland depended on the issue of the war, was uniformly successful, his skilful diplomacy, at the same time, allaying the growing jealousy of the Porte and the Emperor. The details of the war will be found in the following chapter ; here it is only necessary to say that the fruits of his triumph were considerably diminished by the intervention of the papal nuncio Possevino, whom the Curia, deceived by the delusive mirage of a union of the churches, had sent expressly from Rome to mediate between the Tsar and the King of Poland. Nevertheless, by the Treaty of Zapolsk (Jan. 15, 1582), Moscovy ceded to Poland Wielicz, Polock, and the whole of Livonia, but was allowed to retain Smolensk.

It is a melancholy and significant fact that Stephen Báthory's brilliant services to his adopted country, far from being rewarded with the dutiful gratitude of his new subjects, made him absolutely unpopular with both the magnates and the *Szlachta*. Not one word of thanks did the King receive from the Diet for repulsing Moscovy, till Zamoyski put the whole assembly to shame by rising in their midst and delivering an eloquent panegyric in which he publicly thanked his Sovereign, "in the presence of this ungrateful people," for his inestimable services. The opposition was marshalled round the wealthy and powerful Zborowski family, which had monopolised the principal dignities in the kingdom during the short reign of Henry. From the first, they had treated the new King insolently. At a *levée*, held soon after his coronation, the head of the family, the Grand Marshal, Zborowski (the nuncio tells us), "fell to reasoning of good swords, drew forth his own blade from its scabbard, and lauded it as one of the best in the presence of Báthory, who, justly taking offence thereat, suddenly loosed his scimitar from his girdle, and beating down with it the other's sword, flashed the scimitar in his face, remarking that it was a still better blade than his (Zborowski's sword), whereupon, the Marshal, perceiving his error in unsheathing his sword in the royal presence, straightway fell upon his knees and begged pardon." The Zborowscy especially resented the influence of the upstart Zamoyski; and their conduct became so seditious and defamatory that the King was obliged, at last, to take action. His opportunity came when the outlawed homicide, Samuel Zborowski, presumed to return to Poland. Zamoyski at once arrested him, and he was arraigned for high treason before a tribunal presided over by the King. After a scrupulously fair trial, he was condemned to death and duly beheaded at the castle of Cracow, May 26, 1584. The Diet which assembled on January 15, 1585, took up the cause of the Zborowscy; and the whole session was little more than a determined struggle between law and order on one side, as represented by the King and his Chancellor, and anarchy and rebellion as represented by the Zborowski faction, on the other. Ultimately, however, Stephen prevailed; the sentence of Samuel Zborowski was confirmed; and his kinsman, Christopher, was declared infamous and banished (Feb. 22, 1586).

Stephen's policy in religious matters aimed at consolidation and pacification. Devoted Catholic as he was, he nevertheless respected the liberties of the Protestants, severely punished the students of Cracow for attacking their conventicles, and even protected the Jews. A man of culture himself, he justly appreciated the immense value of education and relied especially on the Jesuits, who happened to be the best educational instruments at his command. He established the Order in Posen, Cracow, Riga, and other places, and from their seminaries, whose superiority was speedily and universally recognised (the Protestants themselves sending their children to be educated there), issued those "lions of the spirit," to use Skarga's expression, who were to complete the reconversion of Poland to Catholicism.

High political reasons also bound Stephen Báthory to the Jesuits. They, almost alone, had the intelligence to understand and promote his Imperial designs, which aimed at nothing less than incorporating Moscovy with Poland, and uniting the Kingdoms of Poland and Hungary, with the object of ultimately expelling the Turks from Europe. These grandiose, but, in view of the peculiar circumstances and of Stephen's commanding genius, not altogether impracticable designs, were first suggested by the death of Ivan the Terrible (1584). Stephen's views found an ardent supporter in the new Pope Sixtus V, to

whom the King sent a special mission to expound his plans.
He offered, in return for 3,648,000 ducats, to put on foot
84,000 men-at-arms for the Turkish campaign, and 24,000 for
the conquest of Moscovy.   The Pope thereupon despatched
Possevino on a second special mission to Poland and Russia,
to pave the way for this vast undertaking; and a Diet was
summoned by Stephen to meet at Grodno in February, 1587,
to consider the whole scheme.   The project was for ever
dissipated by the sudden death of Báthory, who was carried
off by a fit of apoplexy on December 12, 1586, at the age of 53.
In his all too brief reign of ten years he had already approved
himself one of the foremost statesmen and soldiers of his age.

The death of Stephen, like the breaking of a dike, let loose
a raging flood of long repressed bitterness and violence.   The
Convocation Diet (Feb. 3–March 13), summoned by the
Primate, was dominated by the Zborowscy, who denounced
"the Pasha"—so they called Zamoyski—as a traitor against
the national liberties.   Only the sudden collapse of a stove,
beneath the weight of the spectators crowding upon it, prevented a free fight in full Senate.   For a time the Zborowscy
continued to be in the ascendant.   Their first act was to banish
all the Báthorys from Poland, thus frustrating the Chancellor's
original intention of raising Stephen's brother, Cardinal Andrew
Báthory, to the throne.

June 29 had been fixed for the assembling of the Election-
Diet at Warsaw; and thither all the chief magnates hastened
with numerous retinues, in full panoply.   The Primate was
escorted by 500 horsemen; Gorka, Palatine of Posen, brought
with him 1086 hussars, *reiters* and cossacks; but Zamoyski, who
had hitherto kept in the background, shewed plainly that he
meant, if necessary, to meet force by force, by marching into
Warsaw at the head of a host of 6000 veteran mercenaries of
all arms, with the best procurable artillery ready for action.
The field of election was now a curious and alarming spectacle.
In the midst of it towered the *okóp* or entrenched pavilion

where the Senate was to hold its sessions. A quarter of a mile off lay the *Czarne Kolo*[1], as the fortified camp of the Chancellor was called. On the opposite side the partisans of the Zborowscy, also armed to the teeth, occupied another camp, the *Generalne Kolo*[2]. The Lithuanians formed a third camp apart. From the first there seemed no prospect of an agreement. The Zborowscy refused to proceed with the election business till Samuel and Christopher Zborowsky had been rehabilitated, which would have been equivalent to the condemnation of Zamoyski. Zamoyski demanded to be heard in his defence. He brilliantly vindicated himself before the Senate; but "the general circle" refused to listen to him. Three weeks were wasted in futile wranglings, the Primate and Senate acting as mediators. On July 22 the Zborowscy refused to listen to any further representations, and proclaimed a *rokosz*[3]. The "Black Circle" protested against this dangerous political novelty; and a pitched battle round the *okóp* of the Senate was only averted with the utmost difficulty. Fortunately, the mass of the *Szlachta* was growing weary of its enforced and expensive detention at Warsaw. A month had elapsed since the assembling of the Diet, and not a step had been taken towards electing a new King. Ugly rumours, too, of the massing of foreign troops on the frontier and of a secret understanding between the Tsar and the Emperor, now accelerated the action of the Electors. The Lithuanians elected Tsar Theodore I, the successor of Ivan the Terrible; but Zamoyski, despite the tempting offers of the Austrian wire-pullers[4], and now greatly strengthened by the accession of the Primate and all the Bishops but one, proposed the election of Sigismund, Prince Royal of Sweden, the nephew of Sigismund II, as the best candidate

---

[1] Black Circle.   [2] The General Circle.

[3] An armed insurrection against the existing authorities. Both the word and the thing were imported from Hungary.

[4] The Court of Vienna offered him the dignity of *Reichsfurst*, and Philip of Spain promised him the Golden Fleece and 200,000 ducats.

available. Moreover, being a Catholic, he was not unacceptable to Rome. On August 19, 1587, Sigismund Vasa was elected King of Poland in the "Black Circle"; on October 7 he landed at Dantzic; on December 27 he was solemnly crowned at Cracow. The Hapsburgs and their supporters, the Zborowscy, were furious. The Archduke Maximilian had been elected King in the "General Circle" on the same day that Sigismund had been elected in the "Black Circle," and he was not disposed to forfeit his newly-won crown without a struggle. But Zamoyski was too quick for him. With the aid of 100,000 gulden, borrowed from Queen Anna, a warm supporter of her nephew's cause, the Chancellor had already raised an army. He hastened southwards and defeated Maximilian beneath the walls of Cracow (Nov. 23). Early in the following year, Maximilian, assisted by a large Polish contingent under Andrew Zborowski, again invaded Poland and laid siege to Cracow; but the Chancellor routed him at the bloody battle[1] of Byczyna (Jan. 24, 1588). Zamoyski was now completely master of the situation; and the throne of Sigismund III was secure.

---

[1] One third of the contending forces on both sides bit the dust.

CHAPTER VII.

IVAN IV, CALLED THE TERRIBLE, 1534–1584.

WE have seen how the Jagiellos laid the foundation of the Polish Monarchy; we have also seen how that monarchy was arrested in its development, and diverted from its purpose, by the centrifugal tendencies of a jealous and undisciplined aristocracy. In Moscovy, meanwhile, the principles of monarchy were gaining steadily in strength. The last vestige of semi-independence disappeared when Pskov, "with much weeping and wailing," was forced, in 1510, to surrender her "assembly bell" and charter, as Novgorod had done a few years earlier. Something also had been recovered from the West. The Grand Dukes of Moscovy, now, occasionally adopting, with caution and circumspection, the higher title of Tsar[1], were pursuing their traditional policy of collecting together the old Russian lands. Both Sigismund I and Sigismund II had been obliged to fall back before the gradual but persistent pressure of their gigantic neighbour, though the capture of Smolensk, in 1514, was the first substantial triumph of the Moscovite over the Pole. But the advance of Moscovy westwards was repeatedly interrupted and retarded by the interference of the Crimean Tatars and their allies. The Giraj dynasty, which reigned in the Crimea, had been willing enough to live

---

[1] The usual title was still "Gosudar (Sovereign) of all Russia," but both Ivan III and his son Vasily III, in their letters to the Emperor, or other foreign potentates, frequently styled themselves "Tsars of all Russia."

amicably with the Grand Dukes of Lithuania and Moscovy so long as they themselves were in constant fear of the Golden Horde of Kipchak and the Sultan-of Turkey. But when the Golden Horde collapsed and the Ottoman Power visibly declined, the Crimean Khans raised their heads once more, claimed to be the Suzerains of Moscovy and Lithuania, and habitually blackmailed the two Grand Duchies with perfect impunity. Even Sigismund I thought it expedient to accept *yarluiki*, or letters of investiture, from the Khan for his Lithuanian provinces, and for years the Lithuanians paid to the Tatars tribute known as *Orduinshchina*, or the "Horde Tax."

Moscovy fared much worse, because the Tatars were nearer neighbours and her powers of resistance were feebler. The military efficiency of Lithuania was still far superior to that of Moscovy; and in the Dnieperian Cossacks she possessed valiant if capricious defenders. The Cossacks of Moscovy, on the other hand, were few, remote, and scattered; and her own untrained and ill-armed levies were rarely a match for the Tatar hordes. Throughout the reign of Vasily III (1505–1533) Moscovy was warring incessantly against these alert and ubiquitous marauders; and in nearly every encounter they were victorious. Kazan was the chief bone of contention between the Khan of the Crimea and the Moscovite Grand Duke. In 1518 the throne of Kazan fell vacant; and Vasily enthroned thereon Shig Ali, the hereditary foe of the Girais, who drove him out in 1521, and placed Saip, brother of the Crimean Khan, Mahomet, on the throne, in his stead. The same year, Khan Mahomet raided Vasily's territory up to the very walls of Moscow, carrying off 80,000 captives who were sold as slaves at Perekop and Kaffa. In the following year, Mahomet conquered Astrakhan, hitherto an independent Khanate; but his allies, the Nogai Tatars, alarmed by his threatening predominance, suddenly turned against and slew him, and ravaged the Crimea terribly. Vasily at once took advantage of this to build a fortress, Vasilsarsk, in Kazan territory as a preliminary to the conquest of the Khanates. But a first expedition of 150,000 men was baffled, in 1524, by the Cheremiss horsemen in the pay of Kazan; and a second expedition, six years later, under Michael Glinsky, which seemed to have every chance of success, failed through the refusal of the Boyars to obey the orders of their Lithuanian commander.

The fact that Michael Glinsky led the second expedition against Kazan shews that his star was once more in the ascendant in Moscovy. He returned to court shortly after the Grand Duke's marriage (in Jan. 1526), with Glinsky's niece Helena, Vasily's first consort, Solomona, having been divorced for sterility, though not without considerable opposition from the Conservatives, and immured in a monastery in 1525. From henceforth Glinsky remained the Grand Duke's chief counsellor; and, on his death-bed, Vasily appointed Glinsky one of the guardians of his eldest son and successor Ivan IV, then a child of three.

Vasily III expired on December 3, 1533. Shortly before his death, he took the monkish habit under the name of Varlam. He seems to have been a kindly Prince of somewhat timid character, with a tincture of letters and no very great liking for war, though unswervingly pursuing the traditional forward policy of his House.

Vasily III had appointed the Tsaritsa Helena Regent during the minority of his son, with a *Duma*, or Council, to assist her. By far the most eminent and capable member of the Council was Michael Glinsky, but, unfortunately, he quarrelled with his niece's equerry and paramour, Prince Ivan Oschin-Telepnev-Obolensky and, as the reward of his presumption, was immured in a dungeon and slowly starved to death, only eight months after Helena's accession to power, August, 1534. It was a' stupid as well as a barbarous and unnatural act on the Regent's part, for both she, as a foreigner, and Obolensky, as an upstart, were detested by the Boyars, who lost no time in plotting against them both, even invoking the assistance of both Turkey and Lithuania against this regimen of women. Nevertheless, Helena maintained her position for four years, when she died suddenly, April 3, 1538. We have very good authority for believing that she was poisoned by enemies who could not get rid of her in any other way. The most notable event of her brief reign was the renewal of the truce with Lithuania for five years, from 1537, after a short and bloody but indecisive war.

The ex-equerry Prince Ivan Oschin-Telepnev-Obolensky now stood alone and defenceless, face to face, with numerous powerful enemies. Of these enemies, the man who hated the upstart most was, naturally, the man who considered himself best fitted to fill the upstart's place. This was Prince Vasily Shuisky. Vasily Shuisky, 24 years earlier, had prevented Smolensk from falling into the hands of the Poles, after the catastrophe of Orsza, by hanging all the principal citizens on the ramparts of the fortress in the sight of the besieging army. A man so energetic in the public service would not be less energetic in the attainment of his private ends. A week after the Regent's death, Shuisky flung her favourite into prison, where starvation and chains of excessive weight soon killed him. The favourite's sister, Agrafina, the little Grand Duke's nurse, was, at the same time, made a nun and sent to the distant monastery of Kargopol. All those who had been proscribed by the late Government were then released, but among them was a Boyar whose presence at court did not promise Vasily Shuisky a long ascendency. This formidable rival was the Boyar Ivan Byelsky, a descendant of the Lithuanian Grand Duke Gedymin, and connected by marriage with the reigning Grand Duke of Moscovy. Byelsky had, moreover, been imprisoned for no fault of his, and he was not the man to forget either his pretensions or his sufferings. A struggle for power immediately ensued. At first the Shuiskies prevailed, and the Byelskies returned to the dungeons from which they had just emerged. Then Vasily Shuisky died, and his brother Ivan took the lead of the Party.

Ivan Shuisky's violence drew a protest from the Metropolitan Daniel, who was promptly suppressed; but Daniel's successor, Josafat, first procured the release of Ivan Byelsky, and then Byelsky and the Metropolitan together succeeded in overthrowing Ivan Shuisky, July 1540. But the Shuiskies had strong supporters among the Boyars of Great Novgorod where the family was very popular (a Shuisky had been the last Governor of independent Novgorod); and a conspiracy was formed against Byelsky and the Metropolitan. Between two and three o'clock in the morning of January 3, 1542, Ivan Byelsky was seized in his house at Moscow, conveyed to Byelozero and there murdered. The Metropolitan sought refuge in the apartments of the Grand Duke. Thither the conspirators pursued and horribly maltreated him, in the presence of the helpless and terrified Ivan, suddenly aroused from his slumbers. The unfortunate Metropolitan, more dead than alive, was finally banished to a distant monastery. Makary, Archbishop of Novgorod, was thereupon made Metropolitan of Moscow in the place of Josafat. The Shuiskies now felt secure; but, twelve months later, their suspicious fears of the Grand Duke's favourite instructor, Theodore Vorontsov, drove them to commit a crowning outrage. On September 9, 1543, while Vorontsov was dining with the Grand Duke in his private apartments, three of the Shuiskies, with their hirelings, burst into the room, seized Vorontsov, tore the clothes from his body, and fell to beating him savagely. They would have killed him outright but for the tears and supplications of Ivan; but, though the young Prince saved Vorontsov's life, he could not prevent the Shuiskies from banishing his friend to Kostroma.

The kidnapping of Vorontsov was the last overt act of violence on the part of the Boyars. A little more than three months later, Ivan, now in his 14th year, asserted his authority by overthrowing the first magnate in the land. On December 19, 1543, he suddenly delivered Prince Andrei Shuisky into the hands of the palace dog-keepers, who beat him to death as they dragged him off to prison. Shuisky's chief counsellors were banished at the same time. A year of suspense ensued. Then a fresh batch of Boyars, who had been concerned in the Vorontsov outrage and the conspiracy against the Metropolitan Josafat, were seized and exiled (Dec. 16, 1544). On September 10, 1545, Athanasy Buturlin had his tongue cut out for indecorous language ; "and henceforth," says the contemporary *lyetopis*, "the Boyars began to fear and obey the Gosudar."

The people with whom Ivan now consorted were his kinsfolk on his mother's side, represented by his grandmother the Princess Anna Glinska and her family. But two things are already patent, the young Ivan's distrust of the Boyars and the higher classes generally, and his independence of character. He listened to advice, but initiated everything. Thus when, in May 1546, his meditated expedition to Kolumna against the Tatars was frustrated by the mutiny of the Novgorodian musketeers, the official selected to investigate the matter was the *dumny dyak*, or clerk of the council, Zakharov —a plebeian. Again, shortly afterwards, Ivan suddenly déclared his intention of assuming the title of Tsar, a title which his father and grandfather could never make up their minds to adopt openly ; and, on January 16, 1547, he was crowned Tsar by the Metropolitan. Previously to this, he had expressed the desire to marry, and, from the scores of virgins sent from every province of the Tsardom to Moscow for his inspection, he chose him to wife Anastasia the daughter of Roman Zakharin-Koshkin, a member of one of the most ancient and loyal of the old Boyar families, better known by its later name of Romanov. The marriage, which took place on February 3, 1547, was a very happy one. A few months after the wedding Moscow was visited by a series of terrible conflagrations, April 12 and 20, June 3 and 21, which reduced half the city to ashes and compelled the Tsar and the Metropolitan to seek refuge outside its walls. On June 26 an enquiry into the cause of the catastrophe was held in the great square of the Kremlin, when the crowd, encouraged by the Boyars, accused the Glinskies of causing the fire by witch-craft. They had, the accusers said, seethed human hearts, torn from living bodies, in boiling water and sprinkled the water about the city. Hence the disaster. The excited mob thereupon murdered Prince Yury Glinsky in the adjoining Uspensky Cathedral, whither he had sought refuge, and then proceeded to the village of Vorobeva, where the Tsar was staying, and demanded that the aged Princess Anna Glinska and the other members of her family should be delivered up. The rioters were dispersed, however, and their ringleaders punished. This mysterious plot, which seems to have been a desperate attempt on the part of the dispossessed Shuiskies to ruin the dominant Glinskies, had very important conse-quences and profoundly affected the young Prince, whose peculiar character, the pivot of the whole situation, it now behoves us to consider a little more closely.

Ivan IV was in every respect precocious, his intellect and his sensibility were equally alert; but, from the first, there was what we should call a neurotic strain in his character which required careful watching and pruning if the gifted child were to develop normally. Unfortunately, from infancy, he was practically left to himself. His father died when he was three, his mother when he was seven; and he grew up in a brutal and degrading environment where he learnt, betimes, to hold human life and human dignity in contempt. He himself has told us, how the leading Boyars wantonly wounded his childish pride and his childish affections; how they rudely sprawled upon his father's bed in their young sovereign's presence; how they made for themselves "vessels of silver and vessels of gold" out of his father's treasures; how, after his mother's death, they trampled upon and tore her clothes to pieces in their search for jewels. "And," he proceeds, "what did not my little brother and I suffer for want of proper food and clothing?

They were never kind to us, they never treated us as children
ought to be treated." He was shrewd enough to observe that
the very men who, in private, treated him as if he were "a deaf
and dumb fool without understanding," in public, at the reception of foreign ambassadors for instance, stood humbly round
the throne in the guise of servants. Those about him, too,
with an eye to their own future advantage, did not fail to
remind him that he was the great Gosudar and that these insolent
and domineering Boyars were, after all, but his subjects. No
wonder then, if, in his impotence, he brooded continually over
his wrongs, and meditated future vengeance on those who were
now usurping his authority. As the eager, inquisitive child
grew older, and read all that there was to be read in those days
—the Scriptures, the Fathers, Church history, Roman history,
Russian chronicles—he sought everywhere, especially in Holy
Writ, for texts and precedents in favour of his own divinely
appointed authority. He looked forward to the day when
he should be, on the throne of Moscow, what Solomon had
been on the throne of Jerusalem, and Constantine or Theo-
dosius on the throne of Constantinople. Ivan IV was, indeed,
the first Tsar, not so much because he first assumed the title at
his coronation, as because he was the first to invent, and
consistently act up to, a regular theory of autocracy focussed in
the person of the Tsar. But, on the other hand, this perpetual
brooding over wrongs and injuries, still unavenged, fostered the
morbid irritability of a passionate nature naturally prone to pride
and cruelty. Hideous stories have come down to us of Ivan's
fiendish treatment of dumb creatures, and of his brutal practical jokes, as, for instance, when he ordered boiling wine to be
poured over the heads of a deputation from Pskov. So far
from any attempt being made to restrain the young savage, his
attendants and domestics seem to have encouraged him to even
worse excesses by their applause. And already there are
current hints of even darker and more disgusting vices. Ivan
himself, in his 20th year, publicly declared, in a moment of

deep repentance: "I cannot describe nor can the human tongue express the vileness of the sins of my youth."

The occasion on which these words were uttered marks a turning point in the life of Ivan IV. The great fire of Moscow had startled a conscience very susceptible to religious terrors. Ivan saw in it a last divine warning, and "a great fear came into my soul and a great trembling into my bones." After consulting the Metropolitan, he summoned representatives from all the Russian towns and provinces to meet on Easter Day, 1550[1], in the Red Square at Moscow. He addressed the multitude from the *Lobnoe Myesto*, or public place of execution. First came a sort of open confession. Then he explained that the bad government of the past had been due to the Boyars, who had misruled the realm during his infancy; but that, henceforth, he was going to rule his people himself in justice and equity. Finally he introduced upon the scene two men of his own choosing, who, henceforth, were to be his chief ministers and instruments, men of humble birth but lofty virtue, "chosen for the health of my soul and...to help me watch over the nation committed to me by God." It was an unheard-of, a revolutionary proceeding, thus to prefer "the lowliest of the people" to the traditional ruling classes; but Ivan had now permanently broken with the Boyars. He was already statesman enough to discern that they could not be fitted into the new order of things which he foresaw must come. The Boyars had shewn themselves incapable of rising to the idea of a commonwealth with equal rights for all. Their outlook was exclusively personal. They had no patriotism, no public spirit. The ties which bound them to their country were of the loosest and feeblest. Ivan meditated the regeneration of Moscovy; and the only men who could assist him in his task were men who would look steadily forward to the future because they had no past to look back upon, men who would unflinchingly obey their Gosudar because they owed their significance, their whole

[1] The first *Zemsky Sobor*, or General Assembly.

political existence to him alone. These men of good will be discovered in Aleksyei Adashev and the monk Sylvester.

We know very little of the antecedents of Adashev and Sylvester. The former is first mentioned in February 1547, when, on the occasion of the Tsar's marriage, he made the nuptial bed and escorted the bridegroom to his praenuptial bath. His influence began at the time of the Great Fire. Sylvester was a simple monk of the Annunciation Monastery at Moscow who attracted Ivan's attention, about the same time, by the earnestness with which he pleaded for those in disgrace, or under condemnation. But, whatever their origin, morally they were, perhaps, the best men in Moscovy of their day; and their influence over the young Tsar, for the next four years, was profoundly beneficial.

The administration of Adashev and Sylvester coincides with the most glorious period of Ivan's reign—the period of the conquest of Kazan and Astrakhan.

From 1539 to 1549 the Crimean Prince, Saip Girai, had been left in undisturbed possession of Kazan. On his death in 1549, Ivan placed Shig Ali, a Kazanian refugee at Moscow, on the throne of Kazan, on condition that all the Christian captives were set free. 60,000 of them were accordingly released, but Ivan was informed that just as many more were still working in chains; and when, in the course of 1551, disturbances broke out in Kazan itself, and one of the two factions offered the Khanate to Ivan, he resolved to take it by force of arms. On June 15, 1552, he quitted Moscow at the head of his host. The hardships of the difficult two months' march through virgin forests and the endless steppe were lightened by the services of the savage Cheremisses and Mordvinians who, overawed by the magnitude of Ivan's forces, offered him submission, built bridges, pointed out fords, and brought him supplies of corn. The rivers abounded with fish, the forests with game; and the elks were so tame that, in the words of the *lyetopis*, "they came and offered themselves up for slaughter." At last, on August 20, Ivan stood before Kazan, with an army of 150,000 men and 50 guns. Kazan was defended only by wooden walls; but behind these walls stood 30,000 fanatical Moslem warriors, determined to sell their lives dearly. At the very beginning of the siege Ivan's fortitude was put to a severe test. A tempest blew down his tents, destroyed most of his boats on the Volga, and ruined his stores. The raw young army was profoundly discouraged. Not so Ivan. He ordered fresh supplies to be brought up from Moscow, declared his intention of spending the whole winter before Kazan if necessary, and put heart into his men by frequent harangues in which he appealed as much to their piety as to their valour. He also reconnoitred the fortress day and night, discovered the most convenient spots for attacking it, and ordered large wooden towers to be built at intervals round the walls, and guns to be planted on the towers. On August 30 a relief force, under the Tatar Prince Yapucha, which had given the besiegers much trouble, was routed and dispersed. On September 4 one of Ivan's German engineers deprived the city of its subterranean water supply by blowing up the gallery by which they gained access to it. A part of the wall was blown down at the same time. But the spirit of the besiegers was still unbroken. They drank muddy water, sheltered themselves in long trenches from the fire of the towers, and, when the trenches were mined, had recourse to *tarasui*, or huge barrels filled with earth, behind which they continued the struggle. On September 30 the *tarasui* were also blown up; and then, for a whole week, not a dart or arrow flew out of Kazan. Then the whole garrison made a sortie and all but pierced the Russian lines, but were repulsed at last, the besiegers at the same time occupying two of the bastions and penetrating into the tower. Sunday, October 2, was then fixed for a general assault, but counter-preparations were made in the fortress the night before; and when Ivan, for the last time, offered a free pardon to the Kazanese if they would do homage, they exclaimed with one voice: "We will not do homage! Russia is on the bastions, Russia is within the walls; it matters not; we will fight to the death!" Shortly before dawn, two terrific explosions brought down a large portion of the main wall, and the Moscovites mounted the breach shouting: "God be with us!" A desperate contest ensued on the walls, in the gates, round every mosque, and in front of the Khan's palace. Ivan was at his devotions when the first explosion filled the air with flying beams and mangled corpses. Messenger after messenger hurried from the fortress to the chapel to urge him to come. "Come, oh Ivan! thy troops wait for thee!"—"Come at once, oh Ivan! to sustain the hearts of thy servants!" they cried. But Ivan, who was no hero, waited till the service was over, and even then he lingered before the ikon of St Sergius and performed a whole series of devotions before he mounted his war-horse. By the time he entered the town the Moscovite banners were already waving triumphantly on the walls; and, though the *mêlée* was prolonged till evening, the victory was virtually won. On October 4, when the city had been cleansed of corpses (not a soul had been left alive), the Tsar visited it for the second time, and on the spot where, with his own hand, he planted a splendid cross, the foundations of the Cathedral of the Annunciation were solemnly laid.

We must transfer ourselves to the sixteenth century to appreciate adequately the full significance of the conquest of Kazan. Ivan's contemporaries regarded it as a mighty feat of arms, rivalling the exploits of the ancient, semi-mythical Russian Princes, those incomparable heroes who had gone forth to conquer fresh dominions, and to whom the later Princes, tributary to the Tatars, looked up with wonder and envy. Russia had already begun to recover land which she regarded as her own, the Lithuanian provinces for instance; but the conquest of Kazan was something quite new, quite different. It was the first territorial conquest from the Tatars before whom Moscovy had humbled herself for generations. It was this which gave to it its extraordinary importance. At last, in the fulness of time, there had arisen in Moscovy a Gosudar who brought back the glorious era of foreign conquest. No wonder then if Ivan IV stood, in the opinion of his contemporaries, so much higher than his immediate forerunners, and, in fact, eclipsed them all.

But, all exaggeration apart, the conquest of Kazan was an epoch-making event in the history of Eastern Europe. At Kazan, Central Asia, in the name of Muhammad, had fought behind its last trench against Christian Europe marshalled beneath the banner of the Gosudar of Moscovy. Kazan fell, and the Volga became a Russian river. Nothing could now restrain the natural advance of the young Russian State towards the east and the south-east. It took, indeed, five years of hard fighting (1555–1560) to conquer the savage Chuvasses, Votiaks, Bashkirs and Mordvinians, between the Oka and the Kama, who had hitherto been subject to Kazan; but Astrakhan fell, almost without a blow, in July 1554, and was formally incorporated with Moscovy in 1557. The conquest of Astrakhan brought Moscovy into direct contact, for the first time, with a whole world of petty, contending principalities in the Caucasus, many of whom hastened to place themselves beneath the protection of the strong Tsar from the North.

Ivan was also the first Tsar who attacked the Crimea. In 1555 he sent Ivan Sheremetev against Perekop with 13,000 men; and Sheremetev routed the Tatars in a two days' battle at Sudbishenska, capturing 80 camels and 60,000 horses. Almost simultaneously the daring raids of the Polish Cossacks, under Rzewuski and Wisniowiecki, who penetrated as far as Oczakow, opened the eyes of the Moscovites to the essential weakness of the Crimean Tatars. Some of Ivan's counsellors, including Adashev and Sylvester, now advised him to make an end of the Crimean Khanate, as he had previously made an end of the Khanates of Kazan and Astrakhan. By so doing, they urged, he would rid himself of chronic freebooters whose incalculable raids not only impoverished the State but made it necessary to keep up a standing army, at an enormous expense. Ivan unhesitatingly rejected their advice ; and there can be no doubt that, in this respect, he saw much further than his counsellors. Kazan and Astrakhan were comparatively easy to conquer, because the Moscovites could approach almost up to their very walls by rivers abounding with fish and flowing through forests full of meat and honey. The Crimea was separated from Moscovy by the endless barren steppe which, in those days, began as far north as Tula and Pronsk. It might be easy for lightly armed and mounted Cossacks, even then, to penetrate thither ; but an army like the Moscovite armies of the sixteenth century would have perished half-way for want of sustenance. And even if, by some extraordinary concurrence of fortunate circumstances, Ivan had succeeded in subjugating the Crimea, how could he have held it against the whole might of the Ottoman Empire with the absolute command of the sea? A century later, the great Golitsuin attempted the same thing, under far more favourable conditions—and failed. A century later still the famous marshal Münnich, with all the appliances of modern warfare at his command, attempted it again—and he also failed. Ivan IV, wiser in his generation, knew that the thing was impossible, and did not attempt it. It was upon Livonia that his eyes were fixed, Livonia which promised him towns by the dozen, fortresses by the score, and above all, a seaboard, and direct communication with the rest of Europe.

Ivan IV, like Peter I after him, clearly recognised the necessity of raising Moscovy to the level of her neighbours. He proposed to do so by encouraging foreigners to settle among his subjects and teach them the arts and sciences of the more highly civilised West. So early as 1547, when only 17, he sent the Saxon Schlitte to Germany to hire and bring to Moscow as many master-workmen and skilled artificers as he could procure. Schlitte, with the permission of the Emperor

Charles V, collected 123 of such men and brought them to
Lübeck for the purpose of shipping them to Moscovy. But
the Livonian agent at Lübeck representing to the Emperor the
danger of such a step, Schlitte was imprisoned and his men
were dispersed. Moscovy's neighbours, Sweden and Poland,
were equally apprehensive of any attempt to civilise her.
Their safety lay in her ignorance and isolation; and they did
their best to keep her ignorant and isolated. Ivan was therefore obliged to help himself as best he could. His opportunity
came on the break-up of the dominion of the Order of the
Sword. During 1557 and 1558 Livonia was systematically
ravaged by the Moscovite hordes, largely composed of savage
Mordvinians and Cheremisses, who reduced everything outside
the walls of the fortresses to ashes, "not even sparing the child
in its mother's womb." The Livonian authorities were too
divided amongst themselves, the nobility and burgesses were
too lazy and selfish, to sustain a vigorous combined resistance,
so that the Moscovites steadily gained ground. Narva and
Dorpat were captured in May and August 1558 respectively;
other fortresses were seriously threatened; the terrified
Livonians, as already recorded, voluntarily placed themselves
beneath the protection of Poland; and, in January 1560,
Sigismund II sent Martin Volodkov to Moscow to bid Ivan IV
cease from molesting Livonia, now a province of the Polish
Crown.

In Moscovy itself, meanwhile, events were happening which
had far-reaching consequences.

Holy fear had prompted Ivan IV, in 1550, to submit himself
to the moral and religious guidance of the monk Sylvester, in
whose motives he had the most absolute confidence. As time
went on, it was very natural that Ivan should also consult this
infallible mentor on political questions. It was equally
natural that Sylvester should expect to be deferred to in
temporal as well as in spiritual matters. But great saints are
not always shrewd politicians, and so now, when Ivan and

Sylvester differed, as they were bound to differ on political grounds, the Tsar happened to be in the right and the monk in the wrong. Sylvester was in favour of the conquest of the Crimea, but opposed the conquest of Livonia, whereas Ivan took the opposite view. Finding that, for once, he could not prevail, Sylvester was offended, and, exchanging arguments for reproaches and prognostications, solemnly declared that all Ivan's subsequent misfortunes were so many divine visitations upon his obstinacy. We know enough of Ivan's character to be quite sure that he would never break with a friend whom he really trusted, but unfortunately Ivan no longer trusted Sylvester. Six years previously, mysterious and still inexplicable circumstances had made an incurable rift in their friendship. In 1553, on returning from Kazan, the Tsar had fallen so ill that he was generally believed to be on the point of death; and all the Boyars and dignitaries were summoned to his bedside to swear allegiance to his infant son Demetrius. But Sylvester raised difficulties. He rather favoured the pretensions of Ivan's cousin, Prince Vladimir Andreevich, though he must have been well aware that Vladimir's accession would mean the removal, perhaps the violent removal, of the infant Demetrius and the ruin of his kinsfolk the Zakharin-Romanovs. Adashev's conduct on the same occasion was most ambiguous. He hesitated for a long time to render the requisite oath of allegiance to Demetrius, and listened, without a word of protest, to the seditious utterances of the large party of Boyars who supported the Pretender. The peculiar conduct of Sylvester and Adashev at this crisis has been ascribed to their jealousy of the Zakharin-Romanovs and their growing ill-will towards their former ally the Tsaritsa Anastasia, whom their adherents openly denounced as a second Eudoxia[1]. But, whatever may have been the cause of their backsliding, it alienated Ivan. Nor can we very much blame him. The very men whom, to use his

[1] *i.e.* the Consort of Arcadius and persecutrix of St Chrysostom. Sylvester was, of course, the second Chrysostom.

own words, he had "raised from the dunghill to set among Princes," the very men whom he had treated not as servants but as friends, and one of whom he had revered as a father, had failed him at the critical moment, had been content to commit the beloved wife and the infant son of their benefactor to certain destruction! We cannot wonder if, after this, he secretly distrusted them, though he continued to employ them for six years longer. Then the Livonian dispute arose and both of them disappear from the scene, Sylvester into a monastery, at his own request, and Adashev in honourable exile as a general in Livonia, where he died the same year (1560).

The ten good years of the Sylvester period (1550–1560) were followed by the ten evil years which saw the establishment of the *Oprichina*, the martyrdom of St Philip of Moscow, and the savage destruction of Great Novgorod (1560–1570). At the very beginning of this horrible decennium, Ivan lost his consort Anastasia and his infant heir Demetrius. Then the Boyars began to murmur because of the absence of Sylvester; and, apparently, for the details are obscure, a plot was set on foot to bring him back. At this, the slumbering demon in Ivan broke loose; and deeds were committed which made the whole Court stand aghast. It was now that Prince Michael Repnin was murdered at a banquet for refusing to wear a mask and dance in public, two things abominable in the eyes of all pious Moscovites. It was now that Prince Jury Kashkin was struck dead in the Cathedral during the reading of the Gospels. It was now that "one little word" from the lips of the Gosudar was regarded as a sentence of death. It was now that Prince Andrei Mikhailovich Kurbsky, Ivan's intimate friend, who shared with him his bookish tastes, fled to Sigismund II, after losing the engagement of Newel, when he heard that the Tsar had "blamed" him. To his treasonable desertion—for so Ivan not unnaturally regarded it—we owe the priceless correspondence which gives us a glimpse into the very soul of the Tsar, but its effect upon Ivan personally was dire indeed. If, he argued, one of the greatest of the Boyars, and his own familiar friend, could betray him first and then abuse him, how could he hope to live in safety among the other Boyars whom he knew to be the sympathisers of Kurbsky? To kill them all was impossible, but he could, at least, live apart from these potential traitors, and this he resolved to do. On January 3, 1565, the Tsar, who had quitted Moscow with his whole Court on December 3, 1564, addressed to the Metropolitan a letter to be read to the people in which he declared that, unable to endure any longer the treachery and villainy of the Boyars, he had resolved to abdicate and seek some safe refuge abroad. The whole population thereupon besought him, with tears, " to rule them as he pleased and take the Government into his own hands," so long as he did not leave them defenceless against their enemies, like sheep without a shepherd. Sure now of the support of the great majority of the Russian people, Ivan consented to remain ; but he entrenched himself within a peculiar institution, the *Oprichina,* or "Separate Estate." Certain towns and districts, or parts thereof, all over Russia, were separated from the rest of the realm ; and their revenues were assigned to the maintenance of the Tsar's new court and household, which was to consist, in the first instance, of one thousand carefully selected Boyars and lesser dignitaries, with their families and suites. In the midst of these Ivan henceforth lived exclusively, those outside the *Oprichina* being denied all access to him. The Boyars and gentry not included in the *Oprichina* were removed from the towns and districts assigned to the *Oprichina* and given estates elsewhere. Even in Moscow itself certain streets and suburbs were taken into the *Oprichina,* and their former owners or occupiers were transferred to other parts of the city. The *Oprichina* was no constitutional innovation. The *Duma,* or Council of Boyars, still attended to all the details of the administration. The old Boyars still retained their old offices and dignitaries. The only difference was that Ivan had cut himself off from them ; they were not even to communicate with him, except on matters of exceptional and extraordinary importance.

The *Oprichina* was founded because the Tsar suspected his great men of hating him, and because he would henceforth be surrounded by none but well-disposed persons.   The Oprich-niki, his exclusive favourites, were bound, in their own interests, to assume an offensive attitude towards everyone outside their charmed circle, were bound to harden the Tsar's heart against all possible disturbers.   Their first notable victim was the Metropolitan Philip, whose saintly life had compelled Ivan to take him from a hermitage to place him on the archiepiscopal throne of Moscow.   Philip now greatly angered Ivan, first, by urging the abolition of so unchristian an institution as the *Oprichina*, and secondly, by repeatedly pleading, with all the fearlessness of holiness, for the victims of Ivan's cruelty. "Silence ! all I ask of you is silence !" the Tsar would cry. "Our silence would lay on thy soul sins which bring forth death !" was Philip's constant answer.   At last Ivan's patience wore out ; and, on November 8, 1568, Philip was dragged, with contumely, from the Uspensky Cathedral and banished to a monastery at Tver.   In 1569 Ivan sent his favourite *Oprichnik*, the infamous Malyuta[1] Skuratov, to ask a blessing of Philip.   Refusal meant instant death, but Philip did not hesitate.   "I bless only the good for their good deeds," he said, and Skuratov strangled him on the spot.

Ivan had stopped at Tver to murder St Philip while on his way to destroy the second wealthiest city in his Tsardom— Great Novgorod.

In the course of 1559, one Peter, a vagabond malefactor from Volhynia, who had been punished at Novgorod for some offence, came to Moscow with a tale that the Magistrates of Novgorod were about to hand over their city to Sigismund II and that proofs of the plot were to be found in a letter signed

[1] *Malyuta* means "stumpy." His real name was Gregory Lyukhanovich.

by the Bishop and concealed behind an *ikon* of the Blessed
Virgin in the Cathedral of St Sophia. The Tsar sent Peter
back to Novgorod with some of the *Oprichniki*; and, sure
enough, the incriminating letter was found in the place
indicated. There is only too much reason to believe that this
document was Peter's own fabrication. Ivan, however, believed
every word of it, and without confronting the Novgorodians
with their secret accuser, without any preliminary enquiry, he
collected an army and set off to punish Novgorod. Late in
December 1569 the Tsar broke into the land, his own land, as
an enemy and ravaged it like a wild beast. From Klina on the
borders of Tver up to the very walls of Great Novgorod everything was destroyed. On January 2, 1570, the advance guard
of the Tsar's bodyguard reached Novgorod and built a strong
and high wall round it so that none might escape. All the
churches and monasteries were sealed up, all the principal
inhabitants were arrested and imprisoned till the Tsar should
come. On the 6th Ivan arrived with 1500 musketeers and
quartered them upon the *Gorodishcha*, or Merchants' Town.
On the 7th all the abbots and priors in the city were publicly
beaten to death on an elevated scaffold, and their dead bodies
sent to their respective monasteries for burial. On the 8th
Ivan proceeded to the Cathedral of St Sophia to hear mass.
The Bishop met him half-way on the Volkhovsky Bridge in full
canonicals surrounded by his clergy, and, as usual, presented
the cross for the Tsar to kiss. "Avaunt thou of evil repute!"
cried Ivan. "That is no cross that thou bearest, but a weapon
to wound my heart!" Ivan then followed the Bishop to the
Cathedral and, after mass, went on to the episcopal palace as
the Bishop's guest. They had scarce sat down to meat, when
the Tsar uttered a terrible yell. It was the signal for the arrest
of the Bishop and the sacking of the Cathedral and all the
intramural churches. This done, Ivan returned to the Gorodishcha and the chief laymen of Novgorod, with their wives and
children, were brought forth for punishment. First they were

singed on "a cunning instrument of fire" which the contemporary *lyetopis* calls "a grill"; then they were dragged in
sledges to the bridge over the Volkhov, bound hand and foot,
the children fastened to their mother's necks, and thrown into
the river, where men in boats despatched them with spears,
axes and boathooks as they came to the surface. This carnage
went on day after day for five weeks. Then Ivan went round
Novgorod and saw that every monastery was systematically and
thoroughly plundered, and the cattle and other property of the
monks destroyed. All the warehouses in the merchants'
quarters were similarly plundered. Then came the turn of the
suburbs. House after house was visited and ransacked; the
doors and the windows were smashed to pieces. The men at
arms simultaneously wrecked all the monasteries, churches and
manor houses within a circuit of 100 miles. At last, on
February 13, the Tsar's wrath was appeased; and he allowed the
miserable remnants of the population of Great Novgorod to go
on living, as best they might, amidst the ruins of their city,
once so mighty and splendid.

The decennium 1560–1570 was on the whole a propitious
period for the Moscovite arms abroad. The interminable
Livonian war, a war of raids and sieges, frequently interrupted
by fruitless negotiations, was waged with equal tenacity and
brutality by Ivan, who won more and more of the smaller
interior towns and castles, but could not reach the coast, where
the Poles, Swedes and Danes had already forestalled him. It
also involved him in indecisive and expensive wars with
Lithuania and Sweden. On February 15, 1563, the Moscovites
captured the important fortress of Polock, additionally valuable
as the great trade emporium of the Dwina district. But the
Poles, as usual, were victorious in the open field; and in 1570
hostilities were suspended by a three years' truce. The war
with Sweden began in 1571. In 1572 Ivan invaded Esthonia
with 80,000 men and captured Wittenstein by storm, on which
occasion his favourite Malyuta Skuratov was slain. In revenge

for this, Ivan burnt all the Swedish prisoners alive. Subsequently Karkus and Nyfort were also taken, but all these successes were neutralised by Klas Totte's victory at Lode, which led to the signature of a two years' truce with Sweden from July 20, 1575. During these years Moscovy suffered terribly from the raids of Devlet Girai, Khan of the Crimea. In May 1571, 120,000 Tatars appeared before Moscow and burnt the whole city, except the Kremlin, when 80,000 people perished and 150,000 were taken captive. In 1572 Devlet again reappeared in the Oka district with 120,000 men; but was routed on the banks of the Lopasna, 50 miles from Moscow, by the Boyars (July 31—Aug. 1).

The Livonian-Lithuanian war was resumed in 1575, in which year Ivan's forces captured Pernau. In the following year Esthonia was again invaded by the Moscovites; and Leal, Lode, and other places fell. In 1577 Ivan failed to take Reval; and in 1578 he was routed at Wenden, by the combined Poles and Swedes, with the loss of a third of his army. It is evident from the extensive preparations which he made for the coming campaign of 1579 that he regarded it as likely to prove decisive of the fate of Livonia. He seems, at first, to have been confident of success. His material resources were immense, and he entertained such a poor opinion of "Obatura," as the Lithuanians called the new King of Poland, Stephen Báthory, that he would not even address him as "my cousin," but contemptuously alluded to him as "my neighbour." What reason had he to fear an obscure stranger from the depths of Transylvania whom he could outnumber a hundred to one? Ivan's envoys had also reported that the new King of Poland was extremely unpopular; that the Pans were disinclined to wage war; and that the Sejm would grant no supplies for offensive operations in Lithuania. The envoys reported truly. Báthory's difficulties were indeed enormous, but it is just because he grappled with and overcame those difficulties that he deserves the name of great. It was he who first made regular infantry the leading arm in warfare in eastern, as it had long been the leading arm in western Europe. Compared with his highly-trained Magyars and Germans, the Moscovite levies were but undisciplined hordes. His artillery too was excellent, his means of transport relatively rapid; and, in the chancellor Zamoyski and his own countryman Gaspar Békés, he had for his lieutenants two of the greatest captains of the age.

In June 1579 Báthory sent Ivan a formal declaration of war for breaking the Livonian truce. In July he resolved, at a Council of War, to recover Polock, the possession of which would enable him to keep open his communications with Riga, and defend simultaneously Livonia and Lithuania. Ivan was diverted towards Livonia by false reports of the King's advance in that direction. Polock was valiantly defended by the Moscovite Voevodes; and the besiegers found it difficult to support themselves in a thinly populated country devastated beforehand. Torrential rains also blocked the roads, and the draft horses died in hundreds. At first, Báthory refused to risk an assault, as failure would mean a shameful retreat; but, at last, his Magyars, encouraged by the promise of a rich reward, crept up to the fortress by night and fired the wooden walls in so many places that the besieged could not extinguish the conflagration. On September 25 the town was taken by assault. Colonel Weigand, one of the King's German officers, who had been at many sieges, said he had never seen so many corpses all together as at Polock. This ended the campaign, and Báthory returned to Wilna. Peace negotiations were now re-opened; but, as Báthory demanded Livonia, Wielkie Luki, Smolensk, Pskov and Novgorod, while Ivan would only surrender 24 Livonian towns and castles, the war was resumed. Báthory could obtain little or no help from his Polish subjects, who were rather alarmed than gratified by his successes. But his brother Christopher, Prince of Transylvania, and his friend Zamoyski liberally supplied him with money and troops, so that he took the field in 1580 with an army of 50,000 men, of whom 21,000 were infantry. Wielkie Luki was now taken by Zamoyski and Zbarasky defeated the Moscovites at Toropets ; but, on the other hand, an attempt to surprise Smolensk led to a Polish defeat at Spasski Lugi. The same year, the Swedes captured Kexholm in Carelia, Padis in Esthonia, and Wesenberg in Livonia from the Moscovites.

Báthory's increasing difficulties (he was now obliged to borrow from the Electors of Brandenburg and Saxony, and from his own vassal the Duke of Prussia) and Ivan's disasters induced them both to reopen negotiations ; but the Tsar still, obstinately, refused to part with the whole of Livonia or pay a war indemnity. In his rage Báthory sent him a letter calling him a "sneaking wolf" and a "vile venomous cur," and challenging him to single combat as the quickest way of ending the war. "Why dost thou not come forth and meet me in the open field," concluded Báthory, "why dost thou not defend thine own subjects? Even a poor little hen covers her chickens with her wings when a hawk hovers in the air above her ; but thou, a two-headed eagle forsooth, for such thy seal proclaims thee, dost nothing but skulk away and hide." Ivan was, indeed, no man of valour. Timidity had been hereditary in his family for generations. But he was wise enough to recognise that, in warfare, quality is superior to quantity, and he prudently avoided pitting his useless myriads against Báthory's handful of veterans. Nor did his political foresight fail him. He had become convinced that in the circumstances, and against such an antagonist as Báthory, the Livonian enterprise was a mistake ; and he was already casting about for an honourable withdrawal from it. Báthory, involuntarily, gave him his opportunity.

The King of Poland had been advised to open the campaign of 1581 by besieging Pskov, but, on pitching his camp beneath the city (Aug. 26), he at once perceived that he was attempting the impossible. Pskov was the strongest fortress in the east of Europe. For whole centuries the chief care of the Pskovians

had been to make it impregnable to the attacks of the Teutonic
Knights. Within its colossal walls was a garrison of 50,000
infantry and 7000 cavalry, provided with an adequate supply
of the best artillery procurable. To make any impression upon
it, Báthory required at least double as many men as he had
brought with him. But to retreat now was out of the question.
On September 1 the first trenches were dug; on the 7th the
first cannonade began; and on the 8th a general assault was
made with such *élan* that two of the principal bastions were
captured, one by the Poles and the other by the Magyars.
For a moment the fortress seemed to be won. But the besieged
were rallied by the Voevode, Prince Ivan Shuisky, and the Igumen Tikhon; the bastions were recaptured; and the assailants
hurled back with the loss of 5000 men, including Gaspar Békés,
a host in himself. Then Báthory's powder ran out, and he had
to wait for weeks till he received fresh supplies from Riga. But
to retreat now was to lose everything; and Báthory declared
his intention to prosecute the siege throughout the winter. A
dangerous mutiny at once broke out in the Polish section of
the army. The *Szlachta*, unused to rigid discipline, demanded
to be led home, and it was only the energetic intervention
of Zamoyski which saved the situation. He punished the
mutineers without the slightest regard for birth or station; and,
when several young nobles had been publicly flogged and a few
more had been publicly hanged, order was restored and the
King was able to go to Poland for reinforcements, leaving
Zamoyski behind him in supreme command. Meanwhile, the
Swedes, operating from Esthonia and Finland, had captured
a whole series of Moscovite fortresses on the Neva, while
Christopher Radziwill, the Grand Hetman of Lithuania, penetrated as far as the Volga. Ivan, now in extremities, invoked
the intervention of Pope Gregory XIII and the Jesuit, Cardinal
Antonio Possevino, appeared at the village of Kierova Gora,
midway between the two camps, where negotiations were
opened in December 1581.

Ever since Schlitte's mission to Germany, the Holy See had had hopes of the conversion of Ivan. In 1561 Pius IV had invited him to send deputies to the Council of Trent and join the Holy League against the Turk. The Tsar, however, made no response to these overtures; and, though he gladly availed himself of the mediation of Possevino, he never had the slightest intention of submitting to the supremacy of Rome. Possevino soon convinced himself of this, and came to the conclusion that Livonia had better be in the hands of a Catholic Prince like Báthory. The 10 years' truce which was finally concluded, on January 15, 1582, at Zapolsk was very favourable to Poland. Ivan surrendered the whole of Livonia, with Polock and Wielicz, to Báthory and received back Wielkie, Luki, Zawolocie and Newel. Thus Poland had succeeded in excluding Moscovy from the Baltic and thus prevented the natural development of the Moscovite State for many years. Ivan at the same time was obliged to conclude a three years' truce, on the river Ilyusa, with Sweden, who thereby retained her Ingrian conquests, Jama, Ivangorod and Koporye, thus cutting off Moscovy from the Gulf of Finland also.

Thus, despite all the efforts of Ivan IV to secure it, the Baltic seaboard was lost to Moscovy. The Tsar had now to be content with the more modest programme of qualifying his subjects to resume the struggle at some future time with a fairer prospect of success. This could only be done by tempting foreign specialists to Moscovy to instruct the Moscovites in the arts of war and peace. It was to England, the one friendly anti-Catholic Power, that Ivan primarily looked for assistance in this respect.

The relations between Moscovy and England began in 1553, when Richard Chancellor discovered the White Sea, was conveyed to Moscow by the astonished natives, and there had an audience of Ivan sitting on his throne in full regalia. In 1555 Chancellor returned to Moscovy as the special envoy of Queen Mary and negotiated a commercial treaty very advantageous to the newly-formed Anglo-Russian Company. Similar favours were granted in England to the first Russian envoy, Osip Nepyea, who brought back with him to Moscovy numerous doctors, master-masons, carpenters and other useful people. In 1570 Sigismund II of Poland warned Elizabeth against assisting a potentate who was increasing in power every year and might, one day, conquer every one if the proper arms were put into his hands. "Your Highness," he concluded, "cannot be aware of the strength of the enemy. Hitherto we have only been able to keep him under because he was a stranger to civilisation." But Elizabeth doubtless regarded these warnings with suspicion as coming from a papist. The same year, when Ivan sounded her on the subject of granting him an asylum in case of need, she assured her "dear brother, the great Emperor and Grand Duke," that she would willingly grant him and his family safe quarters in England, whenever he desired them. After the Peace of Zapolsk, Ivan despatched Theodore Pisemsky to England on a double mission (1582). He was to contract a political alliance with England against Poland, and a matrimonial alliance between Ivan and a kinswoman of the Queen's, preferably Mary Hastings, daughter of the Earl of Huntingdon, concerning whom Pisemsky reported most favourably. Both projects came to nothing. The political alliance was declined as being too adventurous. The matrimonial alliance foundered on the unwillingness of the bride elect to trust herself to a groom of such very ill repute. Elizabeth softened the pill as much as possible in an extremely courteous epistle to Ivan in which his "true friend and dear sister" declared she would fain make his personal acquaintance. She also sent him a number of skilled artificers, engineers, gunners, and one of her own doctors. These politenesses were rendered in the hope of getting, in return, the monopoly of the Russian trade, but the special English envoy, Boyce, failed to obtain any such concession.

In the last years of his reign Ivan was somewhat consoled

for his failure in the west, by the unexpected acquisition of territory in the east.

All this while, the movement of the Russian people towards the Urals had continued uninterruptedly; and beyond the Urals the tidings of the fall of Kazan and Astrakhan had important political consequences. In 1555 Ediger, Khan of the Tatar region of Tobolsk, had placed himself beneath the high protection of the Tsar and engaged to pay a tribute of pelts. Three years later, the wealthy and enterprising firm of Stroganov received a charter from the Tsar to colonise and exploit the vast waste lands extending north-eastwards in the basins of the rivers Kama and Chusovaya, at their own expense. They began by building the fort of Kankor and the town of Kergedan. The latter had wooden walls thirty fathoms thick on stone foundations. In 1572 the Stroganovs suppressed a confederacy of the surrounding savages—Ostiaks, Cheremisses and Bashkirs. In 1573 the Siberian Khan, Mametkul, crossed the Urals and plundered the Ostiak tributaries of the Stroganovs. The Stroganovs retaliated by also crossing the Urals with an armed force and planting a fort on the river Tobola. Thus the colonization of Siberia began. In 1579 fresh outbreaks of the Voguls and other savages compelled the Stroganovs to hire 540 Don Cossacks with their Hetman Ermak, or Yermak, to defend their territories on the Kama; and, after a three years' war (1579–1581), the hostile tribes were reduced to a tributary condition. On September 1, 1581, Ermak, with a force of 840 Cossacks and 300 German mercenaries, was sent to render similar services in Siberia. On the banks of the Tobola, and again on the banks of the Irtuish, the musket prevailed over the bow and arrow. Khan Mametkul was vanquished; his stockaded fortress, Sibir, was taken by assault (Oct. 16); and the Moscovite sphere of influence was extended to the Obi.

Ivan IV did not live to hear the final result of Ermak's triumphs. So early as 1573, when he was only in his 43rd year, he told the Lithuanian Ambassador, Garaburda, that he was already an old man. And, indeed, the horrible life he led, and the hideous diseases which had long been consuming him, must needs have prematurely aged the strongest of men. Ivan's failing health could not have been improved by the miseries and the humiliations of the war with Báthory. His marriage in 1561 with a savage Circassian Princess, christened Maria, did not tend to improve him morally. Maria died in 1569; and in 1571 Ivan married Martha Sobakina, the daughter of a Novgorod merchant, who died within a month. Then, contrary to the precepts of the Orthodox Church, he took unto himself a fourth wife, Anna Koltovskaya, whom, three years later, he shut up in a monastery. In 1580 he married, for the fifth time, Martha Nagaya, who bore him a son, Demetrius. In November the same year, in a fit of insane fury at some contradiction or reproach[1], he struck his beloved eldest surviving son Ivan, a Prince of rare promise, one blow, and the blow proved fatal.

The wretched father, in an agony of remorse, summoned his trembling Boyars, told them of his crime, and declared himself unfit to reign any longer. Then, inasmuch as his second son Theodore was weak-witted, he commanded them to choose the worthiest from among themselves to reign in his stead. But the Boyars, fearing some dark trick, would not hear of his abdication, and vowed they would obey none but him. Ivan survived this catastrophe a couple of years. In the beginning of 1584 he was attacked by a new and indescribably loathsome disease; and a circular letter, addressed to all the churches and monasteries in the Tsardom, implored constant supplications for "the forgiveness and healing of one accursed." In his worst spasms the name of his murdered son was constantly upon his lips. Yet, to the very last, he refused nothing to his vilest appetites. Death released him from his sufferings and his sins on March 18, 1584. Feeling better, he had sat

---

[1] The facts are obscure.

down to a game of chess, when he suddenly fell backwards in his chair and was removed to his bed in a dying condition. As he lay there, he signified his wish to be received into the strictest religious order.   It was as the hermit-monk Jonah that Ivan the Terrible breathed his last.

Ivan IV was undoubtedly a man of genius.   His political foresight was extraordinary.   He anticipated the ideals of Peter the Great, and only failed in realising them because his natural resources, in the long run, proved to be insufficient.   But admiration for his talents must not blind us to his moral ruthlessness.   He himself confessed, "I know that I am evil"; but such a confession, in a man of his strong will and superior education, was a condemnation, not an excuse.   Nor is it right to blame the viciousness and brutality of·Russian society in the sixteenth century for Ivan's excesses.   The same society which produced Malyuta Skuratov also produced St Philip of Moscow. The better class of society in sixteenth century Moscovy reprobated Ivan's misdeeds by the mouth of St Philip; and, by refusing to listen to St Philip, Ivan sank below the moral standard of his age.   Nor is this all.   Ivan left Moscovite society much worse than he found it.   Instead of attempting to heal he stimulated its moral disorders.   He found it cruel and coarse, he left it coarser and crueller still.   With his contempt of human life, with his love of cruel and bloody expedients, with his indifference to the moral responsibility of his high calling, he sowed the terrible seed of that horrible harvest the *Smutnaya Vremya* or "Age of confusion," when the Russian State, torn to pieces by pretenders and adventurers, all but disappeared from the face of the earth[1].

Personally, Ivan was tall and well made, with high shoulders and a broad chest.   His eyes were small and restless, his nose hooked, his beard and moustaches of imposing length.   The habits acquired in later life gave to his face that sinister and troubled expression which so powerfully impressed foreigners;

[1] *See* Chapter IX.

and an enigmatical smile always played around his lips.   His
memory was extraordinary, his energy indefatigable.   The
hardest worked man in his realm, he, nevertheless, made it a
practice to attend to every petition personally ; and every com-
plainant, especially if he belonged to the middle and lower
orders, had free access to him at all times.   Like his father before
him, he loved the relatively learned society of prelates, priests
and monks ; and, in his palace, at Alexandrovna Sloboda, the
whole court was arranged on the model of a monastery, Ivan
himself acting as Igumen, or Abbot.   With the middle and lower
classes, whom, like Louis XI before him, he always favoured
at the expense of the nobles, he was deservedly popular ; and
he was the first Tsar who summoned and took the advice of
national assemblies on important occasions.

CHAPTER VIII.

SIGISMUND III AND THE REPUBLIC, 1588–1632.

THE Jagiellos, after two centuries of almost sisyphean labour, had at last succeeded in welding together, out of the most unpromising and rebellious materials, a new great Power, the *Rzeszpospolita*[1], or Polish Commonwealth. This great Power was exposed from the first to peculiar perils, both external and internal. To begin with, by far the larger part of its vast territories[2] had no natural boundaries. The eastern and northern frontiers, in particular, lay open to the interminable raids of the Tatars, the Turks, and the Moscovites, who, with but moderate initial success, could easily penetrate to the very heart of the unwieldy and ill-defended realm. A strong central Government would have endeavoured to remedy this defect, but, unfortunately, Poland had no strong central Government; and here we touch upon the cardinal organic defect which was the ultimate cause of her ruin. Only sixteen years had elapsed between the death of the last of the Jagiellos and the election of the first of the Polish Vasas; but, in the interval, a momentous political revolution had taken place. Three stormy interregnums had strikingly demonstrated that some 80,000 country squires had become the dominant factor, the motive power, of the Republic. But these rude and ignorant country gentlemen, whose mental horizon rarely extended beyond the limits of their own particular provinces, were naturally at the mercy of

[1] Lit. "res publica."   [2] *See* map I.

every plausible ambitious demagogue; and the inevitable multiplication of such demagogues tended to perpetuate disorder and anarchy. We have seen how Montluc procured the election of Henry, and Zamoyski the election of Stephen and Sigismund III, and how, in two cases out of three, the "King elect" had still to pass through the ordeal of a civil war before he could reach the throne. We shall now see how the representatives of the gentry, assembled in their annual Diets, after cutting down the prerogative to vanishing point, did their best to prevent the King of their own choice from governing at all.

The new King, a young man of 21, ascended his thorny throne under almost every conceivable disadvantage. As a foreigner he was, from the first, out of sympathy with the majority of his subjects. As a highly cultured Prince, fond of music, the fine arts and polite literature, he was unintelligible to the *Szlachta*, who regarded all artists and poets as either mechanics or adventurers. His very virtues were strange and therefore offensive to them. His precocious reserve and imperturbable calmness, almost unnatural in one so young, were branded as stiffness and haughtiness. He looked more like a Spanish Grandee than a Polish King. Certainly, he lacked the tact and *bonhomie* of the Jagiellos, and therefore could never hope to be popular as they were; but, in fairness, it should be added that the Jagiellos were natives of the soil, that they had practically made the monarchy, and that they could always play off their hereditary domain, Lithuania, against Poland. Sigismund's difficulties were materially increased, moreover, by his political views which he had brought with him cut and dried from Sweden, views which happened to be diametrically opposite to those of the omnipotent Chancellor. The coldness between the two men began at their first interview. The jovial, expansive Chancellor was painfully affected by the reticence and ceremoniousness of the young Prince. He complained to his intimate friends that Sigismund was

"possessed by a dumb devil." When their political systems
began to clash, antipathy hardened into antagonism. Sigismund, a zealous Catholic, aimed at a close alliance with the
House of Hapsburg, with the double object of drawing Sweden
within the orbit of Austria, and overawing the Porte by the
conjunction of the two great Powers of central Europe. The
inevitable corollary to this system was the much-needed reform
of the Polish Constitution, without which nothing beneficial,
either to Catholicism or to Poland, was to be expected from
any external political combination. Thus Sigismund's views,
taken as a whole, showed foresight, and were, at least, those of
a practical statesman who clearly recognises present evils and has
a definite plan of his own for remedying them. Zamoyski, on
the other hand, regarded the Hapsburgs with ineradicable,
perhaps exaggerated suspicion. He was also indifferent to any
radical reform of the Polish Constitution. He considered that,
so long as the Austrians were kept out of Poland, Poland would
do very well as she was. A nobleman himself, he placed no
limits to the liberty of the nobility. Every member of a
Republic of gentlemen, he argued, had the right to be as free
as was compatible with the common security. If such liberty
degenerated into licence, he, Zamoyski, who held the Great Seal
and the Grand Hetman's[1] bâton in his own hands, would
simply quell such licence by force, and all would be well again.
Yet he believed in the greatness of Poland, and had a
grandiose but visionary scheme of making her the head of the
Slavonic world by her own unaided efforts. But in the
circumstances, and especially in view of the peculiar national
characteristics of the Poles, Zamoyski's scheme was far more
nebulous than was Sigismund's idea of a pan-catholic league in
Eastern Europe. Personal considerations complicated matters
still further. Zamoyski was, undoubtedly, most jealous of his
influence and dignity; his patriotism, genuine as it might be,
was not always proof against private pique; and, as we shall see,

[1] Commander-in-chief.

though always keeping within constitutional limits, he was never over-scrupulous in his choice of means to an end.

The contest between the King and the Chancellor began during Sigismund's first Diet, the so-called "Pacification Diet," which met at Warsaw in March 1589. Zamoyski presented to this Diet the project of a political combination between Poland, Moscovy, and Bohemia, coupled with a suggestion that in case the present King should die without issue (a somewhat premature and gratuitous assumption in the circumstances) none but a Prince of some Slavonic stock should henceforth be eligible to the Polish throne. The extravagance of a project which could even imagine the possibility of any sort of union between Catholic Poland, Orthodox Moscovy, and semi-protestant Bohemia struck even the majority of the Diet with amazement. It was only explicable at all as a circuitous and clumsy attempt to traverse the Hapsburg influence. The Diet promptly rejected it, accepting instead the royal proposition of a marriage between Sigismund and the Archduchess Anne. The way had already been opened for this *rapprochement* with Austria by the Treaty of Bendzyn (March 9, 1589), negotiated by the Nuncio Ippolito Aldobrandini, afterwards Clement VIII, whereby the Emperor resigned all his claims to the Polish Crown. At the succeeding Diet, which assembled in March 1590, Zamoyski succeeded in persuading the deputies to exclude at any rate the Archduke Maximilian from the succession to the throne. But he had only gained his ends by skilfully frightening them with the bugbears of Austrian intrigues and Turkish threats; and his opponents, headed by the Primate Karnkowski, immediately after the Diet rose, formed a Confederation[1] to protest against its decrees; and a second extraordinary Diet, dominated by the enemies of Zamoyski, met

---

[1] A "Confederation" was an assembly formed to protest against the acts of a Diet. Its decisions were carried by a majority of votes, whereas in a Diet the votes had to be unanimous. On the other hand a Diet had subsequently to confirm the decisions of a Confederation.

at the end of the same year.   It at once proceeded to reverse all the decrees of its predecessor and strike blow after blow at the Chancellor.   Thus the Grand-Hetmanship was placed in commission, the party of Maximilian was amnestied, the Zborowscy were rehabilitated, Zamoyski's friends and supporters were removed from Court, and the chief pillars of the Catholic party in Lithuania, the wealthy Cardinal Radziwill and the newly converted and highly popular Prince James Ostrogsky, were appointed Bishop of Cracow and Castellan of Cracow respectively.   Zamoyski naturally retaliated by means of the same double-edged constitutional weapon which his opponent had used.   On June 1, 1592, he formed a Confederation at Jendrzow, which was more numerously attended than the wedding feast in honour of Sigismund's young Austrian bride the Archduchess Anne, who made her state entry into Cracow, amidst great rejoicings, at the end of May.   All the *Szlachta*, nearly all the senators of Great and Little Poland, and the majority of the orthodox Lithuanians acceded to the Chancellor, so that, at the meeting of the " Inquisition Diet " at Warsaw (Aug. 7) summoned by the King to inquire into all grievances and thoroughly sift the so-called " Austrian cabals," Zamoyski was once more formidable.   Sigismund, supported by the Primate, had still authority enough to stop the inquisition half-way ; but the young Queen's mother, the shrewd and sensible Archduchess Maria, who had accompanied her daughter to Cracow, had made up her mind that Zamoyski was too strong to be set aside, and that therefore the interests of Austria demanded a reconciliation between the King and the Chancellor. This reconciliation was accomplished quietly by Nicholas Firley, Palatine of Cracow, and included all the leading men of both parties.   The rival cardinals Báthory and Radziwill adjusted all their past differences ; Zamoyski was fully reinstated in the Grand-Hetmanship ; and as Grand Chancellor, to the general astonishment, presented to the Diet and eloquently defended all the royal propositions, including Sigismund's request for leave to proceed to Sweden to occupy the throne left vacant by the death of his father John III, on November 17, 1592. This reconciliation lasted a whole decennium, with the happiest results for Poland. Zamoyski, no longer distracted by personal considerations, gave his whole attention to public affairs, and, from 1595 to 1602, achieved some of his most brilliant military and political triumphs.

In 1595 the Papal Court conceived the idea of a new Christian League against the Turk. Certainly the times seemed propitious for such an undertaking. Under a succession of six weak and vicious Sultans (1566–1656), the Ottoman Empire had ceased to be a conquering Power and with difficulty held its own in every corner of its vast domains. But it was still far too strong an enemy for anything less than a league of Christian Princes; and, unfortunately, such a league, in the circumstances, was impossible. The Hapsburg Emperors were absorbed by the double effort of catholicising and germanising their hereditary domains. Venice would not risk losing the trade of the Levant. The Western Powers were indifferent or preoccupied. But the Curia was in an optimistic mood; and, as Poland seemed to be the one remaining great Catholic Power capable of rallying the hesitating and the lukewarm to the holy enterprise, all the efforts of the Curia were directed towards arming Poland in the interests of the League. On February 7, 1595, the Sejm met to consider the question of the Christian League. After six weeks of fruitless debating, the deputies, conscious that the whole burden of a Turkish war would fall upon them, demanded from the Nuncio, as a preliminary, the adhesion of the King of Spain and the Emperor to the project. But they shewed their willingness to co-operate by voting subsidies; making military preparations; and advising the Hetmans to proceed to the Ukraine to look after the Tatars. Meanwhile the prospects of the League grew a little brighter. Early in 1595, Mahomed III mounted the Ottoman throne over the dead bodies of his nineteen strangled brothers, and immediately sent the Grand Vizier, Sinan Pasha, against Hungary, with 150,000 men. He was anticipated, however, by Sigismund Báthory, Prince of Transylvania, who, won over to the League by the eloquence of the Jesuit Alfonso Cariglio and the promise of the hand of an Austrian Archduchess, had already (May 1595) deposed the anti-Austrian Hospodars of Moldavia and Wallachia and annexed both principalities to Transylvania. The Grand Vizier thereupon directed his forces against Transylvania, but was routed by Báthory, at the bloody two days' battle of Mezö Kéresztés ; the Hungarian contingent, under Stephen Bocskay, pursuing Sinan to the Danube and capturing Giurgevo. The Nuncio was now clamorous for the armed co-operation of Poland, but Zamoyski took a more sober view of the situation. He rightly regarded the victories of Sigismund Báthory as Hapsburg victories, and he was determined that Poland should not be made the political catspaw of the House of Austria. With a small army of 8000 veterans he hastened to the Danube, reinstated philo-polish Princes on the thrones of Moldavia and Wallachia; and, in his entrenched camp at Cecora on Pruth, successfully withstood a three days' siege by an innumerable host of Turks and Tatars (Oct. 17–20, 1595), whom he compelled, finally, to come to terms with him. By the peace of Cecora the Hospodars were recognised by the Porte, on condition that Poland refrained from further hostilities; and Zamoyski returned home in triumph. Pope Clement VIII bitterly reproached Sigismund III for ruining the good cause by the Peace of Cecora; but Zamoyski exposed the futility of the Christian League by promising to lead 70,000 men against the Turks in person, as the Nuncio proposed, on condition (1) that Austria should henceforth refrain from all interference in Polish affairs, (2) that, in case of success, Wallachia and Moldavia should be incorporated with Poland, and (3) that in the meantime Breslau and Olmütz should be occupied by Polish garrisons as security for the *bona fides* of the Emperor. As Zamoyski had anticipated, the Nuncio declined to give any such guarantees, and the negotiations fell through. In 1598–1600 Zamoyski again found it necessary to readjust the political situation in the Danubian principalities, where the Gospodar Michael was working in the Austrian interest against Poland. On October 20 he routed Michael, at Tergoviste, and re-established the ascendancy of Poland in those parts. To the same period (July–Sept. 1598) belongs the expulsion of Sigismund from his Swedish kingdom by the Protestant majority there[1], a fresh blow to the hopes of the Curia.

But, though frustrated in its attempts to entice Poland into a highly adventurous oriental policy, the Austro-Ultramontane Party, as it may be called, was now in the ascendant in Poland itself. Towards the end of 1602 Zamoyski's influence had visibly declined. Out of the 142 chief dignitaries of the Republic he could only count absolutely on 30; and his chief opponent, the Grand Marshal, Sigismund Gonzaga Myszkowski, generally detested for his haughtiness and foreign ways which gained him the sobriquet of "the Italian," was one of Sigismund's chief counsellors. Signs of a coming storm were in the air. The *Szlachta* was more than usually suspicious and turbulent. There were loud complaints, not altogether unwarranted, of religious persecutions in Lithuania by the Jesuits; and disquieting rumours were afloat that the King was about to meddle with the Constitution. When, in 1602, Sigismund wedded the Archduchess Constantia, the sister of his first wife, Anne, who had died in 1599, the tempest burst forth. Sigismund's second marriage aroused all Zamoyski's ancient fears and jealousies of the Hapsburgs; and, though now in his 62nd year, he led the opposition during the tumultuous Diets of 1603 and 1605 with his usual spirit and eloquence, but also with quite an unusual unfairness towards his opponents. The utter futility of these two Diets had, at least, the good effect of seriously alarming the wiser heads for the safety of the Republic. At the Diet of 1605 warning voices were even

[1] *See* my *Scandinavia*, pp. 137—139.

raised against the absurdity of the existing Constitution, which demanded absolute unanimity in the decisions of the Diet. "Whether from malice, obstinacy or stupidity," said Ostrogsky, Castellan of Posen, "all our counsels and consultations end in nothing. It is a great glory, no doubt, for the *Szlachta* to be able to obstruct the whole Commonwealth; but it is a great shame for the Commonwealth that, with such a government as ours, anyone can bring about the ruin of the State from sheer obstinacy and stupidity. For God's sake let us not allow the Republic to perish without an effort to save it." Baranowski, Bishop of Plock, supported the Castellan, and declared that the conclusions of the Diet should be decided by a majority instead of by an unanimity of votes. Nothing was done, however, as the Diet regarded any such proposal as a veiled attack upon its most sacred liberties.

Mischievous as the influence of Zamoyski had been during these Diets, his death on June 3, 1605, made matters infinitely worse. A man of his indisputable genius and force of character could always, at a pinch, impose *some* limits on the violence of his partisans. Unfortunately, his mantle fell upon the shoulders of a man who, notwithstanding blameless, even glorious antecedents and many edifying private virtues, was ill-equipped for the duties and the responsibilities of political leadership.

Nicholas Zebrzydowski was related by marriage to Zamoyski and had been one of his close confidants. The youngest of the partisans of the Chancellor, he had hitherto played only a subordinate political rôle; but his career, so far, had been honourable and promising. His zeal and patriotism in the service of Stephen Báthory had been rewarded with the starosties of Stenczyn and Bolislaw. Zamoyski had added to them the still wealthier starosty of Cracow; and, from henceforth, Zebrzydowski attached himself to the victorious standard of the Chancellor. He had distinguished himself during the third interregnum and in the war with Maximilian, and won the favour of Sigismund III, who raised him to the Senate, not so much for his services as for his exemplary piety. A pupil of the Jesuits and intimate with the famous Skarga, Sigismund's court chaplain, he had founded a Jesuit school at Lublin, built the magnificent Calvary monastery near Cracow, renowned through Poland, and was generally regarded, and with justice, as an ornament to the Faith. Unfortunately, his talents by no means kept pace with his virtues. Though a brave soldier, he was no general; though for years a confidant of the plans of the Chancellor he had learnt nothing of diplomacy, and had not a political idea of his own. He claimed to be the spiritual heir of Zamoyski; but all that he had inherited from his master was that master's hatreds and prejudices. Yet, undoubtedly, Zebrzydowski is a very important figure in Polish history. To him belongs the doubtful honour of making constitutional reform in Poland impossible by constitutional means.

At the beginning of 1606, Sigismund III summoned the Diet for the express purpose of reforming the Constitution by substituting decisions by majorities for that unattainable counsel of perfection—absolute unanimity. If Poland was to continue her political existence, the proposed reform, obviously, was urgent and indispensable. Nevertheless, the royal manifesto had scarce been issued when Zebrzydowski summoned a Confederation to protest against an innovation "so destructive of personal liberty." The Confederation assembled first at Stenczyn and then at Lublin (June 4) and was very largely attended by Orthodox Lithuanians, Protestant Poles and political refugees from Hungary. Amongst the most eloquent champions of individual liberty was Stanislaus Stadnicki, surnamed "the Devil," who, to quote a contemporary, "had more sins on his conscience than hairs on his head." This nobleman habitually cropped the noses and ears of offensive small squires, and kept his peasants chained to the walls of subterranean dungeons for months together. Such leaders naturally adopted the most extreme expedients. On August 6 the Confederation moved to Sandomir, where it converted itself into a *Rokosz*, or

"Insurrection," with the avowed object of dethroning the King and electing as his successor Stephen Bocskay, the Protestant Prince of Transylvania, from whom the malcontents got both money and mercenaries.

Sigismund was now obliged to take measures for his personal security. His worst enemies could never accuse him of cowardice, and, with nothing but a lukewarm Diet and a timid Senate to support him against an armed insurrection of at least one half of the Polish gentry, he now shewed what stuff he was made of. First, he summoned to his assistance the *Quartians*, or border troops, from the Ukraine. Then, by the advice of the Senate, he issued a manifesto condemning the " Insurrection " of Sandomir, and at the same time summoned a rival *Zajazd*[1] to meet at Wislica for the purpose of forming a Confederation in defence of the Crown. He then proceeded to Cracow to confront the rebels and, if possible, overawe them.

The resolute conduct of the King was not without effect. The gentry of the palatinates of Russia and Sieradia, enraged at the ravaging of their estates by the " Insurrectionists," acceded *en masse* to the Zajazd of Wislica ; and the " Insurrectionists," alarmed at the diminution of their following, offered to treat and drew up 64 articles, which aimed at still further reducing the royal power. They demanded the protection of Protestant and Orthodox minorities, the equal distribution of offices and dignities irrespective of creeds and nationalities, and the expulsion of the Jesuits from the realm. But Sigismund refused to treat with rebels and took the field against them. In September (1606) he routed Zebrzydowski at Janowiec, whereupon the " Insurrectionists " surrendered and were allowed to renew their homage, after solemnly pledging themselves to disturb the Commonwealth no more. But all these promises were speedily broken ; and, in the course of 1607, the agitation was renewed, and became more widespread than ever. A fresh

---

[1] The Polish equivalent of the Magyar *Rokosz*.

Rokosz was formed at Jendrzejow, at the very time when the Diet was assembling at Warsaw. On May 25, with the consent of the Senate, Sigismund issued an edict demanding its instant dispersion. The "Insurrectionists" retaliated by declaring that a *Rokosz* was as much superior to King and Diet combined as a General Council was superior to the Pope. Consequently, a *Rokosz* was the only legitimate tribunal for the remedy of popular grievances. At this crisis, the Diet, instead of energetically supporting the King in his efforts to re-establish the rudiments of law and order, practically enlisted itself on the side of anarchy. Composed, as it was, of the same elements as the *Rokosz*, its sympathies were with the "Insurrectionists" rather than with the Government; and its edict "De non præstanda obœdientia" (June 17, 1607), which was intended to be a compromise, really amounted to a surrender. This disastrous edict enjoined that, in case of any future malpractices on the part of the King, he was to be twice warned to cease therefrom by the Primate and the Senate, and once more by the succeeding Diet. If he neglected these three warnings, the nation was absolved from its allegiance and free to choose a new Sovereign. But even this did not satisfy the "Insurrectionists." Their personal hatred of so resolute a lover of orderly government as Sigismund III dominated every other consideration, and they would be content with nothing short of his deposition. On June 24 they issued a manifesto at Jeziorna, a village 45 miles from Warsaw, renouncing their allegiance to Sigismund and proclaiming Gabriel Bethlen, Prince of Transylvania, King of Poland.

For the second time, Sigismund's Crown hung on the point of his sword. The Grand and Vice Hetmans, Zolkiewski and Chodkiewicz, were sent against the rebels and, after pursuing them for weeks, brought them to battle at Oransk, near Guzow (April 6, 1608), when a desperate encounter ensued. Once the "Insurrectionists," who were greatly strengthened by a contingent of Hungarian mercenaries, broke the left wing of

B.   10

Sigismund's army and approached the royal camp. The panic-stricken Senators took to their heels, but the King stood firm ; the bulk of the army rallied round him ; and the rebels were routed. Nevertheless, during the next twelve months, fresh "Insurrections" burst forth all over the country; and quiet was only at last restored by the proclamation (1609) of a general amnesty, which punished nobody and decided nothing. The growing unwillingness of the Grand Hetman Zolkiewski "to shed the blood of our brethren" was the cause of this unsatisfactory solution. The helpless King was obliged to concur, and henceforth abandoned all his projects of constitutional reform.

Thus the *Szlachta* had become dominant, and its one exclusive idea was to remain dominant. From the middle and lower classes, whom it had crushed beneath its feet, nothing was to be feared. But the King, as the nominal head of the State, as the controller of foreign affairs through his official counsellors, the Senate and the Chancellors, and, as the head of the army, through the Hetmans, whom he appointed, was still a potential menace to individual liberty as the *Szlachta* understood it. Henceforth, therefore, an unreasonable, incurable suspicion of the Crown, and all the executive instruments of the Crown, is the characteristic, or rather the mania, of every Polish Diet. For its country, as a State, the *Szlachta* had no thought at all. So long as every *Szlachcic*, or squire, was lord paramount in his own parish he cared little for anything beyond it. And what, after all, was the *Sejm*, or Diet, but a collection of some 600 of such squires who met annually at Warsaw or elsewhere, in order to contribute as little as possible to public needs and protest vehemently against everything they did not like or could not understand? So far as they can be said to have had any policy at all, the *Szlachta* was in favour of absolute non-intervention in foreign affairs, as being the cheapest and least troublesome policy to pursue. The unwillingness with which the gentry of Poland parted with their money, especially for armaments, however necessary, was entirely due to the fear lest a popular monarch, at the head of a victorious army, might curtail their privileges. Rather than run such a risk as this, they were ready to avoid every advantageous alliance, forgo every political opportunity, stint their armies, starve and abandon their generals, and even leave the territories of the Republic unguarded and undefended. That this is no exaggeration will be obvious to everyone who takes the trouble to follow the course of events during the long reign of Sigismund III. Then, if ever, Polish statesmen had the opportunity of realising the Jagiellonic dream of Empire. The political situation everywhere favoured them. Livonia, with its fine seaboard and its hundreds of towns and fortresses, had literally fallen into the lap of Poland. Her one serious rival in the north was the rude young Swedish monarchy ; for Moscovy, after the death of Ivan IV (1584), had ceased to be dangerous. The Turk, unless violently shaken, was inclined to slumber. The Emperor and the Western Powers were more or less involved in the Spanish and, subsequently, in the Thirty Years' War. The regular army, if small, was good ; while in the Cossacks Poland had an almost unlimited reserve of the best raw military material. Finally, she possessed, in Zamoyski, Stanislaus Zolkiewski, Jan Karol Chodkiewicz and Stanislaus Koniecpolski, four of the greatest captains of the age. No wonder that the Catholic League expected great things from the Republic. Who could ever have foreseen that the Poles themselves would frustrate the hopes of Poland !

The Livonian question was the first which called for prompt settlement. We have seen[1] how, by the Truce of Zapolsk (1582), Ivan IV ceded Livonia to Poland. But the Swedes also set up claims to the Baltic Provinces, and attempted to enforce them in 1600 when Sigismund III, though expelled from Sweden, refused to relinquish his claims to the Swedish throne. After conquering Esthonia, which, it will be re-

[1] *See* last chapter.

membered, was also part of the territories of the ancient
Order of the Sword, the Swedes invaded Livonia; and by
March, 1601, the whole country, except Riga and Kokenhausen, were in their possession. But, in the beginning of
1602 the tide turned. Zamoyski, supported by his two great
pupils, Zolkiewski and Chodkiewicz, took the field against the
Swedes and recovered so many of the captured fortresses that
Charles IX offered to surrender Livonia if Sigismund would be
equally complaisant with regard to Sweden. Zamoyski, confident of success, advised a vigorous prosecution of the war; but
his hopes were dashed by a sudden mutiny of the Polish army,
which demanded its long outstanding arrears of pay and,
failing to obtain them, dispersed among the Lithuanian palatinates, burning and ravaging as they went. In consequence of
this, the Poles were unable to do anything for two years. Then
Chodkiewicz again took the field, captured Dorpat and routed
the Swedes at Weisenstein (Sept. 15, 1604), for which exploit
he won the grand bâton of Lithuania. In August, 1605,
Charles IX, with an army of 16,000 men, reassumed the offensive
and advanced against Riga. Chodkiewicz, whose army was now
reduced to 3,400 men, mostly cavalry, sent letter after letter
both to Poland and Lithuania for reinforcements. His urgent
appeals remained unanswered; but, recognising clearly that
the fall of Riga would mean the total loss of Esthonia
and Livonia, he resolved to seek his fortune in the field
and risk everything on one desperate venture. Accordingly,
he posted himself two miles from Riga, on the banks
of the Dwina, near a little chapel on an island known
as Kirkholm. Charles hastened thither with all his forces
to administer the *coup de grâce.* The army of the Swedes
consisted almost entirely of infantry. They occupied all the
surrounding hills; their superior artillery commanded all the
fords; they only waited for the enemy to emerge to annihilate
him. At 8 o'clock in the morning, Chodkiewicz suddenly
darted out at the head of his squadrons as if in panic flight

and drew the Swedish army after him into the open field, when he turned swiftly on the disordered ranks of his pursuers. After three hours of desperate fighting, the Swedes scattered in every direction; and the battle became a carnage which lasted till evening.   Barely 5000 of the Swedes escaped; 9000 of them bit the dust.   Sixty standards, eleven guns, all the baggage and the military chest fell into the hands of the Lithuanian Grand Hetman.   Charles IX himself owed his escape to the devotion of Henrik Wrede, who sacrificed his horse, and with it his life, to save his master.

The victory of Kirkholm (Sept. 27, 1605) was a sensational event.   Pope Paul V bestowed his thanks and blessing on Chodkiewicz in an autograph letter.   Sigismund III received congratulatory letters on the glorious success of the Polish arms from a dozen contemporary Potentates, including, somewhat to his surprise, the Sultan and the Shah.   Unfortunately, this signal victory was rendered absolutely fruitless by the "Insurrections," already described, which convulsed Poland during the next three years.   Chodkiewicz's army, still unpaid, again mutinied *en masse*; and it was as much as he could do, with a handful of mercenaries, paid out of his own pocket, to keep the Swedes in check till the theatre of the struggle was, in 1609, transferred to Moscovy.

The details of the Russo-Polish war of 1609–1613 are related in the following chapter.   Here we would only emphasise the fact that the triumphs of Chodkiewicz and of his colleague, the Grand Hetman of the Crown, Zolkiewski, were, throughout that war, perpetually minimised and neutralised by the jealous and fatal parsimony of the Polish Diet.   Thus, Chodkiewicz was sent against the Moscovites with a lilliputian army of 2000 men, though, if there had been a spark of true patriotism in Poland, he could easily have been provided with the requisite 100,000. Nay, the Diet neglected to pay for the maintenance of even the 2000, which consequently mutinied and compelled its leader to retreat through the heart of Moscovy to Smolensk.

Similarly, when Zolkiewski, in 1611, presented the captive Tsar Vasily Shuiski and his family to the Diet, the unwonted sight evoked boisterous enthusiasm from every part of the House; and the Grand Hetman received a perfect ovation from the delighted deputies. But when the Chancellor, Myszkowski, taking advantage of the opportunity, appealed to the liberality of the *Szlachta* and called for subsidies "sufficient to put a roof on so imposing an edifice," they would barely grant enough to fortify the freshly recovered fortress of Smolensk.

But it is only when we come to the dealings of the Republic with its border mercenaries, the Cossacks, that we are able to realise the full folly of a policy which grudged every penny spent on the national defences. The position of the Cossacks in the Polish Republic was peculiar. At the beginning of the sixteenth century the illimitable steppes of south-eastern Europe, extending from the Dniester to the Urals, had no fixed population. The perpetual incursions of the Tatar hordes of Budjak and the Crimea made the Ukraine, or "borderland," as it was called, unsafe to dwell in; but, gradually, as the lot of the serf, both in Poland and Moscovy, grew more and more intolerable, the more energetic spirits among the peasantry sought an untrammelled, adventurous life in the free steppe. Obliged, for fear of the Tatars, to go about constantly with arms in their hands, they soon grew strong enough to raid their raiders, selling the rich booty thus acquired to the merchants of Moscovy and Poland. As time went on, the Cossacks multiplied exceedingly. Their daring grew with their numbers, and they became an annoyance to all their neighbours, frequently involving both Poland and Moscovy in dangerous and unnecessary wars with the Ottoman Porte. Every river of any importance had its own Cossack settlement. Thus, beginning from the extreme east of Europe, we find the Yaitsie Cossacks on the Yaitsa, the Volgan Cossacks, the Terskie Cossacks on the Terek, and, further westwards, the Don Cossacks. The Cossacks of the Yaitsa, the Volga, the Terek and the Don were under the

nominal dominion of Moscovy; but the most important of all
the Cossacks, the Cossacks of the Dnieper, were the vassals of
the Crown of Poland.

The origin of the *Syech*, or Community of the Dnieperian
Cossacks, is still somewhat obscure; but it was of importance, as
a military outpost, so early as the beginning of the sixteenth
century. Not, however, till 1570 do we find the Cossacks
permanently entrenched among the islands of the Lower
Dnieper. The Union of Lublin (1569), which tended to
the polonising of Lithuania, was the immediate occasion of
a considerable exodus to the lowlands of the Dnieper of those
peasants who would escape the taxes of the Polish Government
and the tyranny of the Polish Pans, or overlords. This greatly
increased the number of the Cossacks; and Stephen Báthory converted them into a strong military colony for the defence of the
border by enrolling the pick of them in six registered regiments
of 1000 men each, with allotted districts where they could live
with their families, with their headquarters on and around the
island of Hortica, just below the *porogi*, or falls, of the Dnieper,
whence they were generally known as the *Zaporozhians*, or "Back-
fallsmen[1]." Báthory judged it expedient to leave the Cossacks
alone as far as possible, so long as they fulfilled their chief
obligation of guarding the frontiers of the Republic against the
Tatar raids. The Cossack *Kosh*, or commonwealth, had the
privilege of electing its *Ataman*, or Hetman, and his chief officers,
the *starshins*, annually. The Cossack Hetman received from
the King of Poland direct the insignia of his office, namely, the
bulawa, or bâton, the *bunchuk*, or horse-tail standard, and his
official seal. He was also obliged to follow the Grand Hetmans of
the Crown and of Lithuania to battle whenever called upon to do
so. But, as chief of the *Kosh*, he was responsible to the *Kosh*
alone; and an enquiry into his conduct, during his year of office,
was held, at the expiration of that term, in the *Obshchaya Shkodka*,
or General Assembly, where complaints against him were invited

---

[1] Compare the American " Backwoodsmen."

and considered. Thus the Cossacks were independent of the Polish Diet, though the Diet was pledged to support them as part of the national forces. This privileged position was very odious to the *Szlachta*, who resented the existence of an army which took its orders from the King and yet drew its pay from them.

The Cossacks were from the first a very disturbing and incalculable element in Polish politics. The Republic, with the Porte as its next-door neighbour, was bound to keep the Cossacks within due limits; and this she endeavoured to do by reducing their numbers and setting over them Polish officers. But the Cossacks resented the slightest curtailment of the ancient custom of marauding; and hence collisions between the Polish Government were frequent and bloody. Thus, in 1596, Zolkiewski was obliged to besiege the Cossack Hetman Nalewajko in his camp at Lubus, when 8500 Cossacks out of 10,000 perished after a desperate resistance. In 1613, encouraged by the disorders in Poland, the Zaporozhians undertook a great piratical expedition on the Black Sea, destroyed Sinope and other ports, and returned home with booty of the value of 40 millions of Polish gulden. A war with the Turks now seemed inevitable, but it was averted, for a time, by the courage and vigilance of Zolkiewski, who, by the skilful disposition of his *Quartians*[1], kept back the Tatars, and by imposing demonstrations in the Ukraine overawed the Turks. These operations were conducted almost entirely at his own expense, the Diet turning a deaf ear to most of his appeals for help. Left, thus, to his own resources he was obliged to make the best terms he could with the chronically rebellious Cossacks. Thus, by the compact of Olszawa (1616), he promised them an annual allowance of 1000 ducats and 700 wagon-loads of cloth,

---

[1] The *Quartians*, or *Kwartians*, were border troopers, for the maintenance of which a *kwarta*, or fourth, of the private Crown estates were set aside. The institution was founded in 1562 by Sigismund II to relieve the Diet as much as possible.

on condition that they abstained from piracy; and by the compact of Rastawa (1617), thousands of unregistered Cossacks, mostly runaway serfs, were attached, as auxiliaries, to the registered regiments instead of being compelled to return to their masters as heretofore. This great concession was deeply resented by the landowners and accounts for their persistent hostility to the Grand Hetman. But, though postponed for a time, a war with Turkey, in view of the endless raiding of Turkish territory not only by the Cossacks, but by the Pans themselves, was bound to come sooner or later. The conclusion of the long and wearing Persian war in 1618, gave the Porte a freer hand in Europe; and Sultan Osman, in alliance with Gabriel Bethlen, determined to attack Poland with all his forces. At this critical moment, when the very existence of the Republic was at stake, the malcontent majority of the *Sejm*, instead of voting adequate subsidies, fiercely attacked the Grand Hetman of the Crown in full Diet, accusing him of uselessly protracting the Cossack and Tatar wars to his own advantage. In all these accusations, the result partly of personal jealousy and partly of a suspicion that Zolkiewski favoured the King's political views, there was not one word of truth. The Grand Hetman defended himself with dignity; but, towards the end of his speech, righteous indignation overcame him and, turning towards the throne, he exclaimed, " Of a truth, before dying, I would fain have had some rest and respite not only from many grievous labours, but also from the tongues of men. For four and forty years I have rendered military service, shedding my blood in battles, skirmishes and sieges, yet I, who, methinks, have held up the Republic in my arms, I forsooth! am evil, and those who plunge the Republic into destruction are the better men." It was with a broken heart and a foreboding of disaster that the aged Zolkiewski prepared for his last campaign. Collecting 10,000 men at Bar, he crossed the Dniester at Podbihy and, on September 7, entered Moldavia, whose Hospodar, Gracian, was in the Polish interest and had promised to bring with him an auxiliary force of 25,000. When, then, he joined Zolkiewski with only 500, the Grand Hetman perceived that the original plan of campaign must be abandoned. He entrenched himself, provisionally, at Zamoyski's old camp at Cecora, where, on September 19, 1618, he was attacked by Skinder Pasha and 60,000 Turks. The assault was beaten off; but the situation was now so serious that, at a Council of War, Zolkiewski advised a retreat to Mohilew. But the Hospodar and many of the *Szlachta,* objecting to the perils of so long a march, burst out of the camp and, in an endeavour to cross the Dniester and gain Bessarabia, were cut to pieces by the enemy. With his reduced forces, Zolkiewski then began his retreat through the burnt and barren steppe, harassed at every step by his pursuers. For seven days he fought his way along, when a second mutiny broke out, and the bulk of his forces deserted him after plundering his camp. Then the Turks fell upon the little band which still stood firm, and massacred all but a few generals and dignitaries who were held to ransom. The Grand Hetman himself, fighting to the last and covered with wounds, was finally decapitated by a Turkish scimitar. His head was sent to Stambul as a present for the Sultan.

This terrible disaster awoke at last the conscience of the nation. The Diet of 1619 voted the unprecedented but still inadequate sum of six millions of Polish gulden for war expenses; the Lithuanian Grand Hetman, Chodkiewicz, was appointed to the supreme command; and the Krolowicz, or Crown Prince, Wladislaus, accompanied the army to the Ukraine. Chodkiewicz had demanded at least 60,000 men, but the money voted could equip no more than 35,000; and with this little host he had to confront the pick of the Turkish army, 160,000 strong, led by Sultan Osman in person. At the last moment, however, he was joined by the Cossack Hetman, Sahajadichny, with 30,000 horsemen, and strongly entrenched himself on the Dniester, not far from Chocim, to bar the way of the Ottoman army. The siege, which lasted from September 2 to October 9, was glorious alike to the Poles and the Cossacks.　Chodkiewicz, now in his 61st year, died of exhaustion during the siege, but he lived long enough to hurl back a dozen assaults and so break the spirit of the Turkish host that, on the first fall of autumn snow, Osman opened negotiations.　On October 9, a truce was signed, on a *uti possidetis* basis, which the Janissaries considered to be so humiliating to the Ottoman Empire that they murdered the Sultan on his return to the capital.

"The War of Chocim," as it is called, gave Poland a respite from Turkish attacks for more than a generation, though it was dearly purchased by the sacrifice of two such heroes as Zolkiewski and Chodkiewicz.　Fortunately for Poland she still possessed in Stanislaus Koniecpolski a commander capable of upholding the military traditions of heroic Poland. The pupil and son-in-law of Zolkiewski, he had fought by his side to the last on the bloody field of Cecora, and, after three years' captivity at Stambul, returned to Poland in 1623.　The exploits of Koniecpolski are the most memorable events of the latter years of the reign of Sigismund.　It was he who, on the resumption of the Swedish war, in 1626, with miserably inadequate forces, for three years successfully defended Poland proper against Gustavus Adolphus, whom he defeated in several engagements, notably at Homerstein (1627) and at Trcziana (1629).　A more vigorous prosecution of the war might have rid the Republic of her troublesome northern neighbour.　But the *Sejm* never grasped the significance of the situation, and, instead of enabling Koniecpolski to follow up his victories, concluded with Sweden the six years' truce of Altmark, whereby Gustavus retained possession of Livonia, together with Elbing, a considerable portion of the delta of the Vistula, Braunsburg in West and Pillau and Memel in East Prussia.　Still more important than these territorial acquisitions was the permission conceded to the Swedes of levying tolls at Pillau, Memel, Dantzic, Labiau and Windau, from which they derived, in 1629 alone, no less than 500,000 rix dollars.

But it was in the southern Ukraine that Koniecpolski reaped his most brilliant laurels. In 1623, just before his departure for the Baltic, he routed 65,000 Tatars at Martuinov on the Dniester. Subsequently he devoted himself to the difficult task of chastising the Cossacks, whose pretensions had become insupportable. He broke their power at the great battle of Perejaslawl, and imposed upon them the compact of Kurakow, which reduced the numbers of the registered Cossacks to 6000 men, at an annual cost of 60,000 gulden (1625).

Sigismund III would have intervened in the Thirty Years' War, on the Catholic side, but for the determined opposition of the Diet, expressing itself in fresh insurrections and the refusal of supplies. His intervention would have taken the form of an invasion and, possibly, an occupation of Transylvania, which, under the energetic and ambitious Princes of the Protestant Houses of Bethlen and Rákoczy, was the active ally of the Sultan and equally dangerous to Austria and Poland. The best heads in Poland, including Zolkiewski, warmly approved of the King's policy in this respect, but it proved to be impracticable. The Diet's mania for non-intervention went so far that it refused to grant any subsidies for the Swedish War— with the disastrous consequences already recorded. Towards the end of his reign, Sigismund III withdrew altogether from politics and devoted himself exclusively to family matters. He died, very suddenly, of apoplexy, on April 30, 1632, in his 66th year. He would have made an excellent Sovereign if only his subjects had allowed him to rule them.

CHAPTER IX.

BORIS GODUNOV AND THE PSEUDO-DEMETRIUSES, 1584–1613.

THE death of Ivan IV left Moscovy in much the same position as it had been on the death of his father: in both cases a Regency was necessary, but, in the present instance, the regency had to be permanent; for Theodore, the eldest surviving son of Ivan by Anastasia Romanov, was scarce able to walk, or speak, or indeed do anything but smile unceasingly at the orb and sceptre placed in his hands on state occasions. Such a regency was necessarily the arena of a struggle for power amongst the principal patricians, who fell into two well-defined groups. First came the princely families of the Mstislavskies and the Golitsuins, collateral descendants of Rurik and Gedymin respectively, the prime dignitaries of the land, but without sufficient ability or influence to assert themselves. Next after them came two Boyar families, both closely connected with the Tsarish family, the Romanovs and the Godunovs. The Romanovs were the kinsfolk of the young Tsar's grandmother, and had eminently distinguished themselves in the service of his father. Less pure was the source of the greatness of the Godunovs. Their leader, Boris Theodorovich, a handsome, stately man of great ability, had first won the confidence of Ivan by marrying one of the daughters of his infamous favourite Malyutka Skuratov. The marriage of Boris' sister Irene with the Tsarevich Theodore had brought

Godunov still nearer to the throne; but, during the first two years of the new reign, the dominant personage at court was Nikita Romanov, the young Tsar's uncle. Theodore I was crowned Tsar on May 31, 1584. An attempt to supersede him by placing his young half-brother, Demetrius, the son of Tsaritsa Martha Nagaya, on the throne, was easily frustrated; and the Tsarevich Demetrius, with his kinsfolk, was forthwith banished to his appanage at Uglich. In April 1586 died Nikita Romanov; and Boris Godunov, chiefly through the influence of his sister, Irene, stepped into his place. A combination of all the other Boyars and of the merchants of Moscow, now, thanks to the encouragement of Ivan IV, a power in the State, was immediately formed, to oust Godunov; but the Tsar's relations supported him and he prevailed. In the following year, Godunov, suspecting a fresh conspiracy, struck down his most inveterate enemies, the Shuiskies; and, at the same time, some of the leading Moscow merchants disappeared, no man knew whither. An attempt of the Metropolitan Dionysius to save the fallen Boyars, by an appeal to the Tsar, recoiled on his own head. He was banished to a distant monastery as a simple monk; and Job, Archbishop of Rostov, a creature of Godunov's, was consecrated Metropolitan in his stead. Henceforth Godunov was without rivals. He assumed the title of "Great intimate Boyar" and "Administrator of the Kingdoms of Kazan and Astrakhan," gave foreign powers to understand that if they wanted anything in Moscovy they were to apply to him direct, and exchanged gifts with Sovereign Princes as if he were their equal. In short, the Administrator was now the actual ruler of Moscovy. His vast wealth was an additional guarantee of his stability. His annual income at this period could not have been much below £500,000 a year. He and his family out of their private fortunes could fully equip 100,000 men-at-arms in forty days.

The foreign policy of the Administrator was enlightened in so far as it endeavoured to draw Moscovy out of her isolation by cultivating the friendship of foreign powers, but cautious to cowardice in its endeavours to avoid war except under impossibly favourable conditions. The dread of Stephen Báthory still paralysed Moscovite politics. At the beginning of the new reign, Stephen had demanded Great Novgorod, Pskov, Smolensk and Severia; but the Pans took care that his great designs came to nothing. They chafed and fretted beneath the curb of a strong King, openly declared to a Moscovite embassy, sent to Poland, in 1585, to obtain a prolongation of the truce, their preference for "a gentle and pious Prince" like the young Tsar, and rejoiced indecently at the unsatisfactory condition of Báthory's wounds, which promised to relieve them shortly of that troublesome hero. On Báthory's death, the candidature of Theodore for the vacant throne was seriously discussed in Lithuania, where the orthodox were all in his favour. But the Moscovite deputies who attended the election Diet did not bring sufficient money with them for bribing purposes; and, in any case, there were three insuperable obstacles to the election of a Moscovite, (1) the coronation at Cracow, (2) the precedence of the Polish royal title in the act of homage, and (3) the conversion to Catholicism. The Moscovites succeeded, however, in renewing the Polish truce, for fifteen years, with the new King Sigismund III, who, at the beginning of his reign, was too much harassed by domestic rebels to be dangerous to Moscovy.

With Sweden the new Moscovite government first concluded a truce for four years from December 1585, which, after an indecisive war, was converted into a definitive peace (May 18, 1595), Moscovy retaining Carelia but relinquishing Narva. By the same treaty, free trade was established between the two countries; and the Swedes undertook to allow doctors, artificers and master-mechanics to pass through their territories into Moscovy.

With the other European powers Moscovy had still but little to do. Abroad she was generally regarded as simple and barbarous enough to be exploited, skilfully, by the shrewder and more pushing western nations. Thus, in 1594, the imperial envoy, Varkoch, induced Godunov to send to Prague a quantity of most precious pelts, valued at 400,000 rubles, the proceeds of which were ostensibly to be employed in hiring mercenaries for the grand league against the Turk, Moscovy getting nothing in return. In 1595, and again in 1597, Clement VIII sent the Slavonian Bishop, Komulei, to Moscow on a similar errand. In 1586, Queen Elizabeth, intent on obtaining the monopoly of the Russian trade for her subjects, addressed a very flattering letter to Godunov, through Richard Horsey, in which she called the Administrator "our most dear and loving cousin." Boris more than satisfied the expectations of his "dear cousin" by favouring the English merchants at the expense of their competitors. They were permitted to have their own "courts," or *dépôts,* at Yaroslav, Vologda and Kholmogory, and were freed from the payment of the most usual tolls. In 1588, after Fletcher's embassy, they were even allowed to go through Russia to Persia and Bokhara, while the merchants of other lands were stopped short a hundred miles eastwards of Moscow.

The Tatars, though no longer dangerous, still continued to be troublesome. In 1591 they came against Moscow, but were defeated at Tula, on which occasion all the Boyars concerned were extravagantly rewarded, Godunov receiving a mantle from the Tsar's shoulders and the new title of *Sluga*[1], which was explained to be higher than that of Boyar. In 1592, however, after a Tatar raid of unprecedented severity, the Khan was propitiated by rich gifts; but the Moscovite government now refused to pay a regular tribute.

Contemporaries justly and gratefully acknowledge that the thirteen years of the reign of Theodore I was a period of peace and prosperity. Godunov was an able administrator, and, whenever his personal interests were unconcerned, loved to

[1] Servant.

shew his care for the commonwealth and his hatred of evil doers. He had, moreover, diligent and astute coadjutors in the two *dumnie dyaki,* or clerks of the council, the brothers Shchelkalov. The most salient phenomenon of the reign was the encroachment of the Tsardom upon the steppe in every direction. The fresh territory thus acquired was defended by a series of blockhouses, or fortified settlements, which gradually restricted the area of the Tatar raids. In this way Kursk, Voronezh, Byelogorod, Saratov, Tsaritsuin, and, in Siberia, Tyumen, Chulkov and Tobolsk (1587), sprang into existence. In 1584 Archangel was built and surrounded by wooden walls. In 1589, Astrakhan and, in 1596, Smolensk were provided with stone *Kremls* or citadels. In 1586, the White Town was built round Moscow, forming a third line of circumvallation. The army at this time consisted of 80,000 men, including 12,000 *stryeltsui,* or musketeers, and 300 foreign mercenaries. The chief duties of the troops were garrison-service and "bank-service," that is, the assembling on the banks of the Oka to protect Moscow against Tatar raids.

It is in the reign of Theodore I that the Russian peasant was first bound to the soil. The vastness of the land and the paucity of its cultivators put the agricultural labourer at a premium. Every landed proprietor strove to get and keep as many peasants as possible; and the larger and wealthier proprietors successfully tempted the peasants away from the smaller and poorer proprietors. But the State also suffered considerably from this transmigration. The very numerous class of smaller proprietors held their estates on military tenure. These *Sluzhivuie lyudi,* or serving people, as they were officially called, were obliged, in war time, on the first summons, to assemble in the nearest camp, "with men, horses and equipment." But, as they received no pay for their services and lived entirely on the produce of their estates, the want of adequate peasant labour meant the ruin of their estates and their own consequent inability to perform military service.

The same difficulty had already arisen in Poland where such enticing away of peasants was made a penal offence. In Moscovy the Government tried to meet the difficulty by binding the peasant to the soil. By the Ukase of 1597 it was decreed that fugitive peasants could be pursued and reclaimed within five years after their flight or abduction.

The most important ecclesiastical event of this period was the elevation of the metropolitan see of Moscow to the dignity of a Patriarchate. After the fall of Constantinople there was a general wish among the Moscovites for an autocephalous church of their own. Many even opined that unity with the enslaved oriental churches might be injurious to orthodoxy. This wish grew stronger still when the Jesuits began their propaganda in Lithuania, and reproached the orthodox with being spiritually the subjects of the Turkish Sultan, who regularly sold the Constantinopolitan Patriarchate to the highest bidder. A separate Patriarchate would also be advantageous to Moscovy politically by giving her the preeminence over the more ancient orthodox metropolitan see of Kiev, then under Poland. The wish was gratified when Jeremiah, Patriarch of Constantinople, visited Moscow, partly to collect alms, partly to visit the orthodox churches of the North. After several interviews with Godunov and the Shchelkalovs, he proposed to transfer the Constantinople Patriarchate bodily to Moscow. But his ignorance of Russian, the usefulness of the Metropolitan Job to Godunov—to say nothing of the strong patriotic sentiments of the Moscovites, who disliked the supersession of their own arch-pastor by a foreigner—were so many insuperable objections to this proposal. After six months of discussion and hesitation, Jeremiah consecrated Job first Patriarch of Moscow (Jan. 26, 1589), though it was not till June 1591 that the Metropolitan of Tirnova brought to Moscow the confirmatory epistle from Constantinople.

The century was now running out; and with it disappeared the ancient dynasty of the Ruriks. Godunov had raised himself to power on the ruins of the more illustrious but less intelligent princely families. He had maintained his supremacy by making himself the mouth-piece and the right-hand of the Tsar *fainéant*; but the future was uncertain, and the higher he rose the more terrible was the prospect of a fall. Theodore had no son through whom Godunov might continue to rule; and the rightful heir to the throne was the child Demetrius, Theodore's half-brother, from whom, or, rather, from whose relatives, Godunov had nothing good to expect. It is intelligible with what feelings the Nagais would regard the author of their long disgrace; and they took no pains to conceal their resentment. Not only Godunov but all who owed their advancement to him, and they were many, were equally apprehensive of a future which would bring Demetrius to the throne. Suddenly, in May 1591, the tidings reached Moscow that the young Demetrius was no more. The affair is still somewhat of a mystery, but, according to the contemporary *lyetopis* (and the best critics agree that there is no valid reason for doubting its simple and straightforward testimony), what actually happened was this. After an unsuccessful attempt to poison the lad, Godunov's emissaries were sent to Uglich to take over the government of the town. The Tsaritsa Martha, suspecting their motives, kept strict watch over her son; but his nurse, who was in the conspiracy, took him one day into the outer courtyard, and, while at play there, he was murdered by two of Godunov's emissaries, who, along with eleven accomplices, were immediately afterwards killed by a crowd of people attracted to the spot by the alarm given by a bell-ringer of a neighbouring church, who had witnessed the crime. The child's body was interred in the church of the Transfiguration; and Godunov was duly informed what had happened. He at once told the Tsar that Demetrius had mortally wounded himself in an epileptic fit; and Prince Vasily Shuiski, whom Godunov had sent to Uglich to suborn witnesses in support of the epilepsy theory, confirmed this statement. The Nagais were then haled to Moscow, brow-beaten and tortured ; an ostentatiously elaborate enquiry was opened at which all evidence in any way likely to conflict with the official theory of suicide was suppressed or ignored ; and the Patriarch Job, as President of the tribunal of investigation, declared that Demetrius had died by the visitation of God, and that the Nagais were guilty of treason for killing the Administrator's emissaries.   The Nagais were punished by mutilation and banishment ; the Tsaritsa Martha was forced to take the veil ; the inhabitants of Uglich, as the abettors of the Nagais, were transferred bodily to the new Siberian town of Pelim ; and Uglich itself gradually relapsed into the surrounding wilderness.

The Tribunal had publicly condemned the Nagais, but the Russian nation secretly condemned Godunov. Henceforth he was thought capable of any infamy, so that when Tsar Theodore died a natural death, on January 7, 1598, it was the general opinion that Boris had removed him by poison.

Ever since Tsar Ivan III had declared, "to whom I will, to him will I give the realm," none had disputed the right of the Moscovite Tsars to dispose of their throne. But Theodore had made no sign ; his Tsaritsa Irene, a capable woman whom many considered to be the lawful Regent, had, nine days after Theodore's death, retired into the Novodyevichy Monastery ; and the Patriarch, as the highest dignitary in the land, took over the administration provisionally. But who then was to be Tsar ? The chances were in favour of Godunov. His prosper-ous administration during the last thirteen years was the most convincing proof of his capacity for ruling ; the Patriarch was his friend ; and the whole official class were his creatures. On the other hand, he had powerful enemies among the Boyars, who hated him as an upstart.   When first his sister Irene and the Patriarch united to beg him to accept the crown, he refused it, with ostentatious humility and tears.   On being pressed, he declared that only the choice of the whole land, duly expressed

by its representatives, could induce him to accept "so sublime
an office." This, no doubt, was prudent, for, in the circumstances, only the free and deliberate choice of the whole land
could give him an adequate guarantee for the future security of
himself and his family. Accordingly, forty days after Theodore's
death, a national assembly, representing every class and district
in the Tsardom, was summoned to Moscow. The assembly,
consisting of 474 persons, met on February 17; and, on the
proposal of the Patriarch, Boris was unanimously elected Gosudar. The Boyars would have imposed some limitations upon him,
but they were overawed by an immense concourse of people
which, under violent official and clerical pressure, proceeded to
the Novodyevichy Monastery, where Boris occupied a modest
cell near his sister's, and implored him to accept the throne.
Twice he refused, with protests of unworthiness, flinging
himself down before the sacred ikons and wetting the ground
with his tears. But, when the Patriarch, obviously playing
a preconcerted part, finally threatened him with excommunication, Godunov piously "submitted to the divine will," and
(April 30) took up his residence in the Kreml. With the same
histrionic by-play, he postponed his coronation till he had
given an audience to a Tatar embassy in the plains before
Moscow. He went out to meet them escorted by 70,000 men,
whom he fed every day at his table; and the Tatars had to
traverse seven versts, lined on both sides by troops of all arms, till,
alarmed and humbled, they were admitted "to the presence."
Boris then made his state entry into Moscow with as much
pomp and circumstance as if he had conquered kingdoms. On
September 1, the Moscovite New Year's Day, he was solemnly
crowned Tsar of all Russia.

Boris Godunov had grown up in an unhealthy, enfeebling,
moral atmosphere. He had attained to his boyardom in the
second, evil, half of the reign of Ivan the Terrible, when constant
circumspection and absolute obsequiousness were the conditions
of existence at the Tsarish Court. Ivan's morbid suspicious-

ness naturally infected those of his servants who were pre-disposed to the same malady; and Godunov, for one, was never able to free himself from the pernicious influence of his early environment.   He was, certainly, a clever, far-seeing man. He was more fitted, perhaps, than any of his contemporaries to rule Moscovy.   None recognised her needs so well as he; and in this respect also he was Ivan's best pupil.   He was, besides, a well-meaning, good-natured man, anything but cruel; but he had none of that magnanimity, that elevation of character, which one naturally expects in the founder of a new dynasty, in the elect of a whole nation.   Instead of leaning, fearlessly and securely, on the people who had unanimously raised him to the throne, he saw in everyone around him an enemy to be conciliated or removed.   Hence his extravagant promises and his still more extravagant largesses.   He was, perhaps, the most craven monarch of old Moscovy, though that is saying a great deal; and the constant exhibition of his cowardice, by encouraging his enemies, did more than anything else to undermine what was, originally, a very strong position.

The state of foreign affairs on the accession of Boris was most favourable to Moscovy.   The very two Powers, Poland and Sweden, whose union under one King had lately seemed so menacing, were now at war with each other in consequence of that very union.   It was therefore possible for the Tsar's government in 1601 to obtain a renewal of the existing truce with Poland for 21 years.   Indeed, Livonia might now have been easily recovered, with the willing assistance of Sweden, but for the indecision of Boris, his fear of warfare, and his suspiciousness of all his generals.   Yet, like Ivan IV, he fully recognised the importance of Livonia, and thought of making it a vassal State under Prince Gustavus, the son of Eric XIV, whom he entertained for a time at his court, and would have married to his daughter Xenia but for Gustavus' refusal to abandon the Protestant faith.

The internal administration was tranquil and enlightened.

Boris took especial interest in the colonisation of Siberia, and saw to it that the aborigines were not over-taxed or otherwise oppressed. He also did something for the Russian peasants, by fixing the amount of labour, or its money equivalent, due by them to their masters, and by allowing peasants to flit from one small proprietor to another small proprietor, if maltreated, on St George's Day, in each year (Ukases of 1601 and 1602). He was also the first Tsar to send young Russians to the West to learn arts and languages, and he greatly encouraged the immigration of skilled artisans and learned men, especially doctors. He himself had no fewer than six foreign physicians, whom he treated like princes. The same excessive care for his personal safety induced him never to leave Moscow, if only for a day, without an escort of at least 18,000 musketeers. He kept more foreign mercenaries than any of his predecessors; and his bodyguard was composed entirely of Livonians. The great influx of foreigners, during his reign, was not without its influence on the social habits of the people; and it is now that we first hear of the clipping of beards and the adoption of western modes in clothes, to the lively scandal of the more orthodox.

At first Boris was extremely popular, but his unconquerable suspiciousness was constantly in his way. As the old chronicle quaintly says: "The devil put it into the heart of Tsar Boris to know everything that was going on in the realm of Moscovy." He was suspicious of every sound, of every movement. Hundreds of delators flocked to his court daily. Men of every degree of rank brought each other's evil report to him. Fathers accused their sons, husbands their wives, wives their husbands. The most eminent families were naturally the most defamed. None stood higher than the Romanovs; and the Romanovs were now accused of placing bags full of magical and poisonous herbs in the Tsar's wardrobe. This was sufficient to bring about the ruin and banishment of the whole family, whose principal member, Theodore Nikitevich Romanov, was forced to take the monkish hood under the name of

Philaret (June, 1601). The chief members of the next most eminent family, the Shuiskies, were forbidden to marry, lest the possession of progeny should awaken in them ambitious thoughts.

But this distrustfulness was not peculiar to Boris, it was the salient feature of Moscovite society at the beginning of the seventeenth century. Never had public morality in Moscovy sunk so low. The universal disregard of all social duties and obligations, the universal endeavour to suck the utmost advantage out of the weakness and distress of one's neighbours, did not tend to mutual confidence. Everywhere the welfare of the Commonwealth was subordinated to personal interests. Everywhere there were ominous symptoms of unrest among the anti-social elements of the population, not only among the Cossacks of the Steppe but among those moral Cossacks who, in every society, prefer to live at the expense of the prosperous and the industrious, and whose interest it is to encourage and prolong disorder. The terrible natural calamities of the years 1601–1603, by increasing the popular misery tenfold, fostered still further these anarchical tendencies. For three years running there was a total failure of the crops, with its inevitable consequences, plague, pestilence and famine. The starving people ate grass in summer and straw in winter like cattle. In the later stages of the visitation, parents ate their children, children their parents; and human flesh was exhibited for sale as "beef" in the market places. The Tsar did his duty nobly on this occasion. His mercy and benevolence abounded and overflowed. Corn was collected from all parts of Russia and sold at Moscow at half price; work was found for the myriads who flocked to the capital and were set to build new stone houses in place of the old wooden ones; every day he fed tens of thousands from his own table. But even these liberalities do not seem to have increased his popularity, while his personal enemies put them down to fear of a popular rising. Yet the enemies of Boris were even more craven than he. They wished to overthrow him without seeming to have a hand in it. What they looked for was a pretender strong enough to overthrow Boris, but insignificant enough to be cast aside at the right moment. Nor had they long to wait for such a pretender.

In the course of 1603, a Moscovite fugitive, calling himself the Tsarevich Demetrius Ivanovich, appeared at the Court of the Lithuanian magnate Prince Adam Wisniowiecki. His pretensions were taken for granted; he received royal honours wherever he went, and, finally, settled down at the comfortable mansion of Pan Yury Mniszek, Palatine of Sandomir, to whose eldest daughter Mariana, or Marina, he was speedily betrothed, on condition that he first accepted the Catholic faith. The much enamoured suitor at once complied with this request. His conversion was duly accomplished by the Franciscans; and the Pretender to the throne of Moscovy was received into the bosom of the Catholic Church by Cardinal Rangoni, the papal Nuncio at Cracow, and straightway adopted a Jesuit confessor. In the beginning of 1604 he came to Cracow to be presented to King Sigismund III. Outwardly he was not at all attractive. He was an awkward loutish fellow, with a round common face covered with warts, very red hair and small light blue eyes. Most of the Polish dignitaries looked askance at him. Zamoyski compared him with the low comic rascals in the plays of Plautus and Terence. The King adopted a middle course. Willing enough to use the Pretender as a means of disturbing Moscovy, yet uncertain what to make of him, Sigismund privately acknowledged him as the Tsarevich Demetrius, and allowed him a pension, but refused to support him publicly. Yury Mniszek, a man as low in character as he was high in rank, then took up the cause of his future son-in-law as a private speculation. He undertook to place the Pseudo-Demetrius on the throne of Moscovy in return for one million Polish gulden, the principalities of Smolensk and Severia for himself, and the provinces of Pskov and Great Novgorod for his daughter as her private appanages. A contract to this effect was duly signed by the Pretender, on May 25, 1604 ; and Mniszek began to make the necessary preparations for putting the "Tsarevich" in possession of his patrimony.

But who then was this Pseudo-Demetrius? Of the many conflicting theories concerning him we need only consider three: (1) he was set up by King Sigismund and the Polish Government; (2) he was the instrument of the Polish Jesuits, and (3) he was the tool of Tsar Boris's enemies in Moscovy. The strongest arguments against the first theory are Sigismund's genuine surprise and hesitation when the impostor first appeared, and his anxiety to get rid of him. Moreover, Sigismund had no particular interest in precipitating from the Moscovite throne so pacific and accommodating a Tsar as Boris. The second view is equally unsubstantial. In the first place, it was the Franciscans, not the Jesuits, who converted the Pseudo-Demetrius. In the second place, a pupil and tool of the Jesuits would certainly have issued from their hands with some knowledge of western culture, or, at least, with an excellent knowledge of Latin, whereas the Pretender scarce knew the rudiments of that language, and could not spell the simplest Latin words. It is quite true that the Jesuits subsequently adopted .him with enthusiasm, but it is equally true that they had never seen him before he suddenly plumped down among them as if from the sky. The third view, on the other hand, stands in no need of *a posteriori* hypotheses. We know that the first Pseudo-Demetrius was a Great-Russian, highly educated for his times, and speaking and writing his native language fluently and even eloquently. We know that the first person who pretended to recognise him as the Tsarevich was the fugitive Moscovite Petrovsky, a mortal enemy of Tsar Boris, and therefore interested in raising up rivals against him. We know that Boris himself, always uncommonly well informed, regarded the Pseudo-Demetrius as the tool of the malcontent Boyars. Further, all the Moscovite chroniclers, without exception, maintain that the first Pseudo-Demetrius was a certain person well known at Moscow; and it would be extremely difficult to shake their testimony. Comparing, then, all the existing accounts of the Pretender, and omitting obvious inaccuracies, we arrive at the following conclusion.

The first Pseudo-Demetrius was one Gregory Otrepev, the son of a small Russian squire, Bogdan Otrepev, who met an untimely death in a brawl in the German Settlement at Moscow. The young Gregory grew up, apparently, as a servitor in one or more of the great Boyar families of the capital. His patrons, struck by the lad's bright intelligence and frank fearlessness, seem to have conceived the idea of using him for their political purposes, and brought him up in the belief that he was the Tsarevich Demetrius. In no other way can we account for the extraordinary but indisputable fact that Otrepev always believed himself to be what he professed to be. The alternative hypothesis—that he deliberately made of his whole life a lie incarnate —presupposes him to have been a monster of iniquity, whereas, as a matter of fact, he was a man of so upright and noble a character that, if virtue were the best title to a throne, none so well deserved the throne of Moscovy as the first False-Demetrius. Anyhow, he does not seem to have concealed his aspirations, and was obliged to flee from Moscow to escape from the clutches of the ever-suspicious Boris. For the next few years he led a vagabond life, entered religion, frequented numerous monasteries, where he picked up some Polish and a very little Latin, and finally rejected his monkish habit when he thought that the time for his manifestation had come.

In October 1604 the Pseudo-Demetrius crossed the Moscovite border at the head of 1600 mercenaries and 2000 Don Cossack volunteers. On November 18, by which time his army had swollen to 16,000 men, he defeated the Moscovite host, 50,000 strong, at Novgorod Syeversk. By the beginning of December, he was recognised as Tsar for 600 versts eastwards of the Polish frontier. But now came bad news from

Poland. The *Sejm* protested vehemently against the whole expedition, and recalled Mniszek; and Otrepev was left alone with
his Cossacks. Nevertheless, at Dobruinchui, January 21, 1605,
he gallantly attacked the enormous Moscovite army, which had
been steadily reinforced since the battle of Novgorod Syeversk,
but was badly beaten and shut himself up in Putivl the capital
of Severia. But the Tsar's troops did not follow up their
advantage; and when, after extravagantly rewarding their
modest success, Boris ventured to protest against their cowardly
inaction, they threatened to go over to the Pretender. Boris,
too cowardly to trust himself in his own camp, sent a German
to Putivl to remove the Pseudo-Demetrius by poison; but the
emissary revealed the plot, and immediately afterwards, the
news reached Putivl of the sudden death of Boris himself. On
April 13, as he was rising from table, blood gushed from his
mouth, nose and ears, and he died two hours afterwards in
great agony. His son Theodore, a promising youth whom his
contemporaries describe as "wiser than many grey beards, inasmuch as he was well versed in philosophy and in all bookish
arts[1]," was thereupon proclaimed Tsar, under the title of
Theodore II; and a strongly worded proclamation was issued
denouncing the Pseudo-Demetrius as an impostor.

The reign of Theodore II lasted seven weeks. The generals
appointed by the new government, regarding the cause of the
Godunovs as hopeless, persuaded the army to revolt. The
chief Boyars followed their example. When, on May 19, they
did homage to the Pseudo-Demetrius in his camp at Orel, they
at once recognised him as the monk Otrepev; but it was too late
to go back now. On June 1 the Pretender's envoys, Vasily
Golitsuin and Vasily Shuisky, arrived at Moscow, and announced
to the people, assembled in the Red Square, that Demetrius
Ivanovich had miraculously escaped from his murderers at
Uglich and was already at the gates of Moscow. The people,
agitated but unconvinced, thereupon asked Vasily Shuisky,

---

[1] He was the author of the first map of Russia.

who had actually seen the real Demetrius buried and had solemnly testified to the fact more than once, whether these later tidings were true. Shuisky declared that the real Demetrius had escaped from Uglich, and that the son of a priest had been buried in his stead. The mob, egged on by the envoys, then hastened to the Kreml, the gates of which had, treacherously, been left open. The young Tsar, who stoutly resisted, was literally torn to pieces. His chief supporter, the Patriarch Job, was deposed, and shut up in a monastery.

The Pretender, who was not responsible for these outrages, made his triumphal entry into Moscow on June 20, 1605. The very same day, the perjured Shuisky secretly circulated among the people a rumour that he was an impostor after all. Shuisky's villainy was detected and reported to the new Tsar ; and, after a fair trial before the Council, the treacherous Boyar was condemned to death but reprieved on the very scaffold. On June 24 the Pseudo-Demetrius was officially proclaimed Tsar by the new Patriarch Ignatius. On July 30 he was solemnly crowned. The Tsaritsa Martha, the mother of the real Demetrius, brought to Moscow for the purpose, had already identified him as her son. This she did from fear, for the Pseudo-Demetrius had at once and completely won the hearts of the Russian people. All his measures were liberal, humane and conciliatory. The Nagai, the real Demetrius's kinsfolk, were reinstated at Court. Philaret Romanov was released from prison and made metropolitan of Rostov. The plebeian clerks of the Council, the Shchelkalovs, Godunov's ablest ministers, were retained and, to the general astonishment, ennobled—an unprecedented promotion. The diligence of the new Tsar was exemplary. He presided over the Council every day, and, after listening for hours, with an indulgent smile, to the interminable and unprofitable debates of the Boyars, would, in a few moments, unravel and elucidate the most complicated questions. Sometimes he gently reproached the Boyars with their ignorance. "I must send you abroad to learn things," he would say. He attended to all petitions personally. When his friends the Poles warned him to beware of suspicious characters, he replied: "There are two ways of ruling subjects, by tormenting or by encouraging them: I prefer the latter way." It is true that his retention of Godunov's Livonian bodyguard, his pronounced partiality for foreigners, his dislike of strict etiquette, and his rejection of all unnecessary pomps, produced some murmuring among the upper classes. But the common people excused such eccentricities on the score of youth. Even his public profession of Catholicism did not materially detract from his popularity, though here he obviously stood on very dangerous ground.

Perhaps nothing demonstrates so clearly the intellectual superiority of the first False-Demetrius as his wide religious outlook. Partly from personal motives, partly from calculation, he had accepted the Roman Faith; but of his attachment to Orthodoxy there can be no doubt. It is clear, from all his actions, that he regarded Catholicism and Orthodoxy as very much the same thing; and he seriously believed that the surest way out of his difficulties was to bring about a reunion of the Churches. He frequently expressed his belief in the possibility of another General Council; and, when asked by one of the Boyars whether he intended to build a church for his Polish friends in Moscow, he at once replied: "Why not? Are they not Christians too, and have they not rendered me loyal service?" The Papal Court had great hopes of him. In response to the letter of congratulation which he sent to Paul V on his election, the Pope declared that Demetrius had been fore-ordained to convert to the true faith the great Russian nation, hitherto lying in darkness and the shadow of death, and knowing his desire for the imperial title addressed him as: "*Serenissimus et invictissimus monarcha, Cesar ac Magnus Dux totius Russiae, etc.*" It was the Pope, too, who, at the urgent solicitation of Demetrius, commanded Yury Mniszek and Marina to proceed to Moscow without further delay. When, however,

Demetrius begged that his bride-elect might be permitted to conform outwardly to the Orthodox religion, the Holy Father was inexorable. The Mniszscy arrived at Moscow on May 2, 1606. On May 8, Marina was espoused to Demetrius and crowned Empress, with great pomp and ceremony, according to the old Russian custom. Ten days later, Demetrius was no more. At the very time when, full of enthusiasm, he was preparing to participate, on a grand scale, in a general league against the Turks, Vasily Shuisky, whose life he had so generously spared a few months before, was intriguing to overthrow him. The conspiracy, with the connivance of Sigismund III, who was irritated by the spirited refusal of Demetrius to purchase the help of Poland by large cessions of Moscovite territory, had begun long before the wedding; and the arrival at Moscow of the Novgorod[1] and Pskov divisions of the army, on its way to the Crimea, encouraged the conspirators to take the decisive step. Demetrius by his utter unsuspiciousness played into their hands. Well aware of the devotion of the *stryeltsui* and of the great majority of the population of Moscow, to say nothing of the Poles and Livonians, he disregarded repeated warnings, and took no extra precautions.

At midnight on May 18, Shuisky assembled his partisans in the Red Square. He solemnly assured them that the Tsar was an impostor, and in league with Poland to enslave their country and destroy their holy orthodox faith. Then, at the preconcerted signal, the pealing of the bell of St Elias, they burst into the Kreml, overwhelmed the thirty halbardiers on guard, and brutally murdered the Tsar (who might have escaped but for his solicitude for his wife[2]) flinging the battered, mutilated, corpse into the Red Square. The remainder of the night was passed in attacking the Poles in Moscow who, taken

---

[1] Great Novgorod had for generations been devoted to the Shuisky family.

[2] Marina, a thin little woman, escaped by hiding under the robes of her burly Hofmeisterinn.

unawares, were massacred to the number of 2000. At 6 o'clock
the following morning (May 19, 1606) Shuisky was proclaimed
and, on June 6, crowned Tsar, under the title of Vasily V.

The new Tsar was neither the elect of the nation, like
Godunov, nor even the elect of the capital, as Otrepev had
been. He was but the puppet of a mob of conspirators
hastily assembled in the Red Square at Moscow. In the
provinces he was unknown. It was in vain that he issued
manifestoes proclaiming that Demetrius was an impostor who
had seized the throne by devilish arts; the provincials were
only perplexed by what they heard. What were they to make
of the latest news from Moscow? The late Tsar had been
solemnly declared to be the true Demetrius, and now he was
described as an impostor. Which report was true? And was
Demetrius really dead? Was there, indeed, a new Tsar? and
if so, whence had he sprung and who had chosen him? The
whole affair was so mysterious that the provincials became
incredulous and, still worse, began to lose their old belief and
confidence in Moscow. "And so," as the contemporary
lyetopis puts it, "the whole realm became dark with the
darkness of the Father of lies." Vasily's peculiar vices tended
to increase the general confusion. He was a near-sighted,
nervous, little old man, very shrewd and very stingy, a firm
believer in magic, averse from action and with his ears ever
open to spies and delators. As if his authority was not already
sufficiently limited by his character, he proceeded to limit it
still further by swearing to punish nobody without the consent
of his Council. At the same time he foolishly alienated his
own partisans by withholding from them the promised rewards for their services, although they knew him to be very
wealthy.

In these circumstances, a fresh crop of pretenders was only
a matter of time. As early as May 17, Michael Molchanov,
one of the murderers of Theodore II, had suddenly appeared
on the Lithuanian frontier and proclaimed himself to be

Demetrius, who, he said, had escaped from his murderers.
His statement was confirmed by Gregory Shakovsky, Vasily's
own *voevoda*, who had left Moscow with the great seal in his
pocket; and all Severia declared at once in favour of this second
False-Demetrius.   Shuisky countered the blow by ordering the
remains of the real Demetrius to be exhumed at Uglich and
reinterred in the Archangel Cathedral at Moscow.   But by
this time the insurrection had spread throughout the southern
provinces.   Even the sudden disappearance of the second
Pseudo-Demetrius made no difference.   A Cossack claiming
to be Peter, a purely imaginary son of Theodore I, was set up
by Shakovsky; and the Pseudo-Peter's ablest general, an enterprising ex-galley slave named Bolotnikov, gained several
victories over the Tsarish troops and advanced against Moscow.
As, however, he proclaimed, and practised *en route*, a war of
extermination against the upper classes, the Boyars of Moscow,
despite their contempt for Shuisky, resolved to put up with
him as the lesser of two evils.   Shuisky's one trustworthy
general, his own cousin, Prince Michael Skopin-Shuisky, was
accordingly sent against Bolotnikov, whom he defeated
(December 2, 1606), and drove back to Kaluga.   In the
beginning of 1607, after an unsuccessful attempt to poison
Bolotnikov, Shuisky was forced to take the field against him
with 100,000 men.   He defeated the rebels on the banks of the
Vosina, and shut them up in Tula, which surrendered a few
weeks later, when both the Pseudo-Peter and Bolotnikov were
hanged.

No sooner, however, had Shuisky returned to Moscow than
a still more formidable rebellion broke out against him, headed
by a third Pseudo-Demetrius, a man of infamous character, but
some ability, whose real name seems to have been Gabriel
Verevkin.   From the fact that he could read and write, and
was learned in the Scriptures, he was, most probably, an
unfrocked priest, or monk.   He first appeared at Starodub,
and was quickly joined by 18,000 Polish adventurers, the

remains of Zebrzydowski's dissipated *Rokosz*[1], 28,000 Cossacks eager for pillage, and the scum of the population generally. After defeating the Tsar's army at Bolkhov (May 10 and 11, 1606), he established himself, permanently, in a vast entrenched camp at Tushino, near Moscow, whence he derived the epithet by which he is generally known—"the Thief of Tushino." The Mniszek family were the most zealous supporters in Poland of the new Pretender; and the widowed Marina was induced to recognise him as her husband and live with him at Tushino[2], taking the precaution, however, of being remarried by her Jesuit confessor. Pskov also declared for the new Pretender; and Sapieha, the commander of his Polish allies, proceeded to besiege, happily in vain, the great Troitsa monastery, the most venerated sanctuary and the strongest fortress in Moscovy, which commanded the communications between the capital and the north-eastern provinces.

By this time we have reached the darkest hour of that terrible period which Russian historians aptly call "the anarchy," when the Moscovite State actually passed through the initial stages of disintegration. The Tsardom had ceased to exist. Shuisky at Moscow and "the thief" at Tushino were the merest figure-heads. The former, helplessly shut up in the Kreml with some hundreds of Boyars who openly flaunted him, the latter trembling daily for his life amidst desperadoes who called him an impostor to his face and murdered each other with impunity before his very eyes, helplessly followed the course of events they were powerless to control. The real struggle was between the orderly and the disorderly elements of a society left to itself; between the predatory, vagabond, Cossack element and the landed and trading people who still had something to live and work for. The geographical area of the predatory class was, roughly speaking, the western and southern

[1] *See* Chapter VIII.

[2] Her father had been bribed by the promise of 3,000,000 rubles and the province of Severia, on the success of the enterprise.

Steppe lands, that of the industrious and propertied class the
north and north-eastern forest land, where the larger and older
cities predominated.   But now the Steppe was invading what
remained of civilisation and threatening to submerge it.   In
every direction the Cossacks and their Polish allies levied
blackmail and spread devastation.   Yet, by general consent,
the foreigner was not the worst enemy.   The love of looting or
of adventure had brought the Poles into Moscovy.   Money
and women were what they chiefly looked for.   They had no
particular animosity against the Moscovites.   They were
merciful to their captives ; exacted moderate ransoms ; and
regarded with wonder and horror the unspeakable cruelties
inflicted by their Cossack allies on men of their own language
and religion.   The Cossacks, on the other hand, seemed to
regard all non-Cossacks with a furious hatred which was satisfied with nothing short of their extermination.   It was they
who kindled the torch of conflagration.   It was they who
desecrated the Churches, destroyed, or rendered uninhabitable,
every human dwelling, and trampled beneath their horses' feet
all the corn they could not carry away with them.   It was due
to them that half Moscovy was already a wilderness, in the
deserted villages of which bears, foxes, wolves and hares roamed
fearlessly, while men, women, and children sought a precarious
refuge in the natural haunts of the wild beast, the forest and
the swamp.

Presently, to these horrors was superadded the scourge of
two foreign invasions ; for both Sweden and Poland now
intervened forcibly in the affairs of Moscovy.   The Swedes
were brought in by Shuisky who, in February 1609, through
his cousin Michael Skopin-Shuisky, concluded an alliance
with them at Great Novgorod by the terms of which he ceded
Karelia and renounced his claims to Livonia, in return for the
paid services of 5000 troopers under Pontus de la Gardie,
cooperating with Skopin's Russian contingent.   The Swedes
and Moscovites combined even obtained some victories over

the Poles and Cossacks of "the Tushino thief." Sigismund III naturally could not regard with indifference the intrusion of Sweden in Moscovite affairs; but the *Sejm* limited his operations to the recapturing of the great fortress of Smolensk, the key of the Dnieperian district. Not the royal house but Poland only was to benefit by the war. It is, indeed, very doubtful whether Sigismund ever seriously entertained the subsequent project, emanating from Moscow, of placing his son, the Krolewicz[1] Wladislaus, on the Moscovite throne. In the circumstances, such a project was unrealisable because the conflicting interests of Moscovy and Poland were absolutely irreconcilable. At the very least the Poles would have insisted, beforehand, on large cessions of Moscovite territory, to which the Moscovites would never have consented. Had Wladislaus, as Tsar, insisted on such cessions, he would doubtless have shared the fate of the first Demetrius. On the other hand, had Sigismund pressed the candidature of his son to the throne of Moscovy when circumstances seemed to favour him most, the Poles would, most certainly, have considered their particular interests neglected, and have excluded Wladislaus from the succession to the Polish throne.

On September 21, 1609, Sigismund appeared before Smolensk with 17,000 Poles and 10,000 Cossacks. In his manifesto he declared that he had come not to shed blood but to pacify Moscovy. At the same time he wrote to Shuisky, reproaching him with the massacre of the Poles at Moscow and the conclusion of an alliance with his mortal foe "the Duke of Sudermania." He also summoned all the Poles at Tushino to join him before Smolensk. The ultimate effect of this summons was the break-up of the camp at Tushino (March 10, 1610). Most of the Poles joined Sigismund, most of the Boyars Shuisky, while the Cossacks followed "the Thief" to Kaluga. The Polish Grand Hetman Zolkiewski now appeared on the scene and routed Shuisky's last army, 46,000 strong, at

[1] The Crown Prince of Poland.

Klushino (June 23–24, 1610), the immediate consequence of which disaster was Shuisky's deposition (July 17). The majority of the Council of Boyars, which ruled Moscow provisionally, preferred Wladislaus to "the Thief" as a candidate for the throne. "We will not be ruled by our own slaves," they said. At the invitation of this party, Zolkiewski marched to Moscow, while "the Thief" approached the capital from the opposite direction. The frank and genial humour of the Grand Hetman soon endeared him greatly to the Boyars, and, on August 27, he actually persuaded them to render homage to him as the representative of the Krolewicz. Even when they insisted on the candidate's previous acceptation of orthodoxy, he induced them to submit that and every other point of dispute to the King at Smolensk. But the other principal towns of northern Russia, including Suzdal, Rostov, Vladimir, Yurev, alarmed for the future of orthodoxy, now began to open negotiations with the Pseudo-Demetrius, preferring even an orthodox impostor to a heretical Krolewicz.

From the moment, indeed, of the proclamation of Wladislaus as Tsar, the national movement in Moscovy assumed a religious character which was to traverse all the calculations of the politicians. Sigismund himself involuntarily gave impetus to this new movement. He sent word to Zolkiewski that the election of Wladislaus, on the Moscovite conditions, was impossible, for he meant to keep Moscovy for himself; and he ordered the Grand Hetman to explain his latest views to the Boyars. Zolkiewski did not even attempt to carry out these impossible instructions, the first effect of which would have been the destruction of himself and his little army. But he extricated himself from his extremely difficult position with consummate ability. First he persuaded the Boyars to send to Smolensk a grand deputation of 1246 distinguished persons, including Prince Golitsuin, one of the aspirants to the throne, and Philaret Romanov, Metropolitan of Rostov; thereby getting rid of formidable opponents and at the same time placing valuable hostages in Sigismund's hands.   Next, working on the Boyars' fears of "the Thief's" Cossack host, he induced them to admit the Poles into the Kreml, thus giving them the command of the capital (Sept. 20–21).   But by this time his popularity was so great that the Moscovites were ready to do anything for him ; and, when he made a demonstration against the Cossack army, the premier Boyar of Moscovy, Prince Mstislavsky, with 10,000 Russians, actually followed the standard of the Polish Grand Hetman.   When, shortly afterwards, he quitted Moscow, he took with him, as captives to swell his triumph, the ex-Tsar Vasily Shuisky and his brothers Demetrius and Ivan.   His ablest lieutenant Gonsiewski, with a few thousand Poles, was left in charge of the Kreml.

Meanwhile the grand deputation from Moscow was, on October 10, received in audience by Sigismund outside Smolensk.   The Moscovites were willing enough to accept Wladislaus as their Tsar, but only on condition that he accepted and protected orthodoxy, excluded Catholicism from Moscovy, and came with a gift in his hand in the shape of all the Moscovite territory conquered by Sweden and Poland. Such terms it was impossible for Sigismund to accept without running the risk of losing his own crown.   After months of futile wrangling, the members of the grand deputation were sent as hostages to Lithuania (April 12, 1611) ; and Sigismund seriously took in hand the siege of Smolensk.   On June 3, 1611, a breach was made in the wall, and the fortress was taken by assault, after the garrison had been reduced from 80,000 to 8000. Smolensk, Sigismund's real object, was thus secured ; but the assassination of "the Thief of Tushino" (Dec. 11, 1610), by a vindictive Tatar, led to fresh complications.   The Cossacks, under one Zarucki, adopted "the Thief's" baby son Ivan, born shortly after his death, as their Tsarevich ; and, in conjunction with an independent patriotic army under Lyapunov, a gentleman of Ryazan, moved towards Moscow to drive out the Poles. After a long and bitter struggle (March—May, 1611), in the course of which three quarters of Moscow were burnt, the Poles abandoned the city and retired within the Kreml; but, shortly afterwards, the Cossacks murdered Lyapunov, whereupon the better people separated from the Cossacks and began to act for themselves. The initiative came, in October 1611, from the Troitsa monastery, whence the saintly and heroic archimandrite Dionysius sent circular letters to all the chief towns of the Tsardom, exhorting them, as Orthodox Christians, to be mindful of the true Orthodox Christian faith, and stand firmly together, "against the eternal enemies of Christianity, the Poles and the Lithuanians." " For God's sake," concluded this appeal, "lay aside all your dissensions for a time, and strive, all together, to save the Christian faith. Be merciful brethren, and come and help us with money and fighting men!"

The letters from Troitsa could not but produce an effect. The wretchedness of the last five years had taught all men of good will the necessity of self-sacrifice. The failure of the politicians, the worthlessness of the pretenders, the mischievousness of foreign assistance, turned the thoughts of the serious and the patriotic away from temporal, external protection; and, in the depths of their own hearts, they found that religious inspiration which, in the last resort, is alone capable of saving a sinking nation. From the first, this new movement was not so much political, or even national, as religious. " We are brethren and kinsmen because we have been baptised into the same holy faith"—such was the basis of the league of towns and monasteries which now began to collect money and soldiers for the defence of the faith. Nizhny Novgorod was the first town to respond to the appeal of Dionysius. Here the lead was taken by one of the Starostas, Kuzma Minin, a master butcher by trade. He publicly declared that the time had come to sacrifice everything "for the true orthodox faith," and he set the example by devoting one third of his property to the holy cause. He and 2500 of his friends and colleagues speedily collected 17,000 rubles; and a rich widow of the town surrendered 10,000 rubles out of the 12,000 left her by her husband. But where were they to look for a leader? Minin pronounced in favour of Prince Dmitry Mikhailovich Pozharsky, who was recovering at Suzdal from the wounds he had received at the siege of Moscow. Pozharsky fearlessly accepted the perilous honour and was received with enthusiasm at Nizhny.

Both he and Minin, whom he appointed treasurer, insisted on the absolute obedience of their followers. Pozharsky's first official act was to send out a circular to the other towns inviting their cooperation to drive out the foreigner. He refused to recognise either Wladislaus, or Marina's son Ivan, or a fourth Pseudo-Demetrius who had just appeared at Pskov. Thus his manifesto was directed as much against the Cossacks as against the Poles, and appealed from a portion of the nation to the nation at large. Kazan, out of jealousy of Nizhny, held aloof from the movement; but representatives from most of the other free towns kept pouring in, bringing with them both money and soldiers. But the prevalent confusion could not be overcome in a moment. At the beginning of 1612 there were still three parties in Moscovy, Pozharsky's, the Wladislan Boyars in the Kreml, and the Cossacks under Zarucki who played for his own hand. In March, the Cossack host again advanced upon Moscow, while Pozharsky and Minin wrested Kostroma from the Wladislans, garrisoned Suzdal and fixed their temporary capital at Yaroslavl. The Patriarch Hermogen was starved to death by the philo-Poles at Moscow for blessing the bands of Pozharsky instead of cursing them; but his martyrdom strengthened the national cause. While still too weak to advance on Moscow, Pozharsky skilfully prevented the Swedes, who had now occupied Great Novgorod, from extending their area of conquest by negotiating with them, ostensibly with the view of setting Gustavus Adolphus's younger brother Charles Philip on the Moscovite throne (May—July, 1612). An attempt by the Cossacks to murder Pozharsky (July) determined him to proceed against the Cossack army, now encamped before Moscow, as public enemies. Simultaneously, the famous Lithuanian Grand Hetman, Chodkiewicz, had safely piloted a lilliputian army of 2000 men, through hundreds of miles of wilderness, for the purpose of relieving the Polish garrison at the Kreml, and was now almost within striking distance. On August 18, Pozharsky reached the river Janza, near Moscow, which alone separated him from the Cossack host. On the 21st Chodkiewicz also appeared. On the 22nd, he crossed the river and attacked Pozharsky, the Cossack host looking on without rendering their countrymen the slightest assistance. The Grand Hetman was finally re-pulsed, and all his subsequent determined efforts to reprovision the garrison (which by this time was reduced to feeding on human flesh, kept salted in barrels) were also frustrated. In mid-October, Pozharsky and Minin, with part of the Cossack army as well as their own, made a night attack on Chodkiewicz's camp. It was repulsed. But the Grand Hetman lost 500 men, one fourth of his effective strength, in the struggle, and early next morning he was in full retreat towards Mozhaisk. On October 22 the Polish garrison capitulated, and on November 22, Pozharsky and Minin made their triumphal entry into the capital.

When the news reached Warsaw that things were going amiss in Moscovy, every one hastened to lay the blame upon the King, freely accusing him of carelessness, sluggishness and general incompetence. The Pans insisted that he should at once proceed to Moscow to set matters right, but nobody took the trouble to inform him where he was to find the means for raising an army for the purpose. Nevertheless, Sigismund, after incredible efforts and pledging his personal credit, man-aged to get together 3000 German mercenaries and with this little band set out to reconquer Moscovy. Then, for sheer shame, some 1200 of the *Szlachta* took horse and galloped after him, overtaking him at Vyazma, where the retreating Chodkiewicz also joined him. The combined forces, which did not amount to a single modern army corps, then marched on Moscow; but the city refused to listen to Sigismund, and he returned empty-handed to Poland. Not a single Moscovite fort had opened its gates to him; not a single Moscovite had joined him.

On hearing of the retreat of Sigismund, the Council of Boyars at Moscow sent out circulars summoning representatives of every class of the population to come to the capital to elect a native Gosudar. When sufficient deputies had arrived, a three days' fast was proclaimed. Every one agreed that a prince of a foreign house was undesirable, while the Polish and Swedish candidates were expressly excluded as robbers and truce-breakers. Discord and confusion only began when the names of the native candidates were brought forward. Various factions were formed, but none of them was strong enough to prevail against the others. At last, says the contemporary chronicle, a certain nobleman from Halich laid before the assembly a mandate to the effect that, as Michael Thedorovich Romanov was nearest by kinship to the ancient dynasty, he should be chosen Tsar. A Cossack Hetman thereupon produced another, independent, mandate of the same purport. This decided the matter, and Michael was thereupon elected Tsar (Feb. 21, 1613). Then the senior prelate Theodoret, Archbishop of Riazan, the *Kelar*, or lay administrator, of the Troitsa Monastery, Avram Palitsuin, and the Boyar Vasily Morozov, proceeded to the Red Square and enquired of the people thronging it whom *they* wished to be their Tsar? " Michael Thedorovich Romanov ! " was the unanimous and enthusiastic reply.

CHAPTER X.

THE FIRST ROMANOVS AND WLADISLAUS IV, 1613—1648.

THE possibility of such an election as that of Michael Romanov was an even more remarkable and encouraging fact than the election itself. It was the symptom of awakening public spirit, the presage of a better order of things. The Moscovites had risen superior to all personal and local considerations, and, after purging the capital of foreign foes, had placed themselves, unreservedly, under an autocracy, as being the best conceivable government for themselves in the circumstances. Their choice, at such a time, of an inexperienced youth of sixteen demonstrated that it was not so much the person of the monarch as the principle of monarchy for which they voted. It is not too much to say that the Renaissance of Russia dates from the quinquennium (1613—1618) during which the great men of the realm devoted themselves to the patriotic duty of guiding the footsteps of their young Gosudar, and rallying all the recuperative elements of the nation around the newly established throne.

And now, having elected a Tsar, the next thing was to find him. Not till March 24, did the delegates of the Council discover the young Prince in the Spasovsky Monastery, near Kostroma, under the guardianship of his mother Martha Romanovna. At first, neither mother nor son would accept the gift of the Moscovite throne. Martha protested that her

son was too young and tender for so difficult an office. From
the third to the ninth hour, the Boyars entreated Michael to
accept the throne; and he only yielded, at the last moment,
when they solemnly declared that, if he persisted in his refusal,
they would hold him responsible to God for the utter destruction
of Moscovy.

Michael may well be pardoned for his hesitation. Rarely
has any European country been in such desperate straits as
Russia was in 1613. The Swedes occupied all her Baltic
provinces, as well as Great Novgorod, her commercial
metropolis. The Poles held Smolensk, which commanded
her western provinces. In the extreme south-east the Cossack
Zarucki was carving out a kingdom of his own on the Volga.
Savage hordes of Tatars swarmed in every direction. Throughout the whole northern district of Archangel and Cholmogory
all the churches had been profaned, all the cattle killed, all
the villages burnt. Travellers entering Moscovy from the
West had tales of equal terror to tell. They found every
village between Reval and Novgorod destroyed; and, before
they could shelter from the extreme cold in the ruined way-side
huts, they had to empty them of corpses, often the terrible
stench drove them back to the snow-drifts. But Tsar Michael
had no need to be told of the misery of his people; he could
see it with his own eyes. Every day, on his journey from
Kostroma to Moscow, he encountered hundreds of people of
all classes robbed to the skin, bleeding, blinded, maimed, covered
with bruises and sores. On reaching the Troitsa Monastery,
some 75 versts from the capital, he refused to go any further till
something had been done to stay this effusion of blood. Yet,
in truth, it was not so much horror as penury which detained
him. The Boyars could not provide suitable quarters for him
at the Kreml, because the palaces there were without roofs or
windows, and there was no money in the treasury to pay
carpenters for repairing them. In his extremity, Michael was
compelled to beg the wealthy Stroganovs to supply him with

money, corn, fish, salt, cloth, and all manner of wares, to pay, feed, and clothe his soldiers.   At last (May 13), the Tsar was brought into Moscow by the entire male population, which had gone forth to meet him; and, on July 22, he was solemnly crowned, on which occasion the valiant master-butcher, Kuzma Minin, was ennobled.

The first care of Michael and his council was to clear the land of robbers.   The means for doing this were obtained by a general contribution in money and kind, collected with the utmost difficulty by agents accompanied by soldiers, and additionally fortified by the authority of the Church, which threatened the backward and the disobedient with excommunication.   The most dangerous and audacious of these native ruffians, the Cossack Zarucki, Pseudo-Demetrius V, who had set up a court of misrule at Astrakhan, was defeated and taken prisoner on June 27, 1614, and impaled at Moscow.   Three weeks later, a large Cossack host was routed and scattered on the banks of the Luzha, near Moscow.   After this, the robber-bands, though they continued, for some years, to pillage the central and south-eastern provinces of Moscovy, ceased to be a peril to the State.

The aliens had next to be got rid of, and it was determined to treat with the Swedes first.   So hopeless did the prospects of Moscovy seem in 1611, that Great Novgorod was willing to recognise Charles Philip, the younger brother of Gustavus Adolphus, as the Grand-Duke of a separate Russian State extending from the Baltic to the White Sea, and united with Sweden as Lithuania was with Poland.   The election of Michael Romanov dispelled this dream of a Scandinavian empire.   In June, 1613, Alexis Zyuzin was sent to England to obtain the mediation of James I, who sent John Merrick to Moscovy for the purpose.   The negotiations lasted, with frequent interruptions and perambulations, from January 14, 1616, to March 10, 1617, when a definitive treaty was signed at the now extinct town of Stolbovo, to the satisfaction of both parties. At Moscow, "the surrender of a few places" even though they included Nöteborg, the key of Finland, and three other fortresses in Ingria, was regarded as a trifling matter compared with the retrocession of Great Novgorod and the recognition of Michael as Tsar of Moscovy.

Meanwhile, Moscovy was at open war with Poland. Negotiations opened in September, 1615, under the mediation of the imperial ambassador, Gandelius, had been broken off in January, 1616, amidst fierce recriminations; the Moscovites refusing to accept the Krolewicz Wladislaus as Tsar, and the Poles as obstinately declining to recognise Michael Romanov. In April, 1617, the Polish Diet voted supplies for one year only; and the Krolewicz, with Chodkiewicz as his mentor, set forth "to conquer and incorporate Moscovy." Terror fell upon central Russia at his approach. Dorogobuzh opened its gates to him in September; and in October he made his triumphal entry into Vyazma. Moscow was placed in a state of defence. The national hero, Prince Demetrius Pozharsky, was sent against the Krolewicz. After wintering at Vyazma, Wladislaus, contrary to the advice of Chodkiewicz, advanced against Moscow; but his progress was retarded by the mutiny of his unpaid troops, the *Sejm*, with its usual fatal parsimony, having sent reinforcements without the still more necessary money and supplies. Nevertheless, despite all the efforts of Pozharsky to prevent it, Wladislaus effected his junction, at the Oka, with the hetman Sahajdaczny, who had hurried to his help with 20,000 registered Cossacks; and, on October 18, he made a night assault on Moscow which was repulsed with heavy loss to the Poles. Dread of the approaching winter, and the miserable condition of his half-clothed, half-starved and more than half-mutinous army, then compelled Wladislaus to open negotiations with the Moscovites, at the village of Deulino, 3 versts from the Troitsa Monastery; and, after two months of wrangling, a truce of $14\frac{1}{2}$ years was concluded, each party surrendering too much to consent to a definitive peace. The

Poles provisionally recognised Michael as Tsar, while Michael
surrendered to the Republic a large tract of his central province
extending from Byelaya in the north to Chernigov in the south,
both inclusive, with the fortresses and towns of Smolensk,
Storodub and Novgorod-Syeversk, thus bringing the Polish
frontier appreciably nearer to Moscow.

The most important result of the truce of Deulino, as
regards Moscovy, was the return from his nine years' exile in
Poland, of the Tsar's father, Philaret Romanov, Metropolitan
of Rostov. The tidings of his son's election was, at first, by
no means welcome to him; but, on returning to Moscow, he
both gratified his own ambition and served his country by
reigning conjointly with Michael. Ten days after his arrival
(July 9), he was enthroned as Patriarch by Theophanes,
Patriarch of Jerusalem, and the prelates of the Russian Church;
and henceforth, till his death, in 1633, the established government of Moscovy was a diarchy. In private letters, indeed,
Philaret invariably addressed his son as "your majesty"; and
the name of Michael preceded that of his father in all public
documents. But they both bore the sovereign title of Gosudar;
foreign ambassadors presented their credentials to Tsar and
Patriarch simultaneously; and Philaret frequently transacted
important affairs of State without even consulting Michael.

Naturally, the domination of the experienced and energetic
Patriarch was deeply resented by the clique of courtiers who
had hitherto been nearest to the young Tsar. But all who
hated anarchy and loved good government welcomed the
advent to power of an enlightened statesman who protected
the weak against the tyranny of the strong and was gracious to
all men of learning and ability, irrespective of birth or rank.

The first care of the Patriarch was to secure the succession
by getting the Tsar married. Philaret was bent upon raising
the dignity of the new dynasty by securing a consort for his
son from some sovereign house; and embassies were sent to
Copenhagen and Stockholm for the purpose. But Christian IV

of Denmark refused even to receive the Moscovite envoy; while Gustavus Adolphus, on hearing that his sister-in-law, Catherine of Brandenburg, the lady selected by Philaret, would first have to be re-baptised into the Orthodox Church, declared, with a bigotry not inferior to Philaret's, that the Princess should not sacrifice her soul's salvation even for the Tsardom of Moscovy.   Finally the Tsar gave his hand to Eudoxia Stryeshnevaya, the daughter of a small squire, who thus became the matriarch of the imperial Romanovs.

Philaret's administration must be judged rather by its intentions than its results.   The dilapidation of the land was too great, its resources were too inadequate, to admit of anything more than an attempt to lay the foundations of a better order of things; and this, Philaret conscientiously endeavoured to do.   The tyranny and peculation of the tax-collectors were partially restrained by the compilation of new land registries and the appointment of tax-assessors from among the taxpayers.   A perambulatory commission was also appointed by Philaret to enquire into the condition of the various districts, to remit taxation whenever necessary, but, at the same time, to use every effort to bring the fugitive serfs back to their original dwelling-places.   Hitherto the rights of the oppressed peasantry had to some extent been safe-guarded by Boris Godunov's ukases, which limited the time within which they might be recovered by their former owners.   But now, yielding to the earnest solicitation of the gentry, the Government authorised them to recover their fugitive peasants without fixing any time-limit.   On the other hand, the taxation of those of the *sluzhnuie lyudi*, or military tenants, who chose to settle in the towns, was the first step towards the proportional taxation of the hitherto privileged classes.

In other respects the administration of Philaret was obviously progressive.   He encouraged the publication of theological works, formed the nucleus of the subsequently famous patriarchal library, and instituted a special department for the revision of liturgical books. He also commanded that every archbishop should establish a seminary in his palace, and he himself founded a Greco-Latin institute in the Chudov monastery. He also encouraged learned Greeks to settle in Moscow to instruct the orthodox clergy.

Another great service rendered by Philaret to his country was the re-organisation of the army with the help of foreign officers. The Moscovite gentry had lost whatever of martial instincts it may once have possessed, while still remaining the military caste of Moscovy. The gentry had come to regard their settled peaceful life on their properties as their normal state of existence, and the occasional summons to warfare as an extraordinary and unwelcome interruption. Contemporary writers, not inaptly, compare the Moscovite armies of their day to herds of cattle. The infantry, encumbered rather than armed with heavy, obsolete, blunderbusses, the so-called *pishchal*, or with blunt and clumsy spears and axes, rarely ventured to attack an enemy unless they out-numbered him by four to one, while the cavalry was " a shameful thing to look upon." Mounted on sorry hacks, and armed with primitive carbines, or simply with the *saadak*[1], they considered it a great victory if they managed to kill half a dozen Tatars—that is to say, if they fought at all; for the great aim of the Russian soldier was to get home again as quickly as possible. In vain a whole series of statutes threatened deserters with the knout, exile and confiscation; the generals were constantly complaining of shameless and wholesale desertion in the course of every campaign. Yet we know from a somewhat later, but equally trustworthy, source that the Russian infantry, when properly trained, would follow its foreign officers through fire and water.

The gentry formed the bulk of the Tsar's forces; the peasants and tradespeople were rarely recruited, being far too valuable to the state as taxpayers; but in the *stryeltsui*, or musketeers, the Tsar possessed a peculiar and superior sort of

[1] A bow with its quiver of arrows.

militia composed of able-bodied volunteers outside the agricultural class. In times of peace, the *stryeltsui* lived in their own quarters on the outskirts of the towns, with their wives and families, carrying on various trades, toll-free, and, at the same time, acting as police and firemen. In Moscow alone there were 20,000 of them, divided into *prikazui* or companies. The *stryeltsui* had a fixed salary as well as a special allowance for clothes and salt. Their chief officers were always selected from among the Boyars.

But the proved inefficiency of the Russian fighting-man compelled Tsar Michael, like Tsar Boris before him, to introduce foreign mercenaries to teach the native levies European methods. So early as 1614, foreign soldiers began to enter Michael's service. In 1624 we find no fewer than 445 of them in Russia, of whom 168 were Poles, 113 Germans, and 64 Irish. Recruiting officers were also sent abroad to enlist foreign soldiers; but the most orthodox of governments looked askance at Catholic hirelings, and would not allow the recruiting of any of the Roman Faith.

Tsar Michael's army was an improvement upon all previous Moscovite armies ; but, when it came to be tested in the second Polish War, the chief event of Michael's later years, its inadequacy was most painfully demonstrated.

The Peace of Deulino was but a temporary interruption of hostilities postponed by mutual consent. Poland, harassed simultaneously by the Swedes and the Turks, was forced to leave her rebellious vassal (for as such she still regarded Moscovy) unpunished for a time, while Moscovy eagerly awaited the first opportunity of regaining her lost provinces. The death of old King Sigismund III (April, 1632), and the consequent interregnum in Poland, seemed to present that opportunity. Twelve months previously, Alexander Leslie had been sent by Philaret to Sweden to hire 5000 infantry and persuade as many smiths, wheelwrights and carpenters as possible to come to Moscow. Two other emissaries to the same country purchased 10,000 muskets with the necessary ammunition. At the end of 1631, there were 66,000 hired mercenaries in Moscow; and the leading generals were busy inspecting troops in the provinces. In April 1632, one of the national assemblies, which were the great feature of Michael's reign and a sign of weakness and irresolution in the central government, voted large subsidies in money and kind; and Mikhail Shein and Artemy Izmailov were sent to recover the lost towns with 32,000 men and 158 guns, speedily reinforced to twice that number. At first, everything went well; and Shein, who had had some military experience, "picked up fortresses as if they were birds' eggs." Serpyeisk surrendered on October 23, Dorogobuzh six days later, and sixteen smaller fortresses followed their example. But this was the term of Shein's success. The new King of Poland took the field immediately after his election, and he proved a far more formidable antagonist than his father.

Wladislaus IV was the most popular monarch that ever sat on the Polish throne. His election was the merest formality. It was understood from the first that the elder Krolewicz was the only possible successor of Sigismund III. A genuine Pole by temperament, frank, impetuous, mercurial, impressionable, with not a trace of the almost Castilian *grandezza* and punctilio of his father, Wladislaus's naturally noble nature had been refined and matured by excellent tutors with wide views and high ideals. He was absolutely free from caste prejudice; his ardent faith was unspotted by bigotry; and, from an early age, he was remarkable for his sociability, chivalrousness and patriotism. His mind had been still further enlarged by the usual *grand tour*, under excellent guides, which he made in 1624; and he brought back with him to Poland that love of art and letters which was so largely to console him for his political misadventures. Providence seemed to have destined him for great deeds, and the dream of his life was to place on his brows the crown of Vladimir and Monomakh which the Moscovites themselves had pressed upon him in his sixteenth year. He had learnt the science of war under the great Chodkiewicz, and had endeared himself to the common soldiers by the thoroughness and cheerfulness with which he shared their hardships. With the Cossacks he was especially popular, because, in warfare, he made no distinction between them and the *Szlachta*.

But there was another and deeper reason for the rare unanimity with which all parties united to elect Wladislaus. The Poles meanly calculated that so generous and impulsive a Prince would be content with fresh limitations of the royal power ; would be a sort "of King-bee dispensing nought but honey to his subjects " ; would, first, ease all grievances, satisfy all complaints, and then courteously stand aside and consent to be governed rather than to govern. Accordingly, the Coronation Diet, which assembled on September 27, 1632, still further curtailed the prerogative. The *Pacta Conventa* presented to Wladislaus before his coronation bound him never to declare an offensive war, or form alliances, however profitable, or hire mercenaries, though there was no regular army, without the consent of the Estates, or of the Senate as the trustees of the Estates. Moreover, he was to fill up all public vacancies within a certain time and relieve the *Szlachta* from the payment of the land tax and the hearth tax, the sole taxes to which they were still liable, " because the said taxes savoured of servitude." And this, too, at a time when the nobles and clergy between them owned nearly all the land[1] in the Kingdom and there was a deficit in the treasury of 370,000 gulden. The King agreed to all these usurpations, without cavil, and even without comment. The sweetness of popularity and the hope of military glory which, as he supposed, would exalt him still more in the eyes of the nation, and enable him ultimately to lead it whither he would, can alone explain his apparently reckless complaisance on this occasion. The

[1] The clergy owned 160,000 villages out of a total of 215,000, and paid no taxes at all.

niggardliness with which the *Sejm* responded to his magnanimity might have warned him that he was taking the wrong path. The deputies, when they had squeezed everything possible out of him, refused to grant him a single subsidy towards the expenses of the Moscovite War, which had been forced upon the Republic and threatened its very existence. Only by pawning his father's crown for 50,000 gulden, and by selling to the Elector of Brandenburg, for 90,000 more, exemption from personal homage for his Prussian Duchy, was Wladislaus able, at last, to muster 16,000 regular soldiers for the relief of Smolensk, now hardly pressed. Yet, at this very time, there were at least a score of Polish magnates each one of whom could have put 5000 fully equipped soldiers in the field without feeling the expense.

With his 16,000 troopers, reinforced by 15,000 registered Cossacks, Wladislaus hastened to the relief of his chief eastern fortress. The Russian commander, Shein, had distributed his troops in three immense entrenched camps on both sides of the Dnieper. The walls of these camps, according to an eye-witness, were as strong, vast and lofty as the walls of Smolensk itself, and were also defended by forts and blockhouses. After a series of bloody assaults (August 7–22) Wladislaus captured two of the camps, occupied the surrounding hills, and besieged Shein for four months in his main camp, while Kazanowski defeated a relief-army advancing from Dorogobuzh. Finally Shein, who had received nothing from Moscow but promises, yielding to the clamours of his foreign officers, surrendered to the Poles (Feb. 26, 1634). On March 1, the Moscovite army, " without music or the beating of drums, and with arms reversed," issued forth, by companies, and laid 122 banners at the feet of the Polish King, who sat on horseback beneath the triumphant White Eagle standard, the centre of a brilliant ring of castellans and palatines. Next Wladislaus proceeded to besiege the fortress of Byelaya, which resisted so stoutly that the Lithuanian chancellor, Prince Radziwill, declared that,

from henceforth it should be called not Byelaya[1] but Krasnaya[2].
So great was the dearth of food in the Polish camp that the
King ate only half a chicken for dinner so as to save the other
half for supper, while bread, even at the royal table, was a
luxury. And now, too, disquieting news from the south
disposed him to secure his Moscovite conquests by a permanent peace. The Turks were again in arms against the
Republic; and, though the Polish Grand Hetman, Stanislaus
Koniecpolski, in the summer of 1633, had defeated them at
Paniowce, it was rumoured that Sultan Amurath IV, after
publicly insulting the Polish envoy, Trzebinski, at a public
audience, had placed himself at the head of a new army and
was already at Adrianople. Negotiations were accordingly
opened with the Moscovites on the river Polyankova in March
1634, but it was not till May 28 that the treaty was signed.
The Poles conceded the title of Tsar to Michael, but refused the
epithet "of all Russia," arguing, reasonably enough, that as
Russian[3] provinces were to be found in both the Moscovite
and Polish States, Michael should call himself Tsar "of his
own Russia." Territorially, the Poles were now in very much
the same position as after the Truce of Deulino, as they had
little more than recovered what the Moscovites had won at the
beginning of the campaign. The Tsar, moreover, renounced all
his rights to Livonia, Esthonia and Courland, and paid a war
indemnity of 200,000 rubles. Wladislaus, on the other hand,
relinquished all his rights to the Moscovite throne. The
treaty of Polyankova so impressed the Turks that, when
Wladislaus hastened to Lemberg to take up the struggle with
them, they at once made pacific overtures. A truce was concluded in October 1634, on condition that, henceforth, the Poles
should keep their Cossacks under better control, while the

---

[1] White.
[2] Red.
[3] Thus Red and Black Russia belonged, at this period, to Poland, while
White Russia was half in Poland and half in Moscovy.

Sultan undertook to place Hospodars friendly to Poland on the thrones of Moldavia and Wallachia.

The Moscovite and Turkish Wars were no sooner over than events occurred which threatened to draw Poland into the Thirty Years' War. The death of Gustavus Adolphus (1632), and the subsequent rout of the Protestants at Nordlingen (1634), had brought Sweden and France still more closely together and consequently induced the Imperialists to look abroad for fresh allies. The martial King of Poland seemed to Richelieu to be just the man to make a powerful diversion from the east; and the cardinal offered Silesia and the hand of Maria Ludovika Gonzaga, daughter of the Duke of Nevers, one of the greatest of the great dames of France, to Wladislaus IV, if he would accede to the Franco-Swedish alliance and put 10,000 men in the field. Simultaneously, the Maritime Powers tempted Wladislaus with the hand of the ex-Queen of Bohemia. But Poland was desirous of peace, and the *Sejm* rejected both propositions. Unable to gain Poland as an ally yet anxious to prevent her from attacking Sweden while still in difficulties, England, France, and Holland then mediated the Truce of Stuhmsdorf[1], to last for 26 years from September 12, 1635, whereby, without the knowledge and greatly to the indignation of Axel Oxenstjerna, the Swedish Senate retroceded to Poland all the Prussian conquests of Gustavus Adolphus, while retaining Livonia provisionally.

For once the *Sejm* had acted prudently in restraining the impetuous King from plunging into a war which would have brought small advantage to the Republic. But even this solitary act of prudence was entirely dictated by the selfish fear lest Wladislaus's victories might increase the royal power. For precisely the same reason they next opposed his statesman-like endeavour to provide Poland with a navy.

One of Wladislaus's many obligations under the *Pacta Conventa* was to maintain, at his own cost, a fleet on the

---

[1] *See* also my *Scandinavia*, p. 211.

Baltic. He applied all his energy to the provision of this long-felt necessity. Two new fortresses, Wladyslawow and Kazimierzow, were speedily constructed on the north-west of the Gulf of Dantzic; one large and twelve small vessels were purchased at a cost of 381,000 gulden; and, for the first time in Polish history, a Polish fleet appeared in the Baltic. This was a good beginning, but it was only a beginning. The construction and maintenance of an adequate navy were impossible without far more money than the short-sighted *Sejm* was willing to bestow. Wladislaus therefore proposed to re-levy, for the benefit of the Republic, the lucrative tolls which the Swedes had levied during their occupation of Prussia and which had brought them in 3,600,000 Polish gulden per annum, Pillau alone yielding 1,500,000. To this obviously advantageous proposal, which, besides, cost them nothing, the *Senate* at once agreed. But, when Wladislaus announced his intention of levying the tolls, the people of Dantzic at once protested against it, as a violation of the Truce of Stuhmsdorf. They appealed to the signatories of that treaty for protection; and, when the King summoned the rebellious Dantzickers to appear before him and blockaded their harbour with his little fleet, a Danish admiral, acting in collusion with the city, broke the blockade and destroyed the Polish ships. This was the state of things when the *Sejm* assembled in 1638, shortly after the King had wedded the Archduchess Cecilia Renata, daughter of the Emperor Ferdinand III. Wladislaus at once appealed to Parliament to punish Dantzic for thus publicly insulting the Crown and materially injuring the Republic. But the *Sejm* was in a more than ordinarily stupid and suspicious mood. It affected to regard the project of the Baltic tolls as "a Spanish conception." The King, it was said, was acting in the Austrian interest. He meant to suppress Dantzic as a first step towards subduing Scandinavia. A strong fleet would too greatly increase the royal power. The idea of it had been devised by the Chancellor Ossolinski, during his recent secret interview with the Emperor at Ratisbon—and much more to the same effect. Most of the Senators thereupon deserted the King from fear of the *Sejm*; the Dantzic affair was referred to a special commission, which quietly shelved it; and from henceforth nothing more was ever heard of a Polish fleet.

But the real cause of the *Sejm's* distrust of the King was the foundation by Wladislaus, at this very time, of the Knightly Order of the Immaculate Conception, the statutes of which were brought by Ossolinski from Rome, confirmed by Urban VIII. The Order was to consist of seventy-two cavaliers, selected from among the noblest families in Poland, and was obviously meant, in the future, to form the nucleus of a royalist party, by means of which the King might curb the lawlessness of the *Szlachta* and indirectly bring about a reform of the Constitution. A purely Roman Catholic Society like this could not fail to be offensive to the orthodox Lithuanians and the protestant Prussians; but a minority like theirs would have been powerless but for the support of the Catholic magnates themselves, who preferred the domination of the *Szlachta*, which could always be managed or bribed, to the rivalry of a strong King. The united opposition compelled the King to abolish the Order of the Immaculate Conception; and the *Sejm*, out of spite, refused to pay the debts contracted by Wladislaus during the Moscovite war. Not till 1642 did the chancellor Ossolinski succeed in getting the King reimbursed by skilfully waiving the royal claims in return for "a gratification" of 4,500,000 thalers, which roughly represented the amount due.

The disillusioned King, foreseeing clearly the abyss towards which Poland was hastening, but worn out by repeated humiliations, now abandoned politics altogether and sank into a lethargy of indifference from which he was only aroused by the birth of a son, christened Sigismund, in 1640. From henceforth, he became another man, and laboured with all his might first to promote the unity of the nation, and then to bring about a revolution by means of a military *coup d'état*.

He began by attempting to reconcile the various sects in Poland.

We have already seen[1] how the rising tide of Protestantism in Poland receded, towards the end of the sixteenth century, before the opposing forces of race-hatred and the catholic reaction. But there were other dissenters not so easily to be disposed of.

Having conquered the Lutherans and Calvinists, the Jesuits directed their attention to the Greek Orthodox Church, their one remaining spiritual rival in the territories of the Republic. The Princes of the House of Jagiello had, prudently, left their Orthodox subjects alone. Their policy was to strengthen, by every means, the union between Poland and Lithuania; and their statesmanlike instincts told them that any attempt violently to bring together the Roman Church in Poland and the Orthodox Church in Lithuania would only introduce discord where harmony was so essential. The Jesuits thought differently. Their great argument was that the union of the two churches would consolidate the union of the two States; and this argument is set forth, with extraordinary force and eloquence, in the famous book of the greatest of the Polish Jesuits, Peter Skarga, entitled "O jednosci Kosciola Bozego[2]." He proposed a provisional union between the Roman and Greek Churches on three conditions; (1) that the Archbishop of Kiev, the Metropolitan of the West Russian Church, should henceforth be consecrated by the Pope instead of by the Patriarch of Constantinople; (2) that the Russians should acknowledge the supremacy of the Church of Rome; and (3) that the external ceremonies and the liturgical language of the Russian Church should remain intact. A conditional union was considered preferable to an absolute submission as being the easier way of undermining the obstinate attachment of the Orthodox congregations to their ancient faith. The flagrant and manifold abuses in the Orthodox church of Poland seemed to justify the necessity of its union with the better-ordered

[1] Chapter V.   [2] "The unity of the Church of God."

and instructed Roman Church. All contemporary evidence describes its condition in the darkest colours. The bishops, with scarce an exception, were robbers and ruffians; the lesser clergy followed the unedifying example of their ecclesiastical superiors. Prince Constantine Ostrogski, the chief pillar of the Orthodox church, bitterly complained that the common people hungered in vain for the word of God, while Melecy Smotrzycki, Orthodox Archbishop of Polock, declared that he could not lay his hand on three Orthodox preachers, and that, but for the aid of Catholic *postillas*, there would have been no preaching at all. An attempt on the part of the Constantino-politan Patriarch Jeremiah, in 1588, to reform these crying abuses only made matters worse and raised a storm of protest, till the best of the Lithuanian Orthodox, both lay and clerical, began to look longingly towards Rome. After some preliminary negotiations with Sigismund III and Zamoyski, the better class of Orthodox bishops at last took the decisive step. At a synod, held at Brzesc, on June 14, 1595, they drew up two addresses, one to the Pope and the other to the King, in which they declared their willingness to accede to the Union of Florence on condition that their ceremonies and discipline were left intact. Delegated bishops were then sent to Rome to offer the submission of the Orthodox church in Poland to the Apostolic See; and, early in January, 1596, the Bull *Magnus Dominus et laudabilis nimis* received the "Rutheni" into the Catholic Church.

Unfortunately, the bishops did not think fit to take Prince Constantine Ostrogsky into their confidence. As the patron of 600 livings, to say nothing of the inestimable services he had rendered to the Orthodox church by founding academies and issuing a Slavonic translation of the Scriptures, the famous Ostrog Bible, he certainly should have been consulted before-hand. When then he was informed of what had been done after the event, his volcanic indignation threatened to wreck the young Uniate Church at the very outset. He terrified the vacillating Metropolitan Rukoza, formed a close union with the anti-episcopal brotherhoods of Lithuania, and, during the Diet of 1596, at the head of a formidable minority, fiercely opposed the King himself, while Orthodox preachers perambulated Lithuania denouncing the Uniate bishops as traitors and stirring the Orthodox population against them. At the Synod of Brzesc, held on October 9, 1596, the two parties met face to face and excommunicated each other. Thus the immediate result of " the Union " was the division of the West Russian Church into " Uniates " and " Disunited "; but the Orthodox party was now in a much worse position than before, because it was no longer officially recognised, and had to contend against the combined forces of the Uniates and the Catholics. But Ostrogski did not abandon the struggle, and it was due to his efforts that the Warsaw Diet of 1607 granted a " constitution " to the " Disunited " which gave them a quasi-legal status. The death of Ostrogski, in the following year, was a great blow to the Orthodox; and the Uniates redoubled their efforts to " convert " the " Disunited." What their methods were, may be gathered from the warning addressed by Leo Sapieha, chancellor of Lithuania, to the fanatical Uniate Archbishop of Polock, Josephat Kuncewicz, who disregarded it and was consequently murdered, in November 1623, in the streets of Witebsk, by the outraged Orthodox population. Witebsk was duly punished, but no notice was taken by Sapieha of a savage epistle from Urban VIII demanding that " this plague of schism should be extirpated by fire and sword."

Thus Poland once more vindicated her character as a non-persecuting Power in an age of religious intolerance. In process of time, the position of the " Disunited " improved. Thus the Diets of 1631 and 1635, despite the opposition of the Curia, fully recognised the Orthodox Church in Poland as a separate and independent establishment, with bishoprics at Lemberg, Przemysl and Mohilev, and a Metropolitan at Kiev, and confirmed them in the possession of all their property. Wladislaus IV would have gone further still. He proposed, by means of conferences and congresses, to bring about an understanding between the Catholics and all the Dissenters, both Protestant and Orthodox. As regards the Orthodox in particular, the times seemed most propitious as on the Orthodox metropolitan throne of Kiev now sat Peter Mohila, a Moldavian by birth, educated at Paris, and connected by family ties with many of the leading Polish magnates. On the initiative of Wladislaus, a synod of Polish Catholic Bishops assembled at Warsaw in 1643 and invited the Dissidents to meet them at a *colloquium charitativum*, in the following year. The colloquium was actually held at Thorn, on August 28, 1645, under the presidency of the chancellor Ossolinski, but came to naught, owing to the opposition of Pope Innocent X.

To attain his second object, the reform of a mischievous constitution by means of a *coup d'état*, Wladislaus reckoned chiefly upon the Dnieperian or registered Cossacks, who, at any rate, formed part of the irregular forces of the Republic, and were not mere free-booters like their brethren of the Don. The Cossacks liked Wladislaus IV, and he was certain of their whole-hearted support in case of a collision with the *Sejm* against whom the Cossacks nourished many ancient grievances. No doubt the restless predatory, incalculable Cossack was a difficult factor for any statesman to deal with; but, hitherto, the *Szlachta* had frustrated or ignored every attempt to settle adequately the urgent Cossack question. The Pans regarded the Cossacks generally as schismatical, runaway serfs, to whom only the very minimum of tardy justice was to be grudgingly conceded. They did not always remember that these semi-barbarous horsemen were also the sole guardians of the south-eastern Ukraine, or frontier, of the Republic. The condition of the Ukraine was always more or less abnormal; and the slightest accident there, in view of the near neighbourhood of the Turks and Tatars, and the utter defencelessness of Poland, was bound to have the most dangerous consequences.

At the beginning of the reign of Wladislaus IV, the Zaporozhians were more than usually restless. To curb them, the fortress of Kudak was erected, by French engineers, at the confluence of the Samara and Dnieper, to overawe the Cossack *Syech*, or Commonwealth, a little lower down the river. The Polish army then withdrew, leaving this solitary fortress in the wilderness, garrisoned by a few hundred dragoons, at the mercy of the Cossacks, who, on the first stormy night, attacked and destroyed it. For this they were severely punished by the Polish Grand Hetman, Koniecpolski; and Kudak rose again from its ashes. The number of the registered Zaporozhians was now reduced to 6000, and they were promised 100,000 gulden *per annum* for their maintenance. But, despite the repeated warnings of the King, the stipulated amount was never paid regularly; and the result was a series of fresh rebellions, in 1636 and 1638, which were mercilessly repressed. The Diet of 1638, moreover, abolished all the liberties of the Cossacks, including the right of electing their own Hetman; and they were subordinated to a Polish military Commission sitting at Trachtymirov. But no extra precautions, such as the maintenance of an adequate permanent army, or the building of fresh forts, in the now thoroughly disturbed Ukraine, were taken against the possible further consequences of the Government's breach of faith. Everything was left to the discretion of Koniecpolski, who, fortunately for the Republic, was an expert in Ukrainian matters as well as a warrior of renown.

Wladislaus IV largely depended on the cooperation of the Grand Hetman for the consummation of his plans. As originally conceived, these plans were fantastically ambitious. In 1641 he sent Ossolinski to Rome to inform the Pope that he meditated conquering Sweden and Moscovy and pacifying Europe, finally proceeding, at the head of united Christendom, to expel the Turks from Europe and establish his own claims to Constantinople, which he hoped to acquire through Maria Ludovika Gonzaga de Nevers, the last surviving descendant of the Paleologi, whom Mazarin and the Queen Mother of France, in the hope of detaching Wladislaus from the Austrian alliance, had selected to be his second wife.

In the spring of 1646, circumstances seemed to favour the oriental part of the King's designs. In the previous year, the Tatars, enraged at the refusal of Wladislaus to continue the humiliating tribute which the Khan exacted from Poland, invaded the territories of the Republic, but were almost annihilated at Ochmatow by Koniecpolski. Simultaneously, dissensions broke out in the Crimea; and the Turks declared war against Venice. Wladislaus immediately ordered the Cossacks to make ready their boats for a raid upon the Turkish galleys in the Euxine, and sent envoys to Moscow and Venice to conclude a league against the Porte. But Koniecpolski, who was summoned to Cracow to give advice, took a less sanguine view of the situation. He declared that an invasion of Turkey was impracticable unless adequately financed by Venice, at the rate of a million *scudi* down and half a million more *per annum* so long as the war lasted. He urged the King to limit his operations to the acquisition of Moldavia and Wallachia and the subjugation of the Tatars. On March 10, 1646, Maria Ludovika arrived at Cracow and was married to Wladislaus, to whom she brought a very serviceable dowry of 800,000 livres.

At this juncture the sudden death of Koniecpolski deprived the King of his most loyal and judicious co-operator. Still Wladislaus persisted in his designs, leaning now, almost entirely, on the Cossacks, whose deputies arrived at Cracow and held midnight conferences with him and the seven Senators, out of 120, on whom he could depend. In return for a promise of the restitution of their liberties, the Cossacks promised to put 50,000, or even 100,000 men in the field, whenever they were required. Secure in this quarter, Wladislaus next concluded an alliance with the Moscovites for a simultaneous attack on the Budziak Tatars and the Crimea. The plan was well laid and might have succeeded, had not the Venetian ambassador, in order to frighten the Porte, prematurely proclaimed the secret offensive and defensive treaty existing between Venice and Poland. Instantly the whole Polish Republic was in a ferment, and the cry that the Constitution was in danger resounded everywhere. Wladislaus' secret treaty with Venice was undoubtedly a breach of the *Pacta Conventa*; and the Senate, for fear of the Diet, openly turned against the King, declaring they would rather cut off their hands than sign the circular letters directed by Wladislaus to his recruiting agents. Wladislaus' last hope was that the Porte would now declare war against him, or, at least, send the Tatars across the border, in either of which cases he would be justified in using the forces he had collected for the defence of the Republic. But the Porte, well-informed of what was going on in Poland, carefully avoided every appearance of hostility, while the Diet of 1646, convinced that a successful Turko-Tatar war would be " the grave of the national liberties," reduced the standing army to 1200 men and forbade the King to issue any declaration of war whatever without the consent of the Republic. Yet Wladislaus never relaxed his military preparations, hoping against hope that the Turks, or the Tatars, if aggravated, might still play into his hands. But the Sultan ostentatiously proclaimed his desire for peace and sent the Tatars against the Moscovites instead of against the Poles. At the extraordinary Diet of May 2, 1647 the King professed that he did not understand the foreign policy of the deputies. " Here you are," said he, " surrounded on every side by enemies and ill-wishers, and yet you break away from your sole ally, the Venetian Republic !" So tumultuous and unmanageable was this Diet that not a single measure was passed during the session. The death of the little Krolewicz, Sigismund, still further depressed the King, who did not, however, relax his efforts to gain over the Cossacks ; and Ossolinski was sent on a mysterious mission to the Ukraine, probably (for the incident is obscure) to offer the bâton of Hetman of the Zaporozhians to Chmielnicki, who now appears prominently on the scene for the first time.

Bohdan Chmielnicki was the son of a Cossack, Michael

Chmielnicki, who, after serving Poland all his life, died for her on the field of Cecora, leaving to Bohdan the village of Subotow with which the Polish King had rewarded Michael's valour and fidelity. History, in all probability, would never have known the name of Chmielnicki, if the intolerable persecution of a neighbouring Polish squire had not converted the thrifty and acquisitive Cossack husbandmen into one of the most striking and sinister figures of modern times. Failing to obtain redress from the local courts for the raiding of his village, the slaughter of his servants, and the flogging to death of his little son, Chmielnicki sought for justice at Warsaw, whither he had been summoned, with other Cossack delegates, to assist Wladislaus IV, in the projected Turkish campaign. The King, perceiving him to be a man of some education and intelligence, appointed him *pisarz*, or secretary, of the registered Cossacks and chief recruiting officer. Chmielnicki, encouraged by these marks of favour, complained to Wladislaus of the outrages inflicted upon him at Subotow; but, inasmuch as Chmielnicki could not produce any "privilege" entitling him to property actually given to his father for military services, the Polish jurists decided that the non-noble Cossack had no claim against his noble oppressor. Revolted by this instance of aristocratic chicanery, Wladislaus, at a private interview, fastened a sword to the Cossack's side and said to him significantly, "You are a soldier, now, remember! Defend yourself."

Chmielnicki, on his return to the Ukraine, took part in the campaign of Ochmatow under Koniecpolski. But he was now doubly hateful to the Pans, as being a royalist as well as a Cossack, and was deprived of his fair share of booty, accused of meditating rebellion, and thrown into jail, whence he escaped by bribing his jailers. Feeling that neither his life nor his liberty was any longer secure among the Pans, Chmielnicki, in December, 1647, fled to the Zaporozhian settlement on the Dnieper, and sent messages to the Khan of the Crimea, proposing an invasion of Poland by the combined forces of the

Tatars and the Cossacks. This was a contingency which Koniecpolski had always foreseen and Wladislaus IV had always included in his political calculations. When, then, the King learnt that Chmielnicki had been proclaimed Hetman of the Cossacks (April 18, 1648), and was marching northwards at the head of his Cossack-Tatar host, he recognised that his long sought-for opportunity had come at last. After ordering the new Grand Hetman, Nicholas Potocki, to await reinforcements before attacking Chmielicki, he sent off to the Ukraine all his available troops, and was preparing to follow them, when he died suddenly in consequence of a severe chill, caught while hunting in the forests round Mereczko, on May 20, 1648, in his 52nd year.

CHAPTER XI.

JOHN CASIMIR AND THE COSSACKS, 1648-1669.

AT the end of May 1648, the news of a terrible disaster in the Ukraine reached the Polish capital. Stephen Potocki, with the Polish advance guard of 4000 men, was attacked on the banks of the river *Zheltuiya Vodui* by Chmielnicki's countless Cossack and Tatar hordes; and, after a stubborn three days' resistance (May 16, 18-19), his little army was annihilated. A week later, the Hetmans of the Crown, Nicholas Potocki and Kalinowski, were surprised by the Cossack Hetman in the marshy valley of *Kruto Balka*, near the fortress of Korsun, on which they were retreating. Again Chmielnicki triumphed; 8500 out of the 10,000 Poles perished; and both the Hetmans, with a few of their superior officers, were sent in chains to the Crimea to be held to ransom. The immediate result of these Cossack victories was the outbreak of a *Khlopskaya zloba*, or " serf's fury." Throughout the Ukraine, the Polish gentry were hunted down, flayed, burnt, blinded and sawn asunder. Every manor house and castle was reduced to ashes. Every Uniate or Catholic priest who could be caught was hung before his own high altar, along with a Jew and a hog. Every one who shaved his head after the Polish manner, or wore Polish costume, was cut down by the *haidamaki*, as Chmielnicki's bands were called. At Polonny, the Jews were cut up into joints and sold as meat by the butchers. At Bar, the Cossacks roasted and ate little children in the presence of their mothers. The remnant of the panic-stricken inhabitants fled to the nearest strongholds; and soon the rebels were swarming all over the palatinates of Volhynia and Podolia.

Poland was utterly unprepared for a catastrophe which left her without any visible means of defence. The Grand Chancellor, Jerzy Ossolinski, the confidant, some said, the initiator, of the King's martial projects, at once hastened from Warsaw to Lithuania to find the monarch. Midway, he was met by the tidings of Wladislaus' death; and the shock deprived him, for a time, of the use of both hands. Nevertheless, in view of the infirmity of the aged primate, the captivity of the Hetmans, and the absence, or sickness, of the principal senators, he represented the executive, and, rising to the level of his difficulties, proceeded, with characteristic energy, to evolve order out of chaos while every one else was exclaiming: *actum est de republica!*

Jerzy Ossolinski was that rare phenomenon in Polish history—a great diplomatist. Born in 1595, his abilities first impressed his Jesuit instructors at Pultusk, who sent him abroad; and, after frequenting, for eight years, the principal European Universities, he returned to Poland one of the most accomplished scholars and orators of the day. Sigismund III employed him on various diplomatic missions, in all of which he acquitted himself brilliantly, and he was responsible for the foreign policy of Poland during the reign of Wladislaus IV, who made him Vice-Chancellor in 1639, and Grand-Chancellor in 1645. It was Ossolinski who concluded the advantageous truce of Stuhmsdorf with Sweden, arranged the lucrative marriage of Wladislaus with the Austrian Archduchess Cecilia, and preserved unbroken the friendship between the Republic and the Roman Curia in the most difficult circumstances. He was initiated in all the secret revolutionary plans of Wladislaus IV, and, convinced that Poland could only be saved from ruin by a reform of the constitution on a strong monarchical basis, devoted himself to the attainment of that noble ambition, often at the peril of his life.

The first thing to be done was to elect a new King. For

the moment, the Cossack peril had ceased to be acute. The Porte, ignorant of the death of Wladislaus IV, and alarmed at the prospect of a Polish war while the Venetian War was still undecided, had peremptorily ordered the Tatars back to the Crimea; and, Chmielnicki, weakened by their defection, had retired to Czehryn and opened negotiations with Poland to gain time. Ossolinski, whose policy it was to win the Cossacks for the Crown, at once sent peace commissioners to the Ukraine; while the *Szlachta*, who knew and feared the Chancellor's royalist proclivities, determined to crush the Cossacks before they could come to terms with the Government, and so thwart Ossolinski's plans at the forthcoming Election Diet. Thus, within a few weeks of the death of Wladislaus IV, whom they had steadily refused to assist against the Turks and Tatars, the Polish nobility assembled 40,000 horsemen and 200,000 armed camp followers, with 100 guns, at Czolhansk in order to promote their electioneering manœuvres by wiping out the Cossacks. By the time this gorgeous array, in shining armour and flowing, ermine-trimmed mantles, with heron plumes waving from their jewelled caps, their spurs of gold and silver, and their saddles and *shabracks* ablaze with precious stones, set forth "to chase away the Cossack rabble with their whips," the Porte, better informed as to Polish affairs, had permitted the Tatars to rejoin the Cossacks; and Chmielnicki, after contemptuously dismissing the Polish peace commissioners, was advancing northwards. On September 23, 1648, the two armies encountered near Pilyawa; and the glittering Polish pageant was easily scattered to the winds. The steppe for miles around was strewn with corpses; and the Cossacks are said to have reaped 10,000,000 gulden's worth of booty when the fight was over.

The immediate consequence of this disaster was the assembling of the Election Diet, which both parties, from political motives, had, unconstitutionally, postponed for six weeks beyond the usual time. It met on October 5, 1648; and, chiefly through the influence of Ossolinski, Wladislaus IV's eldest half-brother, John Casimir, was elected King on October 13, on condition that he espoused his brother's widow, Queen Maria Ludovika, who paid the expenses of his election out of her immense fortune.

The new King was little known and liked still less in Poland, where he was regarded as an alien adventurer. His career, hitherto, had certainly not been of the sort to inspire confidence in his stability of character. Born in 1609, he had been obliged to seek his fortune abroad because the *Sejm* had refused to allow him an honourable maintenance at home. After fighting in the Thirty Years' War on the Imperial side, he set out for Spain, but was arrested *en route* by Richelieu (1632), and spent the next two years in a French prison. On being released, he proceeded to Rome, where he entered the Jesuit Order and subsequently competed for the dignity of cardinal. On returning to Poland, however, he changed his mind, returned the red hat, which had been sent after him to Warsaw, and was meditating wedlock when the death of his brother gave another direction to his ambition, and made him an aspirant for the Polish crown. Indolent and flighty John Casimir certainly was; and to these personal defects all the calamities of his unhappy reign have been freely but most unjustly attributed. As a matter of fact, John Casimir was almost the only man in Poland who, guided by fixed political principles, endeavoured to do his duty as he understood it. Though no genius like his brother, he was not without fine qualities. His splendid personal valour was distinctly a national asset; and, again and again, he demonstrated that not in vain had he learnt diplomacy in the school of Ossolinski. If he frequently submitted to the guidance of robuster intellects than his own, he had at least discrimination enough always to choose the best counsellors available. But we shall never get at the inner meaning of the labyrinthine complications of this distracting reign if we do not steadily bear in mind this cardinal fact : the great but secret aim of John Casimir, as it had been the aim of Wladislaus IV before him, was to curb the *Szlachta* and reform "the absurd republic" by strengthening the executive at the expense of the legislature.

The most pressing duty of the newly elected King was to endeavour to come to terms with the Cossacks.

After the rout of Pilyawa, all Poland lay at the feet of Chmielnicki ; and the road to the defenceless capital was open before him. But, after capturing the fortresses of Konstantinow and Zbaraz, and blackmailing Lemberg, he wasted two precious months in the vain attempt to capture Zamosc. Meanwhile, John Casimir privately opened negotiations with him and officially recognised him by sending to him the *bâton* and other insignia of the Cossack Hetman. The King furthermore promised his "faithful Zaporozhians" the confirmation of all their ancient liberties if they would retire from Zamosc, break off their alliance with the Tatars, and await fresh peace commissioners at Pereyaslavl. The Pans were furious with the King for thus making friends with "the worst enemy of the Republic"; yet it is hard to say what else could have been done in the circumstances, and Chmielnicki recognised his obligations to the royal House of Vasa by retiring from Zamosc, and consenting to receive the Polish commissioners. They arrived in his camp in January 1649 and found him so intoxicated with success as to be scarcely a reasonable creature. He contemptuously rejected the Polish terms, and was so evidently preparing to invade Poland with the combined forces of the Tatars and Cossacks that the commissioners, at the end of February, returned to Warsaw, and Ossolinski advised the King to proceed to the Ukraine and overawe the rebels by his royal majesty. It seemed, at first, as if this were to be his sole weapon. The *Szlachta* refused even to prepare for war, despite the alarming fact that the Tatars, supported by a threatening letter from Stambul, haughtily demanded the repayment of tribute ; while Chmielnicki, now styling himself "Prince of

Russia," publicly declared his intention of placing George Rákoczy on the Polish throne. Only at the last moment a piteous appeal from the aged primate Lubienski, in the name of religion, induced the train-bands to assemble to the number of 10,000; and John Casimir set off to relieve the Lithuanian magnate Prince Jeremiah Wisniowiecki who was holding the whole Cossack-Tatar host at bay at Zbaraz.

The King encountered the rebels near Zborow, on the banks of the Strypa, the passage of which he forced with irresistible *élan*. A bloody battle ensued on the other side, in which the valour of the King and the skill of his chief artillery officer, Arciszewski, triumphed against tenfold odds. A few days later, the skilful diplomacy of Ossolinski succeeded in buying off the Tatars, who retired from the field; and, checked in mid career though still unvanquished, Chmielnicki now consented to treat with the chancellor. By the compact of Zborow (August 21, 1649) he was recognised as Hetman of the Cossacks; the whole Starosty of Czehryn was ceded to him as an appanage; and the number of the registered Cossacks was raised from 6000 to 40,000, who were to be maintained at the expense of the Republic. The garrison of Zbaraz was ransomed for 400,000 gulden; a general amnesty was proclaimed; and it was arranged that, henceforth, all official dignities in the Orthodox palatinates of Kiev, Chernigov and Braclaw should be conferred solely on the Orthodox gentry. In return for these immense concessions, Chmielnicki did homage to the Polish King on bended knee in presence of both armies, kissing the King's hand; and the chancellor of Lithuania recited his pardon. The Diet, which met at Warsaw on November 22, confirmed the compact of Zborow, after much murmuring, but made no attempt to carry out its provisions. Thus, in spite of all the efforts of the King and Ossolinski, the Cossack question, which, with the exercise of a little tact and equity, might have been adjusted temporarily, continued to be as menacing as before. During 1650, however, the diplomacy of the chancellor greatly improved the position of Poland. He averted a war with Moscovy by threatening her with a Cossack invasion, and, taking advantage of the Venetian victories over the Turks, favourably entertained the project of an alliance between Matthew, Hospodar of Wallachia, the Bulgarians and the Imperial Court. He was about to proceed to Vienna and Rome to consolidate this new league when he died suddenly, leaving none competent to fill his place. Henceforth John Casimir relied principally on the Queen for the furtherance of his plans.

On the death of Ossolinski, the anti-Cossack party, chiefly represented by the Grand and Vice Crown Hetmans, Potocki and Kalinowski, recently returned from their long Crimean captivity, and burning for revenge, gained the upper hand. Chmielnicki's own restless ambition precipitated the rupture. At this time nearly all the minor princes and potentates of south eastern Europe were suitors for the hand of the beautiful Rosanda, the daughter of the fabulously wealthy Basil Lupul, Hospodar of Moldavia. Conspicuous amongst the lady's wooers were some of the most illustrious of the Polish magnates, the Potoccy, the Wisniowiecsy and even the old Vice-Hetman, Kalinowski. Chmielnicki also sought the lady's hand for his son Tymoszko[1]; and, when the Hospodar refused to entertain his proposals, the Cossack Hetman fell suddenly upon him, burnt Jassy, his capital, to the ground and devastated his dominions till the terrified Hospodar gave Rosanda to Timothy. The Polish nobility, enraged to see a low-born adventurer pluck such a prize from their very grasp, were now clamorous for the extirpation of the Cossacks; the Diet of January 1651 voted war subsidies with astonishing alacrity; and, at the beginning of June, John Casimir set out for the Ukraine at the head of 80,000 men. The campaign which ensued was as honourable to the King as it was discreditable to the *Szlachta*. On reaching Beresteczko on Styr, the host entrenched itself and awaited the arrival of Chmielnicki. He

---

[1] Little Tim.

appeared on June 27 with 200,000 Cossacks and Tatars, and made a vigorous reconnaissance, which was repulsed. On the 29th the Poles offered battle and were defeated. The same night the King held a council of war and, overruling the objections of the Hetmans and Senators, resolved to attack the enemy next morning and stake everything on a single hazard. The result was a great Polish victory, which would have been annihilating but for the disobedience of some of the Polish magnates, notably Prince George Lubomirsky, who refused to obey the royal orders in the crisis of the struggle. Consequently the bulk of the Cossacks, some 90,000, contrived to escape; and, when the King proposed to pursue them to their fortresses, a general mutiny broke out, due partly to the fear of the magnates that fresh victories would enhance the royal authority, partly to the effeminacy of the *Szlachta* who were already "longing after their spouses, their firesides and their feather-beds," and partly to the rage of the Vice-Chancellor, Hieronymus Radziejowski, who had been led, by false rumours, to suspect the King of a *liaison* with his wife, and revenged himself by making a successful continuance of the campaign impossible. It was due to his insinuations that the train-bands now quitted the King *en masse*. John Casimir, with only a handful of *quartians*, or regular border-troops, at his disposal, was therefore obliged to make the best terms he could with Chmielnicki. The compact of Bialocerkiewsk—so the treaty was called—amounted to a confirmation and extension of the compact of Zborow.

The mutiny of Beresteczko was the first symptom of that general lawlessness which was now to bring the Republic to the verge of ruin. The first phase of this melancholy record was a struggle between the King and his rebellious Vice-Chancellor.

It was at the court of Queen Cecilia, the first consort of Wladislaus IV, that Radziejowski's wit, *savoir-faire* and agreeable manners had gained him powerful patrons, while his openhandedness and affability made him very popular with the

Szlachta. Though a man of notoriously evil character (he had
been convicted of rape, and all but tortured his first wife to
death) he was already one of the first dignitaries of the
Republic; and his absolute unscrupulousness promised him
still greater eminence in a society where corruption and
simplicity were so strangely intermingled as in seventeenth
century Poland. But he went too far when he accused his
second wife, Euphrosina Wisniowiecka, of adultery with the
King. She at once quitted his roof for the protection of a royal
convent, and instituted divorce proceedings against her sland-
erous consort. Radziejowski thereupon attempted to kidnap
her. But the convent was defended by the royal guards, and for
attacking them he incurred the penalty of *lèse-majesté*, was
summoned before the supreme court, and condemned *in
contumaciam* to lose his life, honour and goods. Never was
sentence so richly deserved, yet public opinion, indoctrinated
by Radziejowski and his creatures who, for months beforehand,
had circulated the most infamous libels concerning the King, was
almost entirely on the side of the felon. John Casimir, however,
did not flinch. He frustrated any attempt at rehabilitation by
treating the lesser seal as vacant and bestowing it on one of his
own adherents, whereupon the Diet, which had just met, was
"exploded[1]" by Wladislaus Sicinski, deputy from Upick, at
the instigation of his patron Prince Janus Radziwill. The
liberum veto had frequently been employed before, but this was
the first time that the right of a single deputy to explode the
Diet was recognised as a matter of principle. Henceforth it was
open to any discontented magnate to put up any petty squire,
or other dependent, to gag the executive by getting rid, at any
time, of an inconvenient Diet. At a later stage, the *Sejmiki*, or
provincial Diets, which elected the deputies to the *Sejm* or
general Diet, frequently included in their mandates to their
deputies an express injunction to "explode" the Diet in

[1] Instead of being dissolved in the usual way at the end of a term fixed
beforehand.

certain contingencies. In the present case the action of Sicinski prevented any further investigation of the Radziejowski affair. The ex-Vice-Chancellor, after vainly attempting, from his exile in Silesia, to negotiate with the King, fled to Stockholm.

Meanwhile both Poland and Moscovy were watching with some apprehension the windings and doublings of the crafty Cossack Hetman, Chmielnicki, who openly interfered in the affairs of Wallachia, Moldavia and Transylvania, assumed the high-sounding and ominous title of " Guardian of the Ottoman Porte" and, in 1652, inflicted a severe defeat on the Polish chivalry at Batoka on the Moldavian frontier. In 1653 Poland made a supreme effort. The *Sejm* voted 17 millions of gulden in subsidies ; and John Casimir led an army of 60,000 into the Ukraine. In the course of the same year the Republic commanded Chmielnicki to break off all relations with the Tatars and send his son as a hostage to Warśaw. The Hetman haughtily refused to obey, and declared that henceforth he would serve "the Lord's anointed, the Tsar of Moscovy." On August 24 he issued "universals" from Pereyaslavl ordering the whole population to rise against the Poles, and soon gathered a countless host around him ; but the Poles defeated him at Zranto, and, in January 1654, he welcomed the Moscovite envoys at Pereyaslavl. On February 19 the Cossack Hetman took the oath of allegiance to the Tsar. The Cossacks were confirmed in all the privileges they had enjoyed under the Polish Crown, including judicial and administrative autonomy ; and their registered number was fixed at 60,000. The Moscovite commissioners refused, however, to bind the Tsar by oath to keep his promises, as Chmielnicki required. It was an unheard-of, impossible thing, they said, for an absolute monarch like the Tsar to swear to be faithful to his own subjects as if he were the sort of King they had in Poland. Thus was accomplished the transference of the free Cossacks from Poland to Moscovy. It was an important political event,

and the first step towards the ultimate subjection of both
"Russia[1]" and Poland by the Tsars. But, as yet, it was only a
first step; and its inevitable corollary was the outbreak of the
long-deferred struggle between the Tsardom and the Republic.
So early as March, 1653, the Tsar's council had determined
upon war with Poland; and, in July, the Moscovite envoys told
John Casimir at Lemberg that the Tsar had decided to take the
Zaporozhians under his high protection, unless the King of
Poland redressed all their grievances forthwith. The Poles
refused to treat any longer "with a thief and a traitor who had
already sold himself to the Sultan," but promised to forgive
him if he resigned his Hetmanship. On October 1–12, 1653,
a national assembly met at Moscow to sanction the war and
find the means of carrying it on. The diminution of the Tsar's
title by the Pans, and their refusal to put to death the author
of various books eulogising the exploits of Wladislaus IV, were
the alleged *gravamina*; but the assembly went to the real root
of the matter by declaring that hostilities were necessary
because the Polish Government had broken its oath to the
Cossacks, and it was to be feared that the Zaporozhians would
turn Mussulmans if Moscovy did not help them against Poland.
Muskets and powder had already been purchased in large
quantities from Sweden and Holland. In May Tsar Alexis,
who had succeeded his father Michael in 1645[2], after weeks of
solemn preparation and humble supplication, set out for the
front.

The war opened favourably for the Moscovites. In Lithuania, Prince Alexander Trubetskoi, aided by 20,000 of Chmielnicki's Cossacks, easily prevailed over the weak and scattered
forces of the Poles, though much hampered by a terrible
outbreak of plague which depopulated the whole Tsardom and
made Moscow a desert during the summer and autumn months
of 1654. In the course of June and July the towns of
Dorogobuzh, Byelaya, Polock and Mstislavl fell into Tru-

---

[1] *I.e.* the Russian provinces of Poland.   [2] See Chapter XIII.

betskoi's hands ; in August he defeated Prince Janus Radziwill
at Szepielwica ; and Mohilew surrendered to Polklowski, who
hesitated to accept the allegiance of the Catholic inhabitants
"because they were not Christians." The ill-provided fortress
of Smolensk, whose feeble garrison of 2000 men found it
impossible to defend the immense circuit of the walls for more
than a couple of months, opened its gates on October 4.
Towards the end of the year Witebsk also áccepted a Moscovite
garrison. In the Ukraine, Theodore Buturlin, sent thither to
co-operate with Chmielnicki against the Khan of the Crimea,
who had definitely broken with the Cossacks after their
surrender to Moscovy, could do little, owing to the friction
between his troops and the Zaporozhians. Moreover the
barbarities of the Moscovite soldiers so revolted the Lithuanians that many of the surrendered towns returned to their
former allegiance. In January 1655 occurred the first Moscovite disaster, when a combined Polish-Tatar host almost
annihilated Sheremetev's army at Ochmatow ; whereupon the
pious Tsar, who had done his utmost to preserve the discipline
and punish the excesses of his troops, deemed it expedient to
return to Moscow to pray before the ikons of the Mother of
God, visit the relics of the saints, and comfort the Boyars and
people by his presence. By the time he returned to Smolensk
the Poles were no longer dangerous.

In the summer of 1655, Charles X of Sweden, from sheer
lust of conquest, forced a war upon reluctant and inoffensive
Poland. There was no real cause of quarrel between the two
countries. The truce of Stuhmsdorf had still six years to run ;
and, since its conclusion in 1635, Poland had carefully avoided
committing any act of war against Sweden. The religious
pretext was absurd and hypocritical. Poland never showed
the least disposition to join any Catholic league except for the
purpose of fighting the Turks ; and Christians of every shade
enjoyed absolute religious liberty within her borders. Charles's
own differences with Poland were insignificant and easily

adjustable.   He could have converted the truce into a permanent peace practically on his own terms ; but he wanted war,
and, after abruptly rejecting equitable conditions for a settlement presented to him by an extraordinary Polish embassy,
expressly sent to Stockholm for the purpose, he fell upon Poland,
in July 1655, with an army of 60,000 men, largely composed
of veteran desperados, ex-soldiers of fortune, whom the close of
the Thirty Years' War had left without occupation and who
rallied with alacrity to the standard of this new *condottiere*.

Radziejowski's well-paid emissaries had prepared the way
for him.   The palatines of Kalisch and Posen, to whom, in the
absence of any regular army, the *Sejm* had committed the
defence of the northern provinces, were the personal enemies
of the King and therefore the personal friends of Radziejowski.
They had raised 24,000 men, who occupied a strong position
among the marshes of the Netze.   At the first summons these
treacherous and craven commanders placed themselves beneath
the protection of the Swedish King (July 25) ; and the Swedes
occupied Great Poland without opposition.   Charles himself,
meanwhile, was marching upon Warsaw.   At Opoczno, John
Casimir courageously attempted to stay his progress ; but the
disastrous result convinced him that the Poles were too
demoralised to fight, even for their country ; and he fled to
Silesia, accompanied by the Queen and a small group of loyal
senators.   Profiting by the cataclysm which had swept the
Polish State out of existence, the Moscovites, unopposed,
quickly appropriated nearly everything not already occupied by
the Swedes.   In July, Wilna was taken ; in August fell Lublin
and Kowno ; in September Grodno ; while Chmielnicki devastated Galicia and blackmailed Lemberg, and Volkonski ravaged
all that remained to be ravaged in central Poland, burning the
towns of Dawuidow, Stolin and Pinsk on his way, and leisurely
returning to Moscovy, at the beginning of October, encumbered
with booty, without losing a man.   By this time, Charles X
had captured Cracow, though valiantly defended for two months

by Stephen Czarniecki, Castellan of Kiev—the only Polish dignitary who did his duty at this crisis—who was allowed to march out with all the honours of war (October 17), and joined John Casimir at Glogau.   On the other hand, the Lithuanian Grand Hetman, Prince Janus Radziwill, a Calvinist, had already, by the compact of Kiejdani, August 18, acknowledged Charles X as his suzerain in the hope of carving a principality out of the ruins of his country.   He now proclaimed himself " Grand Hetman of the Swedish Crown and of the Grand Duchy of Lithuania."   Thus the ruin of Catholic Poland seemed to have been compassed by the unnatural union of Orthodox Moscovites, Calvinists, and Lutherans.

But the end of Poland was not yet ; indeed, before the disastrous year 1655, was out, her deliverance had already begun.   The first gleam of hope came from a quarrel between the Moscovites and the Swedes.   At the end of August, Tsar Alexis warmly protested against the assumption by Janus Radziwill of titles unknown before.   " Lithuania hath never belonged to Sweden," the Tsar's envoy justly observed.   But Charles, with characteristic nonchalance, ignored the very existence of the Tsar.   Not only did he take away Lithuanian towns from the Moscovites and give them to Radziwill, but he entered into direct negotiations with the Elector of Brandenburg, Chmielnicki, and George Rákóczy II, Prince of Transylvania, for the partitioning of Poland among them.   This fantastic project was also a great diplomatic blunder, and excited equal apprehension at Vienna, Moscow and Stambul. Moreover, Austria regarded Charles as the natural ally of her rival France, for the triumph of Charles in Poland meant the triumph of Mazarin.   In October, two Imperial commissioners, Allegretti and Losbach, were sent to Moscow, and arranged a suspension of hostilities between Moscovy and Poland.   In December the Swedish envoys, who had arrived previously, were detained as prisoners ; and a Moscovite embassy was sent to Copenhagen to make common cause with the Danes against the King of Sweden "who was known to be aiming at the sole dominion of the Varangian Sea[1]." The final results of all this diplomatic activity was a declaration of war against Sweden by Tsar Alexis, at the end of May 1656, and an offensive and defensive alliance between the new Emperor, Leopold I, and John Casimir, on May 27, 1657, Austria placing 17,000 men at the service of the Polish King.

Simultaneously, an extraordinary reaction had begun in Poland itself. On October 18, the Swedes invested the fortress monastery of Czenstochowa, which was to Poland what the Troitsa Monastery was to Moscovy. The place was defended as valiantly by the prior Augustin Kordecki, as the Troitsa had been, half a century before, by the Archimandrite Dionysius; and the result was the same—victory and a national uprising. For seventy days Czenstochowa defied all the efforts of Swedish skill and courage; and, on December 27, the besiegers were obliged to raise the siege after suffering very heavily. This success, so astounding that it was popularly attributed to divine intervention, sent a thrill through Poland, and elicited a burst of popular enthusiasm which spread through all ranks of the population and gave the war a national and religious character. The tactlessness of Charles, the rapacity of his generals, the barbarity of his mercenaries, his refusal to legalise his position by summoning a *Sejm*, his negotiations for partitioning the very State he affected to befriend, and the ruinous contributions levied upon the gentry, awoke the long slumbering spirit of the country. The first visible sign of this general reaction was the Confederation of Tyszowiec (Dec. 29) formed by the Hetmans, Potocki, and Lanckoronski, for the defence of "the King, the Faith, and Freedom." Another similar Confederation, in Lithuania, under Paul Sapieha and Gonsiewski, besieged and captured Janus Radziwill in his castle at Tychocin, where he died on the last day of 1655. Thus when, at the beginning of 1656, John Casimir returned from his Silesian

[1] The Baltic.

exile, he was able to attract all the patriotic elements in the country to his standard. On April 1, 1656, he entered Lemberg in triumph, and, at a solemn service in the cathedral, placed himself and Poland beneath the protection of the Blessed Virgin, vowing publicly to use every effort to re-establish and reform the Republic and make it a strong and stable State.

Against such a national resurrection all the military genius of Charles X could avail little. Only by a series of more and more disadvantageous alliances with the Great Elector was he able to make head against the Poles at all. The heroic campaign of 1656, memorable for the capture of Thorn and Elbing, the victory at Golenba over Czarniecki, the miraculous retreat from Jaroslawl to Warsaw amidst three converging armies, and the great three days' battle of Warsaw (July 18–20), when Charles with only 18,000 Swedes and Prussians defeated John Casimir's army of 100,000, was altogether fruitless. The subsequeut victories of the indefatigable Czarniecki at Radom and Rawa, and the suspicious attitude of Frederick William, compelled the Swedish King at last to open negotiations with Poland through the French ambassador Des Lumbrès. But the Poles were now confident enough to refuse Sweden's terms, and the war was resumed. In the spring of 1657, George Rakóczy, with a horde of 60,000 semi-barbarians, joined 17,000 Swedish veterans at Sandomir; but the solitary success of the raid was the capture of Bresc Litewsk ; and, on the departure of Charles, Rakóczy was driven headlong out of Poland by Czarniecki and forced to pay a war indemnity of 1,200,000 gulden to the Republic. On August 15, died Chmielnicki, thus removing for a time the Cossack peril. Finally, Brandenburg was detached from the Swedish alliance by the compact of Wilawa, releasing the Elector from the obligation of doing homage to the Polish Crown for East Prussia, which was henceforth to be independent of the Republic. By the subsequent compact of Bydgoszcz he agreed to place 5000 men at the disposal of John Casimir in return for a small cession of territory, and the temporary mortgage of Elbing. With the Cossacks, also, a better understanding was arrived at. The Cossack officers, accustomed to boundless licence under the loose Polish rule, had already begun to chafe at the more stringent discipline of the Moscovites; and, on the death of Chmielnicki, they elected as their Hetman a Lithuanian gentleman, Wyhowski, who concluded with the Republic the compact of Hadziacz (Sept. 11, 1658). By this compact, the palatinates of Braclaw, Kiev and Chernigov were created into a semi-independent principality, under Polish suzerainty, with Wyhowski as its first ruler; a general amnesty was proclaimed; and the Metropolitan of Kiev and his diocesans were recognised *de jure* as Polish senators. But the rank and file of the Cossacks, together with the orthodox clergy, opposed the arrangement; and, though Wyhowski routed them and their Moscovite allies at the bloody battle of Konotop (July 8, 1659), he was ultimately obliged to resign the Hetmanship and retire to Poland.

Step by step the Republic was emerging from its difficulties. On May 3, 1660, Poland accepted the mediation of Louis XIV and composed her differences with Sweden by the Peace of Oliva, whereby Sweden renounced all her conquests except northern Livonia. Simultaneously, the long-pending negotiations with the Moscovites, whose minimum demands were Lithuania and war expenses, came to an end, and the war was resumed. During 1660 and 1661, the Poles were everywhere victorious. In the north Czarniecki and Sapieha routed the Moscovites at Lachowicz and Bazya and advanced as far as Polock; while, in the south, Stanislaus Potocki and George Lubomirsky routed the Cossacks at Slobodyszcz, and captured the Moscovite general Sheremetev and his whole army in their entrenched camp at Chudnow. The Moscovites thereupon hastily abandoned Kiev, Pereyaslavl, Chernigov and all their other conquests in the Russian provinces of Poland. In the autumn of 1661, the Tsar's army was seriously defeated at Zeromsk, with the loss of 19,000 men, 10 cannons, and all its standards. Before the year was out, Grodno, Mohilew and Wilna were recovered by the Poles ; and Lithuania was almost swept clear of the invader. In the course of 1662, the Moscovites, now in sore distress, sued for peace, but their terms were curtly rejected. However, both Powers were now becoming exhausted by the interminable strife ; and, in the course of 1663, Poland reopened negotiations. On June 12, 1664, a peace congress met at Durovicha, when the Poles demanded the restitution of all the Russian conquests and the payment of a war indemnity of 10 millions of gulden, terms which the Moscovite pleni-potentiaries refused to entertain. At the end of 1666, a second peace congress met at the village of Andrusovo, between Smolensk and Mstislavl ; and, on February 11, 1667, a truce for thirteen years was finally agreed to. Witebsk, Polock, and south Livonia were restored by Moscovy, which was to retain Smolensk, Siewerz, Chernigov, and Kiev for two years, and the whole eastern side of the Dnieper, the territory thus acquired including not only the land lost by the treaty of Deulino, but a large tract north of Chernigov, between the Dnieper and the affluents of the Don, containing the towns of Konotop, Gadyach, Pereyaslavl, Novgorod Syversk, Poltava and Izyum, adding ten millions of rubles to the annual revenue of the Tsar. The Cossacks of the Dnieper were to be under the joint dominion of the Tsar and the King of Poland, whose territories they were to defend. The two Powers also covenanted to restrain the Cossacks from rebelling against either of them, or engaging n piracy on the Black Sea, and to repel any invasion of the Ukraine by the Khan of the Crimea.

The nominal " truce " of Andrusovo proved to be one of the most durable peaces in history, though, but for the per-sistent ill-luck of Poland, at this period, it is doubtful whether it would ever have been signed at all. While the negotiations were still proceeding with Moscovy, the new Cossack Hetman, Doroshenko, the nominee of the Turks, ravaged Poland as far as Lemberg and Lublin with bestial ferocity, carrying off more than 100,000 captives, while the simultaneous warlike preparations of the famous Grand Vizier, Achmet Köprili, drove the Republic to solicit help from all the Western Powers. Yet these were but transient dangers. At the root of the collapse of Poland was the ceaselessly gnawing worm of aristocratic lawlessness. The *Szlachta*, untaught by the most terrible experiences, were now wilfully to reject a last opportunity of putting their house in order, rather than part with the most mischievous of their inordinate privileges.

John Casimir never abandoned the idea of reforming the Constitution. The thirteen years' war with the Moscovites had taught him, however, that the Cossacks were useless for his purposes. Henceforth he meditated carrying out his plan by diplomatic and legislative methods. The first step was to make the Crown hereditary instead of elective and thus obviate the anarchy which prevailed, more or less, during every interregnum.

At first, indeed, the Polish dignitaries themselves, appalled at the sight of the abyss to the edge of which the Swedish war had dragged them, took the matter of constitutional reform seriously in hand. The Diet of 1658 appointed a commission to report upon the expediency of limiting the *liberum veto* and deciding all matters by a plurality of votes. The commission reported to the Diet of 1659 that such reforms were indispensable ; and the Diet of 1660 was preparing to carry them out when, through the intrigues of the Austrian Minister Lisoli, the whole matter was referred to the following Diet.

It was now that " the succession question " came to the front. The Queen proposed to marry her niece to the Duke d'Enghien, son of the great Condé, who, supported by all the influence of France, was to be the last elective and the first hereditary King of Poland. Maria Ludovika had already persuaded many of the leading magnates to join "the French Party," which included such names as Stephen Czarniecki, John Sobieski, now rising to eminence, the royal referendary, Andrew Morsztyn, the leaders of the Lithuanians, Christopher and Michael Pac, and many more, when the project was ruined by the Lord-Marshal and Vice-Hetman of the Crown, Lubomirsky.

George Lubomirsky was a much more respectable malcontent than Hieronymus Radziejowski. He had rendered such eminent services to his country during the Swedish and Russian Wars as to justify the Grand-Chancellor acclaiming him as "Father of the Fatherland" in full Diet. At first he acceded to "the French Party," hoping to be able to control it absolutely; but, jealous of the superior influence of Czarniecki and Sobieski, he as quickly turned against the d'Enghien election project, though it had already received the sanction of the Senate (1661). By dint of the most unscrupulous agitation, Lubomirsky and his partisans easily persuaded the Diet to condemn any alteration of the existing mode of election and inspired the *Szlachta* with such a suspicion of the Court, that it refused to contribute a penny to avert the threatened economical ruin of the country caused by a war which had reduced the best part of Poland to a wilderness. Not one penny would the 500,000 landed proprietors, pleading their privileges as noblemen, consent to pay out of their own pockets; but they levied a poll-tax on the poorest sections of the community, the townsmen, artisans, shepherds, millers and yeomen, to meet the demands of the unpaid and starving army, which claimed 26,000,000 gulden of arrears. The wretched taxpayers broke down under the strain, and the result was a dangerous military mutiny which took the form of Confederations in Poland and Lithuania, levying blackmail on the estates of the bishops and clergy throughout the realm, and refusing to disperse until their claims had been satisfied. Far from attempting to mend matters, the Diet of 1662 re-affirmed the right of free election, condemned as traitors all who should dare to elect a future King during the lifetime of the reigning sovereign, levied a fresh poll-tax on the plebeian classes, and actually took measures to rehabilitate the scoundrel Radziejowski. A period of bewildering confusion ensued. Fresh Confederations were formed ; Lubomirsky pretended to mediate between the Court and the rebels, while forming a host of his own ; and the King, driven to desperation, took the field against him. The rival armies were already face to face at Buichnal, near Jaworow, when the Bishops intervened and brought about a formal reconciliation ; but, at the Diet of 1664, the King demanded the impeachment of Lubomirsky for *lèse-majesté*, and he was sentenced to loss of life, honour and goods by a tribunal appointed by the *Sejm* itself. But it was a long way from sentence to execution. Lubomirsky fled to Breslau, which he made a centre of rebellion ; and when, at the second extraordinary Diet of 1664, the King was proceeding to distribute the vacated dignities of Lord-Marshal and Vice-Hetman of the crown to Sobieski and Stanislaus Jablonowski respectively, Pan Los, the deputy for Plock, interposed his veto and exploded the Diet. The ex-Vice-Hetman thereupon left Breslau, established himself in Lithuania, and collected a fresh army. John Casimir marched against him, and a civil war ensued in which the unlucky King was almost invariably worsted, till the bishops again intervened. By the compact of Lengonice, July 31, 1666, Lubomirsky and his adherents obtained a full amnesty, the discomfited monarch undertaking to pay the troops.

The sudden death of Lubomirsky from apoplexy (January 31, 1667), came too late to improve the situation. The Diet of 1667 rejected all the proposals of the King, who, shortly afterwards, lost his energetic and resourceful consort. Since 1658, Maria Ludovika had been the soul of the French party, which collapsed at her death. John Casimir never recovered from the crushing blow. On September 16, 1668 he abdicated and retired to France, where he died on December 16, 1672. His valedictory address to his subjects rightly threw the responsibility for his failure on their lawlessness, and mournfully predicted the speedy ruin of the Republic which he had done his best to save.

Moscovy had suffered almost as much as Poland from the horrors of the thirteen years' war, but her troubles were not yet over.   Barely six months after the conclusion of the truce of Andrusovo, which brought some respite to the Republic, the Tsardom had to encounter a terrible rebellion of the Cossacks of the Volga and the Don, a rebellion which might have been as damaging to Moscovy as Chmielnicki's rebellion had been to Poland but for the lucky accident that it devastated her eastern instead of her western borders.   Here, unlike Poland she had no powerful neighbours to take advantage of her distress.

The Cossacks, as we have seen, were a perpetual trouble both to the Polish Republic and the Moscovite Tsardom, principally because of their proximity to Mussulman territory which these orthodox vikings, despite the warnings and prohibitions of King and Tsar, regarded as their natural prey. The usual mode of procedure of the Moscovite Cossacks was to sail down the Don into the Sea of Azov, and thence into the Black Sea; but when, in the middle of the 17th century, the Khan of the Crimea closed this outlet by building forts on the lower Don, the Cossacks took to sailing down the Volga into the Caspian Sea instead.   When the Moscovite Government attempted to put a stop to these raids by guarding the mouths of the Volga, the Cossacks dispersed inland, established themselves in a fortress amidst the marshes of the upper Don, inaccessible except in winter, which they called Riga, and plundered all the vessels sailing down the Volga, along 170 miles of its course, from Tsaritsuin to Saratov.   This went on from 1659 to 1665, when the local governors prevailed over the robbers, and the new Riga, which had become a vast depository for stolen property, was attacked and destroyed.

But, in the summer of 1667, a much more formidable malefactor suddenly appeared on the scene.   This was the Cossack Stenka[1] Razin, whom we first hear of, in 1661, on a diplomatic mission to the Calmuck Tatars, and whom we meet,

[1] Steevy.

in the autumn of the same year, on a pilgrimage of a thousand miles to the Solovetsky monastery on the White Sea. After that all trace of him is lost for six years; but, in 1667, the governors of Astrakhan received a warning from the Tsar that a multitude of Cossacks, well provided with arms and ammunition, had settled in the district. The leader of this robber community was the ex-pilgrim Stenka. Fixing his head-quarters at the village of Panshinskoe, between the rivers Tishina and Ilovla, amidst an inaccessible waste of waters, he deliberately set himself to levy blackmail on all the vessels passing up and down the Volga. His first exploit was to attack, overwhelm, and disperse the "Water-Caravan" consisting of the Government treasury-barge, the barge of the Patriarch, and the corn-barges of the rich Moscovy merchant Svorin which were sailing down the river to Astrakhan. Next, he sailed down the Volga himself with a flotilla of 35 *strugi*[1] levying blackmail, as he passed, on the fortress of Tsaritsuin, devastating the country far and wide, and capturing the fortress of Yaitsk by a stratagem. In November, the same year, he scornfully rejected an offer of a free pardon from the Tsar if he would lay down his arms. At the beginning of 1668 he defeated the Tsar's general, Yakov Bezobrazov, and, in the spring of the same year, he embarked on an enterprise which relieved Moscovy of his presence for eighteen months. Sailing into the Caspian, he ravaged the Persian coasts from Derbend to Baku. On reaching Resht he offered his services to the Shah; but an act of treachery of the people of Resht, who surprised and slew four hundred of his followers, induced him to extirpate the defenceless and unsuspecting inhabitants of the wealthy town of Farabat and establish himself, during the spring of 1669, on the isle of Suina, whence he could conveniently raid the mainland. Here, in July, a Persian fleet, with 4000 men on board, attacked Razin but was annihilated, only three ships escaping.

[1] The large, flat-bottomed boats used by the Cossacks on their maritime expeditions.

Stenka was now a potentate with whom monarchs need not disdain to treat. In August, 1669, he appeared in Astrakhan, and magnanimously accepted a fresh offer of pardon from the Tsar. Stenka then remained at Astrakhan and speedily became the hero and the marvel of the city. The common people, whose dull, monotonous life was one ceaseless round of bitter toil, were fascinated by the sight of this fairy-tale paladin and his comrades, fresh from their romantic, oriental adventures, swaggering about the bazaars, arrayed in atlas caftans and jewelled caps, scattering their sequins broadcast, and selling priceless oriental silks at 9*d.* a pound. He was so different from the officials of the Tsar who lived on the sweat and blood of the people and treated them like dirt. He had a good word for every one and feasted the people night and day like a Prince. What booty might not be won at next to no risk under such a *batyushka*[1]? If, as we are told, prosperous merchants on the Don frequently cast their ordinary pursuits to the winds to join in the more lucrative speculation of an ordinary Cossack raid, how much greater must have been the fascination of an expedition under a chieftain who levied blackmail on Shah and Tsar alike? Such an adventurer could always count upon the peasantry, who were of the same stock as himself, as well as upon the ordinary Cossack. Finally, we must remember that the semi-Asiatic " Kingdom of Astrakhan[2]," where the whole atmosphere was predatory, and nine-tenths of the population were nomadic, was the natural *milieu* for such a rebellion as Stenka's.

In the circumstances, the Moscovite government should have rid itself of Stenka at the first opportunity, but they took no active measures against him till he had committed several flagrant acts of rebellion, such as the looting of Tsaritsuin, the building of the fortress of Kagalnik on the Don, and the whole-

[1] " Little Father."

[2] " Tsar of Astrakhan " is still one of the many titles of the Russian Emperor.

sale massacring and plundering of the districts of Tula and Voronezh. The peasantry now flocked to him from every quarter; and in 1670 he was strong enough to capture both the fortress and the town of Tsaritsuin and defeat the Government troops in two engagements. He then proceeded against Astrakhan ; and on January 24, 1670, the Volgan capital was in his hands.

Master of Astrakhan, Razin at once converted it into a Cossack Republic, dividing the inhabitants into thousands, hundreds and tens, with their proper officers, all of whom were appointed by a *Vyeche*, or General Assembly, whose first act was to proclaim Razin their Gosudar. The better classes were then hunted out and massacred, and their widows and daughters given in marriage to the Cossack rabble, Razin's official seal serving in lieu of the blessing of the Archbishop.

After a three weeks' carnival of blood and debauchery, Stenka turned his attention to affairs of State, and, leaving his lieutenant Vaska Us in charge of Astrakhan, set out with 200 barges, escorted by 2000 horsemen, to establish the Cossack Republic along the whole length of the Volga, as a preliminary step toward advancing against Moscow. Saratov and Samara were captured, and the Cossack rule was inaugurated, with the usual ceremonies ; but at Smolensk, the Boyar, Ivan Miloslavsky, held Stenka at bay for twenty-four hours, thus enabling the Government to rally its forces ; and, on the banks of the Sviyaga, after two bloody encounters (October 1 and 4), Prince Yury Baryatinsky routed Razin, who fled away down the Volga, leaving the bulk of his followers to be extirpated by the victors.

But the rebellion was by no means over. The emissaries of Razin, armed with inflammatory proclamations, had stirred up the inhabitants of the modern governments of Nizhny Novgorod, Tambov, and Penza ; and soon, over the whole of the vast region extending between the Volga, the Oka, and the Dwina, a *jacquerie* was raging. The unspeakable horrors of the interregnum of 1611–1613, and of Chmielnicki's rising

in the northern Ukraine, were repeated and exceeded. In all
the villages the sorely oppressed peasantry rose in bands,
butchered the land-owners and joined the Cossacks. The
surrounding semi-Pagan Finnish tribes, the Mordvinians, the
Chuvasses, and the Cheremisses, speedily made common cause
with the native Moscovites in such numbers that in one band
of 15,000 rebels only 100 were Cossacks. Nizhny Novgorod,
which had sent an invitation to the Cossack chief Osipov, was
only saved for the Government by the drastic energy of Prince
Yury Dolgoruki, who terrorised the mutinous city into obedience
by quartering the insurgents inside, and gibbeting them outside
the walls. After purifying the north, Dolgoruki moved southwards, everywhere encountering the most furious resistance,
mostly from behind enormous barricades, some of them three
miles in length. The effusion of blood was horrible. Driven
gradually from lair to lair, the desperate wretches fought like
ravening beasts ; and the slow but steady progress of the Tsarist
generals was marked by hundreds of burning villages and long
lines of wheels and gibbets. One hundred thousand peasants
and Cossacks are said to have perished in these parts. In
April 1671 Stenka was captured in his fortress of Kagalnik and
carried to Moscow. On June 6, after enduring unspeakable
torments with dogged bravado, he was quartered alive.

At Astrakhan there was still no thought of surrender.
When, at the end of August, 1671, the armada of Prince
Miloslavsky appeared before the city, the Cossacks "howled
like savage dogs" at all his offers of mercy. For three months
they beat off the besiegers and, in frequent sorties, damaged or
destroyed the tall wooden towers from which Miloslavsky
attempted to scale the walls. Finally, on November 27, they
obtained their own terms, and an absolute amnesty. Not till
the following year did the Moscovite Government feel strong
enough to hold an enquiry in the city and hang the ringleaders.

Ruffian and freebooter as he was, Stenka, nevertheless,
had within him something of the stuff of which enterprising

colonists and heroic adventurers are made. Indeed, the Cossack element of the Russian nation, with its pioneering audacity and its restless *abandon*, when adequately controlled and directed, was to be largely instrumental in extending the Empire of Moscovy over the barbarians of the central Asiatic steppes.

At the beginning of the 17th century, the Calmucks were the nearest of Moscovy's savage nomadic neighbours. They first penetrated into Siberia in the reign of Vasily Shuisky (1606–1610), and, ultimately, in 1630–1632, settled on the shores of the Volga and the Yaika (though their chief *yurt*, or encampment, lay beyond the Urals) where their depredations speedily brought them into collision with the Moscovite Government. In 1657 they became nominally Russian subjects. In Siberia proper, during the reign of Michael Romanov, the Moscovites, with the assistance of fire-arms, easily subdued the aborigines, who had only bows and arrows, and compelled them to pay *yasak*, or a tribute of pelts. But the authority of the Russians in these remote regions was by no means established; and, from 1634 to the end of the century, scarcely a year passed without an attack of the Calmucks and other races upon the thinly garrisoned Russian settlements. In 1663, the Ostiaks attempted to take Tobolsk and drive the Moscovites out of western Siberia. Not till 1674 were the surrounding tribes brought into something like subjection by Prince Daniel Baryatinsky, who successfully united the forces of the four chief Siberian towns against them.

At the very time when the Moscovite trans-Uralian settlements were fighting for their existence with the Calmucks, Moscovite pioneers were making fresh conquests in the remotest districts of northern Asia. In 1655, after a bloody struggle, the Buriates were subdued by the Cossack Hetman Kolesnikov. In 1661 Irkutsk was founded. From the Yenesei the exploring bands proceeded along the Angora, the Shilka and the Selenga, and round Lake Baikal, conquering and colonising in every direction. In 1648, Simeon Desnev, sailing from the mouth of the Koluimna in search of new lands, was the first successfully to navigate the north-eastern coast of Asia and sail through the narrow strait separating the Chucotch peninsula from the isle of St Laurence, into the northern Pacific, thus anticipating the navigator Bering by sixty years. Rumours of silver and gold mines, and of corn in abundance, attracted the Moscovites to the Amur. The first explorer of these regions was Vasily Poyarkov, sent from Yakutsk, in 1643, in search of fresh *yasak*. Sailing down the rivers Shilka, Ziya, Lina, Aldan, and their tributaries, he entered the Amur unwittingly, taking it to be a continuation of the Shilka. After wintering at the mouth of the Amur, he returned to Yakutsk, bringing rich stores of sables with him and recommending the occupation of the Amur district, which he reported to be rich and populous, abounding with corn, pelts, and fat rivers. Another pioneer, Erothei Khabarov, explored the Amur by way of the rivers Lekhma, Tagir and Ukra. He discovered three or four vast deserted cities and reported that the Amur was even richer in fish than the Volga, while round about it lay lush meadows, rich cornfields, and "large dark forests full of sables." In 1650 Khabarov occupied the fort of Albazin. But the aborigines, who were already the tributaries of China, refused to give *yasak* to the Tsar; and in 1652 Khabarov was attacked, in his winter quarters at Ashansk, by a large Manchurian army under a Chinese viceroy, and obliged to fight his way back into Moscovite territory. In 1653, Onifry Stepanov was appointed governor of the Amur district, and, in 1654, he undertook an expedition down the river; but, though, in March, 1655, he defeated 10,000 Chinese on the river Kamara, a southern confluent of the Amur, he was ultimately starved out of the country, the Chinese Emperor having ordered an exodus from Manchuria of the entire corn-growing population.

Diplomatic efforts to bring about intercourse with China proved equally unsuccessful. Theodore Baikov, sent from

Tobolsk to Pekin (1654–1656) was refused admittance to the imperial presence because he declined to deliver his credentials except in person. In 1675, the Moldavian Greek, Nikola Gavril Spafari, to whom we owe the earliest Russian account of China, Japan and Corea, was sent to the Bogduichan, or Chinese Emperor, to open commercial relations. He reached Pekin on May 16, 1676, and succeeded, with the assistance of the Jesuits, in obtaining two audiences. Nevertheless Spafari's mission proved to be as fruitless as Baikov's. Try as he would, he could not obtain a reply from the Bogduichan to the Tsar. His presents were accepted as "tribute," and he was told not to be surprised thereat, as this was the ancient and immutable custom of the Chinese Court.

CHAPTER XII.

THE AGE OF SOBIESKI, 1669–1696.

THE abdication of John Casimir once more exposed Poland to all the inconveniences of "a free election." For nearly a century the throne had been quasi-hereditary in the Vasa-Jagiello family, for no one had seriously disputed the right of the next heir to succeed Sigismund III and Wladislaus IV. But John Casimir was the last of his race, and all his efforts to establish a new dynasty of foreign origin had failed. His policy was resumed, however, after his retirement, by the principal Senators, headed by John Sobieski, upon whom the late King, a few months before his disappearance, had conferred the grand *bâton* of the Crown, as a reward for Sobieski's brilliant victory over the Cossack Hetman Doroshenko and his Turko-Tatar hordes, at Podhajie—a victory which, for a brief period, re-established the authority of Poland in the Ukraine. The Grand-Hetman and his friends had been won over by French gold, lavishly scattered with both hands, to support any candidate whom Louis XIV might think it worth his while to produce ; but the mass of the *Szlachta* was opposed on principle to any and every foreign candidate. These ignorant but well-meaning country gentlemen, when they saw nearly all the dignitaries of the Republic in the pay of foreign Powers (for Austria and Brandenburg, in their efforts to form their own parties, were almost as liberal as France), dimly felt that the Republic was in no good way. Unfortunately their efforts to stay the progress of foreign influence and foreign corruption were so ill-directed, that their intervention, though momentarily successful, did more harm than good to their unfortunate country.

The Convocation Diet, that is the Diet which convoked the Election Diet, assembled on October 16, 1668. Its tone was violently national. Its first demand was that all the foreign ministers should withdraw from the capital; and one of its members, the starosta Piencanzek, required every member of the Senate to swear that he would accept no bribe from any foreign Potentate. Even the Primate was suspected. The Bishop of Posen openly accused him of having received 50,000 thalers from the French ambassador. The meeting of the Election Diet was fixed for May 2, 1669, on which occasion 80,000 electors assembled in full panoply. Sobieski brought 12,000 armed retainers with him, and the other magnates were similarly supported. Once more, as of old, the field of election resembled a field of battle.

Up to the last moment the greatest uncertainty prevailed as to who should be elected. Most of the magnates were the mercenaries of Louis XIV; but, as the French King vacillated between the Prince of Condé and Philip William Duke of Neuburg, who had married a sister of Wladislaus IV, the French party was uncertain what course to pursue; and, at last, Sobieski went over to the Austrian candidate, Duke Charles of Lorraine. But the *Szlachta* were determined to elect none but a piast, or native Pole; and on June 19, the last day of the Diet, to the general astonishment, Michael Wisniowiecki was proclaimed King of Poland.

Michael, the son of Prince Jeremiah Wisniowiecki, the famous queller of the Cossacks, had neither the material resources nor the personal qualities requisite for the exalted position to which a mere caprice had raised him. He had inherited from his father nothing but a ruined estate and an inordinate fondness for eating and drinking, so that his own

B.

friends, after the excitement of the election was over, would have found it difficult to explain why they had elected him at all. Nevertheless, his intentions were good enough ; and, as the validity of his election was beyond dispute, the least he had a right to expect from his subjects was loyalty. But the Poles were quite unlike other people. No sooner had the new King been solemnly crowned and affianced by his friends to the Archduchess Eleonora, daughter of the Emperor Ferdinand III, with the view of strengthening his position, than all the great dignitaries of the crown united in a conspiracy to dethrone him. At the head of this conspiracy stood the Primate and the Commander-in-chief, Sobieski.

John Sobieski, the youngest son of James Sobieski, Castellan of Cracow, and Theofila, the grand-daughter of the great Crown-Hetman Zolkiewski, was born at Oleska in Galicia in 1624. He rose rapidly to distinction during the wars of John Casimir with the Cossacks, but was one of the first to desert his sovereign in the hour of misfortune. He materially assisted Charles X of Sweden to conquer the Prussian provinces, but perceiving, a few months later, that the position of the Swedes was unstable, he changed sides again and commanded one of the four armies which all but succeeded in capturing the Swedish King on his retreat from Jaroslaw to Warsaw. Henceforth John Casimir made it worth the capable young general's while to remain loyal. On the death of Czarniecki, in 1665, Sobieski succeeded him as Vice-Hetman of the Crown. He had already replaced Lubomirsky as Grand-Marshal, and in 1668 he received the grand *bâton* of the Crown likewise. The same year he married his old love Mary Casimiera, the widow of Jan Zamoyski, Palatine of Sandomeria, and daughter of the Margrave Henri de la Grange d'Arquien. Born in France, in 1637, this beautiful and brilliant girl was educated in Poland at the Court of Queen Maria Ludowika, who initiated her into all the mysteries of political intrigue and spoiled her in the process ; for her essentially petty nature was incapable of taking a broad, detached view of politics, and sacrificed everything to the caprice of the moment. Her influence over her second husband was as absolute as it was mischievous; and the hero of Chocim, whose very name inspired the Turks with terror, was, at home, the obsequious slave of his beloved "Marysienka."

It will be plain, from the brief foregoing sketch, that Sobieski stood on a much lower level than the great captains of the two preceding generations, Zamoyski, Chodkiewicz, Zolkiewski, for instance. He had little or nothing of their sobriety, stability, and self-sacrificing devotion to duty. He could fight as well as the best of them, but he fought for his own hand. His patriotism was far less pure than theirs because it was inextricably bound up with egotism and self-seeking. Inestimable were his services to his country after he had mounted the throne, but he nearly ruined her in the process of getting there. As to his statesmanship, the most convincing demonstration of his utter lack of it is to be found in his hasty and ill-conceived combinations against King Michael from 1669 to 1673.

At the end of 1669, Louis XIV sent the Comte de Lionne to Warsaw to congratulate Wisniowiecki on his accession to the throne. Wisniowiecki was now connected by marriage (February 26, 1670) with the Hapsburgs; and at this juncture the French King, intent on an amicable settlement of the Spanish Succession question, had concluded a secret agreement with the Court of Vienna. Ignorant of this new combination, which ought to have been known to men of their high position, Sobieski and his friends at once jumped to the conclusion that Louis was intriguing against the new King of Poland. They accordingly sent a private memorial to the French King inviting him to assist them to dethrone King Michael, whom, being a friend of Austria, Louis was, as a matter of fact, much more disposed to support. However, he humoured the malcontents at first and even allowed a new French pretender, the Count of Saint Pol Longueville, to send secret agents to Poland to form a party

16—2

there.   At the beginning of 1670 Michael discovered the plot against him, and remonstrated energetically both at Versailles and at Vienna.   Louis thereupon repudiated Longueville ; and the disconcerted conspirators sought refuge at Dantzic or Königsberg, counting on the help of the Elector of Brandenburg.   But the Elector held aloof ; and nothing but the helplessness of the King saved Sobieski and his confederates from the well-deserved penalties of treason.   Only one of the royal counsellors, Christopher Pac, Grand-Chancellor of·Lithuania, had the courage to advise Michael to summon a *ruszenie pospolite* and punish the traitors summarily.   But Michael, who was no warrior, durst not pit the undisciplined levies of the country gentry against Sobieski's veterans, and allowed the Diet of September 1670 to effect a reconciliation.   The rehabilitated Primate consented to crown the young Queen ; the King's uncle Demetrius Wisniowiecki married Sobieski's niece Teofila Ostrogska ; and the Grand-Hetman set out for the Ukraine to wash clean his tarnished honour in Turkish blood.

At this time, the Turkish Empire, after a period of declension and disintegration lasting, roughly speaking, for 100 years, was once more directed by a man of genius in the person of Achmet Köprili, the most illustrious member of a family of soldier-statesmen, sprung from a hardy Albanian stock.   From the moment when, at the unprecedently early age of 26, he succeeded his aged father Mohammed as Grand Vizier (1656), it was his ambition to re-establish the glory and prosperity of his country ; and all Europe was, speedily, to feel the effects of that ambition.   After reducing Transylvania to the rank of a Turkish fief, and adding five counties and as many first class fortresses to Turkish Hungary (Peace of Vasvár, August 1664), Köprili turned his arms against Venice, and began the memorable siege of Candia (1667–1669), which, for the next two years, was to tax to the uttermost the resources of both belligerents, at the same time employing the Tatars and Cossacks to keep Poland occupied till he himself had the leisure to take the field against her. At his command the Cossack Hetman Doroshenko invaded the Ukraine, but was routed at Kalniki by Sobieski, who, at the same time, re-captured Bar, Mohilew and other places. Instead, however, of following up his victories, the Grand-Hetman, with criminal recklessness, returned to Poland to plot once more against King Michael and put De Longueville on the Polish throne. The death of his candidate in the Dutch War and the indifference of Louis XIV, who replied coldly and evasively to Sobieski's urgent letters for assistance, caused the whole conspiracy to end in a fiasco.

While the unhappy Polish King was painfully endeavouring to re-establish law and order, by force of arms, against his own commander-in-chief, Köprili burst suddenly into the territories of the Republic. During the spring of 1672 he collected a host "like the sands of the sea for number and like the stars of heaven for splendour "—in plain prose about 300,000 men—and carrying Sultan Mohammed along with him, to give prestige to the enterprise, invaded Podolia. As something very like civil war was, at that very moment, prevailing in Poland, and as, moreover, the last two Diets had refused to contribute a farthing towards the defence of the country, the issue of the struggle was never doubtful. After defeating Luzecki, Castellan of Podlesia, who commanded the Polish army during the absence of Sobieski, at Czetwertynowka, the Grand Vizier sat down before the great fortress of Kamieniec, the key of Podolia, which had been left with a small garrison of 1000 men and only four gunners to serve 400 guns. Within ten days (August 27) the keys were surrendered; and the Sultan attended a thanksgiving in the cathedral, now converted into a Mosque. Lemberg was only saved by the heroism of its commandant, Elias Lancki. Six weeks later (October 17, 1672), the Republic, by the treaty of Budziak, ceded the Polish Ukraine and Podolia, including Kamieniec, to the Turks, and agreed to pay them an annual tribute.

Without doubt Sobieski was primarily responsible for this shameful treaty. Judging from later events, we may safely infer that, if only he had been in his proper place at the proper time, Kamieniec would never have been taken nor Podolia surrendered. In any other country but Poland a commander-in-chief who had deserted his post, in the hour of utmost danger, in order to play at treason, would have been promptly and justly executed. Even in Poland popular opinion strongly condemned the Grand-Hetman ; and it was with the consent of the majority of the nation that the King now formed a Confederation at Golenbi which deposed the Primate Prazmowski, condemned the other malcontents, and introduced some slight constitutional reform by limiting the operation of the *liberum veto.* Unfortunately, Sobieski was now far too strong, far too indispensable, to be restrained by any constitutional curb. From the 3rd to the 14th October he undertook his famous raid into the Ukraine against the Tatars whom he defeated four times in eleven days. This exploit was generally regarded as "an expiation" of his former misdeeds, and made him so popular that, on his return, he was permitted to do pretty much what he liked. First he formed a Confederation of his own at Szczebrzeszyn, which undid all the work of the reforming Confederation of Golenbi. Next he hastened to Lowicz to the assistance of the Primate, scattering the royal troops on his way, and fixed his head-quarters at the Primate's residence, in threatening proximity to Warsaw.

In the midst of extreme tension the Diet assembled on January 4, 1673. Again the King was obliged to give way. The decrees of the Confederation of Golenbi were revoked ; the full authority of the Grand-Hetman over the troops was officially recognised ; and the Lithuanians, who had steadily supported their countryman, King Michael, were appeased by the distribution of " gratifications " and the passing of an Act to the effect that every third Diet should be held at Grodno under the presidency of the Grand-Marshal of Lithuania. The last obstacle in the way of a reconciliation was finally removed by the convenient death of the turbulent Primate Prazmowski, who

was succeeded by the learned Floryan Czartoryski, the founder
of the fortunes of that illustrious house.

The question of the Turkish war was now seriously taken
in hand. The treaty of Budziak was repudiated; and, on the
motion of Sobieski, an offensive war against the Turks was
resolved upon. Subsidies, sufficient to place 60,000 men in
the field, were voted, and an ultimatum was sent to Stambul.
In August the King reviewed the forces assembled at Gliniani,
near Lemberg, and entrusted the supreme command to Sobieski.
Sending Nicholas Sieniawski against Doroshenko and the
Cossacks, and the Lithuanian army against Halil Pasha, who
had reached Jazlowiec in Galicia, the Grand-Hetman himself
advanced with 30,000 men to the Dniester, and, hastening
through the forests of the Bukowina, united with the Lithuanians
at Chocim, already occupied by the Turkish commander Hussein
Pasha. At dawn on November 11, 1673, Sobieski advanced
with all his forces against Chocim. The Polish artillery, well
directed by Marcin Kontski, prepared the way; and then the
assaulting columns, led by the Grand-Hetman in person, sword
in hand, fell furious , upon the fortress. After an hour's hard
fighting, Chocim was in the hands of the Poles and Hussein
Pasha in full retreat upon Jassy. But Sobieski pursued and
cut him off, and drove him into the flooded Dniester, where he
perished with nine-tenths of his host. The whole of his baggage,
more than 120 guns, and immense treasures, were the spoil of
the victors.

At the moment when the Polish chivalry was singing a *Te
Deum* for the victory of Chocim in the tent of Hussein Pasha,
King Michael had ceased to reign. He had long been ailing,
and on November 10, 1673, he expired, in his thirty-third year.
There could be no doubt as to his successor. The Convocation
Diet (January 1674), enthusiastically supported the candidature
of the hero of Chocim; and, though the Lithuanians favoured
Tsar Theodore III, and the Primate would have set up the
Austrian candidate, the Duke of Lorraine, against him, all
opposition collapsed when Sobieski himself appeared on the

field of election with 6000 veterans and a multitude of Turkish captives. On May 21, 1674, he was elected King of Poland under the title of John III.

The Turkish peril was still so urgent that the new King postponed his coronation and hastened to the frontier immediately after his election. Materially assisted by the diplomacy of Louis XIV, who, anxious to reserve Poland for his anti-Hapsburg plans, persuaded the Sultan to raid Moscovy instead of the Republic during the remainder of 1674, Sobieski employed this welcome respite in efforts to divide his enemies by detaching the Cossacks from the Tatars. He persuaded a considerable section of the Cossacks to garrison the Ukraine fortresses, while he, with his regulars, quickly recaptured Bar, Niemerov and Braclaw, and might even have recovered Kamieniec but for the unwillingness of the Lithuanians to co-operate with him, and the inveterate niggardliness of the Poles, whose martial ardour was already cooling rapidly. In fact the obstinate parsimony of the *Szlachta* defeated all his plans and hampered all his movements, so that when, at the beginning of 1675, he found himself face to face with another Turkish invasion, he was all but helpless. With only 3000 regular troops at his disposal, he could not prevent the junction of Ibrahim Sisman and his 60,000 Turks with the Tatar Khan; but, fortunately, the heroic defence of the fortress of Trembola by Samuel Chrzanowski, an officer of Jewish origin, enabled the King, at the last moment, to collect reinforcements sufficient to compel the Turks to retreat. On October 16, the same year, peace was concluded at Zórawno (heroically and successfully defended by Sobieski from August 28 to October 16), when the Turks retroceded two-thirds of the Ukraine, but retained Kamieniec, which was worth the whole of it. It was after all but a semi-triumph, and for this the nation, not the King, was to blame. "Those who have the greatest stake in this country do the least for it," was Sobieski's sorrowful commentary on the selfish backwardness of his subjects.

But still worse was to come. Sobieski was now to reap to

the full the bitter harvest of treachery and treason, the seeds of which he himself had recklessly sown during the reign of his predecessor.   The *Szlachta*, which had done nothing to help the King to recover Kamieniec, protested violently against the Treaty of Zórawno, yet almost with the same breath they prevented Sobieski from pursuing a more profitable policy in the future by reducing the army from 30,000 to 12,000 men.   In his extremity John III hit upon the desperate, but, in the circumstances, only effectual remedy for existing evils —the establishment with French assistance of an absolute monarchy.   He communicated his views through Bethune, the French ambassador, but Louis XIV replied that he did not see how such a change would suit his own views.   Shortly afterwards (1667) Maria Casimiria brought about an open rupture between the Courts of Versailles and Warsaw because the French King refused to exalt her father to princely rank, and the French influence in Poland was superseded by the Austrian.

In view of the constant peril from the Turks, the political interests of Austria and Poland were, at this time, identical ; and an alliance between them was equally profitable to both. Moreover Innocent XI, the greatest of the later Popes, who ascended the papal throne in 1676, was using all his efforts to form a league of Princes to expel the Turks from Europe ; and it was mainly due to his initiative and enthusiasm that they were expelled at least from Hungary.   His noble ambition was opposed *à outrance* by Louis XIV, with whose anti-Hapsburg plans it directly clashed ; and, for the next thirteen years, the diplomatical battle was fought out at all the Courts of Europe. In 1678, the papal nuncio, Martelli, preached the coming Crusade in Poland ; and the impressionable Diet, which assembled in December of that year, raised the army to 43,000 men and granted subsidies comparatively liberal, but falling far short of actual requirements[1].   The intrigues of Louis XIV did

---

[1] 6,000,000 gulden were still due to the army ; and the initial expenses of the Crusade were estimated at 20,000,000 more.

the rest, and the whole scheme was abandoned. The French King next proceeded to undermine the position of Sobieski. Between 1679 and 1681, Louis is said to have expended no less a sum than fifty millions of livres in efforts to dethrone John III. Most of the great dignitaries of Poland were already in the French King's pay; many of them boasted openly that they were his friends and even his subjects; some of them took their orders direct from him.

The Turkish question became acute, when, in the course of 1682, Emerich Tököly, the leader of the Magyar malcontents, who had long been subsidised by Louis XIV, was proclaimed King of Hungary by the Sultan. Invading that realm at the head of a Hungaro-Turkish army, he captured fortress after fortress, and extended his dominions as far as the Waag. In the spring of 1683 he was joined by the new Grand Vizier, Kara Mustafa, with more than 100,000 men. Sobieski hesitated no longer. The French agent was dismissed from Poland; the French couriers were intercepted; the correspondence of the Polish malcontents with the Elector of Brandenburg, who supported the French policy in Poland, was seized; and, when the partizans of France attempted to explode the Diet by means of the *liberum veto*, the King threatened to form a "Diet on horse-back," or Confederation of all the noblemen in the kingdom, and deliver every traitor into its hands. The French faction thereupon collapsed; and, on March 31, 1683, an offensive and defensive alliance was signed between Poland and Austria, whereby Sobieski agreed to co-operate against the Turks with 40,000 men. Louis XIV exhausted all the resources of diplomacy to prevent John III from succouring the distressed Emperor. John III thereupon, very pertinently, enquired of Louis XIV whether, in case Poland should refuse to help Austria, France would engage to hasten to the assistance of Poland, "when the Turks, after taking Vienna, sit down before Cracow"? In Poland itself, indeed, politicians were by no means agreed as to the expediency of relieving Vienna. At the

Sejm of 1683, many of the deputies protested against fighting
the battles of Austria. "What is it to us," they cried, "if the
Turks *do* extend their empire to the Danube? Ten years ago
did the Emperor move a step when the Turks threatened the
Vistula?" There was some truth in this, no doubt; but
Sobieski, well aware that the danger was pressing, and that
his Polish critics had, as usual, no alternative policy, wisely
resolved to minimise his risks. The alliance with Austria had
been concluded in May. In September he drove the Turks
from Vienna. In October he pursued their retreating forces
through Hungary and severely defeated them at Parkány. Still
there was no sign of surrender at Stambul; and, in September
1684, a Holy League was formed between Poland, Austria,
Venice and the Pope, to which "the most serene Tsars of
Moscovy" were invited to accede. In the spring of 1685, the
Polish and Imperial plenipotentiaries appeared at Moscow.

Prince Vasily Golitsuin, who, during the Regency of the
Tsarevna Sophia[1], directed the Moscovite Foreign Office,
clearly recognised that, in regard to the Eastern Question, the
interests of Moscovy and Poland were identical. Moreover,
Moscovy possessed an excellent pretext for a rupture with the
Porte, in the prevalence of the Tatar raids into the Ukraine.
Every year, thousands of captives and tens of thousands of
cattle were carried off and sold at Kaffa, despite the fact that a
regular tribute was paid to the Khan of the Crimea as a sort of
insurance against such depredations. But Golitsuin was much
too good a diplomatist to sell the Moscovite alliance cheaply.
The negotiations with Poland were protracted till the growing
distress of the Republic constrained her to sacrifice everything
for the co-operation of the Moscovites. Finally, on April 21,
1686, a "perpetual peace was signed at Moscow, by the terms
of which Kiev was surrendered to Moscovy in exchange for
146,000 rubles. But Poland lost much more than Kiev by
this treaty, for it contained a provision binding her to maintain

[1] *See* following chapter.

the liberties of the Dissidents, thus opening the door to the interference of Russia in the domestic affairs of the Republic. Later in the same year, Sobieski, who, after capturing Jassy, had been obliged, from want of money and supplies, to lead his sick and starving army back to Poland, tearfully ratified at Lemberg a treaty from which the eclipse of Poland may be definitely dated.

The Porte had done its utmost to prevent the conclusion of the Russo-Polish alliance. The Patriarch of Constantinople had even been employed by the Divan to dissuade the Tsars from embarking on a war which would, he warned them, call down the vengeance of the Sultan on the Orthodox population of his domains. But neither blandishments nor menaces could avail. Russia had gone too far to retreat ; and, in the autumn of 1687, 100,000 Moscovites under Prince Vasily Golitsuin, set out to reconquer the Crimea. At Samara, Golitsuin was joined by the Cossack Hetman Samoilovich, with 50,000 men ; and the army then plunged into the steppe. There was no sign of the Tatars, but Golitsuin soon encountered a far more terrible enemy in the steppe fires, which destroyed all the grass and make further progress impossible. After traversing eight miles in forty-eight hours, he decided to turn back, and leaving 30,000 men on the lower Dnieper, retired with the rest of his army across the Kolomak, not far from Poltava. According to Patrick Gordon, who accompanied the expedition, Samoilovich was strongly suspected of firing the steppe to compel a retreat, foreseeing that the subjection of the Crimea must inevitably lead to the suppression of the free Cossacks. The Moscovite Government shared this suspicion; and, on July 25, Samoilovich was deprived of his Hetmanship and Ivan Mazepa was then elected unanimously in his stead. Golitsuin solemnly invested him with the usual insignia of office, for which the new Hetman privately paid the prince 10,000 rubles.

At the very time when Golitsuin was ingloriously retreating from the wasted steppe, Sobieski had failed to retake Kamieniec because the *Sejm* would not provide him with an adequate army; but everywhere else the members of the Holy League were brilliantly successful. Defeated in Hungary, Dalmatia and the Morea, the Turks could with difficulty defend themselves even within their own territory. Sultan Mahommed IV fell a victim to an outburst of popular fury which placed Solyman III on the throne (1687), and so great was the confusion that the collapse of the Turkish Empire was confidently anticipated. But, in 1689, the Sultan made Mustafa Köprili, the brother of Achmet (who had died in 1676), Grand Vizier; and the Turkish Empire was saved once more. By Köprili's advice, the dashing Tököly was released from prison and proclaimed Prince of Transylvania; and the victory of Zernyest (Sept. 1690) established the pretender for a time on his unstable throne. Simultaneously Köprili recovered the southern portions of Servia and Bosnia, and replanted the crescent standard on the ramparts of Widdin, Nish, Galambocs, Semlin and Belgrade. In the following year (1691), he resumed the war with redoubled vigour, but perished with the greater part of his army at Zalánkemén (Aug. 9, 1691). Nevertheless, his exploits had given the Turks time to rally and enabled them to carry on the war, with ever diminishing prospects of success, for eight years longer.

Neither Moscovy nor Poland, however, contributed much to the ultimate triumph of the allies. In February, 1689, Golitsuin, for the second time, led more than 10,000 Moscovites into the steppe; but the march was delayed by snowstorms and lack of provisions, and it was not till the middle of May that he encountered the Khan near Perekop. The lightly armed Tatars were easily beaten off; but, with the Crimea open before him, Golitsuin suddenly discovered that there were waterless steppes beyond as well as before Perekop. This fact had never entered into his calculations; and as, moreover, his beasts of burden now began to die off in such numbers as to make him fear for the transport of his baggage, there was nothing for it but to turn back a second time. Yet Moscovy's share in the war had not been altogether useless, for she had prevented the Tatars from co-operating with the Turks ; and the very appearance of a Russian army at the gates of the Crimea was a significant sign that the steppe was no longer an insuperable barrier to Russia's progress southwards.

Still more unlucky was Sobieski. His last campaign, in 1690, undertaken to place his eldest son James on the throne of Moldavia and Wallachia, was an utter failure. But this was but a small part of his misfortunes. Ill-luck persistently dogged him everywhere during the last seven years of his life. Nothing that he put his hand to prospered. Allies and neighbours proved treacherous and ungrateful ; his domestic happiness was ruined by the caprices of his wife and her ceaseless quarrels with her own sons ; and, above all, towered the evil spirit of political discord which he had raised so lightly in his younger days, but was powerless to lay in his miserable old age. Rarely has Nemesis pursued its victim so remorselessly.

Twice his matrimonial projects for the benefit of his son Prince James were frustrated by the Court of Vienna ; and, when John III, revolted by the ingratitude of the Emperor, would have turned to Louis XIV, he found Versailles closed against him. His attempts to convert Poland into a constitutional monarchy, hereditary in his family—certainly the best thing that could have happened—foundered on the determined opposition of the *Sejm.* He had some hopes of success in this respect at the Diet which was to meet at Grodno in 1688 ; but no sooner did his plans get wind, than a Confederation, headed by the chief dignitaries of the Republic, most of whom were under deep obligations to the King, was formed to prevent any such design. The parrot-cry of "the Republic is in danger!" resounded everywhere ; and the application of the *liberum veto* exploded the Diet at the very beginning of the session. At the meeting of the Senate, held immediately afterwards, such a shameless attack was made upon the King that he was provoked to the uttermost and replied in a fulminating address, which concluded with these prophetic words : "Posterity will be stupefied to learn that the only result of so many victories and triumphs, shedding an eternal glory on the Polish name throughout the world, was—God help us!— irreparable ruin and damnation. Yet forty days and Nineveh shall be destroyed."

Yet his worst enemies were the Lithuanians, who could never forgive him for his conduct to their fellow-countryman, King Michael. It was they, represented by the Sapiehas, the Radziwills, and the Pacowe, who perpetually traversed his dearest hopes. Thus they prevented the marriage of his son James with the wealthy young widow Ludowika Radziwill with the result that she married a relative of the Elector of Branden- burg, and her immense fortune passed into German hands. The Diet, on this occasion, was inclined to support the King, whereupon it was exploded by one of the hirelings of the House of Sapieha. Anarchical was the state of Lithuania at this time. Casimir Sapieha, Grand-Hetman of Lithuania, preyed upon his neighbours, lay and clerical, like a feudal baron of the worst type. In his private quarrel with Brzostowski, Bishop of Wilna, he devastated the whole diocese and burnt dozens of churches. When the bishop excommunicated him, Cardinal Radziejowski, Primate of Poland, promptly removed the ban and blamed the bishop. Twice, in 1693 and 1695, the King, indignant at this outrage, summoned Sapieha to answer for his misdeeds before the Diet. On both occasions Sapieha's partisans exploded the Diet before it had time to consider the case. The *liberum veto* had now sunk so low that its principal use was to shelter high-placed felons from the pursuit of justice. With the Grand-Hetman of Lithuania a freebooter and a traitor, there was nobody left to defend the Grand-Duchy from its natural enemies, the Tatars, who raided it every year with perfect impunity. During 1695 they even penetrated as far as Lemberg.

On June 17, 1696, John III expired, in his 72nd year, utterly broken-hearted.   His reign had been a failure, and he foretold, on his death-bed, the ruin of his country.   Three years later, at the Peace of Karlowitz, which ended the long war between Austria and Turkey, Kamieniec, which the Republic had been unable to recover with her own sword, was restored to her by the generosity of the Holy League.

CHAPTER XIII.

THE PRECURSORS OF PETER THE GREAT,
1649–1689.

WHILE Poland had sunk beyond the possibility of recovery, Moscovy, slowly and circuitously, with many a serious hitch and many a ruinous relapse, was creeping forward along the path leading to prosperity and empire. Contemporaries could not be expected to see this. The victories of Sobieski had invested the Polish chivalry with a prestige which it was far from deserving, while Moscovy was generally regarded as a semi-barbarous country, negligible as a political factor, nay, as scarce within the European system at all. Even at the end of the seventeenth century no one could have imagined that, a century later, Poland would have disappeared from the map of Europe, and that Moscovy, under the name of Russia, would have become one of the world's greatest empires. Morally and intellectually, the Moscovites were infinitely below the level of the Western nations ; while their invincible pride and perverted patriotism seemed to exclude the possibility of enlightenment. An iron-bound conservatism, the consequence of a gross ignorance due again to centuries of isolation from the civilised West, fettered every movement, every thought of the national life. It has well been said that existence in old Moscovy, as compared with existence in Western Europe, was as the dull stagnant life of an agricultural district compared with the mobile, inquisitive, enterprising life of a great city.

The only teacher of the Moscovite people at this period was

the Orthodox Church; and, unfortunately, the Orthodox Church, from similar causes, had fallen as far behind other Churches as the Moscovite nation had fallen behind other nations. The only remedy against existing evils which the Church could devise was the rigid application of Byzantine asceticism to every-day life. In 1551 the Synod of Moscow published its *Stoglav*, or "Hundred Articles," severely condemning, among other things, all popular amusements. About the same time, the monk Silvester, now generally identified with Silvester the good genius of Ivan the Terrible during his earlier years, published his *Domostroi*, or "Domestic Economy," which aimed at making every household a monastery, with the father of the family as its prior, or director. Absolute obedience to him, "with slavish fear," was the counsel of perfection enjoined upon his children; and the term "children" included his wife and all who dwelt beneath his roof. The model household was conducted according to strict canonical rules. On every sort of diversion, except a moderate table, the Church looked askance. All music, profane songs, dances and games were banned as sheer idolatry. Draughts and chess were anathematised because they were supposed to be of Chaldean, cards because they were known to be of Latin origin. The position of the women under this régime was pitiable. In general, the Moscovite women were looked upon as permanently immature creatures, to be kept under perpetual tutelage. The wife was not the equal of her husband, but his pupil. As the first of the domestics, she was responsible, indeed, for the government of his household; but, in case of disobedience, he was empowered to chastise her, even "unmercifully" in the case of obstinate disobedience. The Moscovite lady's complete seclusion from the world dates from the end of the fifteenth century. By the beginning of the sixteenth century her domestic incarceration was an accomplished and peremptory fact. By this time, the *terem*, or women's quarters, had become a prison as well as a monastery.

Perpetual tutelage and an absolute want of culture were

almost invincible obstacles to anything like the development of
a free and healthy social life in Moscovy, while the continual
increase of public burdens, and the repression of all popular
amusements, drove the people to seek relief from the grinding monotony of life in habitual drunkenness and the grossest
sensuality.

Intellectually, also, this remorseless discipline proved very
injurious. The mental horizon of the ordinary Moscovite of the
seventeenth century was extraordinarily limited. For centuries
he had lived in a world of phenomena, which he regarded as
unchangeable because they had never changed. The secular
immobility of his surroundings gave to them, in his eyes, a
religious character, and therefore a religious inviolability. Any
alteration of his ancient ancestral customs was to him a sinful
surrender. In these circumstances the only conceivable
chance of improvement lay in the gradual filtration of western
ideas. But this was, necessarily, a very gradual process, de-
pending almost entirely on the superior sagacity of individual
Boyars or Prelates. The first of this little band of pioneers was
the Boyar Boris Ivanovich Morozov, to whom Tsar Michael
Romanov, on his death bed, committed the care of his sole
surviving son Alexis, then a youth of 16, who succeeded him on
July 13, 1645. A more suitable guardian could scarcely have
been chosen. Shrewd and sensible, sufficiently enlightened to
recognise the needs of his countrymen, and by no means
inaccessible to foreign ideas, Morozov stood high above his
fellows. His foreign policy was pacific, his domestic policy was
severe but equitable. The economical condition of Moscovy
at this period was anything but satisfactory. The native
traders, overburdened with taxes, and hampered by all manner
of disabilities, found it very difficult to compete with the highly
privileged foreign merchants. In 1646 they petitioned the
Tsar against the "English Germans[1]," who, being in the

---

[1] " Germans " (*Nyemtsui*) was the name given by the Moscovites to all
the protestants of the North.

possession of unlimited capital, and having at their disposal a whole army of well-paid middlemen, were able absolutely to control the Moscovite market and undersell the native traders. Their worst grievances were redressed in 1648 ; and, in the following year, a beginning was made of the codification of the laws in order to make legal procedure more expeditious and inexpensive. The severity of Morozov's government led, however, to a popular rising against him, in May 1648, when the Tsar was compelled to banish him to the Kirillov-Byelozersky monastery till the storm blew over. But, within two months' time, he was brought back secretly, and, to the day of his death (in 1661), continued to be one of the Tsar's chief counsellors. As the brother-in-law of Alexis (in 1648 he married Anna Miloslavskaya, ten days after the Tsar had married her sister Maria) he was also the Boyar nearest to the throne.

Morozov, for all his sagacity and initiative, was still a Boyar of the old school. The first modern Moscovite statesman was Orduin-Nashchokin.

Athanasy Lavrentovich Orduin-Nashchokin was the son of a poor official of Pskov, of whom we only know that he was greatly in advance of his times, for he saw to it that his son was taught German, Latin, and mathematics, so many abominations to the ordinary Moscovite of the seventeenth century. Athanasy began his brilliant diplomatic and administrative career under Michael as one of the delineators of the new Russo-Swedish frontier after the Peace of Stolbowa in 1642. Even then he had a great reputation at Moscow as one who thoroughly understood "German things and ways." He was one of the first Moscovites who diligently collected foreign books ; and we hear of as many as sixty-nine Latin works being sent to him at one time from abroad. In the beginning of the reign of Alexis he attracted the young Tsar's attention by his resourcefulness during the Pskov rebellion of 1650, which he succeeded in localising as much as possible by sheer personal influence.

At the beginning of the Swedish war, Orduin was appointed to a high command, in which he displayed striking ability, and, as Governor of Drui and Dmitriev, qualified himself for the office of minister and plenipotentiary, to which he was appointed in 1657. His letters to the Tsar during this period are illuminating and do equal honour to himself and his master. With perfect frankness, Orduin warns the Tsar that the atrocities of the Cossacks in Ingria and Livonia are driving even the orthodox inhabitants into the arms of the Swedes; and he urges, repeatedly, that all such orthodox desperadoes should be summarily punished. When the negotiations with Sweden were seriously resumed on the river Narova in 1658, he was the only Moscovite statesman with sufficient foresight to grasp the fact that the Baltic seaboard was worth much more to Moscovy than ten times the same amount of territory in Lithuania; and, despite the ignorant opposition of his jealous colleagues, he succeeded, at the end of December, in concluding a three years' truce whereby the Moscovites were left in possession of all their conquests in Livonia. In 1660 he was again sent, as the chief Moscovite plenipotentiary, to another congress, to convert the truce of 1658 into a durable peace. By this time Sweden had composed her differences with Poland by the Peace of Oliva, an event which modified the political situation very much to the disadvantage of Moscovy; and now the Tsar was nervously anxious to conclude peace with Sweden on any terms, hoping to compensate himself at the expense of Poland. Again Orduin deprecated the sacrifice of the Baltic Provinces. "If any towns be ceded," he writes, "let them be Polish towns. I stand for Livonia." In his opinion, the truce with Sweden should be prolonged, and Charles II of England invited to mediate a Northern Peace "which he would do the more willingly as we had no dealings with Cromwell." Finally, he lays stress upon the immense importance of Livonia for the development of the trade of Novgorod and Pskov. When he was overruled, he retired from the negotiations altogether; and, in the beginning of 1661, other envoys were sent, in his place, to Kardis, a little town between Dorpat and Reval, where, on July 2, 1661, a treaty confirming the Peace of Stolbowa was signed whereby Moscovy ceded all her conquests.   For more than half a century longer Sweden was to dominate the Baltic.

Orduin was next employed as the chief Moscovite plenipotentiary at the abortive Peace Congress of Duroticha, which met, early in 1664, to adjust the differences between Poland and Moscovy; and it was due in no small measure to his skill and tenacity that the subsequent treaty of Andrusovo (1667), so advantageous to Moscovy, was finally concluded.   For this, his greatest diplomatic achievement, he was created a *blizhnui boyarin*[1] and put at the head of the *Posolsky Prikaz*, or Foreign Office, with the extraordinary title of "Guardian of the Great Tsarish Seal and Director of the Great Imperial Embassies." The Russian Chancellor, for that is what the new dignity really amounted to, was now in his proper place.   He was the first Moscovite statesman who gave due importance to foreign affairs, and thus helped to break down the barrier which for centuries had separated Russia from the rest of Europe.

His domestic reforms were also important.   It was he who, as Governor of Pskov, first abolished the excessive system of tolls on exports and imports, established a combination of native merchants for promoting direct commercial relations between Sweden and Russia, and did his best to introduce free trade generally.   He also set on foot a postal system between Moscovy, Courland and Poland, made the Moscow road safe for foreign merchants, and introduced bills of exchange and gazettes.   With his name too is associated the building of ships on the upper Dwina and Volga.   Despite the friendship and protection of the Tsar, Orduin's whole official career was a constant struggle with the jealous enmity of the Boyars and Clerks of the Council who bitterly resented his indisputable superiority.   But Orduin also had his defects.   He rather

[1] One of the Boyars nearest to the Tsar's person.

presumed, sometimes, on his indispensability; and, at last, the Tsar grew weary of his constant complaining, and was not always prepared to admit that the minister's personal enemies were, necessarily, the enemies of the State. In February 1671 he was dismissed, and withdrew to the Kruipetsky Monastery, where he took the tonsure under the name of Antony, and occupied himself with good works till his death in 1680. Morally, as well as intellectually, he was far above the level of his age.

What Orduin was in the department of politics and economics, the Patriarch Nikon, another *protégé* of the "good Tsar Alexis," was in the spiritual and ecclesiastical department of old Moscovy.

In May 1605, in the village of Valmanovo, 90 versts from Nizhny-Novgorod, was born Nikita, the son of the peasant-farmer Mina. Misery pursued the child from his very cradle and prematurely hardened a character not naturally prone to the softer virtues. Nikita's stepmother treated him so inhumanly that the lad had to run away to save his life. And it was a life well worth saving. From a very early age, Nikita gave promise of the extraordinary energy and application which were to distinguish him throughout his career. In the most discouraging circumstances, he contrived to teach himself reading and writing, sure means of advancement in those days of general ignorance. All the books of the period were of a severely religious character. Their favourite theme was the exploits of old-time saints and hermits, and they enkindled in the heart of the young enthusiast an almost overpowering desire to tread in the footsteps of these heroes of the spirit. But the entreaties of his family, who began, at last, to be proud of their prodigy, summoned Nikita back to the world. He was persuaded to take orders and marry, when but twenty; and the eloquence of the young priest soon attracted attention and he was transferred to a populous parish in the capital. For a time, all went well; but, seeing in the almost simultaneous loss of his three little

children a providential call to the higher life, he first persuaded
his wife to take the veil and then withdrew himself to a desolate
hermitage on the isle of Anzersk in the White Sea where he
received the tonsure under the name of Nikon.

In 1643 he was elected *igumen*, or abbot, of the Kozhuzer-
sky Monastery in the diocese of Novgorod. In his official
capacity he frequently visited Moscow, whither his fame had
preceded him ; and, in 1646, he made the acquaintance of the
pious and impressionable young Tsar, who, at once and
entirely, fell under the influence of the famous zealot, twenty-
four years his senior. Alexis appointed Nikon archimandrite,
or prior, of the wealthy and aristocratic Novospassky Monastery
at Moscow, which, as an imperial foundation, was under the
direct control of the Tsar. It was now a part of Nikon's duty
to be present at Mass at the principal church of the monastery
every Friday, and to confer with the Tsar afterwards. Such
conferences were by no means confined to things spiritual; and
Alexis, more and more impressed by the gravity and judgment
of the new archimandrite, made him, first, Presenter of Petitions,
a post of great authority and influence, and, two years later,
procured his election to the metropolitan see of Great Novgorod.
In 1652 the Patriarchate became vacant; and Alexis determined
that "his own familiar friend, the Great Shining Sun, the most
holy Nikon" should occupy that august position. But Nikon
obstinately refused to occupy the patriarchal throne. This was
not, as has so often been supposed, mere affectation, but the
wise determination of a would-be reformer, conscious of the
difficulty of the task before him, to secure a free hand by being
elected on his own terms. Again and again the Tsar sent
prelates and patricians to persuade Nikon, but he remained
immovable. At last the Tsar ordered him to be brought to the
Cathedral by force. Still he persisted in his refusal till the
Tsar, and those who were present, fell at his feet and besought
him with tears to yield to the prayers of the whole community.
Nikon, deeply moved, himself began to weep, and, turning to

the Tsar and the congregation uttered these memorable words:
"...If it seem good to you that I should be your Patriarch, give
me your word and swear to it in this Cathedral Church, before
God our Saviour and His Most Pure Mother...that ye will
keep the evangelic dogmas...and, if ye promise to obey me also
as your chief arch-pastor...in everything which I shall teach you
concerning the divine dogmas and the canons, then will I,
according to your wish and supplication, no longer reject this
great arch-pastorate." The Tsar, the Boyars, and all the
members of the Synod, thereupon swore unanimously upon the
Gospels that they would do all that Nikon commanded them,
and "assist him to edify the Church." On August 1, 1652,
Nikon was elected; and, on August 4, he was solemnly consecrated and enthroned as the sixth Patriarch of Moscow.

Even before Nikon had appeared upon the scene, the
necessity of ecclesiastical reform had been admitted in the
highest circles, and had found advocates in the immediate
entourage of the young Tsar, who was keenly interested in all
theological questions and very willing to learn. Chief among
these would-be reformers were Stephen Vonafitov, the Tsar's
confessor, a relatively learned man, personally of an extremely
austere life, but generally beloved for his gentle disposition;
Ivan Neronov, a bitter zealot, who regarded even Christmas
festivities as "devilish"; and Daniel of Kostroma and Login of
Murom, both of them men of severe morality. The party of the
Protopops, as this group was called, because most of the members
of the group were protopops, or deans, of the numerous cathedrals
within the *Kreml'*, was presently re-inforced and over-shadowed
by the priest Avvakum. This perversely heroic creature, the
proto-martyr of Russian dissent, and one of the most striking
personalities of his age, was born at the village of Gregorovo,
fifteen miles from the place where Nikon was born, a few years
before. From 1643, when he succeeded his drunken father as
parish priest, absolute fearlessness, sublime austerity, and a
perfect fidelity to his religious convictions were to characterise

him throughout life. Nothing in the world could make him condone wickedness, or truckle to the mighty. He possessed, moreover, a rare gift of speech. No other Moscovite ecclesiastic of the seventeenth century could compare with Avvakum as a preacher. He spoke to the people in the language of the people, straight from the heart, in a way which made the rudest feel and tremble. His style was always simple, lucid, vigorous, garnished with racy proverbs, full of quaint and vivid touches, and rising, at times, to flights of irresistible eloquence. His autobiography, one of the most engrossing and pathetic histories ever penned, is, in point of composition, not merely superior to, but centuries ahead of, what passed for style in those days, an unconscious master-piece as well as a historical document of the highest value. Unfortunately, this great and heroic nature was also one of the most narrow-minded of men. Still more un-fortunately, his narrowness was so absolutely conscientious as to be quiet incurable.

With all their good intentions, the Protopops were not the sort of men to initiate even such modest ecclesiastical reforms as were possible in Moscovy in the seventeenth century. Their point of view was erroneous because they were not themselves sufficiently enlightened to be able to pierce to the root of matters, and, nevertheless, shrank from the assistance of their natural teachers, the clergy of Kiev and of Constantinople, because they suspected the former of being crypto-catholics, and knew many of the latter to be scoundrels and impostors. They were therefore thrown back upon Moscovite tradition as represented by the *Stoglav* of the Reforming Council of Moscow of 1551—a Council unrecognised outside Moscovy, and of questionable authority, inasmuch as its members, while professing to follow Greek precedents, had been notoriously ignorant of the Greek language, the very key of orthodox inter-pretation. Thus the antiquity to which the Protopops were never tired of appealing was barely a century old; and the canonicity of their ultimate court of appeal was, at the best, highly problematical. Yet they had pinned their faith implicitly to this purely national Synod, and cut off all possibility of a dignified retreat by accepting the responsibility for the revision of the Church service-books inaugurated by the late Patriarch Joasaf. This was really no revision at all, but a clumsy attempt to apply the hitherto unexecuted canons of the *Stoglav* to the bettering of the liturgies, which resulted in the interpolation of various schismatical prescriptions into five or six of the thirty-eight books so revised, such, for instance, as the *dvuperstia*, or making the sign of the cross with two fingers, and the *sugubaya alleluya*, or two-fold alleluia, to which the Moscovite Church was consequently committed.

Nikon was much more liberal. He shared the Protopops' distrust of the Greek priests and prelates. He was well aware that the bishops without sees, and the archimandrites without monasteries, who appeared, from time to time, at Moscow, with forged letters of recommendation from the Eastern Patriarchs, were, at best, place-seekers and relic-mongers. But he also recognised the fact that, if the morals of these vagabond pastors were detestable, their scholarship was far superior to what passed for learning at Moscovy, and he did not see why he should not sift the gold from the dross. As soon as the Greeks had opened his eyes to the fact that the Moscovite service-books were heterodox in many particulars, he conducted, with the assistance of the learned Epifany Slavenitsky, whom he had specially summoned from Kiev, independent investigations of his own in the patriarchal archives, and arrived at the result that the sooner the Moscovite liturgies were rectified the better. With characteristic energy he summoned, in 1654, a properly qualified synod of experts to re-examine the service-books. The majority of the synod decided that "the Greeks should be followed rather than our own ancients"; but the minority, and several of the old revisers, most of them members of the party of the Protopops, protested vehemently against the decision of the Council. Nikon thereupon addressed six-and-twenty interrogatories to Paisios, Patriarch of Constantinople, enquiring, at the same time, how he should deal with the dissentients. Paisios recommended excommunication, and authorised the holding of a second Council to settle matters, to which Makarios, Patriarch of Antioch, and the Metropolitans of Servia, Nicea and Moldavia, all of whom happened to be at Moscow, were invited. This Council, which assembled in the Uspensky Cathedral, at Moscow, in 1656, sanctioned the revision of the service-books as suggested by the first Council, and anathematised all who still persisted in crossing themselves with two fingers instead of with three. The revision of the service-books was then entrusted to the learned Kievlyan Slavenitsky and the Greek monk Arsenios, and carried out in accordance with the wishes of Nikon.

Nikon was so entirely in the right that it requires a mental effort to imagine how anyone could have seriously believed him to have been in the wrong. The Patriarch stood firm for a real antiquity pruned of all the parasitical excrescences, the outcome of ignorance and misunderstanding, which had overgrown the Moscovite Church in the course of ages. His opponents, blinded by prejudice and suspicion, failed to see that his reforms were but a return to primitive antiquity, and denounced them as the inventions of Anti-Christ. Agreement was impossible. The question at issue had to be fought out to the bitter end. So long as there were men in Moscovy ready to be tortured to death rather than cross themselves with three fingers instead of two, or spell the name of our Lord, in Slavonic, with two iotas instead of with one iota, there could be no peace in the Church, especially as the martyrs of to-day might easily become the persecutors of to-morrow, toleration being accounted by both parties a mortal sin.

The Patriarch certainly shewed the schismatics no mercy. It was a rough age, when gentle methods did not recommend themselves even to the mildest of men. Nikon was hard, if not cruel, and, above all things, he was thorough. His scheme of reform included not only the service-books and the church ceremonies, but the ikons actually in use, which had widely departed from the ancient Byzantine models, being, for the most part, imitations of Polish and West-European models. The Patriarch ordered a search, from house to house, to be made for these new-fangled ikons ; and his soldiers and servants were charged first to gouge out the eyes of the "heretical counterfeits " and then carry them through the town in derision. He also issued an *ukaz* threatening with the severest penalties all who dared to make or use such ikons in the future. Hundreds of pious Moscovites, who had grown up to venerate these holy images, naturally regarded such acts of violence as sacrilege and iconoclasticism.

This ruthlessness goes far to explain the unappeasable hatred with which Avvakum and his followers, ever afterwards, regarded Nikon and all his works.   The protopop was not the man to keep silence under the persecution of Anti-Christ ; and the virulence of his denunciations speedily led to his seizure and imprisonment. During his detention the party of the Protopops was broken up, the weaker members submitting to the Patriarch, while the stronger spirits were flogged, tortured, and exiled in every direction.   On September 16, 1657, Avvakum was banished to Siberia, where, during the next eight years, he endured incredible hardships and persecutions with invincible fortitude.

From 1652 to 1658 Nikon was not so much the minister as the colleague of the Tsar. The whole internal administration, especially during the unlucky Swedish War, when Alexis was absent from the capital, remained in the strong hands of this spiritual Gosudar ; for both in public documents and private letters from the Tsar, Nikon was allowed this sovereign title. So vast was his power and such a free use did he make of it that some Russian historians have suspected him of the intention of establishing " a particular national papacy."   Certainly, he himself always maintained that the spiritual was superior to the temporal power.   It would be grossly unfair to Nikon not to admit that, in many respects, he was no unworthy predecessor of Peter the Great. He loved many branches of learning, especially archaeology and history; and all those arts which minister to religion found in him an intelligent and munificent patron. He enriched with libraries of considerable importance in those days the numerous and splendid monasteries he loved to build. His emissaries scoured Moscovy and the Orient, to search out and bring together precious Greek and Slavonic MSS. Nor did he confine his attention to ecclesiastical documents. Some of his hardly won treasures were the works of profane classical authors, Homer, Hesiod, Aeschylus, Plutarch and Demosthenes.

As an administrator Nikon was indefatigable in purging the church of abuses. His standard of excellence was high. Sloth, immorality, slackness of any kind, found little mercy with him. Unfortunately he never knew when to stop. As the highest interpreter of the Divine Law in Moscovy, he judged all things to be lawful to him; he never paused to consider whether they were also expedient. Hence the charges of cruelty brought against him, exaggerated, no doubt, by his enemies, but true enough in substance. His magnificence and exclusiveness were equally offensive to those—and they were many—who simply envied him because "he held his head high and walked spaciously." Finally, there was the multitude of conscientious adversaries who detested him as a troubler of the Church, and the criminous clerks whose misdeeds he had punished. Against this rising flood of hatred there was but one efficacious barrier, the favour of the Tsar; nor was it an easy task to shake the belief of the most pious of princes in the impeccability of the bosom friend whom he generally addressed as "Great Shining Sun," and before whom he figuratively abased himself in the dust. But there are limits to everything. No sooner was Alexis made to understand that the Sovereign Patriarch was eclipsing the Sovereign Tsar, than he suddenly awoke to a sense of his personal dignity, and began to think less of the

shining virtues of his "own familiar friend." How the change
was brought about is not quite clear, but it was first made
manifest to Nikon in the summer of 1658 when he received no
invitation to a state banquet. On July 19 the same year, the
Tsar, contrary to the practice of years, absented himself from
Mass at the Feast of Our Lady of Kazan. The same day
Nikon informed the people from the Cathedral pulpit that he
was no longer Patriarch, and whosoever henceforth called him
by that name was anathema. He then shut himself up in the
Voskresensky Monastery near Moscow, and there he remained
for two years, absolutely refusing to resume his functions. In
February 1660 a Synod, held at Moscow "to terminate the
widowhood" of the Moscovite Church, decided that Nikon had
forfeited both his patriarchal rank and his priestly orders; and
this sentence, though much criticised at the time, was confirmed,
on December 12 (O.S.), 1666, by an Ecumenical Council—
or the nearest approach to it attainable in the circumstances—
which was attended by Paisios, Patriarch of Alexandria, and
Makarios, Patriarch of Antioch. The Patriarchs of Constantinople and Jerusalem were represented by proxy. This Council
pronounced Nikon guilty of reviling the Tsar, of deserting the
Orthodox Church, of deposing Paul, Bishop of Kolomna,
contrary to the canons, and of beating and torturing his
dependants. His sentence was deprivation of all his sacerdotal
functions; henceforth he was to be known simply as "the monk
Nikon."

Far from being cowed by his sentence, Nikon, who had
abated not a jot of his pretensions, and alienated all but a
very few personal friends by his outrageous violence and
invective, was defiant to the last. He questioned the jurisdiction of the Council, overwhelmed the Greek prelates with
abuse, some of which they certainly deserved, and refused to
make the slightest submission. The same day, he was put in
a sledge and sent away to a distant monastery. He survived
his old friend Alexis, with whom he was subsequently recon-

ciled, by five years, expiring on August 17, 1681, in his seventy-sixth year.

The Council, while deposing Nikon, had, at the same time, confirmed all the Nikonian reforms, and anathematised all who should refuse to accept the revised liturgies, the *troeperstie* [1] etc. Avvakum was among the first to suffer under this decree. He had returned to Moscow in 1662, when Nikon, though not yet dethroned, was in disgrace and powerless. Every one who had any reason to hate the Patriarch hailed the fiery arch-enemy of "Nikonism" as "an angel of God." Even at Court he was received with effusion; and the Tsar frequently begged for his blessing. But, little more than a twelvemonth after his return from exile, the protopop's fanatical violence resulted in his second banishment—to Mezen, a little town near the White Sea. In 1665, by order of the Tsar, all the principal schismatics in exile, were summoned to Moscow to make their peace with the Church. Every conceivable effort was made by the Ecumenical Council to win over its most formidable opponent; for, by this time, Avvakum was regarded by the majority of his countrymen as "a Confessor for Christ's sake." For ten weeks deputations passed between the Council and the protopop, but he answered all their arguments with ridicule and invective. When brought before the Council itself he refused to recognise its authority, and, finally, May 13, 1666, was pronounced a heretic and deprived of his orders. His further sentence was postponed until all the Greek Patriarchs had arrived. Then, for six weeks longer, all the resources of argument and persuasion were employed to convince Avvakum of the reasonableness of the Nikonian reforms. Never was ignorance so proudly invincible. When asked why he held out so obstinately against the whole Orthodox world, he could only taunt the Eastern Patriarchs with their political subjection to "the Turkish Mahomet." Then Avvakum and his three

---

[1] Making the sign of the cross with three fingers according to ancient usage.

principal associates were handed over to the secular arm, and condemned to lose their tongues, and be banished to Pustozersk, on the Pechora, the northernmost town of European Russia. The mutilation, in Avvakum's case, owing to the intercession of the Tsaritsa Maria, was remitted.

For 14 years the great protopop remained at Pustozersk. At first his imprisonment was light and he was allowed to communicate with the outer world. But, when he abused this privilege by threatening the Tsar with the pains of hell unless he repented and restored the exiled schismatics, he was treated with a savage rigour only intelligible on the assumption of a deliberate intention of shortening his life. But the unconquerable spirit of the man sustained him. He added self-inflicted torments to the cruelties of his persecutors. He fasted till power of speech forsook him. He discarded his clothing and lay for hours in ecstatic trances. At last, his very gaolers became his disciples, and assisted in the propagation of his doctrines. The starved and naked anchorite became, in the clay dungeon at Pustozersk, the leader of a vast popular movement, and devoted the whole of his ample leisure to polemical literature. From 1673 to his martyrdom in 1681[1] he composed his autobiography, nine dogmatic treatises, and forty-three epistles. All these works were jotted down on odd pieces of rag which were then secretly conveyed out of the prison, carefully transcribed by the pilgrims who came to him for advice and comfort, circulated in hundreds of copies bound in costly velvet, kept in the schismatical churches close to the holy ikons, and revered like so many divine revelations.

Avvakum's success as a controversialist is not surprising. Although his name will be found in very few histories of Russian literature, he was, undoubtedly, the first Russian who knew how to write his own language. While his literary contemporaries are still struggling in the meshes of an obscure

---

[1] He was burnt at the stake.

and pedantic jargon, Avvakum's diction is a model of lucidity, abounding, moreover, with bold and original metaphors, and expressing every mood and feeling with a simple directness which was bound to catch and hold the popular taste.

But, when we pass from the form to the substance of the heroic schismatic's teaching, we are amazed to find that, literally, there is nothing in it. The whole question turns on the *minutiae* of ceremonial, the veriest mint and cummin of ecclesiastical observance, the true history and bearing of which Avvakum, obviously, is either too ignorant to understand, or too obstinate to wish to understand. There is no question of dogma, no question even of discipline. On all essentials the Avvakumites or " Old Believers," as they now began to style themselves, were really at one with the " Nikonians," or Orthodox.

All Avvakum's writings breathe the fiercest intolerance and exaggeration. " 'Twere better for a man never to be born than to cross himself with three fingers instead of two "—is their constant refrain. He rejoices that the " land of Russia is sanctified by martyr-blood "; nay, he approves of wholesale suicide if there be no other way of avoiding conformity with " Nikonian practices."

Yet, after all, to come to the root of the matter, Avvakum's objections to the Nikonian reforms are political rather than theological. He objects to them not so much because they are anti-christian as because they are anti-Russian. They are heterodox because they run counter to the national tradition; and the national tradition is orthodox because it is the historical development of the belief of the independent Russian people. Thus the whole argument springs from a bigoted patriotism.

The dominant counsellor of Tsar Alexis in his later years was Artamon Sergyeevich Matvyeev.

The early career of this remarkable man is wrapped in impenetrable mystery. His very parentage and the year of his

birth are uncertain.   But, when the obscure figure of young
Artamon first emerges into the light of history, we find him
equipped at all points with the newest ideas, absolutely free from
the worst prejudices of his age, a ripe scholar, and even an
author of some distinction, though nothing but the titles of his
works has come down to us.   How " little Sergy " became the
close personal friend of the Tsar is equally unknown.   We can
only say that, in 1671, they were already on the most intimate
terms, and that, on the retirement of Orduin-Nashchokin,
Matvyeev was entrusted with the conduct of foreign affairs.
In striking contrast to Nashchokin, he was not in too great
a hurry to get on ; and, though courageous enough to sacrifice
his life for his principles, he tactfully avoided riding rough-shod
over other people's prejudices, especially when those other
people were both powerful and stupid.   Matvyeev's house was
a source of never failing delight to the receptive and inquisitive
Tsar.   It was like a bit of western civilisation transferred
bodily into another age and another continent.   Within its
walls could be seen all the wondrous, half-forbidden, novelties of
the West, painted ceilings, rich pile carpets, ingenious clocks,
pictures by French and German artists.   Matvyeev's wife, who
is said to have been a Scotchwoman, moved freely among her
male guests on equal terms, and drove out boldly in a carriage
and pair instead of in a close-curtained litter.   It was here that
Alexis first encountered Natalia Naruishkina, Matvyeev's
favourite pupil, whom the Tsar wedded on January 21, 1672,
three years after the death of his first consort Maria.   At the
end of 1672, on the occasion of the birth of the Tsarevich
Peter, Matvyeev was raised to the rank of *okolnichy*[1].   On
September 1, 1674, he obtained the still higher rank of Boyar.

The influence of Matvyeev remained paramount to the end
of the reign.   Tsar Alexis, stimulated by his handsome young
wife and her wise mentor, advanced along the path of progress
at an accelerated pace which amazed himself.   He who had

[1] The second highest degree of rank in the official hierarchy.

sternly banished even jugglers from his court while still but a youth now, in his old age, gave himself up to such heterodox diversions as stage plays. Yet Alexis had his scruples. His first consort Maria had been a stern rigourist. Gardens and palaces, in her opinion, might be all very well, but spectacles were damnable. But the Tsaritsa Natalia was of a joyous disposition; and the good Tsar did his utmost to gratify his young consort especially as his own inclinations ran in the same direction. So, under the direction of Matvyeev, a *Komidyeinnaya Khoromna*, or "Hall of Comedy," was built at the Tsar's summer residence at the village of Preobrazhensk; and, as Preobrazhensk was difficult of access in the winter, another such Hall was, in 1673, actually constructed in the sacred precincts of the *Kreml'* itself. Here plays of a biblical character[1] were acted by a troupe of German actors directed by Timothy Hasenkrug. A ballet of sixty children and instrumental music were also introduced. The erection of these playhouses was a very important step forward on the path of progress. A Russian historian has even gone so far as to call them "the foundation stones of the regeneration of our social life." Certainly it was an immense advance when the very men who had shrunk from altering a single letter of the old Slavonic Bible were content to look on, complacently, while foreigners and heretics put the Bible itself on the stage before their very eyes.

Tsar Alexis died on January 30, 1676. He was indubitably the most amiable and attractive of all the Moscovite princes. Even foreigners found it difficult to resist the charm of his gentle, humane, and essentially courteous disposition. No man was ever a kinder master, or a more affectionate friend. As a ruler, he was equally remarkable for his conscientiousness and his diligence. His education was necessarily narrow; yet he was learned in his way, read

[1] *e.g.* "Judith and Holofernes," "How Artaxerxes ordered Haman to be hanged," etc.

everything written in the Slavonic language, wrote verses himself, and even began a history of his own times. Finally, Alexis possessed, in an eminent degree, the truly royal gift of recognising and selecting great men. The best of the statesmen who may be called the precursors of Peter the Great were discovered and employed by Peter's father.

Tsar Alexis had thirteen children by his first consort, Maria Miloslavskaya—five sickly sons, three of whom predeceased him, and eight healthy daughters, all of them women of intelligence and character. Theodore III, his designated successor, a lad of fourteen, was greatly to be pitied. He possessed a fine intellect, and a noble disposition; he had received an excellent education, knew Polish as well as his mother-tongue, and even had some Latin. But horribly disfigured, and half paralysed, by a mysterious disease, supposed to be scurvy, he had been a hopeless invalid from the day of his birth.

The deplorable condition of this unhappy prince suggested to Matvyeev the desirability of elevating to the throne the sturdy little Tsarevich Peter, the son of Alexis, by Natalia Naruishkina, then in his fourth year. But the reactionary Boyars, among whom were the Stryeshnevs and the Miloslavskies, the uncles and cousins of Theodore, all of them, more or less, hostile to the upstart Naruishkins, proclaimed Theodore Tsar (his right to the throne was certainly indisputable); and Matvyeev was banished to Pustozersk on an easily established charge of witchcraft. Natalia Naruishkina, with her children Peter and Natalia, were at the same time banished from court.

In 1679 Theodore married his first cousin Agatha, and assumed the sceptre. His native energy, though crippled, was not crushed by his terrible disabilities, and he soon shewed that he was as thorough and devoted a reformer as a man incompetent to lead armies or direct councils, and obliged to issue his orders from his litter or his bedchamber, can possibly be. The atmosphere of the Court ceased to be oppressive ; the light of a new liberalism shone forth in the highest places ; petitioners were forbidden to address the Gosudar with the old servility ; and the severity of the penal laws was considerably mitigated. Theodore also founded an Academy of Sciences in the Zaikonnospasky Monastery, where everything not expressly forbidden by the Orthodox Church, including Greek, Polish and Latin, were to be taught by competent professors.

But the most notable reform of Theodore III was the abolition of the system known as *Myestnichestvo*, which had paralysed the whole civil and military administration of Moscovy for generations.

In old Moscovy the family was everything, the individual nothing. The elders of every family were responsible for the behaviour of all the younger members of the same family, and bound to punish their misconduct, even after they had reached man's estate. If one member of a family were condemned to pay a fine, all the other members contributed to pay it off ; and the elevation or degradation of one member of a family was the elevation or degradation of all the other members. This principle of family solidarity was carried out to its last consequences. Ivan Ivanovich, for instance, would refuse to serve under Semen Semenovich if any single member of Ivan's family had ever held a higher position than any single member of Semen's family ; otherwise Ivan was held to have dishonoured his whole family, and the honour of the family had to be upheld at whatever cost of suffering to the individuals composing it. Thus it came about that the Boyar, slavishly obsequious as he might be to the Gosudar in all other things, would rather quit the Tsar's table than sit below any other Boyar of inferior family ; rather endure imprisonment, or the terrible knout itself, than put himself *bez myest'ye*, "out of place," as the phrase went. To such a point was this principle of priority at last carried, that the members of one family would resort to the most desperate expedients rather than yield precedence to another family, even when that family was obviously entitled thereto.   Thus, to give but a single instance, the great national hero, Demetrius Pozharsky, refused, on one occasion, to admit the pre-eminence of the newly boyared Michael Saltuikov. Out of deference to Pozharsky, the claim was thoroughly examined, when it was discovered that Saltuikov's ancestors were undoubtedly superior to Pozharsky's. Pozharsky had nothing to say for himself, so he took to his bed and feigned serious illness. It is obvious how prejudicial to the public service this *Myestnichestvo* was bound to be ; during warfare, in particular, it frequently paralysed all military operations.   It was no uncommon thing for subordinate officers to refuse to conduct troops to the nearest general because of the inferiority of his family, and petition that they might be sent instead to some other general of loftier origin. For the same reason one general often refused to serve under another general, even though the Tsar had appointed that other general generalissimo. The only remedy devisable against this claim for privileged insubordination was for the Tsar to proclaim beforehand that, so long as the war lasted, and so long only, all the officers without exception were to be *bez myest'ye*, "out of place"—in other words, family rank was not to count during hostilities.

It was Prince Vasily Vasilevich Golitsuin, sometimes called "the Great Golitsuin," especially by foreigners, whom he warmly protected, who first urged the necessity of abolishing *Myestnichestvo*. Golitsuin was unusually well educated. He understood German and Greek as well as his mother-tongue, and could express himself fluently in Latin.   Born in 1643, he entered the service of Alexis at an early age, and in 1676, was created a Boyar. Sent to the Ukraine to provide for its defence against the incursions of the Turks and Tatars, he returned to Moscow with the conviction that *Myestnichestvo* was at the root of Moscovy's deplorable military inefficiency.

The young Tsar was easily convinced by his arguments ; and a special *ukaz* removed, at one stroke, an abuse which had so long appeared unassailable.   Henceforth all appointments were to be determined by merit and the will of the Gosudar. The fact that the dying Theodore could so readily remove so deep-lying and far reaching an abuse is a striking testimony to the steady, if silent, advance of liberal ideas in Moscovite society even since the death of Alexis.   It is often too much taken for granted that Peter the Great created modern Russia. The foundations of modern Russia were laid while he was still in his nursery.

On April 27, 1682, Theodore III died suddenly without issue, and without appointing his successor, so that the throne was left vacant.   By the advice of the Patriarch and with the consent of the people assembled in the Red Square, the Tsarevich Peter was elected Tsar, in preference to his semi-idiotic half-brother Ivan ; and Matvyeev was hastily summoned to return to the capital and occupy the post of chief counsellor to the Tsaritsa Natalia, who had been appointed Regent during the minority of her infant son.   But the elder branch of Tsar Alexis's family, the Miloslavskies, were by no means disposed to submit to the upstart Naruishkins, the younger branch of the same family.   Fear also played a large part in the calculations of the Miloslavskies.   Under Theodore, in their hour of triumph, they had mercilessly persecuted the Naruishkins ; but now the Naruishkins were in the ascendant and might persecute the Miloslavskies in the name of Peter but by the hand of Matvyeev.

It was a portentous sign of the times that the malcontents unhesitatingly looked for guidance neither to Prince Vasily Golitsuin, nor to Prince Ivan Khovansky, the two leading generals of the day, but to a woman of five-and-twenty, who had been educated in the seclusion of the *terem*, and, a genera-tion earlier, would not have dared to leave it.   This product of the new enlightenment was the Tsarevna Sophia, the third daughter of Tsar Alexis. Both Natalia and Sophia had had a relatively superior education. But while, as the pupil of Matvyeev, Natalia belonged to the practical school of the West, Sophia's training, under the guidance of the learned monk, Polotsky, had been on more ecclesiastical lines. But her orthodoxy sat pretty lightly upon her. In emancipating herself from the restrictions of the *terem*, she had, at 'he same time, emancipated herself from its austere morality; and her overwhelming passion for Prince Vasily Golitsuin was already notorious.

A revolt of sixteen regiments of the *Stryeltsui*, or Musketeers, who proceeded to the *Kreml'* to demand arrears of pay, three days after the proclamation of Peter, laid bare the essential weakness of the new Government. The death of Matvyeev, who reached Moscow on May 15th and was torn to pieces, the same day, by the *Stryeltsui*, during a second revolt obviously inspired by Sophia and her friends, put an end to Natalia's regency altogether. On May 23, Ivan V was associated with his brother Peter as co-Tsar. On the 29th he was declared the Senior, and Peter the Junior Tsar, while the Tsarevna Sophia was proclaimed Regent during their minority. As Ivan was hopelessly infirm, half blind, and more than half idiotic, it is plain that this duumvirate aimed solely at the depression and humiliation of the Tsaritsa Natalia. Thus Sophia became the actual ruler of Moscovy. The *Stryeltsui* were not only pardoned for their atrocities but petted. A general amnesty was granted to them; and, at their special request, a triumphal column was erected in the Red Square to commemorate their cowardly massacre of Matvyeev and the Naruishkins on May 15—17.

When, however, the still dissatisfied *Stryeltsui*, in alliance with the more fanatical of the Old Believers, and prompted by the arch-conservative Voevode, Prince Ivan Khovansky, openly rebelled against Sophia, she shewed herself their mistress. After openly confronting them, on July 5, in the "Tesselated

Chamber," the great reception hall of the palace of the *Kreml'*
when she rejected their petitions and confuted their arguments,
she removed for safety's sake, in August, to the village of
Kolmenskoe, where the Court remained till September 1st, the
Russian New Year. By this time Sophia and Khovansky
were at open war ; and the latter was, most probably, aiming at
the crown for himself. In the middle of September, the Regent
felt strong enough to strike the first blow, and she struck
fiercely. The Khovanskies, father and son, were suddenly
seized and summarily executed ; and, when Prince Vasily
Golitsuin prepared to march against rebellious Moscow, the
Stryeltsui sent a deputation to Sophia, begging for forgiveness,
and the rebellion collapsed. On Nov. 6, the Court, satisfied
with the fulness of its triumph, returned to the capital.

During the seven years of her regency, Sophia left the conduct of affairs in the hands of her lover and omnipotent
minister Vasily Golitsuin. For a time all went well. Golitsuin
was a dexterous diplomatist and a wise administrator ; but, as
the paramour of the Regent, he held, from the first, an
extremely difficult position ; and her extravagant favours
gradually raised up a whole host of enemies against him and
made her extremely unpopular. The crisis came after his
disastrous Crimean campaigns in 1687–88[1]. Most of the
malcontents rested their hopes for the future on the young
Tsar Peter, who was the first to benefit by the growing
unpopularity of his half-sister. Twice already they had come
into actual collision. On the first occasion, Peter had objected
to his sister's participation in a solemn procession to the Kazan
Cathedral, which was, indeed, an unheard-of breach of ancient
usage. On the second occasion, he had openly protested
against the ridiculous rewards she had bestowed upon Golitsuin
after a retreat which had only just stopped short of disaster,
and absolutely refused to receive the Prince in audience when
he came to thank Peter for his undeserved promotion. Sophia

[1] See preceding chapter.

was quite alive to the insecurity of her position. To use Solovev's quaint but apt analogy, like those who have sold themselves to the Devil, she might, for a time, enjoy all the good things of this world; but Hell, in the shape of a monastery, awaited her at the end of her pleasant course. She had crowned her brothers in order that she might reign in their names. She had added her name to theirs in state documents, boldly subscribing herself "Sovereign Princess of all Russia." She had officially informed the Doge of Venice that she was the co-Regent of the Tsars. And meanwhile the terrible term of her usurped authority was approaching. Peter was growing up; and Peter's mother, the long despised Tsaritsa Natalia, was beginning to criticise and even censure the doings of the Regent. Nay, she had protested openly against Sophia's assumption of the title of Sovereign. Something had to be done speedily; and, by the advice of her chief ministers, Golitsuin and the clerk of the Council, Shaklovity, she resolved to employ the *Stryeltsui* to dethrone Peter and place herself on the throne. But the *Stryeltsui* were deeply divided in opinion. Many of them regarded Peter as the rightful Tsar; and it was by some of these friendly *Stryeltsui* that warning of the conspiracy against him was brought to Preobrazhensk, where he usually resided. (August 12, 1689.) He at once took refuge in the fortress-monastery of Troitsa, where he was speedily joined by his mother and sister. Presently he was fortified by the arrival of the *Stryeltsui* of the Sakharev regiment and other auxiliaries, and placed the supreme command in the hands of Prince Boris Golitsuin, the cousin of Vasily, a man of superior intelligence and great force of character.

So great was the consternation of the Regent in the *Kreml'*, on hearing that Peter had taken refuge in the famous bulwark of Moscovite orthodoxy and patriotism, that she sent the Patriarch Joachim to Troitsa to mediate. This was a false step, for, by so doing, she converted a valuable hostage into a

formidable opponent.   The Patriarch had long desired to
escape from the treasonable atmosphere of the *Kreml'*, and
his presence at the Troitsa Monastery immensely strengthened
the position of Peter.   From mid-August to September 4,
Sophia attempted to inspire her drooping followers with something of her own spirit.   It was all in vain.   On August 27
the bulk of the *Stryeltsui* deserted her.   On September 4, the
foreign legion in the German Settlement followed their example.
On September 6, her own entourage compelled her to deliver
up Shaklovity, the prime mover of the whole rebellion.   Then
all the Boyars of her party went over to Peter ; and Vasily
Golitsuin hid himself at the Regent's country-house at Medvyed-
kovo.   On the night of September 7, a full confession was
extorted from Shaklovity, who was publicly executed, with his
chief accomplices, on the 11th.   Vasily Golitsuin was spared,
owing to the intercession of his cousin Boris, but was banished
to Kiropol.   Sophia was compelled to retire within the Novody-
evechy monastery, but without taking the veil.

CHAPTER XIV.

PETER THE GREAT, 1689–1725.

Earlier Years.

PETER Aleksyeevich was born on May 30, 1672. In all respects he was a singularly backward child. He was two and a half before he was weaned, and in his 11th year we find him still playing with wooden horses, and struggling with the difficulties of Russian etymology. After 1680 the lad had no regular tutor. From his third to his tenth year, he shared the miseries and the perils of the rest of his family. The stories of innocent children remorselessly persecuted by wicked relatives which other children learn from their nurses with comfortable tremours, were, in Peter's case, terrible experiences. At his second election, scenes of bloodshed were enacted daily before his eyes. He saw one of his uncles dragged from the palace, and butchered by a savage mob. He saw his mother's beloved mentor, and his own best friend, Artamon Matvyeev, torn bleeding from his detaining grasp, and hacked to pieces. The convulsions from which he suffered so much in later years must be partly attributed to the nervous shock and the haunting memories of these horrible days.

Dunce though he might be from the pedagogues' point of view, the child was, nevertheless, of an amazingly alert and inquisitive intelligence. It is plain that he soon felt cramped and stifled in the dim and close, semi-religious, atmosphere of old Moscovite family life. He escaped from the boredom and melancholy of Natalia's *terem* by rushing out into the streets ; and the streets of Moscow in the seventeenth century were very dirty streets. Already we notice what was to become a leading trait of his character, that rollicking joyousness—an exaggeration, no doubt, of his gentle father's sociability—which clutched at life with both hands, and squeezed out of it recklessly all the pleasure it could be made to yield. He surrounded himself with bands of lads of his own age, preferably of the lower, rougher classes, and scoured the country, indulging in all sorts of riotous and scandalous pranks. There was no one near him of sufficient character and authority to keep the passionate, fiery nature within due bounds. From his tenth to his seventeenth year Peter amused himself in his own way at Preobrazhensk. But it was not all amusement. Mother Nature was already teaching him his business. From the first the lad took an extraordinary interest in the technical and mechanical arts, especially in their application to military science. In his twelfth year he built a wooden " toy fortress " on an earth foundation, with walls, bastions and ditches, which he afterwards took by assault at the head of half his band of boys while the other half defended it. By this time his tastes were pretty well known ; and Prince James Dolgoruki, to please him, brought back from Paris the first astrolabe ever seen in Russia. Peter was taught how to use it by a Dutchman, Franz Timmerman, who also instructed him in the rudiments of astronomy and fortification. The same year he began to take that absorbing interest in boats and boating, the final result of which was to be the creation of the Russian navy. The river Yanza, which ran through Preobrazhensk, and was the nearest way to the German Settlement at Moscow, and the large lake at Pereyaslavl, eighty miles away, were the scenes of the indefatigable young navigator's exploits.

The Revolution of 1689 at first made no difference in Peter's pursuits. He had, by this time, found a new friend in the Swiss adventurer, François Lefort, whom he first met in the German Settlement, probably at the beginning of 1690. Lefort was a reckless soldier of fortune, full of the joy of life and infinitely gay and amusing. Peter, who was nothing if not jovial, took to him at once; and their imtimacy was severed only by Lefort's sudden death in 1699. Lefort was certainly not the sort of Mentor that a young man's parents would select for him. It is clear that he initiated Peter into all the mysteries of profligacy in their favourite resort at the German Settlement. Not infrequently the whole company drank hard for three days together behind locked doors. Occasionally some of the guests died during the debauch. It was here, too, that Peter met his first mistress, Anna Mons, a German vintner's daughter. But Lefort was a shrewd as well as a pleasant rascal. He was the first to divine that Peter was a genius who needed guiding to his goal. It was the drunken, disreputable, Lefort who persuaded Peter first to undertake the expedition against Azov, and then to go abroad to complete his education.

It was in 1693 that Peter first saw the sea at Archangel. Here he fraternised with the foreign seamen, added the naval title of "skipper" to his military title of "bombardier" (which latter he had won in 1694 at a "sham fight" of such severity that 24 men were left dead on the field), built and launched his first ship, and bought his first frigate, which was expressly made for him in Holland.

But the White Sea, frozen as it was nine months out of the twelve, also soon became too narrow for Peter; and he began to look about him for more hospitable waters. All sorts of projects were forming in his head. At first he thought of seeking a passage to China by way of the Arctic Ocean. Next he turned his eyes in the direction of the Baltic, but the Baltic was a closed door to Moscovy; and the key to it was held by Sweden, still the second strongest military monarchy in Europe. The Caspian remained, and the best way of tapping the riches of the Orient was to secure possession of this vast inland lake. But so long as Turk, Tatar and Cossack nomads made the Volgan steppes uninhabitable, the Caspian was a possession of but doubtful value, as Stenka Razin's exploits had demonstrated. The first step making for security was to build a fleet strong enough to provide against the anarchical condition of those parts, for which the presence of the hordes of the Khan of the Crimea was mainly responsible. But the Khan was himself the tributary of the Turks, so that a war with the Khan was necessarily a war with the Sultan. Nevertheless Peter did not falter; and, the experience of Vasily Golitsuin having demonstrated the unpromising character of a Crimean campaign, the Turkish fortress of Azov, which could be approached by water from Moscow, became the Russian objective.

The campaign began early in 1695 and ended in unmitigated failure, the Turks surprising Peter's camp during a mid-day siesta and ruining all the Russian siege artillery at the beginning of August, while two subsequent attempts to storm the fortress were repulsed. On September 27 the siege was abandoned. On November 22, the Tsar re-entered Moscow.

Yet from this disaster is to be dated the reign of Peter *the Great*. The young Tsar, fully accepting his defeat, determined to repair it by a second campaign. Immediately after his return, he sent to Austria and Prussia for as many engineers, sappers and miners, and carpenters, as money could get. He meant to build a fleet strong enough to prevent the Turkish fleet from relieving Azov. A model galley was ordered from Holland, and twenty-two copies were speedily made from it. The soldiers of the guards' regiments, and all the workmen procurable, were driven together to the forests of the Don to fell timber and build ships. Difficulties multiplied at every step. Forest fires destroyed the shipping sheds. At the end of March severe frosts, and at the beginning of April heavy snowstorms, were fresh impediments. Yet, a fleet of two warships, twenty-three galleys, four fire-ships, and numerous smaller craft, were safely launched by the middle of April. Peter dwelt in a small two-roomed wooden house at Voronezh, where he lived among his workmen, himself the most strenuous of them all.

On May 3 the "sea-caravan" sailed from Voronezh, "Captain Peter Aleksyeevich" commanding eight galleys of the flotilla from the galley *Principium*, built by his own hand. Nor was all this labour in vain. The new Russian fleet prevented the Turks from relieving Azov by water ; a general attack on the Russian camp was repulsed ; and on July 18 the fortress surrendered on condition that the garrison was allowed to march out with all the honours of war.

The capture of Azov, like the capture of Kazan more than a century earlier, was one of those triumphs which strongly appeal to the popular imagination. It was the first victory won by the Moscovites over the terrible Turks, just as Ivan IV's success had been the first abiding victory won by the Moscovites over the Tatars, and it was of equal significance. On September 30, the Moscovite army made its triumphal entry into the capital. The procession was headed by Admiral-General Lefort and Generalissimo Shein, and behind their gilded sledges walked Captain Peter Aleksyeevich with a pike across his shoulder.

But the real significance of the victory of Azov lay in the fact that it was a triumph of the new system which had brought in the foreign shipbuilders. Peter now felt able to advance along the path of progress with a quicker and a firmer step. At two Councils, held on October 20 and November 4, 1696, it was resolved to consolidate the victory by converting Azov into a first-class fortress, by establishing a new naval station at the head of the Sea of Azov, to which the name of Taganrog was given, and by building a national fleet at the national expense. But it was necessary to guarantee the future as well as to provide for the present. A prolonged war with the Ottoman

B.   19

Porte was a serious prospect for a poor and undeveloped country like Moscovy. It was therefore resolved to send a .grand embassy to the principal Western Powers to solicit their co-operation against the Turk. At the same council it was resolved that fifty young Moscovites of the best families should be sent to England, Holland and Venice, to learn the arts and sciences of the West, especially shipbuilding, fortification and foreign languages, so as to make Russia independent of foreigners in the future. The experiment had already been tried on a smaller scale by Boris Godunov. It failed because the young Moscovites refused to return from civilisation to barbarism. Peter resolved to obviate this by being the pioneer as well as the ruler of his people. He would first be a learner himself that he might be able to teach his people afterwards.

On March 10, 1697, the grand embassy under the leader-ship of Lefort set out on its travels. Peter attached himself to it as a volunteer sailor-man, Peter Mikhailov, so as to have greater facility for learning shipbuilding and other technical sciences. At Libau Peter first beheld the Baltic. Thence he proceeded by sea to Königsberg, where he learnt the practice of gunnery from the great engineer Von Sternfeld. Peter was detained longer than he liked by the election to the Polish throne consequent on the death of Sobieski. The two principal candidates were Frederick Augustus, Elector of Saxony, and the Prince of Conti, who was supported by Louis XIV. Moscovy's policy on this occasion was simplicity itself. It was a matter of indifference to her who sat on the Polish throne so long as he did not abandon the Holy League against the Turks. But France favoured the Turks; and Conti, as the French candidate, held out to the Polish electors the bait of a separate peace with the Porte. Peter was bound to oppose "the nominee of the Turks and Tatars," as he, not inaptly, styled Conti; and he intimated to the Poles that the election of the French candidate would be regarded by Moscovy as a breach of the peace between her and the Republic. Both candidates were elected; and a brief civil war ensued, in which Frederick Augustus, proclaimed as Augustus II, ultimately prevailed. He ascribed his success in a great measure to a second minatory letter from Peter to the *Sejm.*

Peter's five months' stay at Saardam and Amsterdam and his subsequent visit to Deptford have been so often described that there is no need to retell the story here. Suffice it to say that he completed his education as a shipbuilder and returned to Holland in January, 1698, only to find that the Grand Embassy had failed in its main object of obtaining the help of the Western Powers against the Turks. All Europe, divided into two hostile camps, was anxiously awaiting the death of the childless, and long ailing, Carlos II of Spain; and neither France, nor the Grand Alliance pitted against her by William III, was willing to plunge into the distant eastern war, with a war concerning the Spanish Succession at their very doors. At Vienna, whither he next proceeded, Peter was equally unsuccessful. He was about to go on to Venice, to persuade the Signoria to cleave to the fast dissolving Holy League, when he was suddenly recalled to Russia by the revolt of the *Stryeltsui.*

The *Stryeltsui* had long been dissatisfied with Peter's administration. Analysed to its ultimate elements, their dissatisfaction was the protest of indolent, incapable and excessively privileged troops against a new system which demanded from them more work and greater efficiency. Peter, they argued, gave them no rest at all. When actual fighting was over, he set them to building fortresses on the Sea of Azov; and the last straw was added to their burden when he marched off four of their regiments from Azov to the distant Lithuanian frontier in view of a possible war with Poland, and sent other regiments from Moscow to Azov to supply their places. This the *Stryeltsui* regarded as little short of banishment; and 150 of them deserted *en route* and returned to Moscow, on the plea that their pay was in arrear. Driven out of Moscow, they rejoined their regiments at Toropets; and these regiments refused to obey an *ukaz*, subsequently issued by the Boyars, demanding the surrender of the fugitives. Feeling that they had now gone too far to turn back safely, the ringleaders stimulated the other regiments encamped on the Dwina to revolt.   On June 6, 1698, a letter supposed to have been written by the Tsarevna Sophia, urging the *Stryeltsui* to join her in force at the Dyevichesky Monastery, was read to them; and the whole force, 2200 strong, resolved to march against Moscow forthwith and destroy the German Settlement as the source of the new heretical ideas, and the Boyars as the oppressors of the people.   The Gosudar was to be killed because "he goes with the Germans"; and, if Sophia refused to accept the vacant throne, it was to be offered to Prince Vasily Golitsuin, "because he has always been merciful towards us."

There was great consternation at Moscow on the tidings of the approach of the *Stryeltsui*.   By the advice of Boris Golit-suin, the foreign soldiery, 4000 strong, with 25 guns, were sent against the rebels and came upon them at the ford of the river Iskra.   Three volleys sufficed to scatter the *Stryeltsui*.   In an hour's time, all the rebels were in the hands of the Tsar's troops.   It was only after the victory that the real carnage began.   A strict investigation ensued.   Many of the *Stryeltsui* were done to death by torture in their own camp.   The rest were imprisoned to await Peter's good pleasure.   On August 26, Peter arrived at the German Settlement determined to drown all further contradictions in torrents of blood.   The new era of enlightenment was to be inaugurated by a reign of terror.

Peter was well aware that behind the *Stryeltsui* stood the sympathising masses of the Moscovite people, whom it was his mission to reform against their will.   His foreign tour had convinced him of the inherent superiority of the foreigner ; and, this superiority once admitted, imitation of the foreigner was, to his mind, inevitable.   Any such imitation had necessarily to begin with externals ; and Peter, with characteristic insight and thoroughness, at once fell foul of the long beards and oriental costumes which symbolised the arch-conservatism of old Moscovy. In old Moscovy beardless officials had had small chance of promotion. More than one Patriarch had excommunicated those members of their flocks who dared to shave. Against this curious superstition Peter struck with all his might the day after his return to Moscow. On August 16, 1698, the chief men of the Tsardom were assembled round his wooden hut at Preobrazhensk; and Peter, emerging with a large pair of shears in his hands, deliberately clipped off the beards and mustachios of his Boyars. After thus vindicating the claims of common-sense, Peter prudently consented to a compromise. He decreed that, after September 1, 1698, the old Russian New Year's Day, beards might be worn, but a graduated tax was imposed upon their wearers. Thus the beard ceased to be an object of worship, and a new source of revenue flowed into the Treasury.

And now, without giving the reactionaries time to recover from this rude shock, the Tsar proceeded to horrify them by a strange and awful Bacchanalia, the like of which had never been known in Moscovy. From the middle of September to the end of October, 1698, banquets and drinking-bouts alternated with torturings and executions, in which the Tsar and his favourites played the part of inquisitors and headsmen. During these six weeks, no fewer than a thousand of the captive *Stryeltsui* were done to death with every refinement of cruelty. The ringleaders naturally fared worst of all. Their legs and arms were first broken on wheels at Preobrazhensk. They were then conveyed in carts to the Red Square at Moscow, where their backs were broken in the same way; and they were left to die a lingering death, unless shot as an act of mercy by Peter's express command. The corpses were left in the place of execution for five months afterwards.

Peter also seized this opportunity of breaking definitively with the past. The death of his half-brother, Ivan V, in 1696, had left him sole Tsar; but Sophia, even in her monastery, had been a possible source of danger. He determined she should be a danger no longer. An intention, on Peter's part, to implicate her in the conspiracy is transparent from the first; but the most prolonged and exquisite tortures could extract nothing definite from the wretched *Stryeltsui*. The letter supposed to have been sent by her to them turned out to have been written by her elder sister Martha. Both the Tsarevnas were made nuns and shut up for life in nunneries under military supervision.

A leading part in the terrible events of September–October, 1698, was played by Peter's new favourite, Alexander Danilovich Menshikov. This extraordinary man, whom Peter literally plucked from the gutter to set among Princes, was of very base origin. He first emerges into the light of history, at twenty years of age, as a vendor of meat pies in the streets of Moscow. He was introduced to Peter by Lefort and took that favourite's place on his death in 1699. Ignorant, brutal, grasping and corrupt as Menshikov was, it is not too much to say that, after Peter, there was not a more alert, lucid and versatile intellect than his in all Moscovy, while his energy was boundless and inexhaustible. He could turn his hand to anything at a moment's notice. He could drill a regiment, build a frigate, administer a kingdom, and decapitate a rebel with equal facility. During the Tsar's first foreign tour, Menshikov worked by his side in the dockyards of Amsterdam, and, at the same time, acquired a thorough knowledge of colloquial Dutch and German. Henceforth, he became indispensable.

Another useful man who comes forward prominently at this time is Alexis Kurbatov, an intelligent financier of many expedients, who suggested to Peter a new source of revenue by introducing stamped-paper into Moscovy. He was also the first of a new order of officials called *Pribuilshchiki* or "People on the spot," whose duty it was to extirpate corrupt practices by flogging and banishment.

The last year of the seventeenth century saw a notable reform, which drew a sharp line of demarcation between old and new. By the *ukaz* of December 20, 1699, it was ordered that, henceforth, the New Year should not be reckoned from September 1, supposed, as heretofore, to be the date of the Creation, but from January 1, Anno Domini.

Peter had brought home with him in 1698 the conviction that he must conclude peace with the Porte. It was his good fortune at this period to possess a foreign minister of the highest ability in Theodore Golovin, who, like so many others of his countrymen in later times, had learnt the business of a ruler in the Far East. During the regency of Sophia, he had been sent to the Amur to defend the new Moscovite fortress of Albazin against the Chinese. In 1689 he concluded with the Celestial Empire the Treaty of Nerchinsk, by which the line of the Amur, as far as its tributary the Gorbitsa, was retroceded to China because of the impossibility of seriously defending it. On Lefort's death in March, 1699, Golovin succeeded him as Admiral-General. The same year, he was created the first Russian Count; and the conduct of foreign affairs was committed to him.

Golovin's first diplomatic achievement was the conclusion of peace with the Porte. In April, 1699, the Moscovite plenipotentiaries were sent to Stambul, not as usual, by land, but by sea. A man of war, commanded by a Dutch captain, awaited them at the new arsenal of Taganrog; and they were escorted into the Sea of Azov by a fleet of nine warships, among which was the *Apostle Peter* flying the flag of skipper Peter Aleksyeevich. On August 28 a Russian line-of-battle ship sailed for the first time into the Golden Horn, fired a salute, and cast anchor at the very gates of the Seraglio. The negotiations were opened in November, 1699, but, owing to the intrigues of Great Britain and Holland, who feared the commercial competition of Russia in the Euxine and the Levant, and of France, who dreaded her political influence, it was not till July, 1700, that a truce for thirty years was concluded between Russia and the Porte. By the terms of this truce, the Azov district and all the land extending from thence eastwards to the Kuban district for a ten hours' journey were ceded to Moscovy. The tribute to the Khan was waived.

Peter had made peace with the Porte, and relinquished his original project of dominating the Black Sea, in the hope of compensating himself on the shores of the Baltic. The Baltic was nearer both to Russia and the West than the Euxine, and consequently a much more desirable possession. Moreover the Swedish government was now in the hands of an untried lad of sixteen. If the Baltic provinces were to be filched at all, now was the time to filch them. These were the considerations which induced Peter to accede to the league of partition, proposed by Patkul and negotiated by Augustus II of Poland, which resulted in the outbreak of the Great Northern War in 1700. Into the details of this war there is no need to enter. They have been described elsewhere in another volume[1] of this series. Here the Great Northern War can only be considered in so far as it affected or modified Peter's general plans, especially his plans of reform.

Hitherto, historians have regarded the Great Northern War too exclusively from the soldier's point of view; yet it was not so much an arena for the strife of heroes as, in the first place, a training school for a backward young nation, and, in the second place, a means of multiplying the material resources of a nation as poor as she was backward. Peter the Great undertook the war with Sweden in order that Russia might gain her proper place in the Northern Mediterranean. The possession of an ice-free sea-board was essential to her natural development; the creation of a fleet followed inevitably upon the acquisition of such a sea-board; and she could not hope to obtain her due share of the trade and commerce of the world

[1] Scandinavia, Chapter XII.

till she possessed both. Not till after a bitter struggle of twenty-one years was this double object obtained. This struggle Peter rightly regarded as a long apprenticeship. When on September 3, 1721, he broke open the sealed packet containing the Peace of Nystad, sent after him by a special courier, he remarked, half jocularly, half seriously, "most apprentices serve for seven years, but, in our school, the term of apprenticeship has been thrice as long."

In 1700 this long apprenticeship was only just beginning. Russia had still to be educated as far as possible up to the western standard, in order that she might be able to appreciate and utilise the fruits of western civilisation; and thus it was that, during the whole course of the Great Northern War, the process of internal domestic reform was slowly but ceaselessly proceeding. The whole fabric of the State was being changed. New, brand-new institutions, on the western model, were gradually growing up among the cumbrous, antiquated and worn-out machinery of old Moscovy; and new men, capable and audacious, were being trained beneath the eye of the Regenerator to help him in his Herculean task and carry on the work when he had vanished from the scene. At first, indeed, the external form of the administration remained much the same as before. The old dignities disappeared of themselves on the deaths of their holders; for the new men, those nearest to Peter, did not require them. The great drag on the wheels of the Government was its penury, a drag which grew more and more sensible as the war proceeded. The expenses of the fixed embassies at foreign Courts (one of the earliest Petrine innovations) was a particularly severe drain on the depleted treasury. Every expedient to increase the revenue was eagerly snatched at. Taxation was made universal for the first time. The sale of spirits became a government monopoly, the administration of which was first entrusted to the newly instituted Rathhäuser, by means of which Peter hoped to accustom his people to local self-government. A great impediment to commerce was the deplorable state of the currency. The ruble and the *altuin*[1] were the units of account, but neither of them existed, the only coins in circulation being the well-worn silver kopecks and half-kopecks, most of which were further deteriorated by bisection and trisection. The currency was reformed by the coinage *ukaz* of March, 1700, which established mints for the stamping and testing of gold, silver, and copper coins by qualified masters. Previously to 1700, only from 200,000 to 500,000 coins had been annually struck in Russia. In 1700 the number rose to 1,992,000, in 1701 to 2,559,000, in 1702 to 4,534,000.

Peter's two great objects at this period of his reign were external security and internal prosperity. The former he had obtained by the creation of the new army on a European model, the latter he hoped to promote by a whole series of administrative measures. In April, 1702, he issued his celebrated *ukaz* for facilitating the immigration of foreign specialists into Russia on a scale never before contemplated. The invitation was made as tempting as possible, all such visitors being allowed full liberty of worship and permission to be judged by their own tribunals. To the better sort of Russian dissenters Peter was also very tolerant. His attitude towards the chief centre of the *Bezpopovshchina* or "Priestless Community," founded, at the end of the seventeenth century, on the banks of the Vuiga, is characteristic of his general policy. The enterprise and organising genius of this wealthy community enabled it practically to monopolise the rich fisheries and hunting grounds of the White Sea, while the abundant harvests which filled its granaries to overflowing gave this colony the command of the corn market of St Petersburg. All danger from without was avoided by a composition with Peter, the *Vuigovtsui* agreeing to pay double taxes and to work, at set times, for nothing, in the state mines and foundries at Povyenets. In return for these services the Tsar permitted these lucrative

[1] A 3-kopeck piece.

nonconformists full liberty of worship (*ukaz* of 1703) with the use of the old service books.

From the first, Peter did much to promote education, especially education of a practical sort. Schools of mathematics and navigation were established, about 1702, in Moscow; and in 1703 another school was founded, at which geography, ethics, politics, Latin rhetoric and the Cartesian philosophy were taught. Great efforts were made to provide cheap books for the schools, the Pole Ilia Kopiewski, a great admirer of Peter, who set up a Russian press at Amsterdam, about 1697, being the chief worker in this field. In 1703 the first Russian newspaper appeared. It was entitled "Tidings of military and other events worthy of knowledge and remembrance," and consisted, for the most part, of extracts from the foreign gazettes.

A whole series of *ukazes* were directed against social disorders and manifest abuses. In 1702 a regiment was sent to Kostroma to seize freebooters who were also landed proprietors, for committing all manner of outrages, and burning villages wholesale. In the same year, in order to minimise conflagrations, a *ukaz* directed that all houses should, henceforth, be built of brick instead of wood; and fire-hose were introduced. In 1704 *ukazes* were issued forbidding midwives to kill misshapen children, and undertakers to bury corpses till three days after death. Other *ukazes* of the same period endeavoured to raise the tone of public morality and inculcate self-respect. Thus the *ukaz* of 1704 sternly prohibited compulsory marriages, which had been one of the chief scandals and miseries of old Muscovite family life, released women from the captivity of the *terem*, and compelled their husbands and fathers to admit them to all social entertainments.

The death of the Patriarch Adrian in 1700 enabled Peter, by the advice of Kurbatov, to take the first step towards abolishing the Patriarchate, though there is no reason to suppose that Peter meditated doing this at first. Still, the Patriarchate was undoubtedly a danger to Peter at this period.

The enemies of reform could always count upon the acquiescence of the arch-pastor of the Russian Church. The Patriarch Joachim had protested against the employment of foreigners. The Patriarch Adrian had written forcibly against the shearing of beards. Adrian, however, was a timid, slothful man of whom Peter had no fear. An energetic but unfriendly Patriarch, on the other hand, would be the natural leader of a whole army of malcontents; he would be a most dangerous rival, a second Nikon. In January, 1701, therefore, the administration of the temporalities of the Patriarchate was entrusted to a layman, Count Ivan Musin-Pushkin. His appointment was the first step towards a rigid inquisition into the administration of the Russian monasteries, which resulted in the *ukaz* of December, 1701, depriving the religious houses of the control of their estates and making the monks the salaried officials of the government. The care of the spiritualities was entrusted to the learned Kievlyan Prelate, Stephen Yavorsky, with the title of Exarch of the most Holy Patriarchal See. He was at the same time made Metropolitan of Ryazan. Yavorsky, at first, offered no opposition to the work of reform and did much for education. It was he who, as Rector of the Moscow Academy, introduced the teaching of Latin into that institution.

All this time the popular disaffection was steadily growing. As the war proceeded, as the burden of taxation became more and more grievous, and the number of the recruits ever larger, the murmuring of every class of the population grew louder and louder. "What manner of Tsar is this," people said, "who makes our wives and children widows and orphans? If he lives much longer he will ruin the land!" A printer named Grisha Talitsky, encouraged by Ignaty, Bishop of Tambov, actually printed and circulated a pamphlet proving that Peter was Antichrist. Yavorsky at the Tsar's command had to write a formal refutation entitled "The Signs of the Coming of Antichrist." On January 4, 1700, the Tsar irritated the reactionaries still further by issuing the *ukaz* directing the general use of short Saxon, or Hungarian jackets, and French or German hose.   This was followed, in 1701, by the *ukaz* forbidding, from henceforth, under heavy penalties, the wearing of the cumbrous old Moscovite garments.   This change of costume was intended to mark a complete and final rupture with the barbarous past.   But, as Catherine II once remarked to Gustavus III, a century later, there is nothing more difficult than to change the traditional habits of a people ; and Peter's innovation was bitterly resented as being both indecent and irreligious.   In Moscow itself resistance was out of the question ; but at Astrakhan, in July, 1705, a very dangerous rebellion, headed by Old-believers, ex-Stryeltsui, and Cossacks, broke out.   "We of Astrakhan," as the curious document reciting the grievances of the rebels runs, "have risen for the Christian faith, and because of the beard-shearing, and the German clothes, and the tobacco...and because our governors worship Kummerian idols[1] and would make us do likewise, and because of the taxes on our cellars and baths...and because we will not give up our old religion," etc.   It required a whole army to put down this rebellion, which was not crushed entirely till Sheremetev took Astrakhan by assault on March 13, 1706.

The Astrakhan rising was speedily followed by the Bashkir revolt, Bulavin's rebellion, and the treason of Mazepa, at the very crisis of the struggle with Charles XII.   Yet never for a moment was the necessary but dangerous work of reform suspended.   In 1706 the first modern hospital was built on the Yantsa, close to the German Settlement.   In 1707 a commission of Boyars was appointed to devise the best means of dealing with the wholesale vagabondage and universal highway robbery which had ever been among the chief curses of old Moscovy.   And, if eighteenth century Moscovites had little scruple about living on their own countrymen, they naturally

---

[1] These idols turned out to be the exhibited wig-blocks.

had still less about how they treated their country's enemies. Thus, in 1706, Dositheus, Patriarch of Jerusalem, reported to the Tsar that hundreds of Swedish prisoners were regularly sold to the Turks in the slave markets, to the great scandal of the Christian population.

In 1708 Russia was divided into the eight "governments" of Moscow, St Petersburg, Kiev, Smolensk, Archangel, Kazan, Azov, and Siberia, in order that the country might be administered "in a more orderly and peaceable manner." The chief duty of each governor was to see that the taxes were duly collected and transmitted to Moscow. On January 27, 1710, the first Russian Budget was framed, showing an annual revenue of 3,016,000 rubles, or, taking a three years' average, 3,133,000 rubles, while the total expenditure came to 3,834,000 rubles.

Absorbed as he was by the Swedish and Turkish Wars, which required his prolonged absence from Russia, Peter could not attend to the details of the domestic administration; but, as it could no longer be neglected, he instituted (*ukazes* of February 22, and March 2, 1711) a supreme governing board, to which he gave the name of "the Administrative Senate." It was to take the place of the Tsar during his absence, receive the implicit obedience due to himself, and be responsible for the whole burden of the administration.

By the *ukaz* of April 18, 1718, an entirely new public service was introduced, the so-called *Collegia*, or Departments of State. The idea of this administrative reform was first suggested to Peter by Leibnitz. The Colleges were to be, in all points, on the model of the Swedish "Services," so that Peter may be said to have learnt the science of government as well as the science of war from his Scandinavian rivals. As finally constituted, these new public officers were nine in number, and corresponded roughly with the "ministries" of Western Europe. The presidents of the colleges were *ipso facto* members of the Senate, though not every senator was

a minister.   Most of the presidents were Russians, most of the
vice-presidents foreigners, Peter invariably acting on the
patriotic principle, not always followed by his immediate
successors, that natives should always fill the highest posts,
and that no alien should occupy any place that a Russian was
equally capable of filling.

Efforts were also made to simplify local government as
much as possible by subdivision.   Thus the various governments were split up into districts (*uyezdia*), each district
having its own president assisted by a council of assessors
elected by the gentry.   In 1720, *nadvornuie sudbui*, or
courts of justice, were established in every town ; and *Zemskie
Kontorui*, or land-offices, where public account-books had
to be regularly kept, were established in every district.
The land-offices were to supervise the tax-payers, and report,
regularly, to the *Kammer Collegium*, or chief fiscal board of the
Empire.   In 1718 the old *ulozhenie*, or code of laws, which
was found, in many respects, to be incompatible with the new
reforms, was remodelled according to the existing Swedish
Code.   A new law of succession was also introduced, the old
practice of partitioning real estate being abandoned, and the
custom of primogeniture introduced, principally to prevent the
pauperisation of the great families.   By the *ukaz* of January 16,
1721, all army officers, whatever their origin, were ennobled.
But education had previously been declared to be the indispensable qualification for advancement in every branch of the
service.   Nay more, no gentleman was, henceforth, to marry
unless he had first been duly educated.   The famous *ukaz* of
January 20, 1714, saw to this by ordering professors from the
mathematical schools to go the round of the provinces and
teach the children of the gentry arithmetic and mathematics.

The Regenerator also laboured hard to develop and utilise
Russia's latent resources.   All landed proprietors were urged
to search for and work the minerals on their estates, or the
Government would do it for them.   In 1719 we find the silver

mines of Nerchinsk, the iron mines of Tobolsk, and the copper
mines of Kungara in full working order.   At Tula and Kashirsk,
about the same time, Aleksyei Naruishkin founded iron works.
Still more lucrative were the Lipski iron works, which were
bound by contract to turn out 15,000 small arms of all sorts,
including 1000 pistols, per annum.   The Olonets iron foundries
were important because of their proximity to Petersburg.   No
improvement was too small for the attention of the Tsar.   Thus,
in May, 1725, he ordered that corn should, henceforth, be
reaped with scythes instead of with sickles.   In 1716 Nosov
was sent abroad to hire shepherds and cloth-workers.   The
leather-trade had always been of the utmost importance.   In
1716 alone, 133,467 poods were sent to Archangel for export.
Peter did much for the leather industry.   Master-tanners were
sent from Reval to Moscow to teach the people there how to
tan the leather properly; and, after two years of such instruction,
those of the Moscovite tanners who persisted in the old way,
were to be punished by imprisonment and confiscation.

The Government did what it could to protect the serfs from
"their worst enemies, those drunken and disorderly masters
who deteriorate their estates, laying all sorts of unbearable
burdens on their peasants, and beating and tormenting them,
so that they run away from their grievous burdens, for which
cause waste lands multiply and the arrears of taxation increase."
All such "masters" were to be placed under restraint as
lunatics; and their property was to be administered, by their
nearest relatives, or by the State.   Moreover, the *ukaz* of
April 21, 1721, forbade the sale of serfs separately; they were
only to be sold by families.

Peter knew very well that the perennial emptiness of the
Treasury was very largely due to peculation, that ancient and
ineradicable vice of Russian society.   He was not the man to
leave the improvement of public morals to the gradual operation
of time, and he was therefore very speedily committed to a
struggle with the robbers of the Treasury almost as bloody as

his struggle with the rebellious *Stryeltsui*. The vileness of some of the remedies he saw fit to adopt is eloquent as to the extent and virulence of the evil with which he had to cope. By the *ukaz* of August, 1713, informers were invited to report all cases of defalcation to the Tsar, and promised the rank and the property of those whom they denounced. The *ukaz* of December 24, 1714, further encouraged delators to come forward fearlessly, and not to be afraid to report against even their official superiors. The *ukaz* of January 28, 1721, instituted an order of official public-accusers, the Imperial Ober-fiscals, whose principal duties were to protect the revenue and supervise the administration of the Senate itself. On the other hand, owing to the public remonstrances of Archbishop Yavorsky, in 1712, against the abuses of this espionage system, the *ukaz* of March 17, 1714, imposed upon any fiscal, or other delator, convicted of a false accusation, the same penalty which would have been imposed upon the alleged delinquent if *he* had been found guilty.

Villainous as the system was, it certainly brought much rascality to light. Take, for example, the famous Gagarin case, which is typical.

In 1711 the Ober-fiscal, Aleksyei Nestorov, reported to the Tsar that the Governor of Siberia, Prince Gagarin, was plundering the Treasury and had succeeded in monopolising the lucrative China trade for the exclusive benefit of himself and his friends. Nestorov sent a whole chest full of incriminating documents to the Senate for investigation, which Senator Count Musin-Pushkin, whom Nestorov had already reported to the Tsar for malversation, promptly ordered to be destroyed. But the indefatigable Ober-fiscal immediately set about collecting fresh evidence, and, in 1717, he presented a second and much stronger indictment against Gagarin. Peter entrusted the further examination of the affair to Senator Prince Yakov Dolgoruki, but, becoming suspicious of him also, ultimately transferred the case to a committee of the officers of the Guard, whom he could trust implicitly.   A number of merchants were now examined, and they confessed not only that Gagarin had systematically corrupted all the Siberian officials to wink at his depredations, but that many of the Senators and Ministers of State were his creatures.   Peter, now thoroughly aroused, despatched Major Likharev to Siberia to examine Gagarin on the spot.   The Prince was tried and convicted of every sort of dishonesty.   He had bought large quantities of government stores with government funds and then sold them on his own account at an enormous profit.   He had also burnt his account-books and established a system of intimidation which was perfect of its kind.   Peter sent him forthwith to the gallows.

Some of the Tsar's bitterest moments were due to the discovery of peculation on the part of those whom he loved and trusted the most.   His own integrity in money matters was above suspicion.   His pastimes, if rude and coarse, were simple and inexpensive.   Every penny he could spare was devoted to the service of the State.   He had a right to expect that those whom he had exalted and enriched should keep their fingers out of the public coffers.   The worst offender was his own particular favourite, known as "little Alec."   Every time the Tsar returned to Russia he received fresh accusations of peculation against Menshikov.   As early as 1711 he was in disgrace because of his shameful looting in Poland.   Poland, indeed, had by this time become a sort of happy hunting ground, where, as Catherine II once phrased it, you only had to stoop down in order to pick up anything you liked ; but Menshikov's rapacity on this occasion seems to have staggered the Russians themselves.   He had pillaged whole provinces systematically, and carried off waggon-loads of loot, and this too in a country actually in alliance with the Tsar.   On his return to Russia, in 1712, Peter found that even in the new province of Ingria and Petersburg, of which he was Governor-General, Menshikov had winked at wholesale corruption.   "You have represented honest men to me as rogues, and rogues as honest men," wrote the indignant Tsar on this occasion. "I warn you for the last time: mend your ways or you will come to grief!" But he did not mend his ways. In 1714, in conjunction with his principal colleagues and subordinates, he was implicated in astounding frauds on the Treasury. The exasperated Tsar did not spare his hand. Korsakov, the Vice-Governor of Petersburg, was knouted publicly; two Senators had their tongues seared with red-hot irons; and the worst of them, Prince Volkonsky, was subsequently shot. The most distinguished services in the past were not allowed to interfere with condign punishment in the present. Thus, towards the end of the reign, one of Peter's ablest diplomatists, the Vice-Chancellor, Shafirov, was dismissed from office for bribery, condemned to death, and only pardoned on the scaffold itself; while the Ober-fiscal Nestorov, who had brought so many malefactors to justice, was himself broken on the wheel for peculation. Menshikov, by far the most shameless scoundrel of them all, owed his head, on three several occasions, to Peter's partiality and the earnest supplications of the Empress-Consort Catherine.

Extraordinarily difficult during this period of transition and transformation was the position of the Russian Church. As the sworn guardian of Orthodoxy, she was bound, in many respects, to observe a conservative attitude; yet patriotism equally obliged her not to oppose the beneficent civilising efforts of a reforming Tsar. Moreover, the Church herself was very much in need of discipline. The number of unworthy priests had greatly increased in consequence of the influx into the ministry of many gentlemen who evaded military service by becoming candidates for holy orders. Efforts were also made to raise the status of the clergy, which had fallen very low, and to encourage public worship. The *ukaz* of 1716 commanded everyone to go to confession at least once a year under heavy penalties. The *ukaz* of 1718 compelled all parishioners to go to church every Sunday and holiday; and absentees were, henceforth, to be ineligible for public offices. But the real motive of this ordinance was to make the people hear the *ukazes* read after divine service; since in those days of general ignorance, comparatively few could read the *ukazes* posted up on the gates of the towns.

Archbishop Yavorsky, by this time, had fallen somewhat into disfavour for espousing the cause of the unfortunate Tsarevich Alexis and also for protesting, cryptically but still unmistakeably, against such patent irregularities as the putting away of the Tsaritsa Eudoxia. He was therefore to a great extent superseded by Theophan, prefect of the Kiev academy, whom Peter promoted to the archiepiscopal see of Pskov. Henceforth, Theophan, though he was 23 years the junior of Stephen, was the Tsar's chief counsellor among the clergy and enjoyed his unbounded confidence, while his right reverend brother of Ryazan had to be content with the sympathy of the arch-conservative-party and the clergy of the old capital. When Peter, for the better regulation of church affairs, proposed the establishment of a "Spiritual Department," Theophan alone was entrusted with the drafting of the project, so that he may be regarded as the creator of what was subsequently known as "the Holy Synod." The imperial manifesto of January, 1721, subsequently announced that his Majesty deemed it expedient to entrust the conduct of spiritual affairs to a synodical administration, as being more in keeping with the spirit and traditions of the orthodox church. But the real reason of this important innovation is to be found in the sentence which declared that the Synod was substituted for the Patriarchate; "because simple folk cannot distinguish the spiritual power from the sovereign power, and suppose that a supreme pastor is a second Gosudar, the spiritual authority being regarded as higher and better than the temporal."

CHAPTER XV.

PETER THE GREAT, 1689–1725.

Later years.

THE strong and terrible reforming Tsar had triumphed over every obstacle, triumphed so thoroughly that any interruption of his work during his lifetime was inconceivable. But the thought "Will my work survive me?" haunted him persistently. Peter's anxiety was reasonable. His health was uncertain; his half-taught pupils were few and divided; the reactionaries were many and of one mind; and they believed, rightly, that in the heir to the throne, the Tsarevich Alexis, they possessed a secret sympathiser who would, one day, reverse the whole policy of the Tsar Antichrist, and restore the old order of things. It was tragic enough that Peter's only son should be his father's worst ill-wisher; but it is too often forgotten that Peter himself was, to a large extent, responsible for the beginnings of this unnatural hostility. Peter, as we have seen in the case of Menshikov, could forgive everything to those whom he loved. But to those whom he disliked he was inhumanly severe, and he pursued the objects of his hatred with a murderous vindictiveness which was rarely satisfied with anything short of their extermination.

On January 27, 1689, the young Tsar had married, at his mother's command, the *boyaruinya* Eudoxia Lopukhina.

Eudoxia would have made a model Tsaritsa of the pre-Petrine period, but she was no fit wife for such a vagabond of genius as Peter the Great. Accustomed from her infancy to the monastic seclusion of the *terem*, her mental horizon did not extend much beyond her embroidery frame or her illuminated service book. She was one of those Moscovite princesses who were not allowed to receive the foreign ministers lest they should, inadvertently, say something silly. After the birth of their second son, Alexander, on October 3, 1691, Peter practically deserted her, and on his return from abroad in 1698, shut her up in a distant nunnery because she would not consent to a divorce. In June, 1699, the Patriarch Adrian was terrorised into divorcing her; and the Tsaritsa Eudoxia disappeared from the world under the hood of "Sister Elena."

Peter's sole surviving son, Alexis, born on February 19, 1690, was ignored by his father till he was nine years old, when his education was confided to learned foreigners who taught him French, history, geography, and mathematics. In 1703, in order that he might practically apply his lessons, Alexis was ordered to follow the army to the field, as a private in a bombardier regiment, and, in 1704, was present at the capture of Narva. At this period the Tsarevich's preceptors had the highest opinion of their pupil. He was certainly of a precocious intelligence, and his disposition was naturally amiable. Of his ability, indeed, there can be no question; unfortunately it was not the sort of ability that his father could make use of. The Tsarevich was essentially a student, with strong leanings towards archaeology and ecclesiology. He resembled his grandfather Alexis; but, with his knowledge of modern languages, his intellectual vista was wider, and he would doubtless have gone much further than his grandfather. Nevertheless, the quiet seclusion of a monastic library was the proper place for this gentle emotional dreamer, who clung so fondly to the ancient traditions, and was so easily moved by the beauty of the orthodox liturgy.

To a prince of the temperament of Alexis, the restless vehement energy of his father was very offensive. He liked neither the work itself, nor its object. Yet Peter, not unnaturally, demanded that his heir should help to fashion his future inheritance. He demanded from a youth with the nature of a recluse practical activity, unceasing labour, unremitting attention to technical details, the concentration of all his energies upon the business of government, so as to maintain the new State at the high level of greatness to which it had already been raised. In consequence of these stern demands on the one hand, and an invincible repugnance to execute them on the other, painful relations between father and son, quite apart from the personal antipathies already existing, were inevitable.

Then, too, the clergy secretly encouraged Alexis in his resistance to his father. Stephen Yavorsky and the other arch-pastors of the Russian Church openly expressed their disapproval of the Tsar's new and strange ways; and, as a loyal son of the Church, the Tsarevich gladly listened to those who had the power to bind and loose. The person who had most influence over him was his confessor, Yakov Ignatev, a man of considerable force of character, who familiarised the Tsarevich with the idea of parricide. Thus, on one occasion, Alexis confessed to Ignatev that he had wished for his father's death. "God forgive thee!" answered the priest; "yet we all desire his death because there is so much misery in the nation."

On October 14, 1711, Alexis was married, greatly against his will, to Sophia Charlotte of Blankenburg-Wolfenbüttel, whose sister, almost simultaneously, espoused the heir to the Austrian throne, the Archduke Charles. Three weeks later, the bridegroom was hurried off by his father to Thorn, to superintend the provisioning of the Russian troops in Poland. For the next twelve months, Alexis was kept constantly on the move. Evidently, Peter was determined to tear his son away from a life of indolent ease, and make a new man of him.

Alexis was unequal to the strain. When, after returning from Ladoga, where he had been sent to superintend the building of ships, Peter, to see what progress his son had made in mathematics, asked him to produce for inspection his latest drawings, Alexis, to escape the ordeal of such an examination, resorted to the abject expedient of disabling his right hand by a pistol-shot. In no other way could the Tsarevich have offended his father so deeply. He had behaved like a cowardly recruit who mutilates himself to avoid military service. After this, Peter seemed to take no further interest in Alexis, whom he employed no more. Alexis consoled himself with the reflexion that the future belonged to him. He was well aware that the mass of the Russian nation was on his side. All the prelates but one were devoted to him. Equally friendly were the two great families, the Dolgorukis, and the Golitsuins. The Dolgorukis, who had first come prominently forward during the reign of Tsar Alexis, were well represented in every branch of the public service. They detested the all-powerful Menshikov and lost no opportunity of flattering and encouraging the Tsarevich. The Golitsuins were even more illustrious than the Dolgorukis. So far back as the days of Ivan III, their ambition had become a tradition. Their family was also well-placed and had supplied Peter with some of his ablest generals and diplomatists. Most of the other magnates were equally dissatisfied with Peter and equally devoted to Alexis. They argued, and Alexis agreed with them, that all he had to do was to sit still, and keep out of his father's way as much as possible and await the natural sequence of events.

But with Peter the present was everything. He could not afford to leave anything to chance. All his life long he had been working incessantly with a single object—the regeneration of Russia—in view. The more difficult portion of that work was done. All that was required of his successor was sympathy and good-will.

The Tsar gave Alexis what was evidently meant to be a last

chance on the day of the funeral of the Princess Charlotte, who died on October 22, 1715, four days after giving birth to a son, christened Peter. In a letter of terrible severity, Peter reproached Alexis for his negligence and "inattention to military affairs" and threatened to deprive him of the succession, and cut him off "like a gangrenous swelling" if he did not amend the errors of his ways.

It was now that Alexis showed what a poor creature he really was. Following the advice of his friends, he wrote a pitiful letter to his father, renouncing the succession in favour of his baby half-brother Peter[1] (born the day after the Princess Charlotte's funeral) on the plea of ill-health and general incompetence. On January 19, 1716, Peter offered his son the choice between amending his ways or becoming a monk; and Alexis chose the latter alternative. Still Peter did not despair. On the eve of his departure for the Pomeranian campaign, he urged Alexis to think the whole matter over once more and do nothing hastily. Finally, on August 26, 1716, he wrote to his son from abroad commanding him, if he desired to remain Tsarevich, to join the army without delay. Alexis thereupon fled for protection to Vienna; and his brother-in-law the Emperor Charles sent him for greater security to the fortress of San Elmo at Naples. That the Emperor sympathised with Alexis and suspected Peter of harbouring murderous designs against him is plain from his confidential letter to George I of England, whom he consulted in this delicate affair.

Peter's agitation was extreme. The flight of the Tsarevich to a foreign potentate was a reproach and a scandal. He must be recovered and brought back to Russia at all hazards. But the operation was likely to be one of exceptional difficulty. It was therefore confided to the most subtle and astute of all the Moscovite diplomatists, Count Peter Tolstoi.

Three days after his arrival at Vienna, Tolstoi had an

[1] The little Prince died a few months later.

audience of the Emperor and delivered his master's commands so forcibly, that Charles VI, by the advice of three of his most confidential ministers, permitted Tolstoi to proceed to Naples to see the Tsarevich. They also engaged not to prevent the Tsarevich's departure if he went willingly.

On September 24, 1717 Tolstoi arrived at Naples. His instructions were grimly precise. He was to assure the Tsarevich that, if he returned home at once, everything would be forgiven, and he would be restored to favour and have perfect liberty; but, if he refused to return, his father, as his sovereign, would publicly denounce him as a traitor, while the Church would simultaneously excommunicate him as a disobedient son, in which case he might be sure that he would be fit material for the tormentors both in this world and the next. Peter himself wrote to Alexis in much the same strain, reproaching him bitterly for thus exposing his father to shame, but, swearing solemnly "before God and His judgment seat," that if he came back he should not be punished in the least, but treasured as a son.

Threats and promises. notwithstanding, Alexis, though almost insane with terror, still held out. Tolstoi grew impatient. He reported that only the most extreme compulsion could, as he phrased it, "melt the hard frozen obstinacy of this beast of ours"; and we can well imagine what such words meant in the mouth of a man who had not hesitated, when acting as ambassador at Constantinople, to remove an inconvenient secretary by poison. The unfortunate Tsarevich, who felt, instinctively, that he was fighting for his life against merciless enemies, at first stood firm and refused to depart; but, when Tolstoi threatened to take away his mistress, the Finnish peasant girl, Afrosina, the companion of his flight, whom he loved passionately and whose pregnancy was now imminent, he instantly surrendered. He promised to return with Tolstoi to Russia on condition that he should be allowed to live quietly on his estates and marry Afrosina. To these terms, Tolstoi agreed; and Peter himself solemnly confirmed them in a letter to his son, dated Nov. 18, 1717.

Alexis was now hustled out of Italy as stealthily as possible. On January 31, 1718, he arrived at Moscow.

But what was to be done with the Tsarevich? To allow him to live quietly at his country-house was to establish in the heart of Russia a centre of disaffection. And there was another and serious difficulty to be faced. It was inconceivable that Alexis, of his own accord, could have ventured upon so bold a step as flight to a foreign potentate. He must have had aiders and abettors. Who were they? Peter, nervously apprehensive of the designs of the forces of reaction, scented a widespread domestic conspiracy, and determined to investigate the matter to the very bottom.

The first step was to extort a full confession from the Tsarevich. On February 18, Alexis was brought before his father and a council of magnates. Paralysed with terror, he confessed himself guilty of everything, though no crime had yet been imputed to him, and abjectly begged for mercy. Then, on receiving a second promise of full forgiveness, he revealed the names of all his "accomplices," immediately afterwards renouncing his succession to the throne in favour of his half-brother, the infant Grand-Duke Peter Petrovich. The so-called accomplices, torn from their hiding-places and dragged to the torture-chamber, supplied the prosecution with evidence which, nowadays, would never be accepted in any court of justice. Nor did the clergy escape scot-free. Knowing that the eyes of the Orthodox were reverently fixed upon the Suzdal-Pokrovsky Monastery, where the ex-Tsaritsa Eudoxia was imprisoned, Peter resolved to strike a blow at the hierarchy through her which should terrorise all opposition. Accordingly "the nun Elena," together with many of her kinsmen and friends, including Dosithy, Bishop of Rostov, were seized and haled away to Moscow. Prolonged and oft-repeated torture could only extract from these unhappy creatures the fact that they sympathised with Eudoxia and believed in her future restoration. The Bishop had gone so far as to prophesy the coming of the glad event. Dosithy, previously degraded to the rank of a monk, that torture might be applied to him also, confessed that all of them had desired the death of Peter and the elevation of Alexis; but there was no evidence of any conspiracy.

There was a lull in the prosecution of the Tsarevich's affair after the termination of "the Moscow Process," as it was called. On the arrival of Afrosina at Petersburg, however, in April, 1718, the case was resumed. As the mistress and confidante of Alexis, she was the natural depository of all his secrets; and these secrets were easily wormed out of her by Tolstoi and Menshikov. They did not amount to much, but they were sufficient to destroy Alexis. He had rejoiced at the illness of his supplanter, the little Grand-Duke Peter. He had said that when he was Tsar, he would order things very differently. He would have no ships, and keep the army for purely defensive purposes. He had predicted that, on the death of his father, a civil war would break out between the partisans of the old and the partisans of the new system, in which he would prevail. Immediately after this confession was obtained, Alexis was confronted with it. He tried to save himself by saying "yes!" to everything. Yes, he had wished for his father's death; he had rejoiced when he heard of plots against his father; he had been ready to accept his father's throne from rebels and regicides. At last the worst was known. It is true that there were no actual facts to go upon. Evil designs *in foro conscientiae* were all that could be alleged against Alexis. Nevertheless, in the eyes of Peter, his son was now a self-convicted and most dangerous traitor. His life was forfeit. The future welfare of Russia imperatively demanded his extinction.

But now a case for casuists arose. Even if Alexis deserved a thousand deaths, there was no getting over the fact that his father had sworn, "before the Almighty and His judgment

seat," to pardon and let him live in peace if he returned to
Russia.   Did the enormity of the Tsarevich's crime absolve the
Tsar from the oath which he had taken to spare the life of this
prodigal son?

This question was solemnly submitted to a Grand Council
of prelates, ministers and other dignitaries, on June 13, 1718.
Five days later the clergy presented their memorial.   It was
a cautious, non-committal document, plainly inspired by fear,
but unmistakeably inclining to mercy.   If the Tsar would
punish the fallen sinner, he would find numerous precedents
for doing so in the Old Testament, though, on the other
hand, the much injured Tsar David would have forgiven his
persecutor, Absalom.   But, if he were pleased to pardon, he
had the example of Christ Himself, who said, "I will have mercy
and not sacrifice."   "But," concluded the memorial, "the heart
of the Tsar is in God's hand; let him choose what part he will."

It is a significant fact, which says very little for the courage
of the clergy on this unique opportunity of saving their friend
the Tsarevich, that they entirely passed over the strongest, the
most irrefragable, of the arguments in favour of Alexis, namely,
the Tsar's solemn promise of forgiveness to his son, in reliance
upon which Alexis had returned to Russia.   On this crucial
point they had not a word to say, although the Tsar had
explicitly exhorted them to relieve his conscience on this very
point.

Peter was in a dilemma.   There can, I think, be little
doubt that he had, at last, determined to rid himself of his
detested son; but he certainly shrank from a public execution,
the scandal of which would have been enormous and its
consequences incalculable.   The temporal members of the
Council helped him out of his difficulty by expressing a desire
to be quite convinced that Alexis had actually meditated
rebellion against his father.   If this were a genuine desire, it
was, perhaps, a last effort of the Tsarevich's friends to save his
life; but, in view of what ensued immediately afterwards, I am

rather inclined to suppose, that it was a pretext for bringing the Tsarevich to the torture-chamber where he might very easily expire, as if by accident, under legal process. The ordinary method of administrating the question-extraordinary was by means of the knout, a whip made of parchment cooked in milk and so hard and sharp that its strokes were like those of a sword. Practised executioners could kill a man with three strokes. There were few instances[1] of any one surviving thirty. It was to this torture that the Tsarevich, never very robust and severely reduced by prolonged mental anxiety and suffering, was now submitted. On June 19 he received five-and-twenty strokes with the knout, and betrayed his confessor, Ignatev, who was also savagely tortured. On June 24, Alexis received fifteen more strokes, but even the knout could now extract not another word. On the same day, the Senate condemned the Tsarevich to death for imagining rebellion against ´ his father, and for hoping for the co-operation of the common people and the armed intervention of his brother-in-law, the Emperor. The solemn promise of the Tsar, which the clergy had ignored, the Senate sophistically explained away. The Tsar, said they, had only promised his son forgiveness if he returned willingly ; he had returned unwillingly and had therefore forfeited the promise.

This shameful document, the outcome of mingled terror and obsequiousness, was signed by all the Senators and Ministers, including the Tsarevich's secret friends and sympathisers, the Dolgorukis and the Golitsuins, and by three hundred persons of lesser degree. Two days later, June 26, 1718, the Tsarevich died in the Citadel of St Petersburg. The precise cause of his death is still something of an enigma, most of the existing documents relating to it being apocryphal, the outcome of popular excitement and exaggeration. From a comparison and combination of the only two extant genuine documents

[1] Juel : *En Rejse til Rusland,* etc. Juel had frequent opportunities of seeing the punishment inflicted.

which throw any light on the subject, namely, (1) a "Record" of what took place in the office of the garrison-fortress on the morning of the Tsarevich's death, and (2) the official "Rescript" sent by Peter to his Ministers abroad for communication to foreign Powers, I gather the following facts. At eight o'clock in the morning of June 26, 1718, the Tsar, accompanied by some of the chief dignitaries of the Empire proceeded to the fortress, and Alexis was produced and placed before them within the walls of a *zastyenok*[1]. His death-sentence was then suddenly read to him. The shock, acting upon an enfeebled frame, brought on a fit which lasted some hours; on his recovery, he was carried into the close-adjoining Trubetskoi guard-room, where he died. Peter never regretted his abominable, unnatural treatment of his son. He argued that a single worthless life stood in the way of the regeneration of Russia and was therefore forfeit to the commonweal. Thus, all rhetoric and exaggeration apart, we may safely say, taking all the circumstances into consideration, that Peter the Great deliberately cemented the foundations of his Empire with the blood of his son.

However cemented, the Russian Empire was, now at any rate, an established and imposing fact. Its official birth-day dates from October 22, 1721, when, after a solemn thanksgiving service in the Troitsa Cathedral at St. Petersburg, for the peace of Nystad, the Tsar proceeded to the Senate and was there acclaimed "Father of the Fatherland, Peter the Great, and Emperor of All Russia." Some would have pre-ferred to proclaim Peter, Emperor of the East; but Peter himself preferred the more patriotic title.

Prussia, the newest ally, and Holland, the oldest friend of the Tsar, were the first of the European states to recognise Peter's imperial title; but elsewhere the novelty was received with disfavour, especially at Vienna, where the emergence of

[1] A *zastyenok* was the screen, or partition, within which prisoners under arrest were tortured.

a second Empire, which threatened to overshadow the Holy Roman Empire, gave great offence. With his ancient enemy, Sweden, Peter was now on friendly terms. By the Treaty of Stockholm (February 22, 1724), Russia contracted to assist Sweden, in case she were attacked by any other European Power, with 12,000 infantry, 4000 cavalry and nine ships of the line, Sweden undertaking in similar circumstances to assist Russia with 8000 infantry, 2000 cavalry, and six liners. The relations between Russia and France had also become much more cordial than heretofore. It was Peter's ambition to marry his second surviving daughter, Elizabeth, to the young King of France, Louis XV. But Bourbon pride proved an insuperable obstacle; and equally abortive were the efforts of successive French Ministers to bring about a better understanding between Great Britain and Russia. To prevent a renewal of the Anglo-Austrian Alliance, and to isolate the Emperor, were now the chief aims of the French Ministers, especially in view of the anticipated break-up of the Austrian dominions on the death of the sonless Charles VI. France, moreover, was anxious to keep Russia free from complications elsewhere, so that her mercenaries might be available against Maria Theresa, the daughter of Charles VI, to whom, by the Pragmatic Sanction of 1713, he had irregularly transferred the succession to his dominions. A reconciliation between Great Britain and Russia was considered, at Versailles, to be the best way of steadying and restraining Peter. But such a reconciliation was extremely difficult. King George had an ancient grudge against the Emperor of all Russia; and Peter's supposed friendship for the Jacobites was an additional obstacle. Peter himself was anxious to come to terms with Great Britain; but, on the other hand, he did not want to break definitely with the Tories who, as the enemies of his enemy, were his friends. In April, 1722, the Pretender's agent, Thomas Gordon, informed the Tsar that the English nation was ready to rise for its lawful king, if only they had 6000 men and arms for 20,000 more.

But as Peter could not embark upon such a vast enterprise without the cooperation of France, and as France desired to unite England and Russia instead of dividing them, the Jacobite project never had the remotest chance of success. It should also not be forgotten that the Tsar had got all that he wanted in Europe. During the last four years of his reign his policy was predominantly oriental.

Peter never lost sight of the necessity of establishing and extending his influence in the Far East. In 1692 the Dane, Eliazer Isbrandt, was accredited to the Chinese Emperor, Shing-Su, the protector of the Jesuits, but his presents were returned to him because the name of Peter preceded the name of the Grand Khan in his credentials. In 1719 Captain Lev Ismailov was sent to Pekin as the first Russian Minister-Extraordinary; but he was not allowed to establish a regular embassy, or consulates.

Peter, always in want of money, was first attracted to Central Asia by the report of the still unhanged Governor of Siberia, Prince Gagarin, of valuable gold deposits near the town of Erketi on the Amu Daria. The first Russian expeditions into Central Asia were disastrous failures owing to the incapacity of their leaders. In 1716 Colonel Buchholtz was sent to build a fortress on Lake Yamuish, but was driven back by the Calmucks. The same year, Prince Alexander Cherkasky set out to explore the mouths of the Amu Daria and the shores of the Sea of Aral, to win over the Khans of Khiva and Bokhara to the Russian interest, and to attempt to open up a way to India. This expedition excited a general rising of Tatars, Bokharans and Khivans; and, in attempting to suppress it, in 1717, Cherkasky was slain and his little army dispersed.

In the vast district lying between the Black Sea and the Caspian three Powers, Russia, Turkey and Persia, were equally interested. The beginning of the Russian influence in these parts dates from the appointment of the capable Artamon Voluinsky as Russian Minister at Ispahan in 1715. It is clear from his instructions, written by Peter's own hand, that he was sent rather as a pioneer than as a diplomatist. He was to find out what rivers fell into the Caspian and whether he could get to India by such rivers. He was also to take note of Gilyan and the other Caspian provinces, and record his impressions in a regular and copious diary. Voluinsky reported that in Persia rebellion was everywhere rampant, and that the Shah could scarce defend himself against his own subjects. He quitted Ispahan in September, 1717, after concluding a very advantageous commercial treaty with the Shah, and for the next four years vehemently urged Peter to invade Persia. This, however, was impossible during the continuance of the Swedish War. In the beginning of 1722 however, when the Afghans invaded Persia, defeated the Persian troops in two pitched battles, seized Ispahan and dethroned the Shah in favour of his third son Tokmash, Peter hesitated no longer. On July 18 he sailed from Astrakhan to Derbent at the head of 29,000 regular, 70,000 irregular troops and 5000 sailors. On August 23, the Governor of Derbent surrendered the silver keys of the city to the Russian Emperor. But scarcity of provisions, difficulties of transport, and a fierce, persistent north wind, which wrecked most of the lighters, compelled Peter to retrace his steps to Astrakhan, building on his way the new fortress of Svety Krest between the rivers Agrakhan and Sulak.

On his return to Russia, Peter notified the Persian Government that he would clear out all the Kurds and Afghans who were still ravaging the territories of the Shah, if the Caspian provinces of Persia were ceded to him by way of compensation. In December 1722 a Russian army-corps, under Colonel Shipov, began the work of deliverance by seizing the great trading centre of Resht. Simultaneously, General Matyushkin was operating against Baku, which Peter was very anxious to capture as being the key of the south-western Caspian district. The town protested that it had always been loyal to the Shah and could well defend itself against rebels, but it was stormed none the less, and by the Treaty of St Petersburg (September 12, 1723) was ceded to Russia along with Derbent and the provinces of Gilyan, Mazanderan and Astrabad.

The English, Austrian and Venetian residents at Stambul used the Russian invasion of Persia as a means of terrifying the Porte. In August 1722, the Grand-Vizier told Nepluyev, the Russian ambassador, plainly that Russia had better declare war against the Porte at once. The whole of the Tsar's reign, he added, had been one uninterrupted war, in which he had given no rest to any of his neighbours. Subsequently Nepluyev reported to his court that the Turks intended to conquer Persia and Georgia, and drive the Russians out of Daghestan. Fortunately, Turkey was not ready for war; and the acquisition of the Caspian provinces by Russia was a matter of comparative indifference to the Sultan. It was the spread of Russian influence in the Caucasus that he really dreaded. Yet, even so late as the beginning of 1724, war seemed highly probable, as the English Government left no stone unturned to make the Porte declare against Russia, and Nepluyev demanded his passports. Ultimately, however, by the Treaty of Constantinople (June 12, 1724), a compromise was arrived at, whereby the region extending between Shemak and the Caspian was divided between Russia and Persia.

The reform of the internal administration engaged the attention of Peter immediately after the termination of the Swedish War. It began with the highest tribunal of all, the Administrative Senate. In 1722, Peter instituted the office of Procurator-General, whose duty it was to see that the Senators performed their duties "in a faithful, zealous and orderly fashion according to the directions of the standing rules and ukases." Whenever the Procurator-General observed anything irregular, or illegal, in the proceedings of the Senate, he was instantly to admonish the Senate thereof in the plainest terms, and, if they neglected his admonition, he was to report the affair to the Gosudar. "He is in fact to be our Eye," ran the ukase. The first Procurator-General was Paul Ivanovich Yaguzhinsky, the son of the Lutheran organist at Moscow, whom the Tsar probably first encountered in the German Settlement, where he attracted Peter's attention by his immense capacity for work and spirituous liquor, his perennial good humour, and inexhaustible vivacity. Yaguzhinsky was as capable as he was jovial. He was also the only man in Russia who could stand before the Emperor, even in his worst moods, without trembling.

To keep a watchful eye upon defaulters and malingerers among the gentry, the office of Herald-Master was instituted in 1721. This functionary had to draw up lists of all the land-owners in the Empire, shewing who were in the service of the State and who were not, and giving the fullest details as to their families and occupations. A third newly appointed functionary "the Master of petitions," had to examine all the petitions presented to the various departments of State, and see that they were properly attended to. Peter also protected the Synod against the encroachments of the Senate and gave it a more independent position. The office of President of the Synod was abolished, but it received a civil assessor in the person of the "Ober-procurator of the Synod," an office established on May 11, 1722. The training of the clergy, especially of the Black clergy, or monks, the repression of dissent and superstition, and the promotion of the enlightenment of the people, were, henceforth, to be the principal functions of the Synod.

Towards the end of the reign, the question of the succession to the throne caused the Emperor some anxiety. The rightful heir in the natural order of primogeniture was the little Grand-Duke Peter, a child of six ; but Peter decided to pass him over, because, as the son of the unfortunate Tsarevich Alexis, any acknowledgment of his rights would have excited the hopes of those who had sympathised with his father, and the fears of those who had had a hand in Alexis' murder. Time-honoured custom had hitherto reckoned primogeniture in the male line as the best title to the Russian Crown; but by the *ustav*, or ordinance, of 1722, Peter denounced primogeniture as a stupid, dangerous, and unscriptural practice. The will of the reigning Sovereign was henceforth to fix the succession. The *ustav* was but a step to a more sensational novelty. In 1723 Peter resolved to crown his consort the Tsaritsa Catherine, whom he had already designated as his successor, Empress of Russia. The whole question as to what were the proper titles of the Emperor's family had previously been submitted to the consideration of the Senate and the Synod, who decided that Catherine should be called Imperatritsa, or its Slavonic equivalent Tsesareva. On November 15, 1723, Peter issued a second manifesto, in which, after explaining that, from the days of Justinian, it had ever been the custom of Christian Princes to crown their consorts, he proceeded, at some length and in very affectionate terms, to recite the services rendered to him by his Tsesareva in the past, especially during the Turkish War, for which great services[1] he had resolved "by the authority given to us by God to reward our Consort by crowning her with the imperial crown."

On May 7, 1724, the coronation of Catherine took place in the Cathedral of the Assumption at Moscow with extra-ordinary pomp and splendour. The crown worn by Catherine, on this occasion, was the most costly and magnificent ever worn, hitherto, by a Russian sovereign. It was made on the model of the old Byzantine Imperial crown, and was studded with no fewer than 2564 precious stones. Each of its numerous pearls was worth £500, but the most remarkable jewel of all was a ruby, as large as a pigeon's egg, placed immediately beneath a cross of brilliants at the apex of the crown.

In the course of the summer of 1724, the state of Peter's health caused great anxiety. In October, ignoring the warnings

[1] To this day the nature of these supposed services is unknown.

of his medical attendants, he undertook a long and fatiguing tour of inspection over the latest of his great public works, the Ladoga Canal, proceeding thence to visit the iron works at Olonetz, where he dug out a piece of iron 120 lbs. in weight with his own hands. In the beginning of November, he returned to St Petersburg by water. Perceiving, near the village of Lakhta, a boat full of soldiers on their way back to Cronstadt, stuck fast in a sand bank and in imminent danger of being drowned, he plunged into the water to render them assistance and was immersed to the girdle for a considerable time. His paroxysms immediately returned with redoubled violence, and he reached St Petersburg too ill ever to rally again, though he shewed himself in public as late as January 16, 1725. In the evening of the 28th he expired, in great agony.

Peter's educational methods, if rough, were thorough, and they had already begun to leaven the seemingly still inert and sluggish mass of the nation. The Russian nation had really been taught not merely the arts and trades of life, but its duties and obligations also. From the first, the Regenerator, in his ukases, had been very careful to make everything quite plain. He was always explaining why he did this or that; why the new was better than the old, and so on; and we must recollect that these were the first lessons of the kind that the nation had ever received. What the educated Russian of today takes for granted, his forefathers, two centuries ago, first learnt from the *ukazes* and manifestoes of Peter the Great. The whole system of Peter was deliberately directed against the chief evils from which old Moscovy had always suffered, such as, dissipation of energy, dislike of co-operation, repudiation of responsibility, lack of initiative, the tyranny of the family, the insignificance of the individual. All his efforts were devoted to the task of releasing Russians from the leading-strings of an effete tradition, and making them act and think for themselves. They were to walk boldly with swords in their hands, not crawl along on crutches as heretofore.

Ability, wherever he found it, whether in the lowest ranks of his own people, or among foreigners, was, during his reign, the sole qualification for employment and promotion, so that, at last, it was almost a recommendation for a candidate for office to say that he was of no birth, or of alien parentage.   Finally, the disgraceful old Moscovite proverb : "though flight is contrary to honour, it is good for the health," which was of universal application, during the seventeenth century, died out of the language, once for all, during the stress of the Great Northern War, when Russia served her military apprenticeship.

CHAPTER XVI.

THE PUPILS OF PETER, 1725–1741.

As soon as the Empress-Consort Catherine had recognised that the malady of the Emperor must end fatally, she had secretly instructed Menshikov and Tolstoi to sound the other senators as to the succession to the throne, and to take measures on her behalf generally. It was not so much personal ambition as the instinct of self-preservation which made her look to these men for help at this crisis. She knew that they dare not refuse to assist her. Neither Menshikov nor Tolstoi could escape destruction if a reaction set in ; and a reaction was bound to set in if the Grand-Duke Peter were now placed upon the throne. Their interests and perils were therefore identical with those of the Empress. Both ministers, with characteristic energy, at once proceeded to smooth the way to the throne for the only candidate who was likely to maintain the existing Petrine system. Menshikov's first step was to win over the officers of the Guard who had a profound veneration for the dying Emperor and regarded his consort as their comrade. The soldiers were not behind their officers in enthusiasm, especially after their arrears had been paid in full. "We have lost our father," they cried, "but we have still our mother left."

Menshikov meanwhile, with uncommon prudence, had reconciled himself with his numerous enemies, and, assisted by

Tolstoi, succeeded in bringing all the higher clergy over to Catherine's side.   Here, indeed, he met with little difficulty. The arch-prelates of the Russian church and the chief members of the recently instituted Holy Synod were in very much the same position as himself.   No novelties are so detestable to the people at large as ecclesiastical novelties, and for these the archbishops were mainly responsible.   They felt they must, in the circumstances, stand or fall with Tolstoi and Menshikov.

All these measures were taken so quietly and quickly that the faction of the Grand-Duke Peter, which included the larger portion of the aristocracy and the clergy, at least half of the Senate, and many distinguished officers in the army, had no time to make any counter-move.   Unable to obstruct, they were forced to follow the flow of events.   A deputation of the Senate and Nobility accordingly waited upon the Empress, whom they found kneeling, bathed in tears, at the bed-side of Peter, who had just breathed his last.   Respecting her grief, the Deputation withdrew; but presently Catherine rejoined them in the Council-Chamber, weeping bitterly, and recommended herself to their protection "as a widow and orphan." She was immediately proclaimed "Autocrat of all Russia," in accordance with a previous resolution of the Senate.   A few hours later, all the Guards took the oath of allegiance, and the Senate followed their example.

The true origin of the enigmatical woman who now sat upon the Russian throne was, until quite recently, one of the most obscure problems of Russian history.   Briefly, she was one of the four children of a small Catholic yeoman in Lithuania, Samuel Skovronsky, and was born, most probably, in 1683.   In an early stage of the Great Northern War, she fell into the hands of the Russians, and was brought into Sheremetev's camp, wrapped in a corporal's cloak to hide her nakedness.   Menshikov purchased her from Sheremetev as a servant for his wife; and it was at Menshikov's house that

Peter saw and appropriated her. She superseded Anna Mons as the Tsar's favourite mistress; and, after the birth of their first daughter Catherine, Peter made no secret of their relations and resolved to marry her. Catherine Skovronskaya, though coarse and ignorant, was an uncommonly shrewd and sensible woman, with a magnificent physique, an imperturbable good-temper, and an absolute indifference to the hardships of a roving life, just the sort of wife, in fact, for a rough and ready peripatetic Russian soldier like "Peter the Bombardier." Her moral influence over him was extraordinary. She was the only person who had the skill and courage to soothe him in the fits of maniacal fury to which he was always subject. The first step towards regulating the relations of this strange couple was Martha's reception into the Orthodox Church, when she was rechristened Catherine Aleksyeevna. In 1710 she received the title of Gosudaruinya, only given to sovereign Princesses, and in 1711 she was publicly married to Peter. She bore him eleven children in all, of whom Anne, born in 1706, and Elizabeth, born in 1709, alone survived her.

Catherine's safest policy was, obviously, a policy of conciliation; and her earlier measures produced a very favourable impression, and greatly improved her position. A general amnesty was proclaimed immediately after her accession. The heavy poll-tax, which weighed severely on the peasantry, was reduced by one third; and a decree of the Senate forbade, in future, the employment of soldiers in the construction of the Ladoga canal. But her greatest difficulty was to keep the peace among her jealous and turbulent servants, who were continually flying at each others' throats. There can be no doubt, however, that she favoured Menshikov. Nothing was done without his consent, and he had an offensive habit of silencing all opposition in the Senate by suddenly rising and declaring that the opinions he favoured were those of the Empress also. Nevertheless, he was not altogether so omnipotent as has sometimes been supposed. In many things, she preferred to follow the advice of other counsellors. Thus Tolstoi enjoyed her full confidence likewise; and the management of foreign affairs was confided, almost entirely, to Andrei Osterman, a Westphalian, who had entered Peter's service in 1717, succeeded Shafirov as Vice-Chancellor, and was ennobled for his brilliant diplomatic services at the Congress of Nystad. Another confidant of Catherine's was Charles Frederick, Duke of Holstein, the nephew of Charles XII, who had sought an asylum in Russia after the conclusion of the Great Northern War, and, on May 21, 1725, married the Tsesarevna Anne.

The great administrative innovation of the reign of Catherine I was the "Supreme Privy Council," an idea of Osterman's. It was not, as the French Minister Campredon supposed, a move in the direction of limited monarchy, by associating the leading magnates in the government, after the model of an English Cabinet Council; but rather an attempt to strengthen the executive by concentrating affairs in the hands of a few persons, instead of leaving them, as heretofore, to the care of a turbulent and distracted Senate. It was to consist (*ukaz* of February 26) of not less than six and not more than nine members, under the presidency of the Empress. Its powers were immense. No *ukazes* were, in future, to be issued till they had received the approbation of the Council. The control of the War Office, the Foreign Office and the Admiralty was transferred to it from the Senate. Subsequently, the Council received authority to revise the work of all the other Departments of State; even the election of Senators was subject to its approval. The resolutions of the Supreme Privy Council were to be unanimous; but, in case of any difference of opinion, the matter was referred to the decision of the Sovereign, instead of being settled by the majority. The first five members of this august and omnipotent body were Menshikov, Tolstoi, the Grand-Chancellor Golovkin (a mere figurehead), Osterman, and the leader of the reactionaries, Prince

Demetrius Golitsuin, towards whom Menshikov, for personal reasons, was drawing nearer.

The foreign policy of Catherine I, if purely pacific and extremely cautious, was, nevertheless, dignified, consistent and independent.

During the first fifteen years after the close of the Great Northern War, continental diplomacy was dominated by George I of England and the Whigs. George I had rounded off his Hanoverian Electorate by despoiling Sweden in her direst extremity; but his territorial acquisitions had been so recent and so extensive that he was seriously apprehensive of losing them again. It was, therefore, his main object to form a league strong enough to maintain the existing order of things in Europe, against all possible disturbers of the peace. His most obvious confederates were those States which had also snatched something in the general scramble for Sweden's continental possessions, such as Prussia and Denmark. France, exhausted by the ruinous war of the Spanish Succession, was pacifically disposed. The Empire and Sweden were doubtful Powers. Spain was hostile to England, as she could not yet accustom herself to the loss of Gibraltar. The new great northern Power, Russia, was an object of distrust and jealousy to England, whose Baltic trade had suffered severely from the arbitrary restrictions placed upon it by the late Tsar. Russia, too, had given an asylum to the exiled duke of Holstein, and posed as his champion and defender, especially after he had drawn a step nearer to the Russian throne by his marriage with the Tsesarevna Anne. If the Duke chose to assert his ancestral rights, Denmark might be forced to surrender Sleswick-Holstein, when George's enlarged electorate might be in danger. Thus Russia, by the mere force of circumstances, found herself, at the beginning of the reign of Catherine I, at enmity with England; and a contest between the Powers began at all the courts of Europe. On April 30, 1725, Spain concluded an alliance with the Emperor at Vienna, which was looked upon as equally menacing to England and France. The response to the step was the Hanoverian Alliance, concluded at Herrenhausen, September 3, 1725, between England and France, to which Prussia immediately acceded. Russia was the first to feel the bellicosity of the Hanoverian Alliance. In the spring of 1726, Great Britain, startled by unfounded rumours that the Empress's government was massing troops in Finland, and equipping her fleet to promote the interests of the Duke of Holstein, sent an English squadron under Admiral Wager into the Baltic. Wager was the bearer of a letter to Catherine in which his Britannic Majesty declared that the armaments of Russia, in times of profound peace, could not but arouse the suspicions of. Great Britain and her allies. "Our fleet," continued this despatch, "has been sent to preserve the peace of the North and prevent your fleet from putting to sea." Catherine declared, with spirit, that her fleet should put to sea not only that year, but next year also, if only to destroy the poor opinion people seemed to have abroad of the reign of a woman. Her dignified protest had some effect, and Wager withdrew his fleet; but on August 6, 1726, by the advice of Osterman, Catherine acceded to the Austro-Spanish League. Denmark, thereupon, joined the Hanoverian Alliance (Treaty of Copenhagen, April 16, 1727); and, shortly afterwards, Sweden followed her example.

Internally, meanwhile, Russia was being agitated by a question so serious as to dwarf all others—the question of the succession to the throne. The universal popularity of the young Grand-Duke Peter was, indeed, becoming a pressing danger. Anonymous letters reached Catherine and Menshikov daily, pronouncing woe against all who should set aside the lawful heir; and many of the clergy, while mentioning Peter's name in the prayer for the Imperial Family, applied to him the epithet "*blagochestivyeeshy*," given only to reigning monarchs, instead of the proscribed "*blagovyerny*." Both Osterman and Menshikov began to recognise the fact that it would be im-

possible to ignore, much longer, Peter's inalienable claim to
the throne as the last surviving male of Peter the Great's line.
So long as the Empress remained well and strong, there was but
little danger; but, towards the end of 1726, Catherine's health
began to fail, and, though it was apparently re-established in
January 1727, her partisans had received a severe shock and
thought it high time to begin to look after themselves.   The
position of Menshikov in particular was highly critical.   During
the last four months he had ruled almost as an absolute
sovereign.   His enemies were "as numerous as the hairs of his
head"; and his tyranny and violence had revolted them to the
last degree.   He knew that if he made a single false step he
was lost.   At this juncture, he was approached by the Austrian
minister, Rabutin, with a project for securing the succession
of the Grand-Duke Peter, in whom his uncle, the Emperor
Charles VI, took a personal as well as a political interest.
Menshikov eagerly caught at the project, stipulating for himself
the first vacant electorate in the Empire, and, for his daughter
Maria, the hand of the young Grand-Duke when he should
have ascended the throne.   To these conditions Rabutin at
once agreed; and Osterman approved of them.   But even
now Menshikov was not out of danger.   His change of front
had raised up against him a most redoubtable adversary in
Peter Tolstoi, who had even more reason than Menshikov
himself to fear the accession of the Grand-Duke, and now, in
consequence of the desertion of his lifelong colleague, suddenly
found himself dangerously isolated.   After vainly endeavouring
to induce Catherine to repudiate Menshikov's scheme for the
sake of her own daughter, he attempted to form a party of his
own with the object of raising the Tsesarevna Elizabeth to the
throne, with a Council of Regency to guide her.   But Menshikov was too quick for him.   At the end of January 1727,
Catherine had a dangerous relapse; and, though she rallied in
April it was soon understood that there was but little hope
of her recovery.   Menshikov at once surrounded the dying

Empress with his creatures; constrained her to make a will, the authenticity of which was, afterwards, strongly doubted though never actually disputed, appointing Peter her successor; and, when she was already *in extremis*, arrested Tolstoi and his adherents on a charge of *lèse-majesté*, and banished them to various parts of Russia. The *ukaz* pronouncing their condemnation was issued early on May 16, 1727; on the evening of the same day Catherine I expired.

At 7 o'clock the next morning, the members of the Imperial Family, the Supreme Privy Council, the Senate, the Synod, and the chief officers of the Guards, assembled at the Palace to hear the reading of the will of the late Empress declaring the Grand-Duke Peter her successor. As soon as the will had been read, all present kissed the cross in token of their allegiance to the new Emperor, whereupon Peter II, at the head of his ministers, and Privy Councillors, descended into the street and received the homage of the Guards.

Peter II was still only eleven years old, but he was unusually tall and well-proportioned for his age. His grandfather, who hated him because he was his father's son, had systematically ignored him. To do Menshikov justice, it was his first care that the young Tsar should now be adequately trained for his high functions; and Osterman was accordingly appointed his Governor. Even judged by a Western standard, the Russian Vice-Chancellor would have been pronounced a ripe scholar. He devoted himself to his new duties with a zeal and conscientiousness which did him infinite honour, and, easily and completely, won the heart of his pupil. Peter, moreover, had a still more intimate and affectionate mentor in his sister Natalia, who, although only twelve months older than her brother, might well have been twelve years his senior as regards wisdom and prudence. Young as she was, she had already learnt to recognise the value of western civilisation, and to Osterman she was an invaluable coadjutor in his pedagogic labours.

For the first four months of the new reign, the government was entirely in the hands of Menshikov, who, while ridding himself freely of troublesome rivals by banishment to distant places under the guise of honourable employments, endeavoured to attach to himself all able officials who were not over-ambitious, and win over such members of the old nobility as were not too exacting.   Foreign affairs were left in the hands of Osterman.   At the end of August, Menshikov felt strong enough to expel the Duke and Duchess of Holstein from Russia, partly to gratify old grudges, and partly to disarm the suspicions of Russia's enemies and neighbours in the North.   Tyrannous though it might be, the administration of Menshikov was capable, vigorous, and economical, and, best of all, conducted on the lines laid down by Peter the Great. Still it was undoubtedly an usurpation, ignoring as it did the Supreme Privy Council, to which the will of the late Empress had transferred all her authority.   He made himself as secure as he could by appointing himself Commander-in-Chief and literally kidnapping the young Emperor, whom he carried off to his Palace on Vasily Island.   But, at last, the Emperor himself grew tired of the dictator's domination ; and, shortly after Peter's espousals with Maria Menshikovna had been publicly announced, an *ukaz* dated September 20, 1727, deprived Menshikov of all his charges and emoluments for conspiracy against the Crown, fined him 500,000 rubles, and banished him to Kazan.   He was subsequently transferred to Berezov, on the shores of the Arctic Ocean, where he died at the beginning of 1730.

The triumph of Menshikov's enemies proved to be the triumph of the reactionary Russian nobility as represented by the ancient princely families of the Golitsuins and the Dolgorukis. Their domination might have been very mischievous to Russia but for the counteracting influence of Osterman, almost the sole representative in the Government of the Petrine system. The Dolgorukis would have overthrown the Vice-Chancellor if they could, but Peter protected his Governor against all their efforts. Nevertheless, they went very far towards carrying out their reactionary principles. They removed the young Tsar from St Petersburg to Moscow (January, 1728). They recalled to court the long-neglected and half-forgotten ex-Tsaritsa Eudoxia. They appropriated the lion's share of the coronation honours (February, 1728). They usurped an authority unattainable by Menshikov in the plenitude of his power. They had cunningly calculated that the equable climate and pleasant environs of Moscow would make it a much more enjoyable residence than the foggy and humid St Petersburg with its melancholy wastes of bog and fen ; and the young Tsar speedily began to look back upon the new capital as a dungeon, and forbade those about him even to mention the name of St Petersburg. Henceforth there was not even the pretence of study on his part, and he gave himself up entirely to hawking, hunting, and shooting, accompanied everywhere by a dozen or more Dolgorukis. In these circumstances affairs were left to take care of themselves ; and Osterman began to fear lest the removal of the Court to semi-Asiatic Moscow might mean a relapse into barbarism. The Supreme Privy Council did not meet for weeks at a time ; and, on the rare occasions when "their Sublimities" came together, they did little more than drink a dram, nod in their gilded arm-chairs, and refer all business details to the already over-burdened Vice-Chancellor whom alone they had to thank for prosperity at home and tranquillity abroad.

For the reforms inaugurated under Catherine I by Menshikov and Osterman had begun, at last, to bear good fruit. Trade and commerce were reviving ; money was beginning to flow steadily, if slowly, into the Treasury ; the people, relieved of their more oppressive burdens, were happier ; and the land was more prosperous than it had been for years. Abroad, too, such political changes as had taken place were favourable to Russia. On the death of George I, the British Government had, indirectly, hinted at the desirability of resuming friendly relations ; and an unofficial political agent, Claudius Rondeau, was sent to Russia to see how the land lay.   The chief political event of the period was the attraction of Spain to the Hanoverian Alliance by the Treaty of Seville, in 1729, which resulted in the drawing together still more closely of Austria and Russia by way of counterpoise to "the Allies of Seville," as the members of the Hanoverian Alliance were now called. The two Powers agreed to maintain the integrity of Polish territory against the intrigues of Prussia, frustrated the dynastic schemes of Augustus II by exploding the Diet of Grodno, and succeeded in keeping Maurice of Saxony out of Courland.

The principal domestic event of the period was the death of the Grand-Duchess Natalia on December 7, 1728.   This was a severe blow to Osterman, as it removed the last obstacle to the reactionary tendencies of the Dolgorukis.   At the end of November he had said to the Spanish Ambassador, the Duke of Liria, "If we lose the Grand-Duchess, who still possesses a little influence with her brother, and we do not return to St Petersburg, I shall demand my dismissal." A deplorable state of things prevailed at the new capital.   The Swedish minister, Cedercreutz, reported to his government that the galley-fleet was steadily diminishing, the grand or ocean fleet was rotting in the dockyards, and there was such disorder at the Russian Admiralty that it would be impossible to place the navy in its former condition in less than three years. There can be no doubt that the navy was purposely neglected. The Dolgorukis seemed to have gained an absolute dominion over the mind of the young Emperor.   After the death of the Grand-Duchess, they boldly transferred all the Colleges, or Departments of State, from St Petersburg to Moscow as the first step towards a permanent transfer of the seat of government from the new capital to the old.   The Emperor was, at the same time, betrothed to Catherine Dolgorukaya, and the wedding was fixed for January 30, 1730.   All their schemes were frustated, however, by the death of Peter II, of smallpox, very early in the morning of the day that had been fixed for his wedding.

From midnight till 5 o'clock the next morning, the members of the Supreme Privy Council had been in anxious consultation behind closed doors. Death, or misadventure, had reduced the number of their Sublimities to five persons; and the most sagacious of the five, Osterman, after closing the eyes of his pupil, locked himself up in his own apartments where he was immediately laid up with a feigned attack of gout in the hand. In his absence the lead was taken by the one man of character among the remaining Supreme Privy Councillors, namely, Prince Demetrius Golitsuin, who, after patiently awaiting his opportunity for more than thirty years, was now to rule Russia for something less than thirty days. Golitsuin was essentially a Grand Seigneur, a type comparatively rare in Russia, though common enough in Poland. Proud of his ancient lineage, he had always considered himself entitled to fill the highest offices in the State; yet, hitherto, his qualifications had been disregarded. Frowned upon by Peter the Great, passed over by Catherine I, set aside by Peter II, he had had ample leisure to reflect upon the meaning of this singular and exasperating neglect, and had come to the conclusion that such a scandal as the non-employment of one of the noblest magnates in the land was due entirely to favouritism. Autocracy had established favouritism—then autocracy must be abolished. Let the monarchy be made a limited monarchy, and favouritism must disappear. Then, and only then, could the national aristocracy take its proper place beside the throne. Now, apparently, he had the opportunity of carrying out his long-cherished design. The only question was: who should be chosen to fill the vacant throne? That Peter the Great's family must be excluded was to Golitsuin a matter of course. He had never been able to regard Catherine I as Peter's lawful consort; and, consequently, in his eyes, the children of Peter were illegitimate.

It was necessary, therefore, to go back to the elder line of the Romanovs, and seek a successor to the throne from among the descendants of Peter the Great's elder brother Ivan V. Golitsuin fixed upon Ivan's third daughter Anne, the widowed Duchess of Courland. Having quitted Russia twenty years before, as a girl of sixteen, she stood apart from all political factions, and she had, besides, a reputation for sobriety and common-sense. Golitsuin had little difficulty in bringing his four colleagues over to his opinion; and a grand assembly of the Synod, the Senate, the officers of the Guard, and the representatives of the nobility, subsequently convened, proceeded, on the motion of Golitsuin, to elect Anne as successor to the Russian throne. A deputation was sent forthwith to Mittau, to inform the Duchess of her election and conduct her to the Russian capital.

The deputation was provided with secret instructions. They were to inform the Duchess that she could only be elected conditionally upon her subscribing, in their presence, certain Articles which the Council had already drawn up for her signature, whereby she was solemnly to engage, (1) to govern solely through the Supreme Privy Council; (2) not to marry, or appoint her successor, without its consent; (3) to relinquish the prerogatives of declaring war, concluding peace, and conferring appointments; (4) to surrender the command of the army to the Council; (5) not to disgrace any member of the nobility without due cause; and, generally, to do everything which the Council might consider necessary for the good of her subjects.

On February 10, the Council was relieved of much anxiety by the arrival of a courier from Mittau with the Articles signed by the new Empress, and a reassuring promise to observe everything contained therein unreservedly. Then only did Golitsuin make public his audacious political innovation at another assembly of the Senate, Synod, Nobility and Guards which sat in the *Kreml'*. The proposal was received but coldly; and Yaguzhinsky, who, though he had been kept in the background during the last two reigns, had not forgotten that he had once been " Peter's eye," openly protested against the Golitsuin Constitution, and despatched a courier to Mittau advising the Duchess not to submit to the dictation of a handful of usurping aristocrats. His courier was captured, whereupon he was deprived of all his offices and emoluments and sent to the dungeons of the *Kreml'*. The same day, thirty other people were arrested by the Council, on various pretexts; and all the approaches to the Palace, where their Sublimities held their reunions, were guarded by troops. These prompt measures prevented for a time the outbreak of a revolution. The malcontents, though numerous, lacked a leader, and had perforce to keep quiet till the arrival of the Empress-Elect, while "the republican ,gentlemen," as Rondeau calls them, amused themselves, every day, in endeavouring fruitlessly to frame a new Constitution.

Anne speedily shewed her hand. She had evidently been well primed beforehand by her friends and Golitsuin's enemies; and there can be little doubt, that, during the anxious fortnight after her arrival, Osterman, whose keen political instinct told him that a limited monarchy was impossible in eighteenth century Russia, was her secret adviser. On March 8, 1730, her partisans, by a skilful *coup-d'état*, obtained her recognition as Autocrat by the Guards and the Nobility; and she tore "the Articles of Mittau" to pieces with her own hands, amidst loud applause. The Supreme Privy Council was then abolished; and, five weeks later, the Dolgorukis, as being the most forward and insolent of the constitutionalists were disgraced, and banished to various parts of the Empire.

Anne Ivanovna, when she ascended the Russian throne, was in her thirty-seventh year. Her natural parts, if not brilliant, were at least sound; her carriage was dignified and majestic; but her features were coarse and masculine, and her temper was sullen and extremely vindictive. Having lived the best part of her life among Germans, and with her favourite, the brutal German ex-equerry, Ernst Johann Biren, or Bühren, constantly at her side, she could have but little knowledge of or liking for her own countrymen ; and her first experience of the Russian nobility had certainly not predisposed her in their favour.   Naturally suspicious and resentful, she felt that she could never trust the Russians with power after what they had done or attempted to do to her.   She must henceforth surround her throne with persons entirely devoted to her interests ; and these persons, from the nature of the case, could only be foreigners.   Most of these foreigners she brought with her ; but the best of them she found ready to her hand when she arrived.   Two Germans, both of them the pupils of Peter the Great, lent particular lustre to her reign—Osterman, already Vice-Chancellor, and Burkhardt Christoph Münnich, who had settled in Russia, since 1719, by the invitation of Peter the Great, and in 1732 was made a field-marshal and commander-in-chief by Peter's niece.

Under Catherine I and Peter II Russia had stood still, but under Anne her advancement, in every direction, was unmistakable.   Vigorous measures were taken to arrest the decay and repair the damage done to the State during the haphazard sway of the Dolgorukis.   Particular attention was paid to the national armaments.   A College of Cadets was instituted, as a sort of nursery for the Army, at a cost of 30,000 rubles per annum. Special commissioners were appointed to enquire into the condition of the army and the fleet.   The state of the Navy was found to be alarming, scarce twelve liners being in a condition to put to sea.   It was resolved to re-construct the whole fleet, but gradually, so as to lighten the expense as much as possible.

The first foreign event of importance with which Anne's government had to deal was the question of the Polish Succession.

On the death, on February 1, 1733, of Augustus II, the

last act of whose discreditable reign had been an attempted partition of Poland between Prussia and himself, the Primate of Poland, Theodore Potocki, endeavoured, with the aid of France, to replace Stanislaus Leszczynski on the Polish throne. France was not slow to champion a cause which was preeminently her own. As a preliminary measure, 4,000,000 *livres* of secret service money were despatched from Versailles to Warsaw for bribing purposes (the Emperor had already sent a million of ducats in support of the contrary, that is to say the Saxon, interest) ; and the French Ambassador, Monti, succeeded in gaining over to the cause of Stanislaus, the influential palatine of Lublin, Adam Tarlo, by promising him the Grand-Hetman-ship of Poland. The great Lithuanian family of Czartorysky, and Stanislaus Poniatowski, Palatine of Masovia, the one really capable statesman that Poland then possessed, supported the same side. In a circular letter to all its representatives abroad, the French Government declared that it could not regard with indifference the political extinction of a power to whom France was bound by all the ties of honour and friendship, and whose liberties she was prepared to defend against every enemy. Encouraged by this vigorous demonstration, the Polish Primate proceeded to use, freely and fully, his by no means inconsider-able prerogatives ; it was principally due to his efforts that Stanislaus was elected King of Poland for the second time, on September 9, 1733.

When the news of the death of Augustus reached St Peters-burg, a Council of Notables was summoned, which unanimously agreed that the interests of Russia could not permit her to recognise Stanislaus Leszczynski, or any person directly depen-dant on France, as a candidate for the Polish throne. Austria and Russia thereupon made a joint protest at Warsaw against the candidature of Stanislaus ; but as they, at first, had no alter-native candidate of their own to offer, the *interrex* disregarded their menaces and proceeded with the election. Meanwhile the Russian Minister at Dresden had concluded (August 14,

1733) a compact with the Saxon Elector, Augustus, the son of the late King of Poland, whereby, in consideration of his acceding to the Austrian Pragmatic Sanction, Russia and Austria undertook to establish him on the Polish throne. Eighteen regiments of Russian infantry and ten of cavalry were then directed towards the Polish frontier, while 10,000 Cossacks were, at the same time, ordered up from the Ukraine. Stanislaus, having no forces at his disposal (the Polish regular army existing only on paper), thereupon quitted the defenceless capital and shut himself up in Dantzic, with his chief adherents and the French and Swedish Ministers, to await reinforcements from France.

In October 1733, 20,000 Russians, under the command of the gallant Irish adventurer Peter Lacy, reached the right bank of the Vistula and were joined by a band of Polish malcontents who had already placed themselves under the Empress's "august protection," and thus given her a pretext for direct intervention. On the 6th a phantom Diet, consisting of but 15 Senators and 500 of the *szlachta*, assembled at Warsaw, and proclaimed the Elector of Saxony King of Poland.

The Empress had hoped to terminate the Polish difficulty in a single campaign; but this hope had soon to be abandoned. Almost the whole of Poland was in favour of Stanislaus; the country swarmed with his armed partisans; and he himself lay secure in the strong city of Dantzic. It was of paramount importance to Russia that Stanislaus should be driven out of Dantzic before the French arrived; but the fortress was a strong one, and, from the end of 1733 to the middle of March 1734, defied all Lacy's efforts to take it. On March 17, Lacy was superseded by Münnich, but he also could make little impression on the place. On May 9, a vigorous assault was repulsed with the loss of 2000 men and 120 officers. On May 20, the long-expected French fleet arrived, and disembarked three regiments under the command of La Motte Perouse. But this little army could do but little and in the

middle of June was surrounded, forced to surrender, and sent
to St Petersburg as prisoners of war, on the Russian fleet. Two
days later the fortress of Weichselmünde fell; and on June 30,
Dantzic also surrendered unconditionally after sustaining a
siege of 135 days which cost the Russians 8000 men. King
Stanislaus, disguised as a peasant, had contrived to escape.
The war continued to smoulder for another twelve months.
Finally by the Peace of Vienna, Oct. 3, 1735, Augustus III
was recognised as king of Poland.

The War of the Polish Succession was scarce over when
Russia found herself involved in a fresh war with the Porte.

From the beginning of 1733 onwards, the Court of
Versailles exhausted all the resources of its diplomacy to
bring about a simultaneous rupture between Russia and her
northern and southern neighbours, Sweden and Turkey, so as
to prevent her from rendering assistance to the Emperor. A
rupture with Sweden was prevented by the sobriety of the
Swedish Premier, Count Arvid Horn, and the interposition
of Great Britain who, through her minister at Stockholm,
succeeded in renewing for twelve years from 1735 the expiring
treaty of alliance between Russia and Sweden. The diplomatic
struggle at Stambul was more acute, but all the efforts of the
French Ambassador, the Marquis de Villeneuve, were frustrated
by the Russian Ambassador Ivan Nepluyev. Towards the end
of 1735, however, Nepluyev himself advised the Empress to
attack the Turks, who had emerged from the long Persian war
with Kuli Khan much damaged and discredited. He represented the whole Ottoman Empire as weak to the last
degree and even tottering to its fall. His arguments convinced
the Empress and her Council. The way was prepared by a
definitive treaty between Russia and Persia, whereby the former
retroceded Daghestan to the latter and evacuated the fortresses
of Derbend, Baku, and Svyestui Krest. Russia was now
untrammelled in the East; conjunctures were favourable; the
treasury was full to overflowing; and everything promised
success. A formal declaration of war was sent by Osterman to

the Grand Vizier at the end of 1735; and Münnich was ordered
to proceed from the Vistula to the Don to open the campaign.

The Turkish war of 1736–1739 marks the beginning of
that systematic struggle on the part of Russia to recover her
natural boundaries towards the south, which was to last throughout the eighteenth century. A glance at an historical map of
Europe will shew that Turkey, at this time, controlled the mouths
of the five great rivers, the Dniester, the Bug, the Dnieper, the
Don, and the Kuban, that drain southern Russia, and therefore
could control and even suspend, at will, no inconsiderable portion
of her rival's commerce. The Khan of the Crimea, moreover,
from his capital at Bagchaserai ruled over all the Tatar hordes
from the Dnieper to the Don, and let them loose upon Russia
at every opportunity. The approaches to the peninsula itself
were very strongly guarded. As the Turks had the absolute
command of the sea, no danger was apprehended from that
quarter ; on the land side, the lines of Perekop protected the
narrow isthmus which united the Crimea to the mainland, while
the fortress of Azov, at the head of the sea of the same name,
commanded the Delta of the Don and was thought sufficient
to prevent any attack from the north-east.

In the early autumn of 1735, Münnich arrived at the lines
of the Ukraine, the name given to the chain of fortifications,
a hundred leagues in length, connecting the Dnieper and the
Donetz, devised by Peter the Great to keep the Tatars out of
central Russia and completed between 1731 and 1738. Here
Münnich perfected his arrangements for the ensuing campaign.
He and his colleague, Marshal Lacy, were to attack the enemy
simultaneously, the German invading the Crimea, and the
Irishman besieging Azov. On April 20, Münnich began his
march across the steppes to Perekop, a distance of 330 miles,
with 47,000 men, including the Cossacks. On the only
occasion when the Tatars ventured to attack him (at Chernaya
Dolina), they were easily repulsed ; and on May 15, Münnich
sat down before the lines of Perekop, a deep trench, 25 fathoms
broad, and defended by an earthen wall eight fathoms high

and nearly five English miles long.   On May 19, the lines were stormed in less than an hour ; and Perekop itself, which was gorged with merchandise of every description, was abandoned to pillage.   Münnich then marched to Koslov, the chief port on the west coast of the Crimea (where, in 988, the Grand-Duke Vladimir had exchanged bridal rings with the daughter of the Byzantine Emperor) which was occupied without resistance.   On June 17, the Khan's capital was also taken, after a stiff skirmish ; and then want of supplies and a dangerous mutiny in his army compelled Münnich to return to the lines of the Ukraine.   Lacy, meanwhile, had succeeded in storming Azov, though he met with a resistance far more stubborn than anything his brother Marshal had encountered. The campaign was thus completely successful ; but it was extraordinarily expensive, no fewer than 30,000 men, or one half the effective strength of both armies, having perished, though scarce 2000 had been slain by the enemy.

At the end of April 1737, Münnich took the field with 70,000 men, and opened the second campaign, which was to be the bloodiest of the whole war.   His objective was Ochakov, the ancient Axiake, very strongly situated, at the confluence of the Dnieper and Bug, and defended by 20,000 of the best troops of Turkey under the Seraskier Yiagya.   The fortress fell in the course of July, chiefly owing to the valour and skill of James Francis Keith, whom the Empress rewarded with a lieutenant-generalship and 10,000 rubles ; but it was a very costly affair, and when, at the end of August, Münnich returned to the lines of the Ukraine he found his army had diminished by 24,000 men.   In the late autumn General Stoffel, who had been left in command at Ochakov, repulsed a large Turkish army which invested the fortress from October 26 to November 9, and left 20,000 dead beneath its walls.

Glorious as the campaign had been, the Empress was now very desirous of peace, as her Austrian ally had failed to support her adequately, and the expenses of the war were ruinous. A peace-congress met, accordingly, at the little border town of Nemirov; but the Russians asked so much that the Turks preferred fighting to surrender.

The campaign of 1738 was almost entirely barren. This time, Münnich was ordered to hasten to the assistance of the Austrians, the imbecility of whose strategy on the Danube had greatly irritated the Russian Court. But an outbreak of the plague prevented him from getting further than the Dniester; and he lost 10,000 of his men from sickness before the campaign was half over. The Austrians were even less successful than their allies, inasmuch as they had not only been unable to capture Widdin, but lost several of their own fortresses. Both Courts were now ready enough to re-open peace-negotiations, but the Turks, encouraged by their victories in Hungary, would not even listen to the most moderate terms; and the Russian statesmen recognised that another campaign was indispensable. At an extraordinary Cabinet Council, held on March 1, 1739, at which Münnich was in attendance as military adviser, it was unanimously resolved to co-operate energetically with the Austrians by invading Moldavia and proceeding to invest the fortress of Chocim on the Dniester. On quitting the Council, Münnich set out for the Ukraine; and, at the end of May, his army, 60,000 strong, quitted the *rendezvous* at Kiev, and marching straight through Polish territory, without permission, crossed the Dniester at Sinkowcza, about seven leagues distant from Chocim. On August 27, he came in sight of the Turkish camp at Stavuchanak, in a very strong position, which he stormed and captured on the following day, the Russians losing only 70 men in an action which lasted twelve hours, whereupon the fortress of Chocim surrendered unconditionally, at the first summons. On September 9 and 10 Münnich crossed the Pruth. On the 19th he reported the submission of Moldavia. His career of victory was only cut short by the humiliating Peace of Belgrade, Sept. 18, 1739. Russia, unable to carry on the struggle alone, was now obliged to come to terms with the

Turks, and, by the Treaty of Constantinople, 1739, she sacrificed all her conquests except Azov and district[1]. The Porte would not even concede the imperial title to the Russian Empress.

Whilst the energy of Marshal Münnich was defending and extending the limits of the Russian Empire, the Russian people, at home, was trembling beneath the yoke of the Empress's favourite, the Grand Chamberlain Biren. During the latter years of the reign of Anne, Biren increased so enormously in power and riches that he must have been a marvel to himself as well as to others. The climax of his wondrous elevation was reached when, in the course of June 1737, the Estates of Courland were compelled to elect the son of the ostler of Mittau as their reigning Duke. But Biren was fearful in the midst of his triumphs, for he knew that the Russians hated him and suspected them of a desire to overthrow him. It would really seem as if he had had the set purpose of gradually exterminating the leaders of the Moscovite aristocracy, so relentless, so persistent, was his persecution of them. In the course of 1738, the old charges of treason were revived against the Dolgorukis; and, by means of the Secret Chancellery, Biren all but annihilated the whole family in 1739. Demetrius Golitsuin had already (1736) been condemned to death, on the most frivolous of charges; but "the clemency of the Empress" commuted the punishment to imprisonment in the fortress of Schlüsselburg. Anything like independence of attitude was in Biren's eyes an unpardonable offence. Hence, the terrible fate of Artamon Voluinsky, Peter the Great's former plenipotentiary in Persia, who, after a long eclipse, was made a Cabinet Minister in 1735. In 1740 he incurred the enmity of Biren and was decapitated, on a trumped-up charge of treason, despite all the efforts of the Empress to save him. But Anne could now refuse Biren nothing. On her death-bed, at his urgent request, though greatly against her own better judgment, she

---

[1] Azov, too, had to be dismantled. On this occasion the Russian Ambassador, Vishnyakov, induced the Porte to change the old title "Moscovy" into "Russia."

even appointed him Regent, during the minority of her great-nephew Ivan VI, an infant four months old, to whom she left the throne.

Anne died on October 28, 1740. Three weeks later the ex-Regent was on his way to Siberia in consequence of a smart little *coup-d'état* organised by Marshal Münnich, who thereupon proclaimed the mother of the baby Emperor Regent while he himself appropriated the Army, the War office, the Foreign Office and the lieutenant-generalship of the Guards with the title of "Premier-Minister." The new Regent, a shy, stupid and awkward girl of sixteen, was the daughter of Catherine Ivanovna, the niece of Peter the Great, and Leopold Charles, Duke of Mecklenburg. She had been adopted by Anne, settled in Russia, and, in 1733, was received into the Russian Church, changing her German name of Elizabeth Catherine Christina to that of Anne Leopoldovna. In 1739 the Empress married her to Prince Anthony Ulric of Brunswick-Bevern, an utterly insignificant person, despised even by his silly wife and pushed aside by both Biren and Münnich without the slightest ceremony. Anne Leopoldovna found however a friend in the Vice-Chancellor Osterman, whom she reinstated in the direction of foreign affairs by the ukase of February 8, 1741. Münnich, in great dudgeon, believing himself to be indispensable, sent in his resignation (March 14) which, to his surprise, was accepted the same afternoon. The Vice-Chancellor quietly superseded him. "Count Osterman," wrote the French Ambassador La Chetardie, shortly afterwards to his Court, "has never been so great or so powerful as he is now. It is not too much to say that he is Tsar of All Russia." If ever Russia needed the guidance of a great statesman, it was during that troubled and confusing period when France, healed of the wounds inflicted by the War of the Spanish Succession, was endeavouring to regain her former position in Europe.

The first great diplomatic victory of France, after her long eclipse, was the Treaty of Vienna, in 1738, which settled all the

questions arising out of the War of the Polish Succession very
greatly to her advantage[1] and to the disparagement of the
Emperor. The second triumph was the Peace of Belgrade,
concluded in 1739, under her mediation, which humiliated the
Hapsburgs still further, and established, beyond all contradiction,
the momentous fact that the French Monarchy had become,
once more, the paramount continental power. To sever the
Austro-Russian alliance and, if possible, drive Russia back into
the semi-barbarism from which she had scarce emerged, was
the next object that the French statesmen set before them.
" Russia in respect to the equilibrium of the North," wrote
Cardinal Fleury, " has mounted to too high a degree of power,
and its union with the House of Austria is extremely dangerous." The most obvious way of rendering the Russian alliance
unserviceable to the Emperor was by implicating Russia in a
war with Sweden, the second of the northern Powers, and the
permanent ally of France. A first attempt to bring about such
a collision, in 1736, had been foiled by the pacific Swedish Chancellor, Count Arvid Horn. On the outbreak of the War of the
Austrian Succession (1740), the necessity of fettering Russia,
Maria Theresa's one ally, became still more urgent. Again the
French influence was exerted to the uttermost in Sweden, and
this time successfully. At the beginning of August 1741,
Sweden declared war against Russia and invaded Finland.

To embarrass the Russian government still further, a
domestic revolution in Russia itself was simultaneously planned
by La Chetardie, with the object of placing the Tsesarevna
Elizabeth on the throne. The immediate object of this
manœuvre was to get rid of Osterman. Osterman's policy
was based upon the Austrian Alliance. He had therefore
guaranteed the Pragmatic Sanction with the deliberate intention
of defending it. The sudden irruption of the King of Prussia
into Silesia, the defection of France, and the treachery of
Saxony, had surprised him. Old as he was in statecraft, he

---

[1] She acquired, *inter alia*, the reversion of Lorraine.

had not calculated upon such a cynical disregard of solemn treaties. He stigmatised the invasion of Silesia as "an ugly business"; and, when he was informed, officially, of the partition treaty whereby the Elector of Saxony was to receive Upper Silesia, Lower Austria, and Moravia, with the title of King of Moravia, he sarcastically enquired whether this was the way in which Saxony meant to manifest the devotion she had always expressed for the House of Austria? He shrewdly guessed that the Moravian scheme must, inevitably, bring along with it a surrender by the Elector of Saxony of the Polish Crown to Stanislaus Leszczynski, the French King's father-in-law, in which case the interests of Russia would be directly threatened. He sent a strong note of remonstrance to the King of Prussia, and assured the Courts of The Hague and St James's of his readiness to concur in any just measures for preserving the integrity of the Austrian dominions. But, for the moment, he was prevented from sending any assistance to the hardly-pressed Queen of Hungary in consequence of the Swedish War with which the French government had saddled him. Nevertheless the Swedish declaration had found him prepared for every eventuality. More than 100,000 of the best Russian troops were already under arms in Finland; and the victory of Marshal Lacy, at the end of August, at Vilmanstrand, where he utterly routed the Swedish general Wrangel, relieved Osterman of all fears from without. But Osterman's own political career was now nearly run. On the conclusion of a new and more definite treaty of alliance with Great Britain (Nov. 18, 1741), his last official act, he told the English Minister, Finch, that he was about to visit Spa and might then proceed to England and pass the remainder of his days there in philosophical contentment. Ten days later he was arrested in his bed, and before the year was out, he was on his way to the desolate *tundras* of Siberia.

CHAPTER XVII.

ELIZABETH PETROVNA, 1741-1762.

On December 6, 1741, La Chetardie wrote to Amelot, the French Minister for Foreign Affairs, as to the prospects of a *coup-d'état* in favour of the Tsesarevna Elizabeth : "An outbreak, the success of which can never be morally certain, especially now that the Swedes are not in a position to lend a hand, would, prudently considered, be very difficult to bring about, unless it could be substantially backed up." That very same evening, Elizabeth, without any help from without, overthrew the existing government in a couple of hours—a thing carefully to be borne in mind, as most historians, relying on certain *ex-post-facto* statements by La Chetardie, have credited that diplomatist with a leading part in the revolution which placed the daughter of Peter the Great on the Russian throne. As a matter of fact, beyond lending the Tsesarevna 2000 ducats, instead of the 15,000 she demanded of him, La Chetardie took no part whatever in the actual *coup-d'état*, which was as great a surprise to him as it was to everyone else. The merit and glory of that singular affair belong to Elizabeth alone.

Elizabeth Petrovna was born on December 18, 1709, at Kolmenskoe, near Moscow, on the day of her father's triumphal entry into his capital after the victory of Pultawa. From her earliest years, the child delighted everyone by her extraordinary beauty and vivacity. Her parts were good, but, unfortunately, her education was both imperfect and desultory. She managed however to pick up some knowledge of Italian, German, and Swedish, and could converse in these languages with more fluency than accuracy. On the death of her mother, and the departure from Russia, three months later, of her beloved sister Anne (1727), the Princess, at the age of 18, was left pretty much to herself. As her father's daughter, she was obnoxious to the Dolgorukis, who kept her far distant from the Court during the reign of Peter II. Robust and athletic, she delighted in field sports, hunting and violent exercise; but she had inherited more than was good for her of her father's sensual temperament; and the hoyden's life, in the pleasant environment of Moscow, was the reverse of edifying.

During the reign of her cousin, Elizabeth effaced herself as much as possible, well aware that the Empress, of whom she stood in awe, regarded her as a possible supplanter. She was already so popular that the shopkeepers of Moscow frequently refused to take money from her when she bought their wares; but she does not seem to have thought of asserting her rights to the throne till the idea was suggested to her by La Chetardie and his colleague, the Swedish minister, Nolcken, who communicated with her through her French physician, Lestocq. Frequent collisions with the Regent, Anne Leopoldovna, whom she despised, and with Osterman, whom she hated for setting her aside in favour of aliens and foreigners, though he himself owed everything to her father and mother, first awakened her ambition; but her natural indolence was very difficult to overcome. Not till December 5, 1741, when the Guards in the capital, on whom Elizabeth principally relied, were ordered to hold themselves in readiness to march for the seat of war, did she take the decisive step. That same night a hurried and anxious conference of her partisans, chief among whom were her surgeon Lestocq, her chamberlain Michael Vorontsov, her favourite and future husband, Alexis Razumovsky, and Alexander and Peter Shuvalov, two of the gentlemen of her house-

hold, was held at her house.   As a result of their deliberations,
Elizabeth put on a cuirass, armed herself with a demi-pike, and,
proceeding to the barracks of the Guards, won them over by a
spirited harangue at 2 o'clock in the morning.   Then, at the
head of a regiment of the Preobrazhensk grenadiers, she
sledged, through the snow, to the Winter Palace, where the
Regent lay sleeping in absolute security, and arrested all her real
or suspected adversaries, including Osterman and Münnich, on
her way.   The Regent, aroused from her slumbers by Elizabeth
herself, submitted quietly and was conveyed to the Empress's
sledge.   The baby-tsar and his little sister, with their nurses,
followed behind in a second sledge to Elizabeth's own palace.
In less than half an hour, bloodlessly and noiselessly, the
Revolution had been accomplished.   Even so late as 8 o'clock
the next morning, very few people in the city were aware that,
during the night, Elizabeth Petrovna had been raised to her
father's throne on the shoulders of the Preobrazhensk
Grenadiers.

At the age of thirty-three, this naturally indolent and
self-indulgent woman, with little knowledge and no previous
training or experience of affairs, was suddenly placed at the
head of a great Empire, for whose honour and security she was
primarily responsible, at one of the most critical periods of its
existence.   La Chetardie had already expressed his conviction
(and his court implicitly believed him), that, when once
Elizabeth was on the throne, she would banish all foreigners,
however able, give her entire confidence to necessarily ignorant
Russians, retire to her well-beloved Moscow, let the fleet rot and
utterly neglect St Petersburg and "the conquered provinces"
as the Baltic seaboard was still called.   Unfortunately for his
calculations, La Chetardie, while exaggerating the defects, had
ignored the good qualities of the new Empress.   For, with all
her shortcomings, Elizabeth was no ordinary woman.   In many
respects she was her illustrious father's own daughter.   Her
very considerable knowledge of human nature, her unusually

sound and keen judgment, and her diplomatic tact, again and again recall Peter the Great. What to her impatient contemporaries often seemed irresolution or sluggishness, was generally suspense of judgment, in exceptionally difficult circumstances, and her ultimate decision was generally correct. Add to this that the welfare of her beloved country always lay nearest to her heart, and that she was ever ready to sacrifice the prejudices of the woman to the duties of the Sovereign, and we shall recognise, at once, that Russia did well at this crisis to place her destinies in the hands of Elizabeth Petrovna. It is true that, as La Chetardie had predicted, almost her first act was to disgrace and exile all the foreigners who had held sway during the past two reigns, including such illustrious names as Osterman and Münnich (January 29, 1742). But—and this is her justification—she placed at the head of affairs a native Russian statesman, whom, personally, she much disliked, but whose genius and experience she rightly judged to be indispensable to Russia at that particular moment.

Alexis Petrovich Bestuzhev-Ryumin was born on May 2, 1693. Educated, with his elder brother Michael, at Copenhagen and Berlin, he adopted the diplomatic career, and, at the age of 19, served as the second Russian plenipotentiary at the Congress of Utrecht. From 1717 to 1726 he occupied the honourable but peculiar post of Hanoverian Minister to Russia, subsequently representing Russia at Copenhagen till the death of Peter the Great. For the next fifteen years, he was kept in the background and had to be content with the comparatively humble post of Russian resident at Hamburg, while his brother shone as Ambassador Extraordinary at Stockholm. Towards the end of the reign of Anne, Biren recalled him to Russia to balance the influence of Osterman; but he fell with his patron and only re-emerged from the obscurity of disgrace on the accession of Elizabeth. He drew up the Empress' first *ukaz* and was made Vice-Chancellor at the end of the year ; but so insecure did he feel that, in February, 1742, he employed

the good offices of the Saxon Minister, Pezold, to bring about
a good understanding between himself and the reigning (and
now ennobled) favourite, Lestocq, whom, at the bottom of his
heart, he thoroughly despised.

It is a difficult task to diagnose the character of this sinister
and elusive statesman, who took such infinite pains to obliterate
all his traces.   He seems to have been a moody, taciturn
hypochondriac, full of wiles and ruses, passionate when provoked,
but preferring to work silently and subterraneously.   Inordinate
love of power was certainly his ruling passion, but he had to
bide his time till he was nearly fifty.   He was a man who remorselessly crushed his innumerable enemies and never allowed
himself the luxury of a single intimate friend.   Yet, in justice,
it must be added that his enemies were generally the enemies
of his country ; that his implacability was actuated as much by
patriotic as by personal motives ; and that nothing could turn
him one hair's breadth from the policy which he considered to
be best suited to the interests of the State.   And this true
policy he alone, for a long time, of all his contemporaries,
had the wisdom to discern and the courage to pursue.

The first care of the new Empress, after abolishing the
cabinet-council system, which had been in favour during the
reign of the two Annes, and reconstituting the Administrative
Senate, as it had been under Peter the Great, was to compose
her quarrel with Sweden, not only because the Finnish war was
a drain upon her resources, but also because the political
situation required her attention more urgently elsewhere.   The
sudden collapse of Sweden had come as a disagreeable surprise
to the Court of Versailles ; and to baulk Russia of the fruits of
her triumph, by obtaining the best possible terms for discomfited
Sweden, was now the principal object of the French diplomatists
in the north.   La Chetardie was accordingly instructed to offer
the mediation of France, and use all his efforts to cajole the
Empress into an abandonment of her rights of conquest.   Never
for an instant did he doubt of success.   For the first three

months after the Revolution, he was, undoubtedly, the most popular man in Russia. "The first bow here is to her Majesty," observes the English Minister Finch shortly after that event, "but the second is to Mons. de La Chetardie." He saw the Empress almost daily, was closeted with her for hours, and was the only foreign envoy who enjoyed the privilege of accompanying her Majesty on her frequent religious pilgrimages. But when, in February, 1742, he suggested to Elizabeth, at a private interview, that the victorious Russians should sacrifice something for the benefit of the vanquished Swedes in order to satisfy the honour of France, the Empress, very pertinently, inquired what opinion her own subjects would be likely to have of her if she so little regarded the memory of her illustrious father as to cede provinces won by him at the cost of so much Russian blood and treasure? Bestuzhev, to whom the Frenchman next applied, roundly declared that no negotiations with Sweden could be thought of except on a *uti possidetis* basis. "I should deserve to lose my head on the block," he concluded, "if I counselled her Imperial Majesty to cede a single inch of territory." At a subsequent Council it was decided to decline the French offer of mediation and prosecute the Swedish war with vigour. There is no need to follow the course of the campaign of 1742. The Russian advance, under Lacy and Keith, was a triumphal progress. By the end of the year all Finland was in the hands of the Russians. On January 23, 1743, direct negotiations between the two powers were opened at Åbo ; and on August 7 peace was concluded, Sweden ceding to Russia all the southern part of Finland east of the river Kymmene, including the fortresses of Vilmanstrand and Fredrikshamn. Bestuzhev would have held out for the whole Grand-Duchy, but the Empress, fearful of the possible intervention of France and Prussia, overruled him. This was a great blow to France ; and La Chetardie, perceiving that he was no longer of any use to his employers at St Petersburg, presented his letters of recall, and quitted Russia (July, 1742).

The French Government had discovered that it had nothing to hope from Russia so long as Bestuzhev had the direction of affairs. Henceforth, it became the prime object of the Court of Versailles to overthrow him as speedily as possible, especially as it suspected him of a desire to aid the Queen of Hungary. This, indeed, was actually the intention of Bestuzhev. He was as well aware, as Osterman had been before him, that France was the natural enemy of Russia. The interests of the two States in Turkey, Poland and Sweden were diametrically opposed. Russia could never hope to be safe from the intrigues of France in these three border lands. Hostility to France being the norm of Russia's true policy at this period, all the enemies of France were necessarily the friends of Russia, and all the friends of France were her enemies. Consequently, Great Britain, and, still more, Austria, as being a near neighbour and more directly threatened by France, were Russia's natural allies; while the aggressive King of Prussia, who had the disquieting ambition of aggrandising himself at the expense of all his neighbours, and was in alliance with France, had also to be guarded against. It was the policy of Bestuzhev, therefore, to bring about a quadruple alliance between Russia, Austria, Great Britain and Saxony to balance the strength of France and Prussia combined. But here, unfortunately, he was on dangerously slippery ground, where a single stumble meant irretrievable ruin, for the representatives of the three Russophil Powers above mentioned had all been active and ardent supporters of Anne Leopoldovna and had done their best to keep Elizabeth from the throne. Of this the Empress was, by this time, very well aware; her antipathies, therefore, were very naturally directed against the ambassadors of Great Britain, Austria and Saxony, who had been her adversaries while she was only Tsesarevna; and it required no small courage on the part of Bestuzhev to defend a policy, which, indispensable as it might be, was abhorrent to his sovereign for strong personal reasons. Moreover, nearly all the intimate personal friends of the Empress, headed by Lestocq, and extremely jealous of the superior talents and rising influence of Bestuzhev, were already in the pay of France and Prussia, and ready, at the bidding of the French *chargé d'affaires*, D'Allion, to embark in any project for overthrowing the Vice-Chancellor.   The expedient finally adopted was a bogus conspiracy alleged to be afoot for the purpose of replacing on the throne the baby Prince Ivan (who since the Revolution, had been detained, provisionally, with his parents, at the fortress of Dünamunde near Riga), a conspiracy which, very ingeniously, was made to include most of Elizabeth's former rivals, such as Natalia Lopukhina and the Countess Anna Gavrilovna, consort of Michael Bestuzhev, the Vice-Chancellor's brother.   The former Austrian ambassador, the Marquis de Botta, was alleged to be the chief promoter of the affair.   The plot was "miraculously discovered" by Lestocq and burst upon the Empress in August, 1743.   After a rigid inquisition of twenty-five days, during which every variety of torture was freely employed against the accused, "the terrible plot," says the English minister, Sir Cyril Wych, "was found to be little more than the ill-considered discourses of a couple of spiteful, passionate women, and two or three young debauchees." Nevertheless, the two women principally concerned had their tongues publicly torn out before being sent to Siberia ; and the Russian minister at Vienna was instructed to demand Botta's condign punishment.   This was done at a special audience, whereupon Maria Theresa declared, with her usual spirit, that she would never admit the validity of extorted evidence, and issued a manifesto to all the Great Powers defending Botta and accusing the Russian Court of gross injustice.

Thus Lestocq and his principals had succeeded in estranging the Courts of St Petersburg and Vienna ; and the result of the "Lopukhin Trial" was hailed as a great diplomatic victory at Paris.   But the caballers had failed to bring Bestuzhev to the block, or even to "drive him into some obscure hole in the country," as D'Allion had confidently predicted.   At the very crisis of his peril, when his own sister-in-law was implicated, the Empress, always equitable when not frightened into ferocity, had privately assured the Vice-Chancellor that her confidence in him was unabated, and that not a hair of his head should be touched. But Bestuzhev had now a still more formidable antagonist to encounter in Frederick II of Prussia.

From the very beginning of his reign, Frederick II had rightly regarded Russia as his most formidable neighbour. She was also the natural ally of his inveterate enemy the Queen of Hungary. So early as June 1, 1743, he wrote to Mardefelt, his minister at St Petersburg: "I should never think of lightly provoking Russia; on the contrary, there is nothing in the world I would not do in order always to be on good terms with that Empire." A few months later, the neutrality, at least, of Russia had become of vital importance to him. Alarmed for Silesia (his most lucrative province which had cost him nothing and brought him in 3,000,000 thalers per annum) by the Austrian victories in the course of 1743, and especially disturbed by the Compact of Worms (Sept. 13, 1743), which seemed to him a renewed guarantee of the Pragmatic Sanction, he resolved to make sure of his newly-won possessions by attacking the Queen of Hungary a second time, before she had time to attack him. But how would Russia take this fresh and unprovoked act of aggression? That was the question upon which everything else depended. Fortunately, "the Botta conspiracy" provided him with an opportunity of ingratiating himself with the Empress. He wrote an autograph letter to Elizabeth, expressing his horror at the plot against her sacred person, and ostentatiously demanded of the Court of Vienna that Botta, who had been transferred from St Petersburg to Berlin, should instantly be recalled. The Empress was much gratified, and showed it. But Bestuzhev had yet to be got rid of. "I cannot repeat too often," wrote the King of Prussia to Mardefelt (January 25, 1744), "that, until that man has been rendered harmless, I can never reckon upon the friendship of the Empress." And again

(February 29), "It is absolutely necessary to oust the Vice-Chancellor. So long as he is in office, he will cause me a thousand chagrins." Frederick, with the aid of his chief spy, the elder Princess of Zerbst (who in February, 1744, had brought her daughter Sophia Augusta to Russia to wed the Empress' nephew and heir, the young Duke of Holstein), now set his hand to an elaborate intrigue for the undoing of the Vice-Chancellor. The Princess was assisted by all Bestuzhev's other enemies, including La Chetardie, now back again at his post, Lestocq and Mardefelt. "Having regard to the way in which you have concerted measures with the Princess of Zerbst," wrote Frederick to Mardefelt, in February, 1744, "I don't see how the blow can possibly fail." Yet fail it did; and, as the year wore on, and Bestuzhev still held his own, Frederick grew anxious, and then angry. He calls the growing influence of *ce méchant homme* "a mystery of iniquity" which he cannot solve. On June 4, he wrote to Mardefelt, "Pressing circumstances and the prompt execution of my designs absolutely demand that you should change your tactics a little and employ all your *savoir-faire* to win over the Vice-Chancellor"; and he authorised Mardefelt to spend as much as 500,000 crowns for the purpose. Then, trusting to the skill of Mardefelt and the potent influence of the 500,000 crowns, at the end of August he openly threw off the mask and invaded Bohemia at the head of 60,000 men. By the end of September his troops had occupied the whole Kingdom.

In the extremity of her distress, Maria Theresa sent a special envoy, Count Rosenberg, to St Petersburg, to express her horror at Botta's alleged misconduct, and placed herself and her fortunes unreservedly in the hands of her imperial sister. For two months Elizabeth hesitated, while the Lestocq-Mardefelt-Zerbst clique did all in its power to prevent any assistance from being sent to the distressed Queen of Hungary. But Bestuzhev was now much stronger than he had ever been. By the aid of his secretary, Goldbach, he had succeeded in unravelling La

Chetardie's cipher correspondence and furnished the Empress with extracts alluding in the most disparaging terms to herself. These Bestuzhev accompanied by an elucidative commentary. Furious at the treachery of the ever gallant and deferential Marquis, the Empress dictated to Bestuzhev on the spot a memorandum to La Chetardie commanding him to quit her capital within twenty-four hours; and on June 17, 1744, he was escorted to the frontier. Six weeks later (July 26) Elizabeth identified herself emphatically with the anti-French policy of her minister, by promoting him to the rank of Grand Chancellor; their common friend, Michael Vorontsov, being at the same time appointed Vice-Chancellor. Bestuzhev now energetically represented to the Empress the necessity of interfering in the quarrel between Frederick II and the Queen of Hungary. He described the King of Prussia as a restless, agitating character made up of fraud and violence. He had violated the Treaty of Breslau. He was secretly stirring up Turkey against Russia. He had impudently used neutral Saxon territory as a stepping-stone to Bohemia. He had procured the dissolution of the Diet of Grodno to prevent his anti-Russian intrigues from being discovered, thus aiming a direct blow at the supremacy which Russia had enjoyed in Poland ever since the days of Peter the Great. In a word Prussia was now far too powerful to be a safe neighbour. The balance of power in Europe must be restored instantly, and at any cost, by reducing her to her proper place.

Bestuzhev so far prevailed as to persuade Elizabeth to receive the extraordinary Austrian envoy, Rosenberg, and promise to commit the Botta incident to oblivion. In the beginning of 1745 she gave a genuine proof of her reconciliation with Austria by bluntly refusing Frederick a succour of 6000 men, though bound by her last defensive treaty with Prussia to assist him. Bestuzhev then submitted to the British Government an intervention project, which was rejected as too onerous and exorbitant; while Frederick, thoroughly alarmed, offered Bestuzhev 100,000 crowns if he would acquiesce in Prussia's appropriating another slice of Silesia, an offer which the Russian Chancellor haughtily rejected. Frederick's subsequent declaration of war against Saxony greatly agitated the Russian Court; and three successive ministerial Councils (August–September, 1745), inspired by Bestuzhev, unanimously advised an armed intervention. Elizabeth thereupon signed an *ukaz*, commanding that the 60,000 men, already stationed in Esthonia and Livonia, should at once advance into Courland, so as to be nearer the Prussian frontier and ready for every emergency. A manifesto was also addressed to the King of Prussia, warning him that Russia considered herself bound to assist Saxony if invaded by him. But nothing came of it all. Bestuzhev relied for the success of his plan on British subsidies, but the British Cabinet, having already secured the safety of Hanover, by a secret understanding with the King of Prussia, had resolved upon neutrality. This too was the real reason why Great Britain had shrunk from committing herself to a quadruple alliance[1] against Prussia as proposed by Bestuzhev. Elizabeth, who saw much more clearly than her minister on this occasion, bitterly reproached him for trusting too much to England; while Frederick, certain, now, of the neutrality of England, proceeded to devastate Saxony, annihilate the Elector's army, and dictate the Peace of Dresden (December 25, 1745). But the Prussian King was only just in time. Twelve days after the conclusion of the Peace of Dresden, and a week before the news thereof reached St Petersburg, a cabinet council, lasting three days, was held at the Winter Palace, the Empress presiding. At this Council it was unanimously resolved that Bestuzhev should inform Lord Hyndford, the English ambassador, that, if the Maritime Powers would advance Russia a subsidy of six millions, she would at once place 100,000 men in the field, and end the German War in a single campaign.

---

[1] Russia, England, Austria, and Saxony.

But Great Britain would not go so far, and the King of Prussia remained unmolested.

Hampered as he was by the backwardness of England and the misgivings of his own sovereign, Bestuzhev could not prevent the conclusion of a peace which he detested; yet the menacing attitude of the Russian Chancellor had so far impressed Frederick as to make him moderate his demands in spite of his recent victories. Moreover Frederick now played into Bestuzhev's hands by indulging in one of those foolish jests for which he had often to pay so dearly. Before departing for Saxony, he had requested the mediation of Russia and Turkey at the same time, remarking with a sneer, at a public reception, that, in his opinion, the mediation of a Turk was every bit as good as the mediation of a Greek. Elizabeth was wounded in her tenderest point. That she, the devout mother of all the Orthodox, should be placed in the same category with the descendant of the false Prophet revolted her; and her sentiments towards "the Nadir Shah of Berlin," as she called the King of Prussia, underwent a complete change. She had hitherto accepted his effusive compliments without suspicion; but now Bestuzhev gave her frequent glimpses into the deciphered correspondence of Frederick where the references to herself were by no means flattering. Thus political antagonism and private pique combined to make Elizabeth the most determined adversary of Frederick II.

The triumph of the Austrian party at St Petersburg dates from the conclusion of the defensive alliance of June 2, 1745, whereby each of the contracting parties agreed to aid the other, within three months of being attacked, with 30,000 men, or, in case Prussia was the aggressor, with 60,000. Frederick saw in this compact a plan for attacking him on the first opportunity, and, in the course of the same summer, made another determined attempt to overthrow Bestuzhev with the aid of Lestocq, Vorontsov, D'Allion and Mardefelt. But the plot recoiled on the plotters; and the Prussian minister, Mardefelt, received his passports. Bestuzhev's subsequent endeavours to round off his system by contracting an alliance with Great Britain were less successful, Great Britain being by no means so eager to unite with Russia as Russia with her. "The King," wrote Chesterfield to Hyndford, "cannot guarantee to the Queen of Hungary possessions which she herself has relinquished." Nevertheless the victories of Marshal Saxe in the Austrian Netherlands, and the consequent danger of Holland, at last drew Russia and Great Britain more closely together; and the pressing question of the advance of a Russian auxiliary corps to the Rhine engulfed all others. After long and vexatious negotiations, in the course of which Bestuzhev hotly declared that he saw he was about to become "the victim of his own good intentions towards an ungrateful Court," which squabbled over thousands for the alliance, while France would have given tens of thousands for the simple neutrality, of Russia, the British government virtually agreed to his demands. By the Treaty of St Petersburg (December 9, 1747), the Empress, besides agreeing to hold a corps of observation, 30,000 strong, on the Courland frontier, at the disposal of Great Britain for £100,000 a year, consented to send another corps of 30,000 to the Rhine, on condition that £300,000 a year were paid for the troops by England and Holland, four months in advance, as well as 150,000 rix-dollars for their maintenance during their passage through Europe.

On January 28, 1748, the day after the exchange of the ratifications, Prince Repnin, at the head of 30,000 Russians, began slowly to advance through central Europe, so slowly, indeed, that the Courts of London and Vienna were loud in their complaints to the Russian ministers. But, in truth, the subsidiary corps had already accomplished all that was required of it. The news of the approach of Repnin's army induced France, despite her brilliant victories, to accelerate the peace negotiations; and, on April 30, 1748, a preliminary convention was signed between the Court of Versailles and the Maritime Powers, at Aix la

Chapelle, subsequently confirmed by the formal treaty of October 18, to which Austria and her allies reluctantly acceded.

Never yet had Russia stood so high in the estimation of Europe as in the autumn of 1748 ; and this commanding position she owed entirely to the tenacity of purpose of the Grand Chancellor. In the face of apparently insurmountable obstacles, Bestuzhev had honourably extricated his country from the Swedish imbroglio ; reconciled his imperial mistress with the Courts of London and Vienna, her natural allies; re-established friendly relations, on a firm basis, with those powers ; freed Russia from the yoke of foreign influence ; compelled both Prussia and France to abate their pretensions in the very hour of victory ; and, finally, had isolated the restless, perturbing, King of Prussia by environing him with hostile alliances.

The seven years which succeeded the War of the Austrian Succession were nothing more than an armed truce between apprehensive and dissatisfied adversaries, nothing more than an indispensable breathing-space between a past contest which everyone felt to have been inconclusive, and a future contest which everyone knew to be inevitable. Both the Peace of Aix and the Peace of Breslau had been forced from without upon active belligerents. In the first case the unexpected intervention of Russia had arrested the triumphal progress of the French armies ; in the second, the sudden desertion[1] of England had compelled defeated but still defiant Austria to surrender her fairest province to the King of Prussia. The consequences of these prematurely suppressed hostilities were an unnatural tension between the various European Powers, a loosening of time-honoured alliances, and a cautious groping after newer and surer combinations. The determining factor of this universal distrust was the King of Prussia, who alone had profited by the struggle which had convulsed Europe. But Frederick himself was uneasy in the midst of his triumphs, and, far from diminishing his armaments after the war was over,

[1] That is to say, from the Austrian point of view.

prudently increased them. He had nothing to fear, indeed, for the present from exhausted Austria; but the attitude of Russia continued to be as menacing as ever. Bestuzhev did not leave his redoubtable antagonist out of sight for a moment; and the diplomatic struggle between them was carried on with ever increasing acerbity, principally in Sweden, Poland and Turkey.

In Sweden the joint efforts of the British and French Ministers in the course of 1750, prevented Russia from fastening a quarrel upon Sweden, who was supposed at St Petersburg to be about to amend her vicious constitution at the suggestion of the King of Prussia. Frederick, on the other hand, incensed beyond measure by an imperial rescript issued by Bestuzhev, ordering all Russian subjects belonging to the Baltic Provinces but actually in the Prussian service, to return to their homes, deliberately slighted the Russian resident Gross, who was thereupon (October 25, 1750) recalled, and diplomatic intercourse between the two countries ceased.

In Poland and at the Porte, Great Britain and Russia acted together, and their ambassadors successfully resisted all the intrigues of France and Prussia. Purely oriental affairs, however, were of minor importance during the reign of Elizabeth; and even in Poland the one constantly recurring question, the desirability of abolishing the *liberum veto*, excited no more than a languid interest. The Elector of Saxony, in his own interests as King of Poland, desired the abatement of this nuisance; but he dared not move without the consent of Russia, and Russia would consent to no reform of the Polish constitution which might resuscitate her ancient but now moribund rival.

All this while, Bestuzhev had been doing his utmost to promote his favourite project of a strong Anglo-Russian alliance with the object of "still further clipping the wings of the King of Prussia." The negotiations began in 1750, when Great Britain, not without reason, feared that Frederick was about to attack Hanover. But the Empress, who displayed throughout a truer political instinct than her Chancellor, was indisposed to risk a rupture with Prussia simply for the sake of Hanover. For three years, therefore, she returned no answer to the British demands. At last, in May 1753, the negotiations were reopened at the urgent instance of Bestuzhev; but still no progress could be made till June, 1755, when Sir Hanbury Williams arrived from London with secret instructions to conclude a new convention with Russia as speedily as possible. On September 19, 1755, the convention was signed. By the terms of it, Russia engaged to furnish an auxiliary corps of 55,000 men for a diversion against Prussia in return for an annual subsidy from Great Britain of £500,000, besides £100,000 a year for the maintenance of an additional corps on the frontier. This convention was to be ratified two months after signature; but, at the last moment, Elizabeth could not make up her mind to ratify it. She suspected, not without reason, that England required a large proportion of the Russian contingent to fight her battles on the Rhine and in the Low Countries, and she was not disposed to divert her troops thither. Not till February 1, 1756, were the ratifications signed; but the Empress never forgave Bestuzhev for the vehemence and petulance by means of which he forced her hand on this occasion. Yet the very treaty which it had taken nearly six years to negotiate had already become waste paper. A fortnight before the exchange of the ratifications, an event had occurred, at the other end of Europe, which shattered all the cunning combinations of the Russian Chancellor, completely changed the complexion of continental politics, and precipitated a general European war.

Hitherto, broadly speaking, the balance of power in Europe had hung upon the rivalry of the houses of Bourbon and Hapsburg, the determining cause of most of the wars which had convulsed the continent since the days of Richelieu. But the last of these wars, the War of the Austrian Succession, had had strange and unforeseen consequences. Instead of bene-fiting either France or Austria, it had called into existence a new Great Power in the shape of Prussia. France had sought to make a tool of the young Prussian Monarchy, but the young Prussian Monarchy had reversed their respective parts and made a tool of her august and somewhat contemptuous patron and ally. The natural result of this disagreeable surprise was the drawing together of Austria and France, both now animated by a common dread and distrust of Prussia. This astounding *volte-face* was accomplished, not without difficulty (for the prejudices of ages could not be overcome in a moment), by the Austrian Chancellor Wenzel Anton von Kaunitz.

But Frederick had been beforehand with his adversaries. Recognising the fact that decadent France could no longer be profitable to him, and alarmed by the rumours of the impending negotiations between Great Britain and Russia, he calculated that the chances, on the whole, were in favour of the superior usefulness of an English alliance, and (January 16, 1756) signed the Treaty of Westminster with Great Britain, generally known as the German Neutrality Convention, whereby the two contracting powers agreed to unite their forces to oppose the entry into, or the passage through Germany, of the troops of any other foreign Power. The Treaty of Westminster precipitated the conclusion of the Franco-Austrian *rapprochement.* On May 2, 1756, a defensive alliance was signed at Versailles between the French and Austrian governments. On the same day a secret treaty, for the ultimate partition of Prussia, was signed between the same two Powers ; and to this treaty Russia, Sweden and Saxony were to be invited to accede.

The position of the Russian Chancellor was now truly pitiable. He had expended all his energy in carrying through an alliance with Great Britain which was now only so much waste paper. He had repeatedly predicted that Prussia could never unite with Great Britain, or Austria with France, yet both these alleged impossibilities had actually taken place. No wonder if the Empress lost confidence in him, especially as he clung obstinately to a past condition of things and refused to bow to the inexorable logic of accomplished facts. He was well aware that if Great Britain could no longer be counted upon for help against Prussia the assistance of France would be indispensable; yet so inextinguishable was his hatred of France, that he could not reconcile himself to the idea of an alliance with that Power in any circumstances. Consequently, his whole policy was henceforth purely obstructive, and therefore purely mischievous.

His first act, on recovering from the shock of the Treaty of Westminster, was to propose to the Empress the establishment of a *Konferentsia*, or Cabinet Council, as a permanent and paramount Department of State, to advise her on all matters relating to foreign affairs. This he did to compel his opponents to shew their hands openly, instead of secretly intriguing against him. At its second session the Conference decided that England's treaty with Prussia had nullified the Anglo-Russian conventions. At its third session, it determined to invite the Courts of Versailles, Vienna and Stockholm to co-operate with Russia "to reduce the King of Prussia within proper limits so that he might no longer be a danger to the German Empire." It then ordered the army to be mobilised at once, so that Austria might also be spurred on to more rapid action; and the Austrian ambassador was instructed to inform his Court, without delay, that her imperial Majesty was ready to conclude a definite treaty with France whenever invited to do so. Thus the very Council which Bestuzhev had called into existence worked steadily against him from the first.

Great Britain did all she could to counteract the *rapproche-ment* of Russia and France; and Hanbury Williams, her minister at St Petersburg, went the length, during a temporary illness of the Empress, of forming a conspiracy to place on the throne the Grand-Duke Peter and his consort the Grand-Duchess Catherine, both of whom were known to be friendly to the King of Prussia. Contrary to everyone's expectations, how-ever, at the end of October, Elizabeth's health improved and all Williams' schemes to prevent the conclusion of the Franco-Russian alliance instantly collapsed.   On December 31, 1756, the Russian Empress formally acceded to the Treaty of Versailles, at the same time binding herself, by a secret article, to assist France if attacked by England in Europe; France at the same time contracting a corresponding secret obligation to give Russia pecuniary assistance in the event of her being attacked by Turkey.   The secret articles of the partition treaty, as between France and Austria, were not, however, communicated to the Court of St Petersburg.

It is certain that at this crisis of his life the King of Prussia was by no means so well informed as usual.   Indeed, during the first six months of 1756, he acted upon incorrect, or at least incomplete information, and was for a long time in the dark as to the true nature and magnitude of the peril he knew to be impending.   He was well aware, all along, that Austria meant to attack him at the first opportunity, and that Saxony would go with her; but not till towards the end of June did he suspect the existence of the Franco-Austrian League, and, till the end of August, he flattered himself that British influence would prove stronger than Austrian influence at St Petersburg.   He was also mistaken, or misinformed, as to the relative attitudes of Russia and Austria.   He was, for instance, under the false impression that Austria was urging on Russia against him, but that the latter Power was not prepared and would postpone an invasion till the following spring, whereas in reality it was Russia who was urging on dilatory and timorous Austria.

At the beginning of June, Frederick learnt from the Hague, that Russia had definitely renounced her obligations towards England.   Early in July he told Mitchell, the English envoy at Berlin, that Russia was lost to them, and at once resolved to begin what Bismarck has called "a preventive war[1]," certainly his best policy.   On August 31, 1756, he invaded

[1] *i.e.* an aggressive war begun to anticipate an expected attack.

Saxony with 60,000 men, drove back the Austrians into Bohemia (battle of Lowositz, October 1), and occupied the whole Saxon electorate, which he ravaged and blackmailed mercilessly. The Seven Years' War had begun.

It is beyond the scope of this book to enter into the details of the struggle. Here only the salient events, so far as they affected the policy of Russia and the general situation, can be very briefly adumbrated.

The lack of good generals, a fact due to the neglect, during the last three reigns, of Peter the Great's golden rule of forming a school of native generals by carefully training promising young Russian officers beneath the eye of intelligent and experienced foreigners, was the cause of Russia's inefficiency in the field during the first two campaigns. In 1757, the Russian Commander-in-Chief, Stephen Apraksin, accidentally gained the battle of Grossjägersdorf (August 29), one of the most casual victories on record, won as it was by the sheer courage of raw troops suddenly attacked by an enemy whom they were marching to outflank. During the rest of the campaign Apraksin did nothing at all but march and counter-march.

The great political event of the year 1757 was the resumption of diplomatic relations between Russia and France. In June, 1757, the new French ambassador, Paul Galluchio de L'Hôpital, Marquis de Chateauneuf, arrived at St Petersburg at the head of an extraordinarily brilliant suite. His charming manners, ready wit and truly patrician liberality made him a *persona gratissima* at the Russian Court ; and, in conjunction with the new Austrian ambassador, Prince Nicholas Esterházy, he carried everything before him. It was through their influence that Apraksin and his friend Bestuzhev were arrested, early in 1758, on a charge of conspiring with the Grand-Duchess Catherine and her friends to recall the army from the field and hold it in readiness to support a projected *coup d'état* in case of the death of the Empress, who, on September 19, 1756, had had a slight apoplectic stroke after attending mass at the parish church of Tsarkoe Selo.   Bestuzhev's enemies had instantly connected the illness of the Empress with the almost simultaneous retreat of the army, though we now know for certain that the two events were entirely unconnected.   The retreat of the army had been ordered by an unanimous council of war, held a full fortnight previously to the Empress' seizure ; while it is obvious that the Chancellor, especially in his own very critical position, had no object in sparing his old enemy, the King of Prussia.   Bestuzhev succeeded in clearing himself completely of all the charges brought against him.   But the Empress, while admitting his innocence, shewed that she had lost all confidence in him ; he was deprived of his offices, and banished from Court.   He was succeeded as Grand Chancellor by Michael Vorontsov, an honest man of excellent intentions but mediocre abilities.

The campaign of 1758 was a repetition of the campaign of 1757.   After occupying the whole of East Prussia, Apraksin's successor, General Fermor, on August 25, defeated Frederick at Zorndorf, one of the most murderous engagements of modern times, 34 per cent. of the total number engaged being placed *hors-de-combat.*   But Fermor was incapable of making any use of his victory, even after being strongly reinforced ; and, at the beginning of October, he retired behind the Vistula.

The increasing financial difficulties of the Russian Government, in 1759, prevented the army from taking the field till April ; and, on May 19, the incurably sluggish Fermor was superseded by Count Peter Saltuikov, an officer of no experience, who hitherto had been mainly occupied in drilling the militia of the Ukraine.   Frederick the Great communicated this new appointment to his brother Prince Henry, with more than his usual caustic acerbity.   "Fermor," he wrote, "has received by way of appendage one Soltykoff who is said to be more stupid and imbecile than anything in the clod-hopper line which

Russia has yet produced." Yet this same "clod-hopper" was, within three weeks, to reduce the King of Prussia to the last extremity.

Although suddenly pitted against the most redoubtable captain of the age, without having ever commanded an army before, Saltuikov seems to have accepted his tremendous responsibilities without the slightest hesitation. On July 9, he reached headquarters; on July 23, he defeated, near Kay, the Prussian general Wedell, who had attempted to prevent his junction with the Austrians; early in August he united with Laudon at Frankfurt on Oder; and, on August 12, the allies annihilated the army of the King of Prussia at Kunersdorf.

"Only a miracle can save us now," wrote the Prussian Minister Finckenstein to Kniphausen, the Prussian ambassador at London, a few days after the catastrophe. At the urgent request of Frederick, Pitt at once made pacific overtures to Russia on behalf of Prussia, and proposed a peace congress to be held at the Hague. On December 12, the Empress delivered her reply to these pacific overtures. She declared that she and her allies were equally desirous of peace, but of a peace that should be honourable, durable and profitable. Such a peace, she opined, was impossible if things were allowed to remain on the same footing as they were before the war. After this it was plain to the British Ministers that no more could be said at present, and the war must proceed.

Frederick was only saved from instant destruction by the violent dissension between Marshal[1] Saltuikov and the Austrian Commander-in-Chief, Count Daun, who refused to take orders from each other and thus wasted all the fruits of Kunersdorf. Indeed Saltuikov was so elated by his astounding victories that he even refused to submit to the orders of his own court. In spite of urgent rescripts commanding him to follow up his successes without delay, he absolutely refused to remain in Silesia a day longer than October 15, as "the preservation

[1] Kunersdorf gained him his *bâton*.

of his army ought to be his primary consideration." At the beginning of November he deliberately marched off to his magazines at Posen.

It is not too much to say that from the end of 1759 to the end of 1761 the unshakable firmness of the Russian Empress was the one constraining political force which held together the heterogeneous, incessantly jarring, elements of the anti-Prussian combination, and prevented it from collapsing before the shock of disaster.   From the Russian point of view, Elizabeth's greatness as a ruler consists in her steady appreciation of Russian interests, and her determination to promote and consolidate them at all hazards.   She insisted, throughout, that the King of Prussia must be rendered harmless to his neighbours for the future, and that the only way to bring this about was to curtail his dominions, and reduce him to the rank of a Kurfürst. Russia's share of his partitioned dominions was to be the province already in her possession, Ducal Prussia¹ as it was then called; a very moderate compensation for her preponderating services and enormous sacrifices.   On January 1, 1760, the Empress told Esterházy that she meant to continue the war, in conjunction with her allies, even if she were compelled to sell all her diamonds and half her wearing apparel; but she also declared that the time had come when Russia should be formally guaranteed the possession of her conquest, Ducal Prussia. The Court of Vienna was much perturbed.   Maria Theresa was well aware that France would never consent to the aggrandisement of Russia, yet she herself was in such absolute need of the succour of the Russian troops, that she was obliged to yield to the insistence of Elizabeth.   Accordingly, on April 1, 1760, fresh conventions were signed between Austria and Russia, providing for the continuation of the war and the annexation of Ducal Prussia to Russia.   When Louis XV categorically refused to accept these conventions in their existing form, and compelled Maria Theresa to strike out the article relating to

¹ The modern East Prussia.

East Prussia, the Empress-Queen added to the conventions so amended a secret clause, never communicated to the Court of Versailles, virtually reinstating the cancelled article (May 21, 1760). The British ministers were as apprehensive as the ministers of France lest Russia should claim any territorial compensation from Frederick II, for, in view of the unyielding disposition of the King of Prussia, such a claim meant the indefinite prolongation of the war, or, which was even worse and far more probable, the speedy and complete collapse of the Prussian monarchy.

Frederick II has told us that in 1760 the Russians had only to step forward in order to give him the *coup de grâce*. Once more, however, he was saved by the imbecility of the Russian generals. In the course of the campaign of 1760, Saltuikov's mind became unhinged by his responsibilities, and he was superseded by Alexander Buturlin. The occupation of Berlin (October 9–12), which was a financial rather than a military operation (the heavy contributions levied on the Prussian capital helping, as they did, to fill the depleted Russian treasury), and the second abortive siege of Kolberg, were the sole incidents of the campaign.

If France and Austria had only with the utmost difficulty been persuaded to continue the war at the end of 1759, it may be imagined with what feelings they faced the prospect of yet another campaign at the end of 1760. Even in Russia itself there was now a very general desire for peace. On January 22, 1761, the French ambassador at St Petersburg presented a dispatch to the Russian Chancellor from Choiseul to the effect that the King of France, by reason of the conditions of his dominions, absolutely desired peace, especially as the King of Prussia, being at the end of his resources, would now doubtless listen to any reasonable propositions. On the following day the Austrian ambassador presented a memorandum to the same effect. In her reply of February 12, Elizabeth declared that she would not consent to any pacific overtures until the original object of the league, "the essential and permanent crippling of the King of Prussia," had been accomplished. This reply was accompanied by a letter from Elizabeth to Maria Theresa rebuking the Court of Vienna for its want of candour in negotiating with France behind the back of Russia, and threatening, in case of a repetition of such a violation of treaties, to treat with the King of Prussia directly and independently. Elizabeth was not, however, averse from a peace-congress sitting while the war still went on, though she was firmly opposed to anything like a truce as being likely to be "extremely useful to the King of Prussia." To these propositions the allies yielded after some debate. A fresh Russian note, in the beginning of May, laid it down, as an imperative necessity, that France should leave America and the Indies alone for a time and concentrate all her efforts upon the continent. Thus Russia was assuming the lead of continental affairs not only in arms but in diplomacy also.

The equally uncompromising attitudes of Russia and Prussia rendered another campaign inevitable; and, despite the leisurely strategy of the third Russian Commander-in-Chief, Marshal Buturlin, it resulted disastrously for Frederick. During it he lost two first-class fortresses, Schweidnitz in Silesia, and Kolberg in Pomerania, both of which he had deemed impregnable. It is clear from his letter to Finckenstein of January 6, 1762, that he now gave himself up for lost: "Methinks," he wrote, "we ought now to think of preserving for my nephew, by way of negotiations, whatever fragments of my possessions we can snatch from the avidity of my enemies. Be persuaded that if I saw a gleam of hope...of re-establishing the State on its ancient foundations, I would not use such language, but I am convinced that...it is impossible." This means, if words mean anything, that Frederick had resolved to seek a soldier's death on the first opportunity, and thus remove the chief obstacle to a peace for want of which Prussia was ·perishing. He was spared the heroic sacrifice. A fortnight later, he received the tidings of the death of the Russian Empress, who had expired on January 2, 1762—and he knew he was saved. Almost the first act of Elizabeth's nephew and successor, Peter III, a fanatical admirer of Frederick, was to reverse the whole policy of his aunt, to grant the King of Prussia peace on his own terms (May 5, 1762), and contract a regular defensive alliance with "the King my master." Four months later (July 9) Peter was overthrown and made away with by his consort, Catherine II, but the change came too late to modify the situation. Despite her enormous expenditure of blood and money, Russia gained nothing but prestige from her participation in the Seven Years' War.

CHAPTER XVIII.

FINIS POLONIAE, 1733-1794.

WHILE Russia had thus become a great Empire, with a dominant voice in the European concert, Poland had almost ceased to exist politically. The thirty years of the reign of Augustus III (1733-1763) were a period of sheer stagnation. There was no government to speak of. The King rarely visited his kingdom; and his chief minister Heinrich Brühl, omnipotent in Saxony, was powerless in Poland. And, if there was no executive, there was also no legislature. The *Sejm* continued, indeed, to be elected and assembled as usual, every two years; but it was so regularly exploded by the application of the *liberum veto* that no laws had been passed and no business done for more than a generation. Thinking men had shaken their heads in the reign of Augustus II, when no fewer than seven Diets had thus been extinguished; but in the reign of Augustus III not one of the fifteen Diets which solemnly assembled at Warsaw or Grodno, did anything at all, and all for the same reason.

The long-sought political utopia of the *szlachta* had, in fact, at last been realised: they lived in a land where every gentleman had nothing to do but please himself. All onerous restrictions had long since been removed. The army had virtually been abolished because the Polish squire would not pay for it. The diplomatic service had been done away with because he did not see the use of expensively maintaining any regular intercourse with foreign powers. On leaving school, with nothing in his head but a smattering of Latin, the young *szlachcic*, or squire, hastened to the court of the nearest Pan, or Lord, who ruled like an independent prince in his own district, and there swelled the numberless mob of the great man's retainers and hirelings. These little courts—and there were hundreds of them—were now the focuses of whatever of social and political life still survived in Poland. Many of the Polish magnates were fabulously wealthy. The estates of the Potocy, in the Ukraine alone, extended over thousands of square miles. The Radziwills were equally opulent. One member alone of that princely house, Michael Casimir, was worth 30 millions sterling. It would have been a small thing to many of these great nobles to have contributed towards the national defence by training to the use of arms a few thousands of the heydukes, cossacks and poorer gentlemen who ate the bread of idleness in their service ; and never was the Republic so sorely in need of a military police as during the reign of the second absentee King of the Saxon dynasty. That period was for central Europe a period of almost incessant warfare ; Poland, unfortunately for herself, lay in the direct path of the belligerents ; and, despite her neutrality, her territories were systematically traversed, exploited, and ravaged as if the Republic were a no man's land which everybody might make free with. Yet what could be expected from private enterprise when the Grand-Hetman, Potocki, the dignitary officially responsible for the defence of the country, would not even place an observation corps on the threatened Silesian frontier for fear of provoking hostilities, and when even such a friend of reform as Waclaw Rzewuski, who resigned a high position in order the better to serve his country, could flippantly exclaim, "The Republic died long ago, only it has forgotten to tumble down."

In justice to the Saxon Court it must be admitted that it attempted to strike at the root of the prevalent anarchy by abolishing the *liberum veto*, especially after the peace of Aix la Chapelle, when Augustus III had somewhat strengthened his position by matrimonial alliances with the Courts of Vienna and Versailles. But all these efforts foundered on the opposition of the Austrian Court and the determined opposition of the Poles themselves.

In Poland itself the standard of reform was conscientiously upheld by the Czartoryscy, a princely family of Lithuanian origin, which, though akin to the ancient Jagiellos, had only risen to eminence towards the end of the 17th century. Its principal members were prince Michael, Grand-Chancellor of Lithuania, the statesman of the family, and Prince Augustus, its chief military celebrity, who had been decorated with a sword of honour by Prince Eugene for pre-eminent valour at the storming of Belgrade, and, on returning home, had rehabilitated the somewhat drooping fortunes of his House by espousing the great heiress, Sophia Sieniawska. Their sister, Constantia, was married to Stanislaus Poniatowski, the father of the future king of the same name.

The Czartoryscy were superior to all their Polish contemporaries in ability, patriotism and public spirit. They warmly sympathised with the new ideas of enlightenment which came from the banks of the Seine; they encouraged and supported the great educational reformer, Stanislaus Konarsky, who was familiarising his countrymen with these ideas. Their palaces were schools for promising young men selected from every class, and carefully trained to be their political pupils; for the end and aim of all the efforts of "The Family[1]" was the reform of the constitution, an object which they rightly regarded as indispensable. But they clearly recognised that only by educating, and thereby transforming public opinion could they hope to realise their aspirations.

At first the Czartoryscy co-operated with the Saxon Court where from 1733 to 1753 their influence was predominant. But, when their opponents in Poland exploded every Diet

[1] The name generally given in Poland to the Czartoryscy to mark their pre-eminence.

favourable to them, and nullified all their confederations by counter-confederations, while the Saxon Court, fearful of losing Poland altogether, refused to interfere on their behalf, then they fell out with their old friend Brühl and began to plot against Augustus III. They endeavoured to dethrone him, with the aid of Russia, to whom they appealed, through Kayserling, the Russian minister at Warsaw, for help to reform the constitution, promising, in return, to recognise the Russian imperial title, a thing the Republic had hitherto steadily refused to do. There is no reason whatever to question the *bona fides* or the patriotism of the Czartoryscy on this occasion. But that they should seriously have believed that Russia would consent to strengthen and rehabilitate her ancient enemy (for that is what their appeal amounted to) is the strongest proof of their incompetence as statesmen. They were, in fact, sentimental dreamers, mere children in politics, utterly without practical experience, hopelessly blind to the realities of the situation.

Catherine II, whose own situation, for some months after her accession to the throne, was somewhat precarious, declined to interfere till after the death of Augustus III. That event took place on October 5, 1763, whereupon the Czartoryscy immediately resumed their appeal to the Russian Empress. At the end of February, 1764, they went still further, and demanded an army-corps to protect them against the violence of their enemies. Their demands were supported by the new Russian ambassador at Warsaw, the energetic and masterful Prince Nicholas Repnin, who reported that, in view of the state of parties, the presence of a Russian army in Poland was indispensable. In March, 8000 of the Empress' troops entered Poland; in June a general confederation, formed by the Czartoryscy, declared that only a native candidate was eligible; while their Russian allies simultaneously suppressed all the enemies of "The Family." The elective Diet met at Warsaw (August 16–26) and elected, unanimously, Stanislaus Poniatowski, the nephew of the Czartoryscy, King of Poland. The issue could scarce be otherwise, as the electors were overawed by the proximity of 8000 Russian veterans.

The new king was a strikingly handsome man, thirty-two years of age, brilliantly educated, brimful of the noblest ideas of the new era of enlightenment, but prone to luxury and indolence, and with no force of character, though he had a much better judgment than either of his uncles, and, in the course of his royal career, learnt to be a very fair diplomatist. He had first made the aquaintance of Catherine in 1755, at St Petersburg, whither he had come, nominally in the suite of the new English minister, Sir Hanbury Williams, but really as the secret agent of the Czartoryscy. The Grand-Duchess, as she then was, at once appropriated the Polish Adonis, body and soul; and he was mixed up in the mysterious intrigues which resulted in the fall of Bestuzhev and very nearly in the ruin of Catherine herself. On discarding the sentimental Poniatowski for the more virile Orlov, Catherine sent the former back to Poland with a promise of the Polish crown on the death of Augustus III. She already read her paramour through and through. She described him, subsequently, to Frederick the Great, as "the candidate most suitable for our purposes"; and it is clear, from her instructions to Prince Nicholas Repnin, that she meant the crowned Stanislaus to be the mere tool and hireling of Russia. Stanislaus was certainly not of the stuff of which heroes are made; but it is only fair to add that, as King, he tried to do his duty to his country so far as his almost absolute financial dependence upon the Russian Empress (who allowed him 3000 ducats per annum to start with) would permit him to do so.

Their candidate thus established on the throne, the Czartoryscy now insisted upon the prompt carrying out of their reforms, which included the limitation of the *liberum veto* and the establishment of an hereditary monarchy. Stanislaus also privately represented to Catherine that such reforms were indispensable. But, if constitutional reform was the vital question for Poland, the vital question for Russia was the establishment of her own hegemony in Poland, which she proposed to bring about by placing the few and scattered religious Dissidents there on an equality with the overwhelming Catholic majority. The success of such a project, she argued, would not only win for her the suffrages of the Orthodox population of Poland, but would make her extremely popular in Russia also; and popularity was what this new sovereign, of German origin, was most in need of. In reply therefore to the King and his uncles, she declared that the constitutional question must be postponed to the question of the religious Dissidents. So important indeed did the adjustment of the Dissident question seem to Catherine, that, in case of success herein, she was not unwilling to permit some amelioration of the Polish constitution. Compared with her policy, at this period, the policy of her Prussian ally seems narrow and selfish, aiming as it did at pure aggrandisement. But the policy of Prussia was, anyhow, easy because of its very simplicity, whereas the Dissident question ultimately proved too difficult even for Catherine because she overrated the number and importance of the Polish Dissidents and underrated the force of Polish catholicism.

At this time, too, there was no thought at St Petersburg of any regular partition of Poland. At the council summoned immediately after the death of Augustus III, Count Zachary Chernuishev did indeed suggest the advisability of a "rectification" of the frontiers of the Republic; but the idea was scouted because the Russian Cabinet, and the Empress herself, were under the influence of Count Panin, who preferred to fit Poland into his ingenious "Northern Accord" system instead of destroying her.

Nikita Ivanovich Panin was a pupil of Bestuzhev whose "system" he had followed with brilliant success as ambassador at Copenhagen and Stockholm. Towards the end of the reign of Elizabeth, he was appointed to the important post of

Governor of the little Grand Duke Paul, whom, on the fall of Peter III, he would have placed on the throne instead of Catherine, had he been able to do so. Panin's intimate acquaintance with European diplomacy made him indispensable to Catherine when she ascended the throne. He was her political mentor during the first half of her reign, and, though never made Chancellor or even Vice-Chancellor, he stood on an altogether different footing to the counsellors of her later years, who were very little more than superior foreign-office clerks, though some of them, Alexander Bezborodko for instance, were even superior to Panin in sagacity. Panin on the other hand steadily resisted the generally pernicious influence of the imperial favourites, which none of his successors had the courage to do.

Panin was the inventor of the famous "Northern League or Accord " which aimed at opposing a combination of Russia, Prussia, Poland, Sweden and, if possible, Great Britain, against the Bourbon-Hapsburg League, so as to preserve the peace of the North. Such an attempt to bind together, indissolubly, nations with such different aims and characters was doomed to failure. Frederick the Great, in particular, deeply resented what he regarded as an attempt to fetter his liberty of action ; while Great Britain could never be persuaded that it was as much in her interests as in the interests of Russia to subsidise the anti-French faction, the "Caps," in Sweden. Yet the idea of the "Northern Accord," though never realised, had important political consequences, and influenced the policy of Russia for many years. It explains, too, Panin's strange tenderness towards Poland. For a long time, he could not endure the thought of destroying her, because he regarded her as an indispensable member of his "Accord," wherein she was to supply the place of Austria, especially in case of oriental complications. There can also be little doubt that, if the plan could have been realised, it would have been good for Poland. It might even, perhaps, have saved her from being partitioned, and given her a chance of re-establishing herself.

But in order to become serviceable Poland had first to be made subservient. In February 1765, Panin warned Repnin that he must be prepared to support the cause of the Dissidents by force of arms, and that, consequently, the Russian troops must remain in Poland and be quartered on the anti-Dissidents. But it was only now that the difficulties of Repnin began. On September 19 the Russian, Prussian, British, and Danish Ministers waited upon the Primate and the Senate to demand equality of rights for the Dissidents. The Czartoryscy replied that they would willingly promise toleration, but to grant equality was impossible. Even when Repnin threatened to seize their estates they replied, with dignity, that they were ready to be ruined, if necessary, but they could not gratify Russia in this particular.

The Diet of 1766 was of the same mind, and, in spite of considerable pressure, dissolved after referring the whole question to the decision of the bishops. Violence and corruption were now the weapons which Repnin unscrupulously employed. Troops were quartered on the estates of the bishops and magnates. With great difficulty and considerable expense, so-called Dissident confederations were formed at Thorn and Slucz. The royal referendarius, Gabriel Podoski, Repnin's secretary and hireling, and the most despised ecclesiastic in Poland, was, through Russian influence, raised to the primacy to she~ that "the friends of Russia might expect anything and everything." All the enemies of the Czartoryscy were recalled to Poland, professed themselves "the humble servants of the Empress," and (July 12, 1767) formed a confederation at Radom which petitioned Catherine to guarantee the national liberties, including the *liberum veto*, assist the Dissidents to their rights, and contract a protective alliance with the Republic. On the other hand the new papal nuncio, Durini, armed with an encyclical from Clement XIII, urging the faithful to uncompromising resistance, and supported by the bishops, prominent among whom was the courageous Kajetan Ignaty Soltyk, Bishop of Cracow, frustrated all the efforts of Repnin. During the elections, the few partisans of Russia were only saved from destruction by the Russian soldiers; and the Diet of 1767 met, on September 23, in a white heat of religious enthusiasm.

But the elections had still further damaged the Russian cause by laying bare the utter artificiality of the Dissident agitation. One of the most disconcerting novelties of the political struggle was a spontaneous petition from the Dissidents themselves to the Diet protesting against being forced to accept high office; and Repnin was compelled to admit in his correspondence with Panin, that, at present, they certainly were unfit for political equality. "For some time," he writes, "I have been trying to find among them someone even moderately capable, but up to now I have been unable to find anybody. They are all tillers of the soil and without any education. If you want a Polish Orthodox gentleman you must look for him in the Russian monasteries." The Dissident question was consequently subordinated to the question of political supremacy on the basis of the confederation of Radom. A Russian army corps was stationed within five miles of Warsaw; a regiment of grenadiers was quartered in the capital; and all opposition in the chamber itself was silenced by the arrest of four bishops, including Soltyk, three senators, and the Grand-Hetman of the Crown, Rzewuski, and his son, all of whom were deported to Russia (October 13, 1767). It is due to Repnin to add that he did not like his work and despised himself for doing it. He reported that all the best people were in favour of a limitation of the *liberum veto*; and that to guarantee the old constitution would be to alienate them for ever and convince the nation at large that Russia only desired its ruin. He concluded by observing that, personally, he believed in the possibility of combining politics and philanthropy. Catherine, somewhat impressed, now declared her willingness to consent to some limitation in the *liberum veto* in regard to financial affairs; and on the strength of this half-promise, Repnin finally induced the helpless and leaderless Diet of 1768 to repeal all the edicts against the Dissidents, to declare free elections and the *liberum veto* essential and irrevocable articles of the Polish constitution, and to place that constitution, in its entirety, under the guarantee of Russia (Feb. 24, 1768).

But now, just as the triumph of Russia seemed most complete, alarming news reached Warsaw from the distant Ukraine.

On February 29, 1768, a score or so of country gentlemen, some hundreds of peasants and a few priests and monks assembled at the little Podolian fort of Bar, and formed, beneath the banner of the blessed Virgin, a Confederation to protest against the resolutions of the last Diet. Without money, influence or organisation—for not one of the magnates or prelates adhered to it—the Confederation of Bar appeared at first sight insignificant enough. But it owed its real importance to the fact that it was a genuine popular rising, inspired by a patriotism and a devotion utterly unknown to the official classes ; and its consequences were momentous and far-reaching. The original Confederates were, indeed, easily scattered by the Russian troops ; but, stamped out in one place, the insurrection instantly burst forth in half a dozen other places, and, at last, the whole Republic was, as Repnin put it, "ablaze with the fire of Bar." Presently, fresh complications arose. At the end of 1768, a band of Cossacks, in pursuit of the Confederates, crossed the border and destroyed the Turkish town of Galta ; whereupon the Grand Vizier, already seriously alarmed by the recent events in Poland, delivered an ultimatum to the Russian ambassador Obryezkov, threatening Russia with war if she did not instantly cancel the guarantee and withdraw her 40,000 troops from the territories of the Republic.

Almost simultaneously, Choiseul, very jealous of the upstart young Empire which had dared to traverse the designs of the ancient French monarchy, promised to send the Confederates money and officers ; and, during an interview with Krasinski,

Bishop of Kamieniec, one of Repnin's victims, undertook to advance 3,000,000 livres to any party in Poland strong enough to overthrow Stanislaus and place the Prince of Condé, or some other French candidate, on the Polish throne.

Catherine was seriously embarrassed. Unable to prevent the inconvenient and unexpected outbreak of the first Turkish War[1], which absorbed for a time all her forces, she felt obliged to make some concession to the Republic. On March 31, 1769, Repnin was superseded by Prince Michael Volkonsky, who was instructed to be conciliatory and pacific without making the slightest concession. From the Russian point of view the supersession of Repnin was a mistake, as the change of ambassadors necessarily implied a change of system. Fortunately for Russia, the extreme weakness of Poland minimised the consequences of the blunder. Stanislaus was so poor that he was glad to borrow 10,000 ducats from Volkonsky[2] soon after his arrival; and the Grand-Hetman Rzewuski accepted 3000 ducats more in order to put the liliputian Polish army on a war footing, Rzewuski undertaking to defend Kamieniec in case the Turks attacked it. Nevertheless, it was quite clear that neither the King nor the Czartoryscy would submit much longer to Russian dictation. When Volkonsky asked Stanislaus whether he imagined he could keep his throne without the aid of the Empress, the King simply shrugged his shoulders. The Senate too, at the suggestion of the Czartoryscy, after despatching an embassy to St Petersburg complaining that the treaty of 1768 had been extorted by the violence of Repnin, endeavoured by diplomatic means to secure the good offices of Great Britain at Stambul, and assured the Porte, by a special envoy, that the Republic would remain neutral during the war.

It was only now, when Poland seemed about to break with Russia, and Russia herself was immeshed in the Turkish War,

---

[1] See next chapter.
[2] He had already borrowed 13,000 from Repnin.

that the partition project, which had long been in the air, suddenly became a prominent political factor.

So early as the end of 1768, the Courts of Vienna, Versailles and Copenhagen became aware that the King of Prussia was about to "compensate himself" at the expense of Poland for the subsidies that he was bound, by treaty, to pay the Russian Empress on the outbreak of the Turkish War. The first partition scheme, the so-called Lynar project—though it was not the Saxon Minister Lynar but Frederick himself who was the real author of it—was sent to Count Solms, the Prussian Minister at St Petersburg, at the beginning of 1769. Panin, however, was not much pleased with it. The territory of Russia, he said, was so vast already, that he doubted whether it would be any advantage to her to increase it. His real objection to it was that it ran counter to his "Northern Accord." He preferred to keep Poland Russianised but intact. Frederick was profoundly irritated. He wanted an increase of territory sufficient to counterpoise any possible acquisitions of Russia from Turkey, and, above all, he wanted it without the risks of war. For the Frederick of 1769 was a very different man from the Frederick of 1741 or 1756. The terrible experiences of the Seven Years' War had converted the brilliant military adventurer into a cautious, almost timorous, statesman, whose invincible dread of war coloured the whole policy of his later years. Of the "bears of the Holy Roman Empire [1]" whose mortal hug had all but crushed him to death at Kunersdorf, he was particularly fearful; while Poland then, as Turkey is now, "the sick man of Europe," seemed expressly at hand to adjust all differences and reconcile all ambitions. With Russia on his side, he had no reason to apprehend the interference of the other European Powers, who regarded the partition of Poland as an unavoidable and, indeed, not altogether undesirable event of the near future, as it might have an equilibrating effect. The only question was, which of the Powers should benefit by it, and

---

[1] The name he gave the Russians after Kunersdorf.

how.   The Court of Vienna at first considered it disadvantageous
for Austria to transgress her natural boundaries, the Carpathians,
by annexing the Polish lands beyond; but it was willing to
allow Frederick a free hand in that direction if only he first
restored Silesia.   Saxony wanted a slice of Poland big enough
to enable her Elector to assume the royal title; she was
indifferent as to what became of the rest.   Choiseul, in order to
anticipate what Panin called "the sordid designs of the King
of Prussia," suggested that Austria should take the first step
and appropriate as much of Polish territory as she wanted—and
Choiseul was ostensibly the friend of Poland! Even the Porte,
which had actually taken up arms on behalf of the Republic,
proposed (in 1770) that Austria and Turkey should partition
Poland between them in order to circumvent Russia and
Prussia.   Great Britain had no interest in the matter except in
so far as it might affect her commerce.   Thus, oddly as it may
sound now, the only serious opposition to a partition came from
Russia.

   Joseph II's fear and jealousy of Frederick, and the aged
Kaunitz's desire to go down to posterity as a famous acquisitor
of territory, especially after it became quite clear to him that
nothing could be gained by pretending to advocate the cause
of Turkey, were the causes of Austria's final adhesion to the
partition project.   But Maria Theresa revolted at the idea
of despoiling a friendly Catholic Power.   Only the urgent representations of her son and her chancellor, who assured her that
Austria could not safely sit still while Russia and Prussia
aggrandised themselves at the expense of Poland, only the
sophistries of her spiritual directors who drew subtle distinctions
between political and private morality, induced the devout and
scrupulous old lady to put her hand to a deed which she
abhorred.   The subsequent alacrity of Austria to secure her
share of the spoil certainly contrasted strangely with her
previous backwardness.   The new understanding with Prussia
was cemented at the meeting between Frederick, Joseph II and

Kaunitz, at Neustadt in Bohemia, at the beginning of September 1770; and immediately afterwards Austria formally[1] annexed the Zips counties, a district in north Hungary, which had been mortgaged to Poland in 1412 and never redeemed. The occupation of Zips was followed up by Frederick's proposed joint mediation of Prussia and Austria between Russia and the Turks (September), and the despatch of Prince Henry of Prussia to St Petersburg (October) to accelerate the adhesion of Russia to the partition project. Catherine resented being hurried into a compact for which she had no great relish. At the end of December she shewed Prince Henry that she had penetrated the designs of his brother by hinting, facetiously, that as Austria had already seized Polish territory, Prussia might just as well follow suit. In January 1771, Frederick applied still further pressure by informing the Court of St Petersburg that he could not guarantee the neutrality of Austria if the Turkish war continued, and at the same time dictated the terms with which he thought Russia should be content. Catherine was justly indignant. " Be firm ! " she wrote to Panin, " not one step backwards ! If we are hurried into a peace it will be a bad peace." Although it is highly probable that the details of the first partition were settled with Prince Henry, it is evident that Catherine and Panin would have separated the Polish from the Turkish question and spared Poland as much as possible. The Russian government was even inclined to compensate Poland with Moldavia and Wallachia ; but Prussia and Austria would allow Russia neither to retain those conquered provinces herself nor to transfer them.

On the other hand, though Frederick was quite capable of seizing Polish territory as unceremoniously as he had seized Silesia, he was not insensible to the outcry which such an act of political brigandage would inevitably call forth. It was necessary, therefore, that the spoil should be shared with the two Empires. Common action would be the safest course to follow in the

[1] She had seized it just before the Neustadt conference.

present, and the best guarantee for the future. But the hand of the Russian government was still held back by some scruples of honour. In February 1771, Panin, in reply to another impatient reminder from Potsdam, informed the Prussian Minister, Solms, that the Empress had so often and so solemnly guaranteed the territorial integrity of the Republic, that the open violation of that principle must produce everywhere the most unpleasant effect. He added that Frederick's suggestion that Russia should compensate herself in Poland for losses sustained elsewhere was regarded at St Petersburg as "hard and offensive." March, April and May passed; and still there was no further reply from the Russian Court. During this time Panin was struggling against a combination of all his enemies in the cabinet, including the War Minister Chernuishev and the Orlovs, whose chief and incontrovertible argument was the ease and profitableness of a partition. At length they prevailed, and Catherine directed Panin to carry out the details of the partition. It was a hard blow for the old minister thus to violate the principles of his "Northern Accord"; but he comforted himself with the reflection that, even after a partition, Poland would still be a considerable Power, and he saw to it that both Prussia and Austria abated their "claims" considerably, at the last moment[1].

Panin's public justification of the Empress's change of front was the damage done to Russia by the Polish Confederates, for which Russia claimed to be recouped by the ungrateful Republic shé had vainly endeavoured to serve. The Confederates, who, up to 1770, had been favoured by Austria, who had allowed them to make their headquarters at Eperies in Hungary, and by France, who had sent Dumouriez to organise their undisciplined bands, were now promptly suppressed at the end of 1771, by Suvarov, just as they threatened

---

[1] Thus he prevented Frederick from annexing Dantzic and Thorn, and Austria from incorporating the whole of Galicia.

to become most dangerous[1]. A general "pacification" was indeed the necessary preliminary of a partition.

Poland, meanwhile, was the only country in Europe where there was still no suspicion of the coming partition. Stanislaus and the Czartoryscy naively imagined that the Republic was far too essential a part of the continental system to be dealt with thus summarily. Even when military cordons began to be formed, along the Netze by Prussia and on the Galician border by Austria; even when the suave and courtly Volkonsky was superseded by the brutal Saldern and the contemptuous Stackelberg, they failed to discern a fresh change of system at the Russian Court, and obstinately shut their eyes to facts. On September 7, 1771, Stackelberg presented the partition project to the Polish Ministers, who, in their utter helplessness, could only fall back on passive resistance and procrastination. At the end of October the Russian Minister put fresh pressure upon the King at a private interview. Stanislaus, characteristically, took to posing and haranguing. "I would beg your Majesty to leave Plutarch and antiquity alone," interrupted Stackelberg, "and deign to consider the history of modern Poland and of Count Stanislaus Poniatowski." He then assured him that his political existence depended upon two things, the summoning of a Diet at Grodno to consider the propositions of the Powers, and his own abstention from intrigue[2] in the future. Nevertheless, two days later, Stanislaus made a last desperate effort to save his country by sending a secret embassy to Versailles. But Choiseul, the only French Minister who, even now, might have seriously embarrassed the partitioning powers, had been dismissed from office scarce twelve months before (Dec. 10, 1770) for failing to show proper respect to the infamous Du Barry; and the Polish

---

[1] Some of the magnates had now joined them. Their last exploit was the capture of the citadel of Cracow (Feb. 2, 1771). Then they made a crazy attempt to abduct the King, which came to nothing (Nov. 3).

[2] *i.e.* efforts to obtain extraneous assistance.

envoys brought home with them nothing but polite con-
dolences. There was now nothing for it but to submit.

After innumerable declarations and diplomatic notes had
been exchanged between the three Powers, the definite treaty
of partition was signed at St Petersburg on August 5, 1772.
On September 18, 1773, the miserable shadow of a Diet,
which assembled at Grodno beneath the "protection" of
Russian bayonets, was forced to confirm it. By the first
partition Poland lost about 214,000 square kilometres of her
total territory (751,000). Austria got the lion's share, consisting
of the palatinates of Lemberg and Belz, half the palatinates of
Cracow and Sandomir, and parts of Podolia and western
Galicia, together with 70,480 square kilometres with a population of 2,700,000 and a revenue of 1,408,000 Polish gulden.
Prussia got the modern West Prussia, exclusive of Dantzic and
Thorn, with the Netze district, altogether 34,741 square kilometres with a population of 416,000 and a revenue of 534,750
thalers. Russia got Polish Livonia, the palatinates of Witebsk
and Mstislavl and half of the palatinates of Polock and Minsk,
altogether 108,750 square kilometres, with a population of
1,800,000 and a revenue of 920,480 Polish gulden[1].

None of the contemporaries of the first partition seems to
have regarded it unfavourably either from a political or from
a moral point of view. The general condemnation of it was
of a later date and largely due to a growing dislike of
Catherine's policy in general, and Panin's methods in particular.
Russia comes the best out of the wretched business. She
prevented the partition as long as possible, and she won her
share of it (which, by the way, consisted entirely of old Russian
lands) at least by right of conquest, whereas Austria and
Prussia got their portions of the spoil by no right at all.
It is therefore unfair and humiliating to Russia to place her
in the same class as her accomplices. In fact the hand of

[1] These figures differ materially in the different accounts of the partition.
I have taken the most probable items.

Catherine was forced by Frederick II, who, taking advantage of her difficulties with his usual astuteness and unscrupulousness, compelled her to sacrifice her interests to those of Prussia. Catherine never forgave Frederick for this exhibition of tactical superiority, and, diplomatically considered, the first partition of Poland marks the beginning of the estrangement between Russia and Prussia, and its corollary, the re-approximation of Russia and Austria.

It cannot fairly be said that the diminution of the Polish State was, in any way, injurious to the Polish people. Panin's contention that the wrested provinces would benefit by the transfer was perfectly true ; and it must also be added that the new constitution adopted by the Diet of 1775, which the Russians invented to meet the new conditions of the Republic, was, sentiment apart, far superior to anything of the kind which the Poles themselves had ever been able to devise.

The throne continued, indeed, to be elective, though the candidates were to be limited to native Poles, always excepting the sons and grandsons of the reigning King. The *liberum veto* was also retained. But everywhere we trace the hand of Panin endeavouring to make Poland a serviceable but not too formidable an ally. The executive was intrusted to a *Rada Nieustajaca*, or Permanent Council of State, consisting of 36 members, 18 senators and 18 deputies, elected biennially by ballot and subdivided into the five departments of War, Justice, Foreign Affairs, Police and Finances, on the model of the Swedish constitution overthrown by Gustavus III in 1772. The King was to preside over the Council, summon the Diet with its consent, and select all senators, ministers and bishops from a list of three candidates submitted to him by the Council. For the first time in Polish history the King received a decent civil list and the chief officers of state adequate, but not extravagant, salaries. The yearly budget was fixed at between 32,000,000 and 35,000,000 Polish gulden[1].

[1] A Polish gulden = about 1*s*. 3*d*. of our money.

The regular army was to consist of 30,000 men of all arms, a force five times as large as it used to be when Poland was in the plenitude of her power.

On the whole, then, the new Polish constitution, though it restricted the Republic within a very moderate political programme, made for order, economy and stability. But, whatever its merits, it was, after all, the invention of the enemy, and therefore abominable to Polish patriotism. The opportunity of replacing it by something better did not occur, however, till fourteen years later, when (in 1787) the insolent and provocative policy of Catherine II suddenly involved herself and her ally Joseph II in a second war with the Turks, far more dangerous than the first, which speedily engrossed her attention.

It was therefore in the most favourable circumstances conceivable that the famous *Czteroletni Sejm*, or Quadrennial Diet, assembled at Warsaw on October 16, 1788. The patriots were justified in hoping much from a national assembly which differed materially and advantageously from all its predecessors. Its benches were crowded by youthful enthusiasts, elected under the immediate stimulus of agitating events, and brimful of public spirit. Their first act was to elect, as Marshal, Stanislaus Malachowski, almost the only nobleman in the land quite free from aristocratic prejudices, whose civic virtues had won for him the title of "the Polish Aristides." These young reformers grouped themselves round Adam Casimir Czartoryski and Ignatius Potocki. The conservatives and reactionaries followed the lead of the immensely wealthy Grand Hetmans, Felix Potocki and Xavier Branicki, both of them avowed Russophils who had fought without shame against their own countrymen in the open field and been liberally rewarded by Catherine for their valuable services during the time of the first partition. The King had his own party. He was in favour of an alliance with Russia, but a free and independent alliance, on equal terms, which would not exclude constitutional reform. It is quite clear that Stanislaus grasped the whole political situation far better than any of his Polish contemporaries; unfortunately, the correctness of his views was more than counterbalanced by the instability of his character.

The first political acts of the *Sejm* were the repudiation of the Russian guarantees of 1775, and the rejection of a proposal from St Petersburg for a new alliance—hazardous proceedings so long as Poland did not possess a stable government and a powerful army of her own. But it must be remembered that the Poles of 1788 were 'prentice hands in the trade of politics, with no practical knowledge of foreign affairs, and animated by a fierce and very natural hatred of Russia. They were encouraged in these sentiments by Frederick William II of Prussia and his ministers, who, uneasy at the ambition of Catherine II and Joseph II, were disposed to make use of Poland as a political cat's-paw. It was the Prussian envoy Lucchesini who first suggested that the *Sejm* should demand the withdrawal of the Russian troops from Poland—another foolish step which needlessly irritated Russia without bestowing any corresponding benefit on Poland. Then Frederick William, going a step further, renounced Prussia's guarantee of the constitution of 1775, and recognised, in the most emphatic way, the right of the *Sejm* to frame a constitution of its own. Emboldened by this neighbourly support, the patriots proceeded to abolish the Permanent Council of State (Jan. 19, 1789). The brilliant victories of the Russians and Austrians over the Turks, in the course of 1789[1], so frightened Frederick William and Hertzberg that they attempted to form a political combination, strong enough to compel the allies to make peace with Turkey on the basis of the *status quo*. The combination failed ultimately because Pitt refused to accede to it, but it drew Poland completely within the orbit of Prussia.

The Prussian "system" was based on a complicated

[1] See next chapter.

scheme of territorial exchanges. Poland was to surrender
Dantzic and Thorn to Prussia, and receive back Galicia from
Austria, who, in her turn, was to be compensated, at the
expense of Turkey, by the restoration of the Passarowicz
frontier, while Prussia and Austria were to assist the Porte
to get the best terms procurable from Russia. Lucchesini, the
Prussian minister at Warsaw, was instructed to caress and
flatter the Poles to the top of their bent, and insinuate the
Dantzic-Thorn exchange project at every convenient opportunity. Great Britain regarded the proposed cession favourably,
and offered, in case of Polish compliance, herself to conclude,
and to make Prussia conclude, treaties of commerce so advantageous to the Republic that her economical rehabilitation, by
means thereof, would only have been a matter of a few years'
time. Prussia at the same time offered to conclude an
offensive and defensive alliance with Poland, guaranteeing
her territorial integrity; and Pitt, on this occasion, said to
Oginski, the Polish minister in London : " I will speak plainly
to you. I mean to coerce Russia if you will oblige Prussia."

It is obvious that for such services as Prussia was prepared,
for her own sake, to render to Poland, the weaker confederate
was bound to pay handsomely. Moreover, the Frederician tolls
had so ruined the trade of Dantzic and Thorn, that those
cities were now mere skeletons of their magnificent former
selves, and of no advantage whatever to Poland. Unfortunately,
the Diet, misled by a false patriotism, refused to make the
required sacrifice ; and Frederick William II, unable to obtain,
by an open, amicable agreement, what he so keenly coveted,
henceforth sought to secure it by underhand treacherous ways.
Nevertheless circumstances prevented him from breaking with
Poland immediately. The growing interest which Austria, under
the new Emperor Leopold II (Feb. 1790 to March 1792),
took in the welfare of the Republic seriously alarmed Frederick
William. On March 20, 1790, a defensive alliance was
concluded between Prussia and Poland whereby they engaged

to guarantee each other's possessions; and, when the Polish Diet proclaimed the new Constitution, the King of Prussia officially congratulated the King of Poland on the success of "the happy revolution which has, at last, given to Poland a wise and regular government." He declared, at the same time, that it should henceforth be his "chief care to maintain and strengthen the ties which unite us."

The May Constitution was the result of a *coup d'état* skilfully conducted by the patriots and the royal faction combined. The experience of the last three years having convinced all men of good will in Poland that the small reactionary[1] minority of the Diet would never consent to a sweeping revolution, they took advantage of the Easter recess when most of the malcontent magnates were out of town, and (May 3, 1791), suddenly bringing the question of a reform of the Constitution before the Diet, demanded urgency for it. Before the Opposition could recover from its surprise, the Marshal produced, and read aloud, the latest foreign despatches, which unanimously predicted a fresh partition; and, while the excitement caused thereby was at its height, Ignatius Potocki, as pre-arranged, arose and solemnly adjured the King to provide for the safety of the Republic. Stanislaus thereupon produced a form of constitution, originally drafted by himself, in French, on the model of the British constitution. In a perfervid speech from the throne, he exhorted the deputies to accept this new constitution as the last and best means of saving their country, and himself set the example by taking an oath on the Gospels to defend it. The Diet, in an access of enthusiasm, followed suit, whereupon the whole Assembly marched in procession to the Church of St John where a Te Deum was sung, amidst salvos of artillery.

The Revolution of May 3, 1791, converted Poland into an

---

[1] It was never more than 72 in a house of 354 members, and ultimately it sank to 20.

B.

26

hereditary[1] limited monarchy, with ministerial responsibility and biennial parliaments. The *liberum veto* was for ever abolished. All invidious class distinctions were done away with. The franchise was extended to the towns. Serfdom was ameliorated, as a first step towards its abolition. Absolute religious toleration was established, and every citizen was declared equal before the law.

The alarm of the Russian Empress was the most conclusive testimony to the excellence of the new Polish constitution. Cobenzl, the Austrian minister at Petersburg, writing to his Court immediately after the reception of the tidings at the Russian capital, describes Catherine as full of consternation at the idea that Poland, under an hereditary dynasty, might, once more, become a considerable power. But Turkey still engaged her anxious attention, so she was obliged to watch, in furious impotence, the collapse of her party in Poland, and submit to the double humiliation of recalling her ambassador and withdrawing her army from that country. Even after the Peace of Jassy (Jan. 9, 1792) she waited patiently for the Polish malcontents themselves to afford her a pretext for direct intervention. She had not long to wait. The Constitution of May 3, 1791, had scarce been signed, when Felix Potocki, Severin Rzewuski and Xavier Branicki, three of the chief dignitaries of Poland, hastened to St Petersburg, and there entered into a secret convention with Catherine, whereby she undertook to restore the old constitution by force of arms, but, at the same time, promised to respect the territorial integrity of the Republic. On May 14, 1792, the conspirators formed a so-called[2] Confederation at the little town of Targowicz, in the Ukraine, protesting against the Constitution of May 3; and, almost simultaneously, the new Russian minister at Warsaw

[1] On the death of Stanislaus the crown was to pass to the family of the Elector of Saxony.

[2] It consisted, in the first instance, of only ten persons besides the three original conspirators.

presented a formal declaration of war to the King and Diet. The Diet met the crisis with dignity and firmness. The army was at once despatched to the frontier; the male population was called to arms; Ignatius Potocki was sent to Berlin to obtain the assistance stipulated by the treaty of March 19, 1791; and, after declaring the King Dictator so long as the war lasted, the Diet dissolved so as to leave the executive perfectly free. A few days later Ignatius Potocki returned from Berlin empty-handed. The King of Prussia (having, in the meantime, privately come to terms with Russia) now declined to defend a constitution which " had never had his concurrence."

All that Poland now had to depend upon was a small, ill-provided army of 46,000 men, whose only possible strategy, in the circumstances, was to keep the enemy, some 100,000 strong, at bay, till the King came to their assistance with the reserves. Mistakes were made at first, and there was some treachery among the higher officers, but, on the whole, the brief campaign was most creditable to the Poles. For three months the southern army, under Prince Joseph Poniatowski, the King's nephew, and Thaddeus Kosciuszko, in their slow retreat on the capital, skilfully and valiantly retarded the advance of the Russians. At Polonna the enemy was repulsed with the loss of 3000 men. At Dubienka, Kosciuszko, with only 4000 men, defended the line of the Bug against 20,000 for five days; and Kochovski's unsuccessful attempt to cut off the hero's retreat cost him 4000 men. The northern army, too, under Judycki, made good its retreat through the fens and forests of Lithuania. Both armies, converging upon Warsaw, were about to risk everything in a great general engagement, when the King, despairing of success, and hoping thereby to receive better terms for Poland, acceded to the Confederation of Targowicz. Most of the Polish officers thereupon threw up their commissions and fled to Saxony, where they were joined by the principal members of the Quad-rennial Diet (see p. 499). The army was then dispersed all over the country. Throughout the autumn the Russians poured by thousands into eastern Poland, while the Prussians occupied Great Poland. The two Powers then declared their intention of annexing the occupied territory, and summoned a carefully selected assembly of renegades and reactionaries, who represented only 17 out of 32 palatinates, "to come to an amicable understanding." Yet even this helpless and debased assembly revolted against its tyrants. Only after twelve weeks of the most brutal violence was the second partition-treaty signed (Jan. 4, 1793), whereby Russia gained 250,700 and Prussia 58,370 square kilometres more of Polish soil[1]. The miserable remnant of the ancient kingdom was then compelled to re-accept its vicious old constitution under the guarantee of the partitioning Powers.

The first partition of Poland has sometimes been plausibly defended as a regrettable necessity, but no sophistry in the world can extenuate the villainy of the second partition. The theft of territory is its least offensive feature. It is the forcible suppression of a national movement of reform, the hurling back into the abyss of anarchy and corruption of a people who, by incredible efforts and sacrifices, had struggled back to liberty and order, which makes this great political crime so wholly infamous. Yet here again the methods of the Russian Empress were less vile than those of the Prussian King. Catherine openly took the risks of a bandit who attacks an enemy against whom he has a grudge ; Frederick William II came up, when the fight was over, to help pillage a victim whom he had sworn to defend.

But Poland was not to perish utterly without one last exhibition of splendid valour whose very failure was far more glorious than all the victories of her enemies.

After the second partition the Polish refugees made Leipsic their headquarters. They now placed all their hopes in revolutionary France. Here again their simplicity and inex-

_____
[1] See map 3.

perience misled them. They imagined that republican France was the natural ally of all republics, their own included. They discovered that the Jacobins regarded them as aristocrats, and were far more inclined to make peace with Prussia, even at the expense of Poland, than to help the Polish patriots. Hence the inevitable failure of Kosciuszko's mission to Paris at the beginning of 1793. Nay, it was worse than a failure, for, coinciding as it did with the execution of Louis XVI, it prejudiced all the other Powers against Poland.

Kosciuszko would have waited for better times, but his hand was forced by a popular rising in Poland itself, headed by the officers and soldiers of the disbanded Polish regiments. He blamed severely the impetuosity of his countrymen, but leave them in the lurch he could not; and on February 12, 1794, he appeared at Cracow, with a brigade of volunteers. His first act was to attend mass at the Church of the Capuchins, where the prior, according to ancient custom, solemnly consecrated the arms of the patriots to the service of God and their country. From March 24 to April 1 Kosciuszko remained at Cracow organising his forces, which consisted entirely of small squires, citizens of Cracow, and peasants, armed only with scythes and pikes. Yet with this rude army he routed General Tormasov at Raclawice (April 5), the scythemen capturing all the Russian guns by an impetuous rush. For the next two months necessity detained him in his camp at Pinczów. He depended for everything on the voluntary offerings of a depressed and impoverished people, for the insurrection of 1794 was entirely a popular rising; not one of the great nobles joined it, for fear of losing his estates in case of disaster. But the people flocked to Kosciuszko in thousands ; the churches and monasteries sent him their gold and silver plate for the mint; and, as the news of Raclawice spread through the land, the Polish officers and soldiers, incorporated in the various Russian regiments, broke away from their colours and hastened to join the Liberator whose first manifesto had proclaimed the emancipation of the serfs. By the middle of June his army had increased to 14,000 men, of whom 11,000 were regulars.

The nation too had, by this time, declared for him. On April 17 the citizens of Warsaw rose and expelled the strong Russian garrison. On April 22–23 Wilna followed the example of Warsaw. Soon all Poland, except Podolia, Volhynia and the Ukraine, was at the Liberator's disposal.

In all his proclamations, Kosciuszko had been careful to indicate the Moscovite as the sole irreconcilable enemy who must be fought *à outrance.* Austria he looked upon as a possible friend, Prussia as a neutral. He never suspected that both these Powers had already resolved to profit by the insurrection and assist Russia to repress it as speedily as possible. His eyes were first opened when, on June 5, at Szczekocina he and his 14,000 Poles came upon the combined Russian and Prussian forces, 26,000 strong, with 124 guns, where he had only expected to find the Russian division of General Denisov. At nightfall, after a desperate encounter, the Poles fell back upon Warsaw leaving 1000 dead and eight guns upon the field. What was still more serious, four out of their six best generals had been placed *hors-de-combat.* And now Job's messengers came hurrying in from all parts of the country. On June 8 Zajonczek had been defeated at Chelm. Shortly afterwards Cracow was taken. Loud cries of treachery were raised at Warsaw; and the provisional government could or would not prevent the mob from dragging the political prisoners out of prison and hanging them without a trial. Then fierce dissensions broke out among the Poles themselves, the moderates accusing the radicals of Jacobinism, and the radicals retorting by denouncing the moderates as traitors. It was as much as Kosciuszko could do to restore even the semblance of order; and by the time he had drafted 10,000 of the mob into his army, and compelled the two conflicting factions to work together harmoniously for the common weal, the Prussians were already beneath the walls of Warsaw, with 25,000 men and 179 guns, exclusive of an auxiliary Russian division of 16,000 men and 74 guns, and a covering army of 11,000. To these forces Kosciuszko could only oppose 26,000 men, of whom 16,000 were regulars and 9000 volunteers from Warsaw. But his position was strong; his skill in engineering was great; and the whole population was transformed by his enthusiasm.

The siege of Warsaw lasted from July 9 to September 6. Two unsuccessful attempts to storm the city were made on August 28 and September 1, and then the tidings of a general rising in Great Poland induced Frederick William II to raise the siege. This was Kosciuszko's last great victory. Everywhere else the Poles had been worsted, not so much by overwhelming numbers as by their own insane and incurable dissensions. A general, however able, had only to suffer a temporary and unavoidable reverse, to be instantly suspected of treason by the central government, and superseded. Kosciuszko alone did his duty heroically to the very end. The Quadrennial Diet, with all the resources of the Republic at its disposal, could only put 65,000 men into the field, whereas he, in a few month's time, had organised and equipped 149,000. Both as an administrator and as a soldier he performed prodigies; and his unconquerable optimism and inexhaustible energy put heart into thousands who but for him would long since have despaired. It was he who planned the invasion of Prussia by Prince Joseph Poniatowski and Jan Henrik Dombrowski, which resulted in the storming of Bydgoszcz and the retreat of General Schwerin. At one time, the Prussian government even feared Dantzic was lost. But the victorious Russians were now close upon the capital; and, in attempting to save it with his little army, Kosciuszko was routed, wounded and taken prisoner at the battle of Maciejowice (Oct. 10, 1794). Three weeks later, Suvarov, at a fearful cost, stormed the fortified suburb of Praga; and the whole insurrection collapsed in torrents of blood[1] (Nov. 3, 1794).

Poland lay at the feet of her conquerors; and, now that Panin and the Emperor Leopold II were both dead, there was no one to plead for or protect her. The jealousy and rapacity of the three partitioning Powers (the demands of Prussia, in particular, were monstrous) nearly led to a war over the distribution of the spoil; but, chiefly owing to the firmness of Catherine, all disputes were finally adjusted.

On January 3, 1795, Russia and Austria concluded their treaty; and Prussia, after holding out for nine months longer, and seriously counting the cost of a war against the two Empires combined, acceded, on October 24, to the January compact. Prussia got the whole district between the Oder, Bug and Niemen[2], 54,898 square kilometres with a population of 1,000,000; Austria got Cracow, with the palatinates of Sandomir and Lubelsk, also with a population of 1,000,000; and Russia the remainder, 111,780 kilometres with a population of 1,200,000.

---

[1] 20,000 innocent non-combatants were ruthlessly massacred at the storming of Praga.

[2] See Map 3.

CHAPTER XIX.

CATHERINE II, 1762-1796.

So enormous were the gains of Catherine II from the partition of Poland, that all her other acquisitions fade into insignificance by comparison. Yet, as we have seen, a partition of Poland did not originally enter into .her calculations; it was forced upon her from without, and was as much due to fortuitous circumstances as anything in politics can well be. As a matter of fact, it was Constantinople, not Warsaw, upon which the longing gaze of Catherine II was steadily fixed. It was as the restorer of the Greek Empire, not as the subjugator of so feeble a foe as Poland, that she desired to go down to posterity. How was it that a sovereign, commonly supposed to be one of the shrewdest statesmen of her age, could be so irresistibly attracted by this splendid mirage as frequently to subordinate to it her own advantage and the prosperity of her subjects? The answer to this question may perhaps be found in a brief preliminary scrutiny of the personal character of the Empress herself.

On February 14, 1744, the Princess Sophia Augusta Frederica of Anhalt-Zerbst, then in her 14th year, arrived at Petersburg as the *fiancée* of the young Grand-Duke Peter, the heir to the Russian throne, to whom she was duly wedded on August 21, 1745. She had previously (July 8, 1744) been received into the Greek Orthodox church under the name of Catherine Aleksyeevna. The alert, piquant, but by no means artless little creature tells us in her memoirs that she had already made it "a rule of conduct" to win every person worth winning; and to this eminently prudent rule she adhered religiously throughout life. She possessed a peculiar gift of attraction which very few could resist; and her numerous admirers, who were generally clever as well as handsome men, continued to be her political partisans long after they had ceased to be her lovers. Her first adventure in politics, in her 29th year, was, however, singularly unfortunate. Calculating wrongly as to the powers of recuperation of the sick Elizabeth in 1758, she had joined the mysterious Bestuzhev-Williams conspiracy[1], which was apparently intended, on the death of the Empress, to place Catherine on the throne instead of her consort. But Elizabeth recovered; and, for a moment, the aspiring little Grand-Duchess was in extreme peril. Only her remarkable cleverness and the indulgence of the kind-hearted Empress saved her from banishment to the obscure German home the very memory of which was detestable to her. During the brief reign of her husband (January to July 1762) she was a nonentity. Peter III had every reason to detest a wife who ridiculed as well as deceived him; and, though generous to her in money matters, he kept her at a safe distance. There can be no doubt that she was accessory to his murder after the Revolution of July 17, 1762 had placed her on the throne; nor, we must believe, would the custodians of her last remaining rival, the semi-imbecile Ivan VI, have dared to strangle him in his prison at Schlüsselburg (August 5, 1764) unless the Empress had been privy to it.

From the moment when, in the prime of life, she mounted the Russian throne, Catherine II resolved to make herself a great name in every department of public life. Richly endowed by nature, audacious to a crime, and with a native sagacity which would have been an unerring guide but for frequent deflecting gusts of passion and the obsession of a

[1] See Chapter XVII.

boundless vanity, nothing seemed impossible to her whom Joseph II called "the Catherinised Princess of Zerbst."

In diplomacy Catherine's inexperience compelled her, during the first half of her reign, to be the pupil of Nikita Panin who, at first, exercised somewhat of a restraining influence. But in every other department of affairs the Encyclopædists were her teachers ; and to win their homage by realising their precepts was the motive power of all her actions. It is evident from her correspondence with Grimm, Voltaire, Diderot and D'Alembert that their approval, or rather adulation, was what Catherine valued most of all ; and the *philosophes* were well content to be the advertisers, and even the sycophants, of a monarch so enlightened and also so exceedingly bountiful. Catherine consulted her oracles almost day by day. All her enterprises and adventures, nay, her very thoughts, feelings, ideas, sentiments, friendships and amours, were minutely chronicled for their benefit and admiration, with an abundance of personal detail, which gives them, now, considerable historical value ; and they are written in a style, less correct perhaps, but infinitely more piquant and original, than the correspondence of her French friends.

All Catherine's grand schemes and magnificent projects, when directed towards the amelioration of the Russian people, came to naught partly because the Empress grew tired of them before they were half finished, and partly because, in the latter part of her reign, foreign affairs claimed her exclusive attention. But, in point of fact, Catherine lacked the moral earnestness of the true reformer, without which the most alert intelligence is powerless. We cannot imagine her sacrificing her life for the benefit of her people after the heroic example of Peter the Great. Unlike him, too, she had very little sense of duty apart from the desire for her own gratification. She did a great deal, no doubt, but she did it only to be talked about. She must also incur the just condemnation which falls on one who begins to build before he has counted the cost. All her most ambitious undertakings proved miserable failures. Catherine II was a very bold and a very clever woman, but the epithet "great" is woefully misplaced when applied to her. A glance at her domestic administration will, perhaps, justify a judgment which certainly runs counter to the common opinion.

Catherine began with an attempt to recodify the laws of Russia by means of a "Grand Commission" of 564 members, to be elected from every class all over the country, who were to bring with them to Moscow lists of their grievances for consideration and redress. She herself had previously drawn up an elaborate *nakaz*, or "guide," for the instruction and direction of this Commission, every sentence of which is directly inspired either by Beccaria's *Dei delitti e delle pene*, or by Montesquieu's *L'Esprit des Lois*. The latter book, which she called the "Prayerbook of Princes," was an especial favourite of the Empress. The more practical of Catherine's advisers, specialists like Alexander Bibikov for instance, made no secret of their dislike of the whole project, which they regarded as premature and unworkable. Their criticisms, especially as regards the proposed emancipation of the serfs, contained in the manuscript draft of the *nakaz*, were so unsparing that the Empress abandoned that part of the scheme, and it was omitted from the printed *nakaz* altogether. On the other hand she insisted upon the abolition of judicial torture, on humanitarian grounds.

It soon became clear that the nation at large was rather puzzled than pleased by the notion of a "Grand Commission" which was to collect their grievances and present them before the throne as a basis for remedial legislation. Not a tenth part of the proposed electorate took part in the elections. Most of the electors did not understand the meaning of the thing; the gentry and the Cossacks suspected an insidious trick for curtailing their privileges. Finally however, though not without considerable difficulty, the whole 564 were got together. One hundred and fifty of the deputies were landowners; 50, retired soldiers ; 200, citizens of the towns. Most of the others belonged to the official class. Oddly enough, there was but a single priest among them all, namely Dimitry, Metropolitan of Novgorod, President of the Synod.

The elections took place from February to April 1767 ; and the " Grand Commission " assembled at Moscow on July 30. Catherine opened it in person and appointed the Presidents and Vice-Presidents. The reading of the imperial *nakaz* occupied the first seven sessions, whereupon the official wire-pullers moved that the Empress should be acclaimed " Great and most wise Mother of her country." The motion was carried unanimously ; and there the achievements of the Grand Commission ended. After holding seventy-seven sessions at Moscow, it was transferred (Feb. 18, 1768) to St Petersburg, and dismissed on December 18, the same year, to enable its military members to take part in the first Turkish War. That was the last of it.

But, indeed, the " Grand Commission " was bound to fail. Bibikov, its marshal, justly observes that it was too stupid and ignorant even to understand what was required of it. So desultory and irrelevant were the very occasional debates, that it was often very doubtful what was the point actually under discussion. Most of the time was taken up in listening to the reading of the minutes of the last session, or to extracts from Catherine's *nakaz*. Of any official guidance there is scarce a trace. There was no rule of procedure ; there were no general directions. No propositions had been prepared beforehand for the consideration of the Commission. In fact the government seems to have had no general plan at all. The Presidents and Vice-Presidents knew not how to direct the Assembly and had no control over it. The deputies, so far as they were able to formulate an opinion at all, were strongly in favour of the existing penal code, on the ground that any mitigation thereof would only encourage evil doers and make life and property everywhere insecure. All of them, except a few of the nobles, were in favour of terrorism and severity. Yet they were as obsequious as they were barbarous, for, the moment that Bibikov drew their attention to the fact that the Empress was of a contrary opinion, they immediately veered round and fully acquiesced in her Majesty's humanitarian principles. Their grievances were the ancient ones: official tyranny and corruption, judicial chicanery and procrastination, and, above all, the grievous burden of excessive taxation. Taxation the Empress could not afford to remit ; the other abuses she was well aware of already. In fact the "Grand Commission" was a solemn farce and benefited nobody but Catherine herself, whose western admirers now professed to regard her as a second Justinian.

It was the same with all other matters of purely domestic interest. To take a single instance, Shcherbatov has severely, but not unjustly, commented upon the uselessness to Russia of Catherine's paedagogic theories. Here again Voltaire and Diderot were her directors. The latter even drew up an elaborate plan for her to work upon. She meditated crowning her educational system by the erection of universities at St Petersburg and Dorpat. The sole result of all these ambitious projects were a few seminaries for young ladies of the upper classes, which aimed rather at outward show than at serious and regular training.

But the most striking and curious contrast between promise and performance is to be seen in the history of the building of Ekaterinoslav. This new city, as its name[1] implies, was to be a perpetual memorial of Catherine's glory. Its construction was confided to Potemkin, the most extravagant of her satraps, in 1786. It was to be the capital of the southern Ukraine and to eclipse St Petersburg itself in magnificence. Its cathedral was to be built on the model of St Peter's at Rome, but on a grander scale. Its courts of justice were to be imitations of ancient Basilicas. It was to have an Academy or *Conservatoire*

[1] " The Glory of Catherine."

more splendid than any in Europe. The famous musician
Sarti was to be its first director with a salary of 3500 rubles.
There was also to be a fully equipped University at a cost of
300,000 rubles, while 250,000 more were to be spent on the
residences of the professors and their families. The city was
to have an area of 25 square miles, its streets were to be 30
fathoms wide. It was, moreover, to be a great trade emporium
as well as a south-slavonic metropolis; and 340,000 rubles were
actually spent in the erection of its stocking factories alone.
The foundations of the city cost the Russian Treasury 71,000
rubles[1]. The Emperor Joseph II, who was present at the
ceremony of inauguration in 1787, observed to a friend that the
Empress had laid the first stone of the new city and he himself
the second—and last. The sarcasm was prophetic. Shortly
afterwards the work was stopped. Even in 1795 the only
inhabitants of Ekaterinoslav were a few officials, a few soldiers,
and a few peasants. All that remained of the original dream
were the imposing palace and the expensive orangeries of
Potemkin, on which millions had been wasted.

These gigantic operations naturally swallowed up enormous
sums of money. In 1763 the imperial budget was something
under 17,000,000 rubles; in 1796 it considerably exceeded
80,000,000. The assistance of foreign capitalists soon became
indispensable; and though, in 1771, the Empress was able to
repay the Dutch bankers the loan by means of which she had
carried on the first Turkish War, her financial position, even
then, was anything but satisfactory. How could it well be
otherwise at a Court which was the most extravagant in Europe?
But for the territorial acquisitions from Poland, which placed
fresh millions at Catherine's disposal, she would never have
been able to meet her liabilities. Even so she was forced (so
early as 1769) to issue *assignats* so recklessly that, at last, the
paper ruble was worth only a 142nd part of its face value.

---

[1] The ruble was then equivalent to nearly 6*s*. English.

Sievers, her chief financial adviser, used frequently and bitterly to complain that the Empress could never be made to realise the injury she did to the national economy by her financial operations.

It was naturally the peasants, paying, as they did in the long run, for everything, who suffered most from this state of things.

Catherine had no particular liking for the peasants. They were, in her eyes, rather subjects for experiment than fellow human beings. The Empress Elizabeth, on the occasion of her pilgrimage to Kiev in 1744, had exclaimed, with perfect sincerity, at the sight of the mob which crowded round her: " Do but love me O God! as I love this gentle and guileless people." Catherine, during her triumphal progresses, had the people kept at a safe distance. When she alluded to them at all it was generally to ridicule them. For all her public professions of humanity, she winked at the cruel practice of selling the members of peasant families separately—an abuse which Peter the Great, who never claimed to be a philanthropist, had sternly forbidden. Yet Catherine seems to have meant well to her subjects in a general, impersonal sort of way; and it is due to her to add, that the favourites and adventurers by whom she was always surrounded took good care to hide from her the real condition of the Russian people. During her frequent journeys through her domains, everything was presented to her *en fête*, in an artistic, or rather an artificial environment. This was especially the case throughout her famous excursion to the southern Ukraine in 1787, when whole cities sprang up in her path in a single night; and, in the whole course of her progress, she saw nothing but smiling rustics and happy aborigines in their most picturesque costumes, for the simple reason that her courtiers had taken the precaution to threaten with the knout and a dungeon all who dared to approach the Sovereign with complaints and petitions. Only once, indeed, during the reign of Catherine, did the misery of the nation find a natural outlet, namely in the Pugachev rebellion.

Emilian Pugachev, the son of a Don Cossack, born about 1726, enlisted in the Cossack forces in his 18th year. He served through the Seven Years' War with some distinction, but subsequently resumed the usual vagabond life of a Cossack. Then, tiring of this also, in 1773 he suddenly proclaimed himself to be Peter III. The assumption of this title was a mere symbol or watchword. The story of Pugachev's strong resemblance to the murdered Emperor is a later legend. Pugachev called himself Peter III the better to attract to his standard all those— and they were many—who attributed their misery to Catherine's government. Peter III was generally remembered as the determined opponent of Catherine; any one therefore who professed to be Peter was bound to be in opposition to the government of Peter's arch-enemy. As a matter of fact, however, Pugachev and his followers were opposed to any form of settled government. The one thought of the destitute thousands who joined the new Peter was to sweep utterly away, in a general anarchy, the intolerably oppressive upper classes. In a word, the rebellion of Emilian Pugachev was a repetition of the rebellion of Stenka Razin[1], in very similar conditions.

Pugachev's story was that he and his principal adherents, having escaped from the clutches of Catherine, were resolved to redress the grievances of the people, give absolute liberty to the Cossacks, and put Catherine herself away in a monastery. He held a sort of mimic court at which one Cossack personated Panin, another Zachary Chernuishev, and so on. He also frequently alluded to his son Paul, whom he hoped to see again shortly at Moscow. The Government at first made light of the rising. At the beginning of October 1773, it was simply regarded as a nuisance; and 500 rubles were considered a sufficient reward for the head of the troublesome Cossack. At

---

[1] See Chapter XIII.

the end of November, 28,000 rubles were promised to any one who should bring Pugachev in alive or dead; and the Court could talk about nothing else. Even then, however, in her correspondence with Voltaire, Catherine affected to treat " L'affaire du Marquis de Pugachev " as a mere joke; but, by the beginning of 1774, the joke had developed into a very serious danger. All the forts on the Volga and Ural, including Samara, were now in the hands of the rebels; the Bashkirs had joined them; and the Governor of Moscow reported great restlessness among the population of Central Russia and a general sympathy with the rebels. Shortly afterwards, Pugachev captured Kazan, reduced most of the churches and monasteries there to ashes, and massacred all who refused to join him. It had become evident that the rebellion must be put down at any cost. General Peter Panin, the conqueror of Bender, was forthwith sent against the rebels with a large army; but difficulties of transport, want of discipline, and the gross insubordination of his ill-paid soldiers, paralysed all Panin's efforts for months, while the innumerable and ubiquitous bands of Pugachev were victorious in nearly every encounter. Not till August 1774 did General Mikhelson succeed in inflicting a crushing defeat on the rebels near Tsaritsuin, when 2000 of them fell on the field and 8000 were taken prisoners. Panin's savage reprisals, after the capture of Penza, completed their discomfiture. Pugachev himself was seized and delivered up by his own Cossacks, on attempting to fly to the Urals (September 14), and was executed at Moscow on January 10, 1775.

Catherine's domestic policy was unsuccessful because it was unreal. To see her at her best, we must follow her foreign policy. Here, undoubtedly, she shone. The ceaseless permutations and combinations of diplomacy strongly appealed to her penchant for speculation and adventure; the element of risk was an additional spur to her audacity; and even her fathomless vanity was satisfied by triumphs which, achieved as they were on a world-wide field, were consequently world-renowned.

When Catherine first entered the arena of diplomacy, her most puissant antagonist was France. From the first, French diplomacy had instinctively recognised the rising Russian Empire as an intruder who might one day become a rival. After the Seven Years' War, the Court of Versailles could no longer shut its eyes to the disagreeable fact that the new northern State was the strongest power in Europe. But the ancient French monarchy could not endure the thought of surrendering its time-honoured political hegemony to this upstart young Empire, and henceforth, always and everywhere, steadily opposed it. These principles were personified in François Etienne de Stainville, Duc de Choiseul, the last great statesman of old France, who was responsible for the conduct of her foreign affairs from 1758 to 1770. Hampered as he was, at every step, by the lack of material resources—for the worn-out Bourbon autocracy was already sinking into its grave—he still had at his disposal a delicate but deadly weapon in the brilliant corps of diplomatists, a legacy from Richelieu which, under his masterly direction, did something to veil the decrepitude and revive the prestige of France. His means were limited, but he made the most of ·them. If he was unable to prevent, he could at least retard the triumphs of his northern rival. He could not meet the irritating and provocative challenge of "The Northern Accord[1]," but he crippled it by preparing the way for the Swedish revolution of 1772, which Panin always regarded as the greatest reverse of the reign of Catherine II. He could not detach Prussia from Russia; he could not obviate the election of Stanislaus Poniatowski as king of Poland; but he could and did assist the Confederates of Bar, he could and did prevail upon the Sublime Porte to embarrass the Russian Empress by declaring war against her.

The diplomatic struggle between France and Russia, in Turkey, began in the very year after Catherine's succession, namely in 1763. The Marquis de Vergennes, one of the great

[1] See Chapter XVII.

names of French diplomacy, then represented Louis XV at the Porte, while Catherine was represented by Obryezkov, who could boast of fifteen years' experience and a unique acquaintance with the methods and mysteries of the Divan and the Seraglio. The high-handed interference of Catherine in Poland, after the death of Augustus III, had profoundly disturbed the Porte, which had learnt, since the days of Peter the Great, to regard, rightly enough,. the Polish question as an essential part of the Eastern question. The Turkish ministers fancied, at the outset, that Catherine had made Stanislaus a king as a first step towards making him her husband; but Obryezkov solemnly protested that the mere rumour was "a blasphemy against her sacred person." Vergennes, however, had already opened the eyes of the Porte to the dangers of "a free election" in Poland so long as Russia was the mistress there, and insinuated how glorious it would be for the Sultan to place his own candidate on the Polish throne. In 1765 the well-informed Crimean Khan, Krum-Giraj, strongly advised the Porte to declare war upon Russia forthwith; whereupon both Austria and Prussia, more and more jealous of Russia, offered to assist Turkey in such an eventuality. The Prussian envoy Rexin, under secret instructions, even tried to alarm the Porte still further by mendaciously representing that Russia was about to reform and strengthen Poland by abolishing the *liberum veto.*

Catherine was quite justified after this in calling Frederick "a disloyal scoundrel"; and Solms, the Prussian minister at St Petersburg was dumb when Panin informed him of "this low trick." Nevertheless, despite disquieting rumours from Poland, and a fresh offer of alliance, this time from France and Austria, the summer of 1765 passed away tranquilly enough; but in October the Hospodar of Wallachia reported the massing of Russian troops on the Turkish border, and Soltyk, Potocki and other Polish patriots demanded the protection of Turkey against Moscovite tyranny. At the same time the Khan reported that 40,000 Russian troops were living in Poland and treating the country as if it

belonged to them.   But Obryezkov's arguments and ducats prevailed over the warnings of the Khan and the French ambassador.
The Porte ultimately decided not to interfere in Poland unless
Russia attempted to aggrandise herself territorially at the
Republic's expense.   This apathy continued until, in 1768, the
Confederates of Bar began to be troublesome all along the
northern border of Turkey ; but even then Obryezkov, by means
of a bribe of 3000 ducats, persuaded the Reis Effendi to refuse
them the least assistance.   When, however, in the autumn of
the same year, the Cossacks pursued the Confederates across
the border and pillaged and burnt the Turkish town of Galta,
a wave of fanaticism passed over the Ottoman Empire.   The
Grand Vizier and the Reis Effendi were dismissed, and French
diplomacy was once more triumphant.   After a stormy interview with the new Grand Vizier, Hamza Pasha, Obryezkov,
who refused to guarantee the withdrawal of the Russian troops
from Poland, and the abolition of the laws in favour of the
Polish Dissidents, was thrown into the Seven Towers[1] ; and
20,000 men were despatched to the Danube.

The Turkish declaration of war came upon Catherine as a
painful surprise ; but she accepted the challenge with spirit and
confidence.   At the first session (November 4, 1768) of a
council of ministers and magnates, which, from and after 1769,
became a permanent institution, it was unanimously resolved
to anticipate the enemy by offensive operations ; and Prince
Alexander Golitsuin, who had served his military apprenticeship during the Seven Years' War, was appointed Commander-
in-chief.   It was hoped at St Petersburg that the Turks would
not open the campaign till the spring of 1769 ; but in January,
the Khan of the Crimea began hostilities by endeavouring to
bring 70,000 Tatars to the help of the Confederates of Bar.
But this, the last Tatar raid, was easily repulsed ; and early in
the year Azov and Taganrog were captured.   The sluggishness
of the Grand Vizier, Mohammed Emine, who remained idle for

[1] The usual mode of declaring war at Stambul in these days.

weeks in his camp, near Jassy, though he had 150,000 men at his disposal, materially assisted the Russians to concentrate their forces on the Dniester. In the autumn, however, Mohammed was strangled in his camp by the command of the Sultan ; and the new Grand Vizier, Ali Bogdancsi, an ex-brigand of great courage and ferocity, boldly crossed the Pruth and advanced irresistibly to the Dniester. But he was encountered and defeated by the new Commander-in-chief, Count Peter Rumyantsev (who had superseded the over-cautious Golitsuin on August 13), and compelled to fall back on the lower Danube. Immediately afterwards Chocim, which Golitsuin had failed to take, surrendered voluntarily; and the Russians occupied Jassy, Bucharest, the whole of Moldavia and the left bank of the Danube as far as Braila, but failed to take Bender, on the capture of which Catherine had set her heart. "Give me Bender this autumn," she wrote to the naturally despondent Rumyantsev, "and the business will already have been half done."

At the second meeting of the Russian council it had been decided to support the land operations by a great naval expedition to the Mediterranean. The chief promoter of this adventurous scheme was Gregory Orlov, the reigning favourite ; and Catherine, who was as proud of the Russian fleet as ever Peter had been, supported it with enthusiasm.

The whole story of this risky circumnavigation, except the denouement, which was very different, has a curious and striking resemblance to the Rozhdestvensky adventure of 1905. The Russian fleet, consisting of seven liners, one frigate and some smaller vessels, left Cronstadt on July 26, 1769, under the flag of Admiral Spiridov. At the beginning of August, when off the Isle of Gottland, the newest ship, the Svyatislav, could go no further and put back to Reval. The rest of the fleet was a long time reaching Copenhagen and a still longer time in leaving it. The Russian envoy, Filosofov, reported that all the officers wanted to go back instead of forward ; that the Admiral had lost all control over them; and that the men were ignorant, inefficient and full of terror at the unknown peril before them. When the fleet anchored in the Humber, some 20 miles from Hull, Chernuishev, the Russian ambassador in England, boarded it to try and put some heart into its officers, whom he found "very melancholy and unhappy." Out of the complement of 5000 sailors 1500 were too ill to work. Most of them he describes as raw recruits, taken straight from the plough, with no idea of seamanship. Only a few skippers and fishers from Archangel were equal to their duties. The next stoppage was Portsmouth, where some curiosity and much amusement were caused by the unwonted spectacle. Many distinguished persons, including the Duke of Cumberland, went on board. Chernuishev's reports became still more pessimistic. "Since 1700 we have spent 10,000,000 rubles on the fleet, and what have we got for it?" he wrote. "With grief, shame, and confusion I must confess that her Majesty's instructions have not been carried out." Catherine, in great annoyance, severely scolded Spiridov. "If you eat up all your provisions on the way, and half the crews die before they see the enemy, the whole expedition will be covered with shame and dishonour. For God's sake pull yourself together and don't put me to shame before the whole world!"

Catherine's irritation was more than excusable. Success in this dangerous war, with which her enemies had saddled her, meant very much more to her than it could possibly have meant to an hereditary and long-established sovereign. After all, what was she but a *parvenue*, who had won the reputation of an extraordinary woman by ascending the throne in a sensational way? Let but one serious reverse ruin her reputation for greatness, and the consequences to her, both at home and abroad, might be very serious. Fortunately, the fleet, in the long run, justified her confidence in it. In February 1770 it arrived' safely at Leghorn. It was to have proceeded to the Morea, in the first instance, to support a general rising of the

Greeks, preparations for which had been made by the Orlovs ever since 1763. But the Greeks proved to be a broken reed to lean upon; and both they and their Russian confederates were easily worsted on the mainland by the Turks. The fleet arrived just in time to find that it was useless there; and Admiral Spiridov's relations with the British officers[1], who had volunteered to help him, now threatened to ruin the fleet altogether. Discipline and confidence were only restored when Alexis Orlov[2], the Empress's plenipotentiary, took over the supreme command himself by Catherine's express orders, and, eager to avenge the Morean disaster, deliberately went in search of the Turkish fleet. He discovered it at dawn, on June 24, at anchor along the Anatolian shore of the Straits of Chios, beneath the guns of the little fortress of Chesme. It consisted of sixteen liners, six of them with 80 and the rest with 70 guns, six frigates and a number of smaller vessels. Orlov frankly confessed to the Empress that his first feeling at the sight of such odds was fear; but he instantly gave the order to attack, and, after a furious encounter, lasting four hours, in which the Russian flagship Evstafy was blown up, the Turkish fleet was scattered. Two days later it was pursued and, with the aid of fireships, utterly destroyed. The impression at St Petersburg was all the greater because the fleet had only been intended to support the Morean rising. Orlov, as a reward for the success of his brilliant impromptu, received permission to quarter the imperial arms in his shield. Here, however, the triumph of the fleet ended. An attack upon the isle of Lemnos was beaten off; and nothing very important was attempted during the remainder of the war, though a dozen of the Ægean Islands were captured.

Equally signal were the Russian successes on land during the campaign of 1770. Plague delayed the advance of the

---

[1] Elphinstone, Greig, *etc.*

[2] It was he who took the chief part in the murder of Peter the Third. He was certainly the ablest member of the Orlov family.

army till the early summer; but, on July 7, Rumyantsev defeated a large Turkish force at the junction of the Pruth and Larga; and on the 21st he earned his marshal's *bâton* by routing 150,000 Turks with only 17,000 Russians near Trajanopolis, when 140 cannon were taken on the field and 127 more in the pursuit. This victory led to the fall of a whole series of fortresses, Ismaila being taken by Potemkin, Kilia by Repnin, and Akkerman by Igelström, while Braila was evacuated by the Turks themselves on the approach of the Russians. Bender, however, occupied the whole attention of the second army, under Golitsuin, from July to the middle of September. Golitsuin finally took it by assault (Sept. 16), but he was severely blamed for losing one-fifth of his army in the operation.

During the winter of 1770–71 Catherine was somewhat disquieted by the aggressive attitude of the King of Prussia, who affected to regard the Russian terms of peace as exorbitant, and declared openly that he could not guarantee the neutrality of Austria much longer. Desirous as she now was for peace, Catherine felt that the best answer to the veiled menaces of her neighbour was another successful campaign. But her resources were limited; her generals, especially her best general, Rumyantsev, were growing despondent; and the army was in a deplorable condition, owing to the breakdown of the commissariat. The soldiers, in the depth of winter, were without boots and underclothes, and had to be put on half rations of bread made of damaged millet and maize. There were no horses for the guns and wagons. Rumyantsev declared it was impossible to repeat the triumphs of 1770. Catherine, however, besides encouraging them by letters full of fire and courage, worked night and day to remove all obstacles from the paths of her commanders. New recruits were promised; fresh stores were obtained from Poland; every penny that could be obtained was spent upon the army; and, after superhuman efforts, Rumyantsev was able to take the field again in 1771 with an imposing force.

The Russian army was in three divisions. The right wing occupied the district between the Sereth and the Aluta. The left wing, under Wiessman, guarded the course of the Danube from the Pruth to the Black Sea. The centre, under Rumyantsev, with its head-quarters at Maksiminaki on Sereth, was to lend help to whichever of the wings might need it most. But the Turks were too weak to attack in force ; and the whole campaign was consequently of a guerilla character in which the Russians were invariably victorious. The fortresses of Giurgevo and Tulcea were also taken after repeated attempts, but not without terrible loss of life. In October the army went into winter quarters round Jassy. On June 14, the second army, under Prince Vasily Mikhailovich Dolgoruki, stormed the lines of Perekop, which were defended by 7000 Turks and 50,000 Tatars, and compelled the Khan Selim Giraj to sue for a truce.

In the autumn of 1771, Austrian diplomacy was very busy in the east, and Kaunitz' notes to the Court of St Petersburg grew more and more dictatorial. "The time has come to end this Turkish War," he said. An Austro-Turkish Alliance was even concluded by Thugut, the Austrian Minister at Constantinople, Turkey engaging, in return for active assistance, to cede Little Wallachia to Austria and give the Court of Vienna 34,000,000 gulden in subsidies, 11,000,000 of which were actually paid. It was this "sly trick" of Thugut's, as Panin called it, which forced the hand of Catherine and, in conjunction with strong and persistent pressure from Frederick, inclined the Empress to abate her claims upon Turkey and compensate herself at the expense of Poland. On December 5, 1771, Catherine virtually gave way when she declared by the mouth of Panin, in full council, that the Turks were disposed towards peace. Austria, thereupon, cynically threw over Turkey, to the just indignation of the Sultan, who promised, nevertheless, not to demand back the eleven million gulden he had already paid for the Austrian alliance, if Moldavia and Wallachia were retroceded. In February 1772, Panin reported to the council the pleasing intelligence that Austria would co-operate with Russia and Prussia in the peace negotiations, and that the Turkish plenipotentiaries were on their way to a peace congress, which ultimately met at Fokcsani in Moldavia. The congress lasted from July to August and then dissolved because Russia claimed more than the Turks could concede. On October 19 a second congress met at Bucharest. Catherine was now very anxious for peace. She feared that a war with Sweden was inevitable in consequence of the Revolution of 1772, whereby Gustavus III had emancipated himself from the thraldom of a party supported and subsidised by Russia. Catherine had actually detached nine infantry regiments from Rumyantsev's army on the Danube and sent them to Pskov in view of an expected Swedish invasion. But the Turks, secretly encouraged by Austria and Prussia, refused to surrender the Crimean towns; so the second congress also proved abortive. Peace was, however, finally concluded (July 21, 1774) at a third congress held at the little Bulgarian town of Kuchuk-Kainardje, twenty miles from Silistria. By the peace of Kuchuk-Kainardje, Turkey recovered most of her conquered territory, but was obliged to recognise the independence of the Tatars of the Crimea and the Kuban, and the protectorate of Russia over the Christians of Moldavia and Wallachia, and to cede the Crimean towns of Kertch and Yenikale to Russia.

The thirteen years' interval between the first and second Russo-Turkish Wars was marked by a growing alienation between Russia and Prussia and a corresponding approximation between Russia and Austria. Catherine never forgave Frederick II for his treacherous, underhand proceedings during the first twelve years of her reign. His effusive compliments after the conclusion of the first partition of Poland and the first Turkish War must have seemed to her sarcastic compliments after what had gone before. Nevertheless, circumstances compelled her to renew her alliance with him in 1777 and assist him vigorously, if only diplomatically, in his quarrel with Austria concerning the

Bavarian succession, a quarrel ultimately composed, under Russian mediation, by the peace congress of Teschen (May 3, 1779). This, however, was the last of the many services she rendered to an ally who had always been more of a hindrance than a help to her ; while for his shifty, sentimental successor, Frederick William II (1786–1797), who with all the will to damage her had not the courage, she always entertained a wholesome contempt. Panin, meanwhile, had completely forfeited her confidence by his mischievous subserviency to Prussia in his later years ; and she dismissed the old statesman (May 1881) with the firm resolve, henceforth, to be her own Minister of Foreign Affairs. The younger generation of politicians, who henceforth surrounded her, were little more than the executive instruments of her sovereign will, superior Foreign Office clerks in fact. The most remarkable of these "pupils" was Alexander Bezborodko, who entered her service in 1774, contrived to ingratiate himself with the reigning favourite Potemkin, and, though he never held any very high official position till after Catherine's death[1], was, towards the end of her reign, generally recognised as the soul of her cabinet and the subtlest diplomatist whom Russia had yet produced. He was as superior to Bestuzhev and Panin in resourcefulness and versatility as he was inferior to them in honesty, courage and personal dignity. He was especially admired by the Emperor Joseph II, into whose plans he pretended to enter enthusiastically ; while the wonderful lucidity and literary excellence of his political memorials and despatches greatly attracted Catherine, and largely influenced her decisions.

Apart from mutual attraction, the great bond of union between Catherine and Joseph II was the grandiose "Greek Project." Joseph simply desired to partition the Turkish Empire between Catherine and himself by way of eclipsing the fame of Frederick II ; Catherine's more romantic imagination

---

[1] Paul made him Grand-Chancellor and a Prince. Catherine allowed him, however, to accumulate millions.

dreamed of re-establishing the Greek Empire under her grandson Constantine. The scheme seems first to have been mooted at Catherine's meeting with the Emperor at Mogilev in 1780.

In 1782 a formal understanding as to the disposal of the Ottoman Empire was arrived at between the two Courts without any formal treaty. The anarchical and dilapidated condition of Turkey, since the last war, was taken to justify the most impudent depredations. Russian warships passed up and down the Dardanelles with impunity. New forts were built all along the Turkish frontier. Russian agitators, in the guise of consuls, perambulated the Turkish provinces, stirring up the Christian population to revolt.

On April 8, 1783 the Crimea was deliberately incorporated with the Russian Empire by Potemkin; and the last Khan became a subject of the Empress. Austria had long since annexed the Bukovina (May 7, 1775). The Porte, anxious above all things to avoid another war, meekly protested, and that was all. The correspondence of the two sovereigns reveals a prodigious appetite for fresh territory. Joseph had no objection to the restoration of the Greek Empire under Constantine Pavlovich, but he coveted for himself (Nov. 30, 1782) Chocim, Little Wallachia, Orsova, Belgrade, and everything contained within a straight line drawn from Belgrade to the Gulf of Drina, inclusive. He also proposed to take all the insular and continental possessions of Venice "as the only way of unifying the Austrian dominions." Venice was to be compensated for this rather severe amputation by the Morea, Candia and the Aegean islands, in other words with parts of Catherine's prospective Greek Empire. To this she very naturally objected; and a certain coolness ensued in consequence.

The finishing touch was given to "the Greek Project" at the magnificent and prolonged picnic of potentates and princes whom Catherine in 1787 took with her to the shores of the

Euxine to admire her new arsenal at Kherson and marvel at the brand-new fleet, which Potemkin, in an incredibly short time, had constructed and fully equipped for battle, in the harbour of Sebastopol.   Unfortunately the immediate effect of this pleasant triumphal progress was to rouse the long-suffering Turk from his apathy and precipitate a war for which Catherine was totally unprepared, though she had done everything to provoke it.

It was the seizure of the Crimea in 1783 which first awoke the Turks to a sense of their extreme peril.   They at once proceeded to reorganise their forces; and, with the assistance of numerous English and French officers, the Ottoman army was soon a disciplined host instead of a disorderly mob.   Moreover, the new and energetic Kapudan Pacha succeeded in practically rebuilding the fleet.   It was now that Great Britain assumed the rôle of chief Turcophil which France had sustained for more than 300 years.   From the outset, the British Government had been suspicious of Catherine II.   It had looked with indifference upon "the Northern Accord" of Panin; the refusal of the Russian Empress to assist in the subjugation of "His Majesty's misguided subjects in America" had increased the coolness between the two Powers; and, when Catherine, with the aid of Bezborodko, began to apply the principles of the Armed Neutrality of the North to British commerce, public opinion in Great Britain was profoundly irritated against the Russian Empress.   Great Britain, moreover, was rightly jealous of Russia's increasing influence in the Mediterranean, which threatened to injure the English Levant trade; so that, when the second Turkish War broke out, it was obviously the correct policy of the cabinet of St James's to assist the Porte as much as possible by multiplying Catherine's embarrassments.   Prussia, especially disturbed by the new Austro-Russian alliance, laboured assiduously, and not very scrupulously, with the same object in view.

The critical year was 1787.   While Catherine perambulated

the Ukraine, scattering rubles and epigrams in every direction, Great Britain and Prussia were helping to bring about a Swedo-Turkish alliance ; and millions of piastres found their way to Stockholm from Stambul, by way of Amsterdam and Hamburg, to enable Gustavus III, who had his own very real grievances against Russia, to put his fine fleet and by no means inconsiderable army in motion. It was hoped that Turkey and Sweden would declare war against Russia simultaneously ; but Gustavus was prevented by constitutional trammels from invading Finland till July 1788, whereas the Turks began hostilities by besieging, ineffectually, the fortress of Kinburn in October 1787. The real tug of war did not come, however, till 1788, when Joseph II, acting as his own generalissimo, poured his troops through the Transylvanian and Wallachian passes into Turkish territory. The upshot showed that the Emperor was no general, and that the Turks had lost nothing of their ancient valour. The imperial troops suffered bloody defeats in Bosnia and Wallachia, and were driven back headlong into Hungary, whose southernmost towns and villages were reduced to ashes. Had not Marshal Laudon taken over the supreme command at the last moment, the Austrian army would have been annihilated. As it was, Joseph, at the combat of Karansebes, owed his life solely to the fleetness of his charger. The Russians were more fortunate. Rumyantsev and the Prince of Coburg took Chocim by assault ; the Prince of Nassau-Siegen destroyed the Turkish fleet at the mouth of the Dnieper ; and Suvarov put 30,000 Turks to the sword at the storming of Ochakov. In the North, too, the course of events was favourable, a rebellion of the Swedish army placing Gustavus III *hors de combat* for nearly twelve months.

Still the Turks were not discouraged. At the beginning of 1789, the incapable Abdul Hamid I was succeeded by Selim III, an enlightened and patriotic sovereign, who had been well educated by French tutors. He was the only Sultan of the eighteenth century who could dispense with Dragomans. His first act was to place at the head of the army a new Grand Vizier, Hassan Pasha, whose dogged valour heroically sustained the terrible disasters of the campaign of 1789. In that year the combined allies were everywhere victorious. In April Derfelden defeated the Turks on the Pruth and captured Galatz. But the left bank of the Danube was the chief theatre of operations. On August 1, Suvarov and the Prince of Coburg defeated Hassan Pasha at Fokcsani, when 10,000 Turks bit the dust, and the whole Turkish camp fell into the enemies' hands. Nevertheless even this overthrow did not dismay Hassan. In less than a month he had assembled around him another army of 100,000 men. In September he encountered the allics at Martineste on Rimnik, where was fought the bloodiest and best contested battle of the whole war. But again Hassan was routed, this time with the loss of 22,000 men and 60 guns. The result of these victories was the fall of the fortresses of Belgrade, Bender and Akkerman. Simultaneously Prince Repnin defeated the Turks at Isakhi and began the siege of Ismaila.

The Turks had now lost their last field army, the remains of which were distributed among the garrisons of the strong Danubian fortresses, the last defence of the Empire. A speedy peace on the best terms obtainable had become a vital necessity to the Porte. But Catherine was scarcely less anxious to end the war. The political horizon was darkening everywhere. Gustavus III had recommenced hostilities in Finland in June 1789; and things were going badly with the Russians. Poland had thrown off the Russian yoke and contracted an alliance with Prussia. It seemed possible that Catherine might have to sustain a third war with Frederick William II and the Republic combined. Her victorious armies had been decimated, and all the energy and ingenuity of Bezborodko were taxed to the uttermost to supply the gaps in the ranks. A serious blow too was the death of Joseph II on February 20, 1790. In these circumstances the Turkish War languished. Not till the late autumn could the campaign of 1790 begin. The only triumph won by Russia, though a very considerable one, was the storming of Ismaila by Suvarov, on which occasion the carnage was so awful that the Empress doubted whether she should reward or rebuke the victor. She contrived, however, by the end of the summer, to draw "one paw out of the mire." On August 14, 1790, the Peace of Värälä rid her of Gustavus III, who was actually threatening her capital[1].

In 1791 Austria withdrew from the struggle by the peace of Sistova, concluded on a *status quo ante bellum* basis (August 4). Despite the brilliant victory of Prince Repnin over the Grand-Vizier, at Machin, in July, Catherine continued the negotiations with the Turks which had already been opened at Jassy; and here (January 9, 1792) the faultless diplomacy of Bezborodko ensured a very advantageous peace for Russia. The Porte formally surrendered the Crimea and along with it Ochakov and the district lying between the rivers Bug and Dniester. Thus, for the first time in history, the whole of the northern shore of the Euxine became an integral part of the Russian Empire.

The last years of Catherine II were absorbed, as we have seen[2], by the Polish question, whose final solution only took place a few months before her death. By that time she had quite outlived her pseudo-liberalism and had become the most reactionary autocrat in Europe. Yet, in truth, she had never been anything else, at heart; and this is no reproach to her, for in those days, as she very well knew, an autocracy was the only possible government for Russia. Her fear and hatred of the French Revolution are therefore perfectly intelligible, though she agreed with Bezborodko that Russia's proper political attitude towards revolutionary France was strict neutrality. But she lavished millions on the legitimist *emigrés* and heartily

[1] See "Scandinavia" in this series, Chapter XIII.
[2] See Chapter XVIII.

approved of the anti-Jacobin Crusade of Gustavus III, with whom she came to be on very amicable terms. Indeed it was the wish of her heart, in her extreme old age, to marry her granddaughter Alexandra to the young King Gustavus IV. The frustration of this design, in somewhat humiliating circumstances, undoubtedly accelerated her death.

Catherine II expired, very suddenly, on November 17, 1796. Enough has already been said to give some idea of her character. If she does not rightly deserve the epithet " Great " (she was too flighty to be an administrator, too fanciful to be a statesman of the highest rank), none can deny to her the title of "extraordinary." Everything she did, from first to last, was out of the common. Whether she did more harm than good to Russia, on the whole, is still a matter for debate among the Russians themselves. Of her many fascinating and commanding qualities, her wit, humour, serenity and *savoir-faire*, her courage, insight, resoluteness, high public spirit, and intimate knowledge of human nature, there never can be any doubt at all.

BIBLIOGRAPHY.

Askenazy, Sz. Die letzte polnische Königswahl, 1767. Göttingen, 1894.

——. Polish-Prussian treaties (Pol.). Lemberg, 1900.

Bain, R. N. The Daughter of Peter the Great. Westminster, 1899.

——. The first Romanovs, 1613–1725. London, 1905.

——. Peter III, Emperor of Russia. Westminster, 1902.

——. The Pupils of Peter the Great. London, 1897.

Bilbasov, V. A. Geschichte von Katharina II. Berlin, 1891.

Bobrzynski, M. and Smolka, S. Jan Dlugosz (Pol.). Cracow, 1893.

Bogoslavsky, M. The provincial reforms of Peter the Great (Rus.). Moscow, 1902.

Bourrée, M. D. Un diplomat français à la Cour de Catherine II, 1775–1780. Paris, 1901.

Brueckner, A. Bilder aus Russlands Vergangenheit. Leipsic, 1887.

——. Die Europaisierung Russlands. Gotha, 1888.

——. Geschichte Russlands bis zum Ende des 18 Jahrhunderts. Gotha, 1896.

——. Materials for a life of Count Panin (Rus.). St Petersburg, 1888.

Bulgakov, Ya. Correspondence (chiefly from Constantinople). 1779–1798. St Petersburg, 1885.

Catherine II. La Cour de Catherine. Ses collaborateurs. St Petersburg, 1899.

——. Political correspondence (Rus. and Fr.). Collections Imp. Rus. Hist. Soc., vols. XLVIII, LI, LVII, LXVII, LXXXIV, XCIV. St Petersburg, 1885, etc.

Celichowski, Z. Contributions to the history of the reign of Sigismund I (Pol.). Posen, 1900.

Choloniewski, A.   Tadeusz Kosciuszko (Pol.).   Lemberg, 1902.

Collections (Sbornik) of the Imperial Russian Historical Society (Rus., Fr., Eng., Ger.).   St Petersburg, 1881, etc.

Czermak, W.   In the days of John Casimir (Pol.).   Lemberg, 1893.

——.   Wladyslaus IV's plans for the Turkish War (Pol.).   Cracow, 1895.

Dembicki, L.   Pulawy, 1762–1830 (Pol.).   3 vols.   Lemberg, 1887–1888.

Dembinski, B.   Documents relatifs à l'histoire du deuxième et du troisième partage de la Pologne.   Lemberg, 1902.

——.   Russia and the French Revolution (Pol.).   Cracow, 1896.

——.   Stanislaus Augustus and Prince Joseph Poniatowski (Pol.). Lemberg, 1904.

Dubrovin, N.   Pugachev and his confederates (Rus.).   St Petersburg, 1884.

Finkel, L.   Fontes rerum polonicarum.   Lemberg, 1899.

——.   Bibliografia Historyi Polskiej.   5 vols.   Lemberg, 1891–1906.

Gloger, Z.   Historical geography of the former Polish lands (Pol.). Cracow, 1900.

Grigorevich, N. I.   Chancellor Prince Alexander Bezborodko (Rus.). 2 vols.   St Petersburg, 1879–1881.

Gumplowicz, M.   Zur Geschichte Polens im Mittelalter.   Innsbruck, 1898.

Heyking, C. H.   Aus Polens und Kurlands letzten Tagen.   Berlin, 1897.

Hirschberg, A.   The false Demetrius (Pol.).   Lemberg, 1898.

Ikonomov, V. I.   On the eve of the reforms of Peter the Great (Rus.).   Moscow, 1903.

Ilenko, A. K.   The beginning of the end of Poland (Rus.).   St Petersburg, 1898.

Ilovaisky, D. I.   The anarchic period of the Muscovite realm (Rus.).   Moscow, 1894.

Janicki, I.   Acta historica res gestas Stephani Bathorei illustrantia. Cracow, 1881.

Jarochowski, K.   History of the reign of Augustus II (Pol.). Posen, 1890.

Kalinka, W. J.   Der vierjährige polnische Reichstag.   2 vols. Berlin, 1896–1898.

Kluczycki, F.   König Johann vor Wien.   Cracow, 1883.

Kochanowski, J. K.   Casimir the Great (Pol.).   Warsaw, 1900.

Kochubinsky, A. A.   Count Osterman and the partition of Turkey 1735–1739 (Rus.).   Odessa, 1899.

Korwin, S.   Materials for the history of the last century of the Polish Republic (Pol.).   Cracow, 1890.

Korzeniowski, J.   Catalogus actorum et documentorum res gestas Poloniae illustrantium.   Cracoviae, 1889, etc.

——.   Analecta romana quae historiam Poloniae saec. XVI. illustrant.   Cracow, 1894.

Korzon, I.   Domestic history of Poland, 1764–1794 (Pol.).   2 vols. Cracow, 1897–1898.

——.   Fortunes and misfortunes of John Sobieski (Pol.).   Cracow, 1898.

Kostomarov, N. I.   Bogdan Khmelnicki (Rus.).   St Petersburg, 1884.

——.   Russische Geschichte in Biographien.   Leipsic, 1885.

Kozlowski, S. G.   Stanislaus Zolkiewski, 1547–1620 (Pol.).   Cracow, 1904.

Kraszewski, J. I.   Poland during the time of the three partitions (Pol.).   3 vols.   Warsaw, 1902–1903.

Kraushar, A.   Prince Repnin and Poland, 1764–1768 (Pol.). Warsaw, 1900.

——.   Two historical sketches of the age of Stanislaus Augustus (Pol.).   Warsaw, 1905.

Kulish, P. A.   The defection of Little-Russia from Poland (Rus.). 2 vols.   Moscow, 1888–1889.

Kurakin, I. A.   The eighteenth century (Rus. and Fr.).   Moscow, 1904.

Larivière, C. de.   Catherine le Grande d'après sa correspondance. Paris, 1895.

Leliwa, L. P.   John Sobieski and his age (Pol.).   2 vols.   Cracow, 1882–1885.

Lopukhin, A. V.   Sketch of the Congress of Jassy, 1791 (Rus.). St Petersburg, 1893.

Maikov, N. M.   I. I. Betskoy (Rus.).   St Petersburg, 1904.

Mezhov, V.   Bibliographie des livres russes d'histoire.   3 vols. St Petersburg, 1892–1893.

Milyukov, P. N.   Essais sur l'histoire de la civilisation Russe. Paris, 1901.

Morfill (W. R.). A history of Russia from the birth of Peter the Great to the death of Alexander II. London, 1902.

Nepluyev, I. I. Correspondence (from Constantinople), 1725–1740 (Rus.). St Petersburg, 1893.

Nicholas, Grand Duke. Count P. A. Stroganov, 1774–1817 (Rus.). St Petersburg, 1903.

Nyström, A. K. Striderna om Östra Europa mellan Ryssland, Polen och Sverge. Stockholm, 1901.

Pantenius, I. H. Der falsche Demetrius. Bielefeld, 1904.

Pawinski, A. Poland in the XVIth century (Pol.). 2 vols. Warsaw, 1883–1886.

Peter the Great. Papers and correspondence (Rus.). In progress. St Petersburg, 1887, etc.

Pierling, P. Un arbitrage pontificial au XVIe siècle entre la Pologne et la Russie, 1581–1582. Bruxelles, 1890.

——. L'Italie et la Russie au XVIe siècle. Paris, 1892.

——. Papes et Tsars, 1547–1597. Paris, 1890.

Polkowski, J. The warlike deeds of King Stephen Báthory (Pol.). Cracow, 1887.

Potemkin, G. A., Prince. Papers, 1774–1793 (Rus.). 2 vols. St Petersburg, 1893–1895.

Potocki, P. F. The last Polish ambassador at the Porte, 1789–1792 (Pol.). Paris, 1894.

Rambaud, A. N. History of Russia. London, 1886.

Radziwill, K. I., Prince. Correspondence (Pol.). Cracow, 1898.

Rembowski, A. The insurrection of Zebrzydowski (Pol.). Cracow, 1893.

Russian Archives, The. (A periodical.) (Rus.) Moscow, 1881–

Schiemann, T. Russland, Polen u. Livland bis ins 17 Jahrhundert. 2 vols. Berlin, 1885–1887.

Shcherbachev, Y. N. Russian documents, 1514–1687. St Petersburg, 1897.

Shmurlo, E. F. Collection of documents relating to the reign of Peter the Great (Rus.). Dorpat, 1903.

Smolenski, W. The Confederation of Targowicz (Pol.). Cracow, 1903.

Sobieski, W. The Tribune of the country gentlemen (i.e. Jan Zamoyski). Warsaw, 1905.

Sokolowski, A. Illustrated history of Poland (Pol.). Vienna, 1896–1900.

Solov'ev, S. M. History of Russia (Rus.). St Petersburg, 1895.

Sorel, A. Le partage de la Pologne et le Traité de Kainardji. Paris, 1889.

——. La question d'Orient au XVIIIe siècle. Paris, 1889.

Szelongowski, A. Growth of the Polish realm in the XVth and XVIth centuries (Pol.). Lemberg, 1904.

——. The struggle for the Baltic, 1544–1621 (Pol.). Cracow, 1904.

Szujski, J. Works (Pol.). 5 vols. Cracow, 1885–1894.

Szymanowski, O. K. Beiträge zur Geschichte des Adels in Polen. Zurich, 1884.

Tikhomirov, E. The first Russian Tsar, Ivan IV (Rus.). Moscow, 1888.

Tourneux, M. Diderot et Catherine II. Paris, 1899.

Tsvyetaev, D. V. Tsar Vasily Shuisky (Rus.). 2 vols. Warsaw, 1901–1903.

Volkonsky, S. Pictures of Russian history. Boston, 1897.

Waliszewski, K. Archives of French Foreign Office (relating to Poland), 1674–1696. Cracow, 1881.

——. La Dernière des Romanovs. Paris, 1902.

——. Marysienka, reine de la Pologne. Paris, 1898.

——. Les Origines de la Russie moderne. Paris, 1904.

——. Pierre le Grand. Paris, 1897. (English translation. London, 1898.)

Wejle, C. M. Sveriges politik mot Polen, 1630–1635. Upsala, 1901.

Wittichen, P. Die polnische Politik Preussens, 1788–1790. Göttingen, 1899.

Zajonczek, J. History of the Revolution of 1794 (Pol.). Lemberg, 1881.

Zamoyski, A. The Archives of Jan Zamoyski (Pol.). Warsaw, 1904.

INDEX.

Index

CAMBRIDGE: PRINTED BY JOHN CLAY, M.A. AT THE UNIVERSITY PRESS.

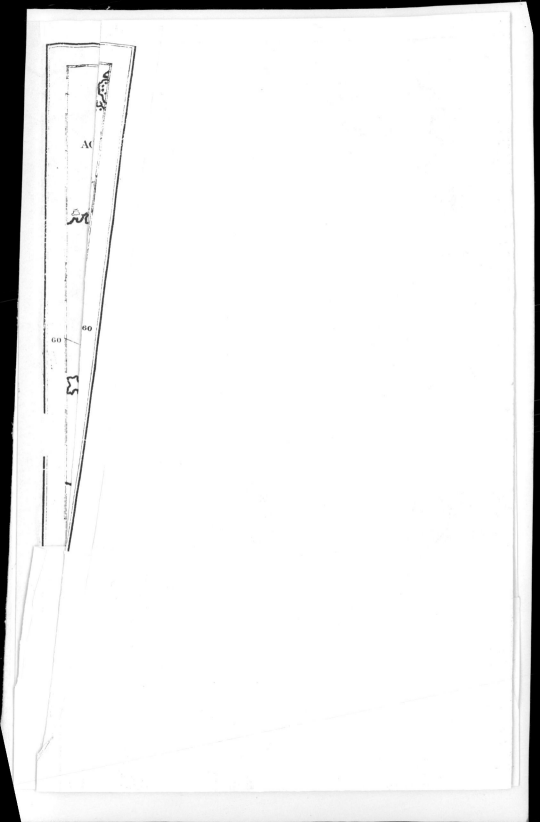